Financial Accounting
for Non-Specialists

We work with leading authors to develop the
strongest educational materials in accounting,
bringing cutting-edge thinking and best learning
practice to a global market.

Under a range of well-known imprints, including
Financial Times Prentice Hall we craft high quality
print and electronic publications which help readers
to understand and apply their content, whether
studying or at work.

To find out more about the complete range of our
publishing, please visit us on the World Wide Web at:
www.pearsoneduc.com

Financial Accounting
for Non-Specialists

Peter Atrill
and
Eddie McLaney

An imprint of **Pearson Education**

Harlow, England · London · New York · Reading, Massachusetts · San Francisco · Toronto · Don Mills, Ontario · Sydney
Tokyo · Singapore · Hong Kong · Seoul · Taipei · Cape Town · Madrid · Mexico City · Amsterdam · Munich · Paris · Milan

Pearson Education Limited

Edinburgh Gate
Harlow
Essex CM20 2JE

and Associated Companies throughout the world

Visit us on the World Wide Web at:
www.pearsoneduc.com

Second edition published 1999 by Prentice Hall Europe
Third edition published 2002 by Pearson Education Limited

© Prentice Hall Europe 1999
© Pearson Education Limited 2002

ISBN 0273 65587 6

British Library Cataloguing-in-Publication Data
A catalogue record for this book is available from the British Library

Library of Congress Cataloging-in-Publication Data
Atrill, Peter.
    Financial accounting for non-specialists / Peter Atrill & Eddie McLaney.—3rd ed.
        p. cm.
    Includes bibliographical references (p.) and index.
    ISBN 0-273-65587-6
    1. Accounting.   I. McLaney, E. J.   II. Title.

    HF5635 .A884 2002
    657—dc21   2001054784

10 9 8 7 6 5 4 3 2 1
06 05 04 03 02

Typeset in 9.5/12pt Stone serif by 35
Printed by Ashford Colour Press Ltd., Gosport

Contents

Preface

Financial accounting is concerned with the provision and use of information that should help those outside an organisation (that is, not managers) to make both better judgements and decisions about that organisation. This book seeks to introduce financial accounting, particularly to those people who wish, or need, to have an understanding of the subject, without going into a lot of technical detail.

The book is directed at non-accounting students who are following a course in financial accounting, perhaps as part of a university or college course majoring in some other area. It is also directed at readers who are studying independently, perhaps with no qualification in mind. Specialist accounting students should also find the book useful as an introduction to the main principles of financial accounting.

In writing the book, we have been mindful of the fact that most of the book's readers will not have studied financial accounting before. We have, therefore, tried to write in an accessible style, avoiding technical jargon. Where technical terminology is unavoidable, we have tried to give clear explanations.

The book is written in an 'open learning' style. That is to say, it tries to involve the reader in a way not traditionally found in textbooks. The book tries to approach its contents much as a good lecturer would do. We have tried to introduce topics gradually, explaining everything as we go. We have also included a number of questions and tasks of various types to try to help readers to understand the subject fully, in much the same way as a good lecturer would do in lectures and tutorials. More detail of the nature and use of these questions and tasks is given in the 'How to use this book' section immediately following this preface.

The open learning style has been adopted because we believe it to be more 'user friendly' to readers. Irrespective of whether they are using the book as part of a taught course or for personal study, we feel that this approach makes it easier to learn.

In writing the third edition, we have taken account of helpful comments and suggestions made by lecturers, students and other readers. We have expanded certain parts of the book so as to include topics of growing importance such as social reporting. We have also tried to improve the presentation of the book. Although the book looks at financial accounting from the perspective of a user of financial information, we have included in this third edition an appendix that deals with the principles of double entry and outlines the recording system for financial transactions. This has been included for those who wish to find out more about the preparation of financial statements.

We hope that readers will find this book readable and helpful.

Peter Atrill
Eddie McLaney

How to use this book

We have organised the chapters to reflect what we consider to be a logical sequence and, for this reason, we suggest that you work through the text in the order in which it is presented. We have tried to ensure that earlier chapters do not refer to concepts or terms that are not explained until a later chapter. If you work through the chapters in the 'wrong' order, you will probably encounter concepts and terms that were explained previously.

Irrespective of whether you are using the book as part of a lecture/tutorial-based course or as the basis for a more independent mode of study, we advocate following broadly the same approach.

Integrated assessment material

Interspersed throughout each chapter are numerous **Activities**. You are strongly advised to attempt all these questions. They are designed to simulate the sort of quick-fire questions that your lecturer might throw at you during a lecture or tutorial. Activities serve two purposes:

■ To give you the opportunity to check that you understand what has been covered so far.
■ To encourage you to think about the topic just covered, either to see a link between that topic and others with which you are already familiar, or to link the topic just covered to the next.

The answer to each Activity is provided immediately after the question. This answer should be covered up until you have deduced your solution, which can then be compared with the one given.

Towards the middle/end of each chapter there is a **Self-assessment question**. This is more comprehensive and demanding than any of the Activities, and is designed to give you an opportunity to check and apply your understanding of the core coverage of the chapter. The solution to each of these questions is provided in Appendix D at the end of the book. As with the Activities, it is important that you attempt each question thoroughly before referring to the solution. If you have difficulty with a self-assessment question, you should go over the relevant chapter again.

End-of-chapter assessment material

At the end of each chapter there are four **Review questions**. These are short questions requiring a narrative answer or discussion within a tutorial group. They are intended to help you assess how well you can recall and critically evaluate the core terms and concepts covered in each chapter. Answers to these questions are provided in a seperate Lecturers' Manual.

At the end of each chapter, except for Chapter 1, there are eight **Exercises**. These are mostly computational and are designed to reinforce your knowledge and understanding. Exercises are graded as 'more advanced' according to their level of difficulty. The basic-level questions are fairly straightforward; the more advanced ones can be quite demanding but are capable of being successfully completed if you have worked conscientiously through the chapter and have attempted the basic exercises. Solutions to five of the exercises in each chapter are provided in Appendix E at the end of the book; these five are identified by a coloured exercise number. Here, too, a thorough attempt should be made to answer each exercise before referring to the solution. Solutions to the other three exercises and to the review questions in each chapter are provided in a separate Lecturers' Manual.

Content and structure

The text comprises nine chapters. The market research for this text revealed a divergence of opinions, given the target market, on whether or not to include material on double-entry bookkeeping techniques. So as to not interrupt the flow and approach of the chapters, an appendix on recording financial transactions (including activities and exercises) has been provided.

Supplements and website

A comprehensive range of supplementary materials is available to lecturers adopting this text.

- **Solutions Manual**
  - Solutions to all the exercises not provided in the text.
- **PowerPoints**
  - Over 55 colour slides comprising all the Figures and Exhibits from the text, which can be downloaded from the Web site and printed as OHPs, as well as specially prepared summary lecture notes.

Acknowledgements

We should like to thank those lecturers who reviewed the second edition of the text and who made numerous useful comments. We believe that this third edition has benefited significantly from their help and advice.

We should also like to thank the Association of Chartered Certified Accountants for permission to include questions from the Certified Diploma in Finance and Accounting as well as those organisations that have allowed us to use extracts from accounts, news items and other material to help illustrate issues dealt with in the book.

We are grateful to the following for permission to reproduce copyright material: Exhibit 2.3 from the 2000 annual report, Manchester United plc; Exhibit 3.4 from Ong, A. 'The problems of accounting for intangible assets in the food and drink industry' in Atrill, P. and Lindley, L. (eds.), *Issues in Accounting and Finance*, 1997, Ashgate Publishing Ltd; Exhibit 4.2 from the 2000 annual report, Kingfisher plc; Exhibit 4.4 from the balance sheet, 31 December 1999, Nichols plc; Exhibit 4.5 from the 1999 annual report Rolls Royce plc; Exhibit 5.2 from the balance sheet 31 December 1999, GlaxoSmithkline plc; Exhibit 5.5 from the 1999 annual report, National Express Group plc; Question 5.1 from the 2000 annual report, J. Sainsbury plc; Exhibits 5.6–5.10 from operating review for 2000, Monsoon plc; Exhibit 7.4 from the 2000 annual report, Tate & Lyle plc; Exhibit 8.1 from the 2001 annual report, De La Rue plc; Exhibit 8.3 from the 2000 annual report, Rexam plc; Exhibit 8.4 from the 2000 annual report, Cadbury Schweppes plc; Exhibit 9.1 from the 2000 annual report, Railtrack plc; Exhibit 9.3 from the *Safety, Health and Environment* report 2000/2001, British Energy plc; Exhibit 9.4 from *Accounting and Business*, March 1998, reproduced with permission of *Accounting and Business*, the professional journal of ACCA; Exhibits 9.5 and 9.8 from *Value Report 1997*, The Body Shop International plc; Exhibit 9.6 from BAA plc web site.

In some instances we have been unable to trace the owners of copyright material, and we would appreciate any information that would enable us to do so.

Finally, we should like to thank Vera Iordanova Atrill for her help in developing the graphs and diagrams contained within the book.

CHAPTER 1

Introduction to accounting

Introduction

In this first chapter, we shall begin by considering the role and nature of accounting. We will identify the main users of accounting information and discuss the ways in which accounting can improve the quality of the decisions that they make. We will then go on to consider the particular role of financial accounting and the differences that exist between financial and management accounting. As this book is concerned with financial accounting for private-sector businesses, we shall also examine the main forms of business enterprise.

OBJECTIVES

When you have completed this chapter you should be able to:

- **Explain the role and nature of accounting.**
- **Identify the main users of accounting information and discuss their needs.**
- **Distinguish between financial and management accounting.**
- **Identify and discuss the main forms of business enterprise.**

What is accounting?

When studying a new subject, it is often helpful to begin with a definition. The literature contains various definitions of **accounting**, but the one we find most appealing is that provided by the American Accounting Association, which defines accounting as:

> the process of identifying, measuring and communicating information to permit informed judgements and decisions by users of the information.

This rather broad definition is appealing because it highlights the fact that accounting exists for a particular purpose. That purpose is to help users of accounting information to make more informed decisions. If accounting information is not capable of helping to make better decisions, then it is a waste of time and money to produce. Sometimes, the impression is given that the purpose of accounting is simply to prepare financial reports on a regular basis. Whilst it is true that accountants undertake this kind of work, it does not represent an end in itself. The ultimate purpose of the accountants' work is to influence the decisions of users of the information produced. This decision-making perspective of accounting is a major theme of this book and will shape the way in which we deal with each topic.

Who are the users?

For accounting information to be useful, an accountant must be clear about *for whom* the information is being prepared and *for what purpose* the information will be used. There are likely to be various user groups with an interest in a particular organisation, in the sense of needing to make decisions about that organisation. The most important groups that use accounting information about private-sector businesses are shown in Figure 1.1.

Figure 1.1

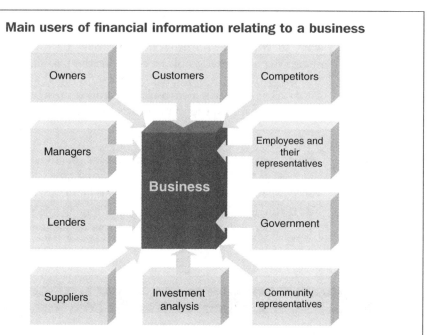

Main users of financial information relating to a business

The figure shows that there are several user groups with an interest in the accounting information relating to a business. The majority of these are outside the business but nevertheless they have a stake in the business. This is not meant to be an exhaustive list of potential users; however, the user groups identified are normally the most important.

Activity 1.1

Why do each of the user groups identified in Figure 1.1 need accounting information relating to a business?

Your answer may be as follows:

User group	Use
Customers	To assess the ability of the business to continue in business and to supply the needs of the customers.

User group	Use
Competitors	To assess the threat to sales and profits posed by those businesses. To provide a benchmark against which the competitor's performance can be measured.
Employees (non-management)	To assess the ability of the business to continue to provide employment and to reward employees for their labour.
Government	To assess how much tax the business should pay, whether it complies with agreed pricing policies and whether financial support is needed.
Community representatives	To assess the ability of the business to continue to provide employment for the community and to purchase community resources. To assess whether the business could help fund environmental improvements.
Investment analysts	To assess the likely risks and returns associated with the business in order to determine its investment potential and to advise clients accordingly.
Suppliers	To assess the ability of the business to pay for the goods and services supplied.
Lenders	To assess the ability of the business to meet its obligations and to pay interest and to repay the amount borrowed.
Managers	To help make decisions and plans for the business and to exercise control so that the plans come to fruition.
Owners	To assess how effectively the managers are running the business and to make judgements about likely levels of risk and return in the future.

You may have thought of other reasons why each group would find accounting information useful.

The conflicting interests of users

There may be conflicts of interest arising between the various user groups over the ways in which the wealth of the business is generated and/or distributed. For example, a conflict of interest may arise between the managers and the owners of the business. Although managers are appointed to act on behalf of the owners, there is always a risk that they will put their own interests first. They may use the wealth of the business to furnish large offices, buy expensive cars or whatever. Accounting information has an important role to play in reporting the extent to which various groups have benefited from the business. Thus, owners may rely on accounting information to check whether the pay and benefits of managers are in line with agreed policy. A further example of potential conflict is between lenders and owners. There is a risk that the funds loaned to a business will be used for purposes that have not been agreed. Lenders may, therefore, rely on accounting information to check that the funds have been applied in an appropriate manner and that the terms of the loan agreement are being adhered to.

Activity 1.2	Can you think of other examples where accounting information may be used to monitor potential conflicts of interest between the various user groups identified?

Two possible examples that spring to mind are:

■ Employees (or their representatives) wishing to check that they are receiving a 'fair share' of the wealth created by the business and that agreed profit-sharing schemes are being adhered to.
■ Government wishing to check that the profits made from a contract which it has given to a business are not excessive.

You may have thought of other examples.

Not-for-profit organisations

Although the focus of this book is accounting as it relates to private sector-businesses, there are many organisations that exist with their prime purpose not being the pursuit of profit yet they produce accounting information for decision-making purposes. Examples of such organisations include charities, clubs and associations, universities, local government authorities, churches and trade unions. Accounting information is needed by user groups that are often the same as, or similar to, those identified for private-sector businesses. These groups may have a stake in the future viability of an organisation and may use accounting information to check that the wealth of an organisation is being properly controlled and used in a way that is consistent with the objectives of the organisation.

How useful is accounting information?

No one would seriously claim that accounting information fully meets the needs of the various user groups identified. Accounting is a developing subject and we still have much to learn about user needs and the ways in which these needs should be met. Nevertheless, the information contained within accounting reports should reduce uncertainty in the minds of users over the financial position and performance of the business. It should help to answer questions concerning the availability of cash to pay owners a return for their investment or to repay loans, and so on. Often, there is no close substitute for the information contained within accounting reports and so the reports are usually regarded as more useful than other sources of information that are available regarding the financial health of a business.

| Activity 1.3 | What other sources of information might users employ to gain an impression of the financial position and performance of a business? What kind of information might be gleaned from these sources? |

Other sources of information available include:

- Meetings with managers of the business
- Public announcements made by the business
- Newspaper and magazine articles
- Radio and TV reports
- Information-gathering agencies (for example, Dun and Bradstreet)
- Industry reports
- Economy-wide reports

These sources can provide information on various aspects of the business, such as new products or services being offered, management changes, new contracts offered or awarded, the competitive environment within which the business operates, the impact of new technology, changes in legislation, changes in interest rates and future levels of inflation. It should be said that the various sources of information identified are not really substitutes for accounting reports. Rather, they should be used in conjunction with the reports in order to obtain a clearer picture of the financial health of a business.

There is convincing evidence and arguments that accounting information is at least *perceived* as being useful to users. There has been a number of studies that ask users to rank the importance of accounting information in relation to other sources of information for decision-making purposes. Generally speaking, these studies have found that users rank accounting information more highly than other sources of information. There is also considerable evidence that businesses choose to produce accounting information for users that exceeds the minimum requirements imposed by accounting regulations (for example, businesses often produce a considerable amount of management accounting information, which is not required by any regulations). Presumably, the cost of producing this additional information is justified on the grounds that users believe this information is useful to them. Such evidence and arguments, however, leave unanswered the question as to whether the information produced is actually being used for decision-making purposes – that is, whether accounting information has a direct effect on *behaviour*.

It is normally very difficult to assess the impact of accounting on human behaviour; however, one situation arises where the impact of accounting information can be observed and measured. This is where the **shares** (that is, portions of ownership of a business) are traded on a stock exchange. The evidence reveals that, following an announcement concerning a business's accounting profits, the price and volume of its shares traded often change significantly. This suggests that investors change their views about the future prospects of the business as a result of this new information and that this, in turn, leads them to either buy or sell shares in the business.

Thus, we can see that there is evidence that accounting reports are perceived as being useful and are used for decision-making purposes. However, it is impossible to measure just how useful accounting reports really are to users. Accounting information will usually represent only one input to a particular decision and the precise weight attached to the accounting information by the decision maker and the benefits that flow as a result cannot be accurately assessed. We shall see below, however, that it is at least possible to identify the kinds of qualities that accounting information must possess in order to be useful. Where these qualities are lacking, the usefulness of the information will be diminished.

Accounting as a service function

One way of viewing accounting is as a form of service. Accountants provide economic information to their 'clients', who are the various users identified in Figure 1.1. The quality of the service provided will be determined by the extent to which the information needs of the various user groups have been met. It can be argued that, to be useful, accounting information should possess certain key 'qualitative' characteristics. These are:

➡ ■ **Relevance**. Accounting information must have the ability to influence decisions. Unless this characteristic is present, there is really no point in producing the information. The information may be relevant to the prediction of future events (for example, in predicting how much profit is likely to be earned next year) or relevant in helping confirm past events (for example, in establishing how much profit was earned last year). The role of accounting in confirming past events is important because users often wish to check on the accuracy of earlier predictions that they have made.

➡ ■ **Reliability**. Accounting should be free from significant errors or bias. It should be capable of being relied upon by users to represent what it is supposed to represent. Although both relevance and reliability are very important, the problem that we often face in accounting is that information that is highly relevant may not be very reliable, and vice versa.

Activity 1.4	To illustrate this last point, let us assume that a manager is charged with selling a custom-built machine owned by the business and has recently received a bid for it. What information would be relevant to the manager when deciding whether to accept the bid? How reliable would that information be?

The manager would probably like to know the current market value of the machine in order to decide whether or not to accept the bid. The current market value would be highly relevant to the final decision, but it may not be very reliable because the machine is unique and there is likely to be little information concerning market values.

Where a choice has to be made between providing information that has either more relevance *or* more reliability, the maximisation of relevance should be the guiding rule.

➡ ■ **Comparability**. This quality will enable users to identify changes in the business over time (for example, the trend in sales over the past five years) and also to evaluate the performance of the business in relation to other similar businesses. Comparability is achieved by treating items that are basically the same in the same manner for measurement and presentation purposes, and by making clear the policies that have been adopted in measuring and presenting the information.

→ ■ **Understandability**. Accounting reports should be expressed as clearly as possible and should be understood by those at whom the information is aimed.

Activity 1.5	Do you think that accounting reports should be understandable to those who have not studied accounting?

This may prove to be an impossible challange for those preparing accounting reports. The complexity of financial events and transactions cannot normally be that easily reported. It is probably best that we regard accounting reports in the same way as we regard a piece of modern art (an interesting thought!). To understand both, we really have to do a bit of homework. Generally speaking, accounting reports assume that the user not only has a reasonable knowledge of business and accounting but is also prepared to invest some time in studying the reports.

→ ■ **Materiality**. When preparing accounting reports, we should make sure that all material information is provided. Information will be regarded as material if it is likely to have an influence on the decisions made by users. If information is not regarded as material, it is best to exclude it from the reports as it will merely clutter up the reports and, perhaps, interfere with the users' ability to interpret the financial results.

Costs and benefits of accounting information

In the previous section, the five key characteristics of relevance, reliability, comparability, understandability and materiality were identified. However, there is a key characteristic that is also very important. It is raised in Activity 1.6.

Activity 1.6	Suppose an item of information is capable of being provided. It is relevant to a particular decision, it is also reliable, comparable, understandable and material. Can you think of any good reason why, in practice, you might choose not to produce the information?

The reason that you may decide not to produce, or discover, the information is that you judge the cost of doing so to be greater than the potential benefit of having the information.

For example, suppose that you wish to buy a particular audio-cassette player, which you have seen in a local shop for sale at £20. You believe that other local shops may have the same model on offer for as little as £19. The only ways in which you can find out the prices at other shops are either to telephone them or visit them. Telephone calls cost money and involve some of your time. Visiting the shops may not involve the outlay on money, but more of your time will be involved. Is it worth the cost of finding out the price of the cassette player at various shops? The answer is, of course, that if the cost of discovering the price is less than the potential benefit, it is worth having that information. Supplying accounting information to users is similar.

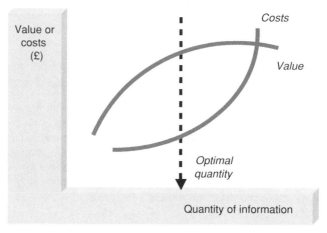

Figure 1.2

Relationship between costs and the value of providing additional financial information

The figure shows how the benefits of financial information will eventually decline. The cost of providing information, however, will rise with each additional piece of information. The optimal level of information provision is where the gap between the value of the information and the costs of providing it is at its greatest.

In theory, financial information should be produced only if the cost of providing that piece of information is less than the benefit, or value, to be derived from its use. Figure 1.2 shows the relationship between the cost and value of providing additional financial information. The figure shows how the value of information received by the decision-maker eventually begins to decline, perhaps because additional information becomes less relevant or because of the problems that a decision maker may have in processing the sheer quantity of information provided. The cost of providing the information, however, will increase with each additional piece of information. The point at which the gap between the value of information and the cost of providing that information is at its greatest (indicated in the figure by the dotted line) represents the optimal amount of information that can be provided. This theoretical model, however, poses a number of problems in practice, as discussed below.

The provision of accounting information can be very costly. However, the cost is often difficult to quantify. The direct, out-of-pocket costs such as the salaries of accounting staff are not really a problem, but these are only part of the total cost involved. There are also less-direct costs such as the cost of managers' time spent on analysing and interpreting the information contained within the reports. In addition, costs will also be incurred if the accounting information is used to the disadvantage of the business. For example, if suppliers were to discover from the accounting reports that the business is in a poor financial state, they may refuse to supply further goods or may impose strict conditions.

The economic benefit of having accounting information is even harder to assess. It is possible to apply some 'science' to the problem of weighing the costs and benefits (see Figure 1.3), but a lot of subjective judgement is likely to be involved. Although no one would seriously advocate that the typical business

Figure 1.3

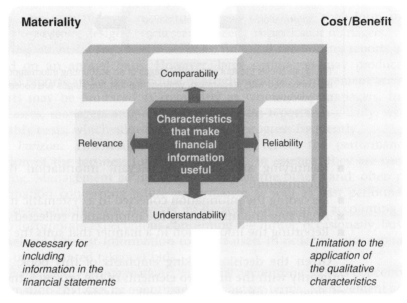

The characteristics that influence the usefulness of accounting information

Materiality

Cost/Benefit

Comparability

Characteristics that make financial information useful

Relevance

Reliability

Understandability

Necessary for including information in the financial statements

Limitation to the application of the qualitative characteristics

The figure shows that there are four main qualitative characteristics that influence the usefulness of accounting information. In addition, however, accounting information should be material and the benefits of providing the information should outweigh the costs.

should produce no accounting information, at the same time no one would advocate that every item of information that could be seen as possessing one or more of the key characteristics should be produced, irrespective of the cost of producing it.

When weighing the cost of providing additional financial information against the benefit, there is also the problem that those who bear the burden of the cost may not be the ones who benefit from the additional information. The cost of providing accounting information is usually borne by the owners, but other user groups may be the beneficiaries.

Accounting as an information system

We have already seen that accounting can be viewed as the provision of a service to 'clients'. Another way of viewing accounting is as part of the total information system within a business. Users, both inside and outside the business, have to make decisions concerning the allocation of scarce economic resources. To ensure that these resources are allocated in an efficient and effective manner, users require economic information on which to base decisions. It is the role of the accounting system to provide that information, and this will involve both information-gathering and communication.

The **accounting information system** is depicted in Figure 1.4. It has certain features that are common to all information systems within a business. These are:

- *Regulations*.   Financial reports, for many businesses, are subject to accounting regulations that exist to try to ensure that they are produced according to a standardised format. These regulations are imposed by law and the accounting profession. Because management accounting reports are for internal use only, there is no regulation from external sources concerning their form and content; they can be designed to meet the needs of particular managers.

- *Reporting interval*.   For most businesses, financial accounting reports are produced on an annual basis. However, large companies may produce semi-annual reports and a few produce quarterly reports. Management accounting reports may be produced as frequently as required by managers. In many businesses, managers are provided with certain reports on a daily, weekly or monthly basis, which allows them to check progress frequently.

- *Time horizon*.   Financial accounting reports reflect the performance and position of the business for the past period. In essence, they are backward-looking. Management accounting reports, on the other hand, often provide information concerning future performance as well as past performance. It is an oversimplification, however, to suggest that financial accounting reports never incorporate expectations concerning the future; occasionally, businesses will release forecast information to other users in order to raise capital or to fight off unwanted takeover bids.

- *Range and quality of information*.   Financial accounting reports concentrate on information that can be quantified in monetary terms. Management accounting also produces such reports, but is also more likely to produce reports that contain information of a non-financial nature, such as measures of physical quantities of stocks and output. Financial accounting places greater emphasis on the use of objective, verifiable evidence when preparing reports. Management accounting reports may use information that is less objective and verifiable in order to provide managers with the information that they require.

We can see from the above that management accounting is less constrained than financial accounting. It may draw from a variety of sources and use information that has varying degrees of reliability. The only real test to be applied when assessing the value of the information produced for managers is whether or not it improves the quality of decisions made.

Activity 1.7	Do you think a distinction between management accounting and financial accounting may be misleading? Is there any overlap between the information needs of managers and the needs of other users?

The distinction between management and financial accounting suggests that there are differences between the information needs of managers and those of other users. Although differences undoubtedly exist, there is also a good deal of overlap between the needs of managers and the needs of other users. For example, managers will, at times, be interested in receiving an historic overview of business operations of the sort provided to other users. Equally, the other users would be interested in receiving information relating to the future, such as the forecast level of profits, and non-financial information such as the state of the order book and product innovations.

The distinction between the two areas reflects, to some extent, the differences in access to financial information. Managers have much more control than other users over the form and content of information they receive. Other users have to rely on what managers are prepared to provide or what the financial reporting regulations state must be provided. Although the scope of financial accounting reports has increased over time, fears concerning loss of competitive advantage and of user ignorance concerning the reliability of forecast data have led businesses to resist providing other users with the detailed and wide-ranging information that is available to managers.

The changing nature of accounting

We are currently witnessing radical changes to both financial and management accounting. In the past, financial accounting has been criticised for lacking rules based on a clear theoretical framework. In addition, the accounting rules developed have been criticised for being too loose, for lacking consistency and for failing to portray economic reality. These weaknesses have been highlighted by a number of financial scandals over the years. The accounting profession has responded by trying to develop a framework that provides a clearer rationale for the subject and for the way in which accounting information is prepared and presented. This framework tries to address fundamental questions such as: 'What is the nature and purpose of accounting?', 'Who are the users of financial reports?', and 'What kinds of financial report should be prepared and what should they contain?' Although much work has still to be done, by answering these questions we will have the foundations necessary to develop accounting rules and practices in a more logical and consistent manner. This framework is considered in more detail in Chapter 7.

Management accounting has also been confronted with radical change. The environment in which businesses operate has become increasingly turbulent and competitive, and there have been rapid advances in production technology. These developments have, in turn, resulted in radical changes to the way in which businesses are organised and to the marketing and manufacturing strategies employed. Increasingly, successful businesses are distinguished by their ability to secure and maintain competitive advantage. In the face of such changes, management accounting has had to develop new approaches. In order to provide relevant information to managers, it has had to become more outward-looking. In the past, information supplied to managers has been largely restricted to that collected within the business. Increasingly, however, information relating to market share, innovations, customer evaluation of services provided, and costs of production compared with those of competitors is supplied to managers in many businesses. Changes in the environment have also created a need to develop more sophisticated methods of measuring and controlling costs. Businesses can no longer risk the damage to competitive advantage that might occur where decisions are based on inaccurate and misleading information, particularly when information technology can now help to provide sophisticated costing systems at relatively low cost.

Nowadays, we have a more questioning attitude to conventional rules and methods, and the result is that the boundaries of accounting are being redrawn.

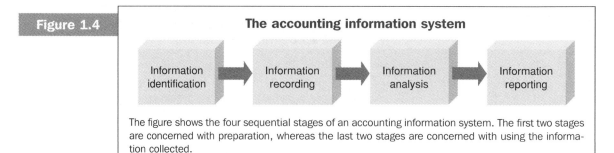

Figure 1.4

The accounting information system

Information identification → Information recording → Information analysis → Information reporting

The figure shows the four sequential stages of an accounting information system. The first two stages are concerned with preparation, whereas the last two stages are concerned with using the information collected.

- Identifying and capturing relevant information (in this case economic information).
- Recording the information collected in a systematic manner.
- Analysing and interpreting the information collected.
- Reporting the information in a manner that suits the needs of users.

Given the decision-making emphasis of this book, we shall be concerned primarily with the final two elements of the process – the analysis and reporting of financial information. We will consider the way in which information is used by, and is useful to, users rather than the way in which it is identified and recorded.

Financial and management accounting

Accounting is usually seen as having two distinct strands:

- **Management accounting**, which seeks to meet the needs of a business's managers.
- **Financial accounting**, which seeks to meet the accounting needs of all of the other users identified in Figure 1.1.

The differences between the two types of accounting reflect the different user groups that they address. Briefly, the major differences are as follows:

- *Nature of the reports produced.* Financial accounting reports tend to be general-purpose reports. That is, they contain financial information that will be useful for a broad range of users and decisions rather than being specifically designed for the needs of a particular group or set of decisions. Management accounting reports, on the other hand, are often specific-purpose reports. They are designed either with a particular decision in mind or for a particular manager.
- *Level of detail.* Financial accounting reports provide users with a broad overview of the position and performance of a business for a period. As a result, information is aggregated and detail is often lost. Management accounting reports, however, often provide managers with considerable detail to help them with a particular operational decision.

The changes that have taken place in recent years, and those that are currently taking place, are largely in response to changes in the external environment in which accounting exists. Given the increasing rate of change in the external environment, accounting is likely to change at an even faster pace in the future.

Scope of this book

This book is concerned with financial accounting rather than management accounting. In Chapter 2 we begin by introducing the three principal financial statements:

- Balance sheet
- Profit and loss account
- Cash flow statement

These statements are briefly reviewed before we go on to consider the balance sheet in more detail. We shall see that the balance sheet provides information concerning the wealth held by a business at a particular point in time and the claims against this wealth. Included in our consideration of the balance sheet will be an introduction to the **conventions of accounting**. Conventions are the generally accepted rules that accountants tend to follow when preparing financial statements. Chapter 3 introduces the second of the major financial statements, the profit and loss account. This statement provides information concerning the wealth created by a business during a period. In this chapter we shall be looking at such issues as how profit is measured, the point in time at which we recognise that a profit has been made and the accounting conventions which apply to this particular statement.

In the UK and throughout much of the industrialised world, the limited company is the major form of business unit. In Chapter 4 we consider the accounting aspects of limited companies. Although there is nothing of essence which makes the accounting aspects of companies different from other types of private-sector business, there are some points of detail that we need to consider. In Chapter 5 we continue our examination of limited companies and, in particular, consider the framework of rules that must be adhered to when presenting accounting reports to owners and external users.

Chapter 6 deals with the last of the three principal financial statements, the cash flow statement. This financial statement is important in identifying the financing and investing activities of the business over a period. It sets out how cash was generated and how cash was used during a period.

Reading the three statements will provide information about the performance and position of a business. It is possible, however, to gain even more helpful insights to the business by analysing the statements using financial ratios and other techniques. Combining two figures in the financial statements in a ratio and comparing this with a similar ratio for, say, another business, can often tell us much more than just reading the figures themselves. Chapter 7 is concerned with techniques for analysing financial statements.

Many of the larger businesses in the UK are a group of companies rather than just a single company. A group of companies will exist where one company controls one or more other companies. In Chapter 8 we shall see why groups exist and consider the accounting issues raised by the combination of companies into groups.

Finally, we shall consider the way in which the reporting of financial information has expanded in recent years. The increasing complexity of business and the increasing demands of users for additional information have led to a number of supplementary financial reports being produced. In Chapter 9 we shall consider some of the more important of these.

Forms of business unit

Businesses may be classified according to their form of ownership. The particular classification has important implications when accounting for businesses – as we shall see in later chapters – and so it is useful to be clear about the main forms of ownership arrangements that can arise.

There are basically three arrangements:

- Sole proprietorship
- Partnership
- Limited company.

Sole proprietorship

➡ **Sole proprietorship**, as the name suggests, is where an individual is the sole owner of a business. This type of business is often quite small in terms of size (as measured, for example, by sales generated or number of staff employed), however, the number of such businesses is very large indeed. Examples of sole-proprietor businesses can be found in most industrial sectors but particularly within the service sector. Hence, services such as electrical repairs, picture framing, photography, driving instruction, retail shops and hotels have a large proportion of sole-proprietor businesses. The sole-proprietor business is easy to set up. No formal procedures are required and operations can often commence immediately (unless special permission is required because of the nature of the trade or service, such as running licensed premises). The owner can decide the way in which the business is to be conducted and has the flexibility to restructure or dissolve the business whenever it suits. The law does not recognise the sole-proprietor business as being separate from the owner, and so the business will cease on the death of the owner. Although the owner must produce accounting information to satisfy the taxation authorities, there is no legal requirement to produce accounting information relating to the business for other user groups. However, some user groups may demand accounting information about the business and may be in a position to have their demands met (for example, lenders requiring accounting information on a regular basis as a condition of a loan). The sole proprietor will have unlimited liability which means that no distinction will be made between the proprietor's personal wealth and that of the business if there are business debts that must be paid.

Partnership

➡ A **partnership** exists where there are at least two individuals – but usually no more than twenty – carrying on a business together with the intention of making a profit. Partnerships have much in common with sole-proprietor businesses. They are often quite small in size (although partnerships of accountants and solicitors can be large as they are permitted to have more than twenty partners). Partnerships are also easy to set up as no formal procedures are required (and it is not even necessary to have a written agreement between the partners). The partners can agree whatever arrangements suit them concerning the financial and management aspects of the business, and the partnership can be restructured or dissolved by agreement between the partners.

Partnerships are not recognised in law as separate entities and so contracts with third parties must be entered into in the name of individual partners. The partners of a business usually have unlimited liability, although it is possible to grant limited liability to partners who have no say in the running of the business.

Activity 1.8	What are the main advantages and disadvantages that should be considered when deciding between a sole proprietorship and a partnership?

The main advantages of a partnership over a sole-proprietor business are:

■ Sharing the burden of ownership.
■ The opportunity to specialise rather than cover the whole range of services (for example, a doctors' practice).
■ The ability to raise capital where this is beyond the capacity of a single individual.
■ The ability to limit the liability of owners who are not engaged in running the business.

The main disadvantages of a partnership compared with a sole proprietorship are:

■ The risks of sharing ownership of a business with unsuitable individuals.
■ The limits placed on individual decision making that a partnership will impose.

Limited company

➡ **Limited companies** can range in size from quite small to very large. The number of individuals who subscribe capital and become the owners may be unlimited, which provides the opportunity to create a very large-scale business. The liability of owners, however, is limited (hence 'limited' company), which means that those individuals subscribing capital to the company are liable only for debts incurred by the company up to the amount that they have agreed to invest. This cap on the liability of the owners is designed to limit risk and to produce greater confidence to invest. Without such limits on owner liability, it is difficult to see how a modern capitalist economy could operate. In many cases, the owners of a limited company are not involved in the day-to-day running of the business and will only invest in a business if there is a clear limit set on the level of investment risk.

The benefit of limited liability, however, imposes certain obligations on such a company. To start up a limited company, documents of incorporation must be prepared that set out, amongst other things, the objectives of the business; furthermore a framework of regulations exists that places obligations on the way in which such a company conducts its affairs. Part of this regulatory framework requires annual financial reports to be made available to owners and lenders and an annual general meeting of the owners to be held to approve the reports. In addition, a copy of the annual financial reports must be lodged with the Registrar of Companies for public inspection. In this way, the financial affairs of a limited company enter the public domain. With the exception of small companies, there is also a requirement for the annual financial reports to be subject to an audit. This involves an independent firm of accountants examining the annual reports and underlying records to see whether the reports provide a true and fair view of the financial health of the company and whether they comply with the relevant accounting rules established by law and by the accounting profession.

The features of limited companies will be considered in more detail in Chapters 4 and 5.

Activity 1.9   **What are the main advantages and disadvantages that should be considered when deciding between a partnership business and a limited liability company?**

The main advantages of a partnership over a limited company are:

- The ease of setting up the business.
- The degree of flexibility concerning the way in which the business is conducted.
- The degree of flexibility concerning restructuring and dissolution of the business.
- Freedom from administrative burdens imposed by law (for example, the annual general meeting and the need for an independent audit).

The main disadvantages of a partnership compared with a limited company are:

- Restrictions placed on the number of partners, which can limit the ability to raise capital.
- The fact that it is not possible to limit the liability of owners who play an active part in running the business.

In this book we will be concentrating on the accounting aspects of limited liability companies, because this type of business is by far the most important in economic terms. However, the accounts of limited companies are more complex than those of partnerships and sole proprietorships and so it is not really a good idea to introduce the basic principles of accounting using examples based on this form of business unit. The early chapters will, therefore, introduce accounting concepts through examples based on sole-proprietor businesses, this being the simplest form of business unit. Once we have dealt with the basic accounting principles, which are the same for all three types of business, we can then go on to see how they are applied to limited companies.

Summary

This chapter has identified the main users of accounting and examined their information needs. We have seen that accounting exists in order to improve the quality of economic decisions made by users. Unless accounting information fulfils this purpose, it has no real value. We considered two views of accounting that help us to understand its essential features. The first view is that accounting is a form of service and that the information provided should contain certain key characteristics or qualities to ensure its usefulness. The second view is that accounting can be seen as part of the total information system of a business which is concerned with identifying, recording, analysing and reporting economic information. These two views are not competing views of the subject. By embracing both views we can achieve a better understanding of the nature and role of accounting.

We considered the particular role of financial accounting and distinguished it from its close relation management accounting. We saw that financial accounting reports tend to be general-purpose reports which provide a broad overview of the position and performance of the business. These reports are usually constrained by the regulations imposed by law and the accounting profession.

Finally, we considered the three main forms of business enterprise. We saw that limited companies are the most important of the three forms discussed and, for this reason, will be the main focus of this book.

 Key terms

Accounting p. 1	Accounting information system p. 9
Share p. 5	Management accounting p. 10
Relevance p. 6	Financial accounting p. 10
Reliability p. 6	Conventions of accounting p. 13
Comparability p. 6	Sole proprietorship p. 14
Understandability p. 7	Partnership p. 15
Materiality p. 7	Limited company p. 15

Further reading

If you would like to explore the topics covered in this chapter in more depth, we recommend the following books:

Financial Accounting, *Bebbington J., Gray R.* and *Laughlin R.*, 3rd edn, Thomson Learning, 2001, chapter 1.

Management Accounting, *Atkinson, A., Banker, R., Kaplan, R.* and *Young, S.*, 3rd edn, Prentice Hall International, 2001, chapter 1.

Fundamentals of Corporate Finance, *Brealey, R., Myers, S.* and *Marcus, A.*, 2nd edn, McGraw Hill, 1999, chapter 1.

Financial Accounting and Reporting, *Elliott, B.* and *Elliott, J.*, 5th edn, Financial Times Prentice Hall, 2001, chapter 1.

Accounting Theory: Text and Readings, *Schroeder, R.* and *Clark, M.*, 5th edn, Wiley, 1995, chapter 1.

? REVIEW QUESTIONS

1.1 Identify the main users of accounting information for a university. Do these users, or the way in which they use accounting information, differ very much from the users of accounting information for a private-sector business?

1.2 What, in economic principle, should be the determinate of what accounting information is produced? Should economics be the only issue here? (Consider who are the users of accounting information.).

1.3 Financial accounting statements tend to reflect past events. In view of this, how can they be of any help to a user in making a decision when decisions, by their very nature, can only be made about future actions?

1.4 'Accounting information should be understandable. As some users of accounting information have a poor knowledge of accounting, we should produce simplified financial reports to help them.' To what extent do you agree with this view?

CHAPTER 2

Measuring and reporting financial position

Introduction

We begin this chapter by providing an overview of the major financial statements. We shall see how each of these statements contributes towards providing users with a picture of the financial position and performance of a business. We shall then turn our attention towards a detailed examination of one of these financial statements – the balance sheet. We shall examine the principles underpinning this statement and see how it is prepared. We shall also consider its value for decision-making purposes.

OBJECTIVES   When you have completed this chapter you should be able to:

■ Explain the nature and purpose of the major financial statements.
■ Prepare a balance sheet and interpret the information contained within it.
■ Discuss the accounting conventions underpinning the balance sheet.
■ Identify the limitations of the balance sheet in portraying financial position.

The major financial statements – an overview

The major financial statements are designed to provide a picture of the overall financial position and performance of the business. To provide this overall picture, the accounting system will normally produce three major financial statements on a regular basis. These are concerned with answering the following:

■ What cash movements took place over a particular period?
■ How much wealth (that is, profit) was generated by the business over a particular period?
■ What is the accumulated wealth of the business at the end of a particular period?

These questions are addressed by the three financial statements, each of which deals with one of them. The financial statements produced are:

➡ ■ **The cash flow statement**
➡ ■ **The profit and loss account**
➡ ■ **The balance sheet**

When taken together, they provide an overall picture of the financial health of a business.

Perhaps the best way to introduce the financial statements is to look at an example of a very simple business. From this we shall be able to see the sort of information that each of the statements can usefully provide.

Example 2.1

Paul was unemployed and was unable to find a job. He therefore decided to embark on a business venture. Christmas was approaching and so he decided to buy gift-wrapping paper from a local supplier and sell it on the corner of his local high street. He felt that the price of wrapping paper in the high street shops was excessive and that this provided him with a useful business opportunity.

He began the venture with £40 in cash. On the first day of trading he purchased wrapping paper for £40 and sold three-quarters of his stock for £45 cash.

■ **What cash movements took place in the first day of trading?**

On the first day of trading a cash flow statement, showing the cash movements for the day, can be prepared as follows:

Cash flow statement for day 1

	£
Opening balance (cash introduced)	40
Proceeds from sale of wrapping paper	45
	85
Cash paid to purchase wrapping paper	(40)
Closing balance	45

(Note that a bracket round a figure as shown with the second £40 here, means that it is to be deducted. This is common in accounting statements, and we shall tend to use it throughout the book.)

■ **How much wealth (profit) was generated by the business in the first day of trading?**

A profit and loss account can be prepared to show the wealth (profit) generated on the first day. The wealth generated will represent the difference between the value of the sales made and the cost of the goods (the wrapping paper) sold:

Profit and loss account for day 1

	£
Sales	45
Cost of goods sold ($\frac{3}{4}$ of £40)	(30)
Profit	15

Note that it is only the *cost* of the wrapping sold that is matched against the sales in order to find the profit and not the whole of the cost of wrapping paper acquired. Any unsold stock (in this case $\frac{1}{4}$ of £40 = £10) will be charged against future sales of that stock.

■ **What is the accumulated wealth at the end of the first day?**

To establish the accumulated wealth at the end of the first day, we can draw up a balance sheet. This will list the resources held at the end of the day:

Balance sheet at the end of day 1

	£
Cash (closing balance)	45
Stock of goods for resale ($\frac{1}{4}$ of £40)	10
Total business wealth	55

We can see from the financial statements in the example that each provides part of a picture which sets out the financial performance and position of the business. We begin by showing the cash movements. Cash is a vital resource that is necessary for any business to function effectively. Cash is required to meet maturing obligations and to acquire other resources (such as stock). Cash has been described as the lifeblood of a business and movements in cash usually attract scrutiny by users of financial statements.

It is clear, however, that reporting cash movements alone would not be enough to portray the financial health of the business. The changes in cash over time do not give an insight into the profit generated. The profit and loss account provides information on this aspect of performance. For day 1 in Example 2.1, we saw that the cash balance increased by £5, but the profit generated, as shown in the profit and loss account, was £15. The cash balance did not increase by the amount of the profit made because part of the wealth generated (£10) was held in the form of stock.

To gain an insight to the total wealth of the business, a balance sheet is drawn up at the end of the day. Cash is only one form in which wealth can be held. In the case of this business, wealth is also held in the form of a stock of goods for resale. Hence, when drawing up the balance sheet for our example, both forms of wealth held will be listed. In the case of a large business, there will be many other forms in which wealth will be held, such as land and buildings, equipment and motor vehicles.

Let us now continue with our example.

Example 2.2	On the second day of trading, Paul purchased more wrapping paper for £20 cash. He managed to sell all of the new stock and half of the earlier stock for a total of £38.

The cash flow statement on day 2 will be as follows:

Cash flow statement for day 2

	£
Opening balance (from day 1)	45
Cash proceeds from sale of wrapping paper	38
	83
Cash paid to purchase wrapping paper	(20)
Closing balance	63

The profit and loss account for day 2 will be as follows:

Profit and loss account for day 2

	£
Sales	38
Cost of goods sold (£20 + $\frac{1}{2}$ of £10)	(25)
Profit	13

The balance sheet at the end of day 2 will be thus:

Balance sheet at the end of day 2

	£
Cash	63
Stock of goods for resale ($\frac{1}{2}$ of £10)	5
Total business wealth	68

We can see that the total business wealth had increased to £68 by the end of day 2. This represents an increase of £13 (that is, £68 – £55) over the previous day – which, of course, is the amount of profit made during day 2 as shown on the profit and loss account.

Activity 2.1

On the third day of his business venture, Paul purchased more stock for £46 cash. However, it was raining hard for much of the day and sales were slow. After Paul had sold for £32 stock that had cost £23, he decided to stop trading until the following day.

Have a try at drawing up the three financial statements for day 3 of Paul's business venture.

Cash flow statement for day 3

	£
Opening balance (from day 2)	63
Cash proceeds from sale of wrapping paper	32
	95
Cash paid to purchase wrapping paper	(46)
Closing balance	49

The profit and loss account for day 3 will be as follows:

Profit and loss account for day 3

	£
Sales	32
Cost of goods sold	(23)
Profit	9

The balance sheet at the end of day 3 will be thus:

Balance sheet at the end of day 3

	£
Cash	49
Stock of goods for resale £(5 + 46 – 23)	28
Total business wealth	77

Note that at the end of day 3 the total business wealth had increased by £9 (that is, the amount of the day's profit) even though the cash balance declined. This is owing to the fact that the business is now holding more of its wealth in the form of stock rather than cash compared with the end of day 2.

Note also that the profit and loss account and cash flow statement are both concerned with measuring flows (of wealth and cash respectively) over time. The period of time may be one day, one month, one year, or whatever. The balance sheet, however, is concerned with the financial position at a particular moment in time (the end of one day, one week, etc.). Figure 2.1 illustrates this point.

Figure 2.1

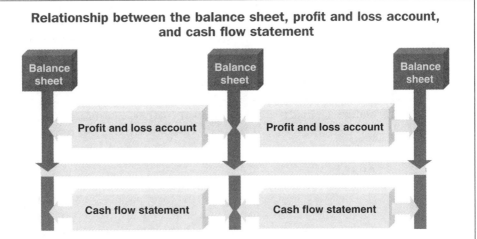

Relationship between the balance sheet, profit and loss account, and cash flow statement

This figure shows how the profit and loss account and cash flow statement are concerned with measuring flows of wealth over time. The balance sheet, however, is concerned with measuring the stock of wealth at a particular moment in time.

The profit and loss account, cash flow statement and balance sheet, when taken together, are often referred to as the **final accounts** of the business.

For external (that is, non-managerial) users of the accounts, these statements are normally backward-looking and are based on information concerning past events and transactions. This can be useful in providing feedback on past performance and in identifying trends that provide clues to future performance. However, the statements can also be prepared using projected data in order to help assess likely future profits, cash flows and so on. The financial statements are normally prepared on a projected basis for internal decision-making purposes only. Managers are usually reluctant to publish these projected statements for external users, as they may reveal valuable information to competitors.

Nevertheless, as external users also have to make decisions about the future, projected financial statements prepared by managers are likely to be useful for this purpose. Managers are, after all, in a good position to assess future performance and so their assessments are likely to provide a valuable source of information. In certain circumstances, such as raising new capital or resisting a hostile takeover bid, managers are prepared to depart from normal practice and issue projected financial statements to external users. Where publication occurs, some independent verification of the assumptions underlying the forecast statements is often provided by a firm of accountants to help lend credibility to the figures produced.

Now that we have considered an overview of the financial statements, we shall consider each statement in more detail. In Chapter 3 we shall look at the profit and loss account, and in Chapter 6 we shall go into more detail on the cash flow statement.

The balance sheet

The purpose of the balance sheet is simply to set out the financial position of a business at a particular moment in time. (The balance sheet is sometimes referred to as the 'position statement' because it seeks to provide the user with a picture of financial position.) We saw earlier that the balance sheet will reveal the forms in which the wealth of the business is held and how much wealth is held in each form. We can, however, be more specific about the nature of the balance sheet by saying that it sets out the **assets** of the business, on the one hand, and the **claims** against the business on the other. Before looking at the balance sheet in more detail, we need to be clear about what these terms mean.

Assets

In everyday language, the term 'asset' is used to denote something that is of value. Thus, for example, you may hear someone say 'She is a tremendous asset to the organisation,' meaning that the individual is making a valuable contribution to the work of the organisation. In accounting, however, the term is used in a much more narrow sense than this. For accounting purposes, the term is used to describe a resource held by a business that has certain characteristics. The major characteristics of an accounting asset are set out next:

- *A probable future economic benefit exists.* This simply means that the item is expected to have some future monetary value. This value can arise through its use within the business or through its hire or sale. Thus, an obsolete piece of equipment that can be sold for scrap would still be considered an asset, whereas an obsolete piece of equipment that could not be sold for scrap would not be regarded as an asset.
- *The business has an exclusive right to control the benefit.* Unless the business has exclusive rights over the resource, it cannot be regarded as an asset. Thus, for a business offering holidays on barges, the canal system may be a very valuable resource; however, as the business will not be able to control the access of others to the system, it cannot be regarded as an accounting asset of the business. (The barges owned by the business would be regarded as assets.)
- *The benefit must arise from some past transaction or event.* This means the transaction (or other event) giving rise to the business's right to the benefit must have already occurred and will not arise at some future date. Thus, an agreement by a business to purchase a piece of machinery at some future date would not mean that the item is currently an asset of the business.
- *The asset must be capable of measurement in monetary terms.* Unless the item can be measured in monetary terms with a reasonable degree of reliability, the item will not be regarded as an asset for inclusion on the balance sheet. Thus the loyalty of customers may be extremely valuable to a business, but is usually impossible to quantify and so will be excluded from the balance sheet.

We can see that these conditions will strictly limit the kinds of item that may be referred to as assets for accounting purposes. Certainly, not all resources exploited by a business will be accounting assets of the business. This is viewed by many as a weakness of accounting as it means that valuable resources are being excluded from the financial statements of businesses. (We shall return to this point later in the chapter.) Once an asset has been acquired by a business, it will continue to be considered an asset until the benefits are exhausted or the business disposes of it in some way.

| **Activity 2.2** | State which of the following items could appear on the balance sheet of business A as an asset. Explain your reasoning in each case. |

(a) £1,000 owing to business A by a customer who will never be able to pay.
(b) The purchase of a patent from an inventor that gives business A the right to produce a product designed by that business. Production of the new product is expected to increase profits over the period in which the patent is held.
(c) The hiring of a new marketing director by business A who is confidently expected to increase profits by over 30 per cent over the next three years.
(d) Purchase of a machine that will save business A £10,000 per annum. It is currently being used by the business but has been acquired on credit and is not yet paid for.

(a) Under normal circumstances a business would expect a customer to pay the amount owed. Such an amount is, therefore, typically shown as an asset under the heading 'debtors'. However, in this particular case, the debtor is unable to pay. Hence, the item is incapable of providing future benefits, and the £1,000 owing would not be regarded as an asset. Debts that are not paid are referred to as 'bad debts'.
(b) The purchase of the patent would meet all of the conditions set out above and would, therefore, be regarded as an asset.
(c) The hiring of a new marketing director would not be considered the acquisition of an asset. One argument against its classification as an asset is that the business does not have exclusive rights of control over the director. Nevertheless, it may have an exclusive right to the services that the director provides. Perhaps a stronger argument is that the value of the director cannot be measured in monetary terms with any degree of reliability.
(d) The machine would be considered an asset even though it is not yet paid for. Once the business has agreed to purchase the machine and has accepted it, the business has exclusive rights over the machine even though payment is still outstanding. (The amount outstanding would be shown as a claim, as we shall see below.)

The sorts of item that often appear as assets in the balance sheet of a business include:

- Freehold premises
- Machinery and equipment
- Fixtures and fittings
- Patents and trademarks
- Debtors
- Investments

Activity 2.3	Can you think of three additional items that might appear as assets in the balance sheet of a business?

Some items that you might have identified are:

- Motor vehicles
- Copyright
- Stock of goods
- Computer equipment
- Cash at bank
- Cash in hand

Note that an asset does not have to be a physical item – it may also be a non-physical right to certain benefits (for example, patents and copyright). Assets that have a physical substance and that can be touched are referred to as **tangible assets**. Assets that have no physical substance but, nevertheless, provide expected future benefits are referred to as **intangible assets**.

Claims

A claim is an obligation on the part of a business to provide cash, or some other form of benefit, to an outside party. A claim will normally arise as a result of the outside party providing funds in the form of assets for use by the business. There are essentially two types of claim against a business. These are:

- **Capital.** This represents the claim of the owner(s) against the business. This claim is sometimes referred to as the owners' equity. Some find it hard to understand how the owner can have a claim against the business, particularly when we consider the example of a sole-proprietor business where the owner *is*, in effect, the business. However, for accounting purposes, a clear distinction is made between the business (whatever its size) and the owner(s). The business is viewed as being quite separate from the owner, irrespective of the form of business. This means that when financial statements are prepared, they are prepared from the perspective of the business rather than that of the owner(s). Viewed from this perspective, therefore, any funds contributed by the owner to help finance the business will be regarded as a claim against the business, in its balance sheet.
- **Liabilities.** Liabilities represent the claims of individuals and organisations, apart from the owner, that have arisen from past transactions or events, such as supplying goods or lending money to the business.

Once a claim has been incurred by a business it will remain as an obligation until it is settled.

Now that the meaning of the terms assets and claims has been established, we can go on to discuss the relationship between the two. This relationship is quite simple and straightforward. If a business wishes to acquire assets, it will have to raise the necessary funds from somewhere. It may raise the funds from the owner(s) or from other outside parties or from both. To illustrate the relationship let us take the example of a new business as set out in Example 2.3.

Example 2.3

Jerry and Co. deposits £20,000 in a bank account on 1 March in order to commence business. Let us assume that the cash is supplied by the owner (£6,000) and an outside party (£14,000). The raising of the funds in this way gives rise to a claim on the business by both the owner (capital) and the outside party (liability). If a balance sheet of Jerry and Co. is prepared following the above transactions, the assets and claims of the business would appear as follows:

Balance sheet as at 1 March

	£			£
Assets			**Claims**	
Cash at bank	20,000		Capital	6,000
			Liability – loan	14,000
	20,000			20,000

We can see from the balance sheet that the total claims are the same as the total assets. Thus:

$$\text{Assets} = \text{Capital} + \text{Liabilities}$$

This equation – which is often referred to as the **balance sheet equation** – will always hold true. Whatever changes may occur to the assets of the business or the claims against the business, there will be compensating changes elsewhere that will ensure that the balance sheet always 'balances'. By way of illustration, consider some further possible transactions for Jerry and Co. Assume that, after the £20,000 had been deposited in the bank, the following transactions took place:

2 March   Purchased a motor van for £5,000, paying by cheque
3 March   Purchased stock in trade (that is, goods to be sold) on one month's credit for £3,000
4 March   Repaid £2,000 of the loan from outside party
6 March   Owner introduced £4,000 into the business bank account

A balance sheet may be drawn up after each day in which transactions have taken place. In this way, the effect can be seen of each transaction on the assets and claims of the business. The balance sheet as at 2 March will be as follows:

Balance sheet as at 2 March

	£			£
Assets			**Claims**	
Cash at bank	15,000		Capital	6,000
Motor van	5,000		Liabilities – loan	14,000
	20,000			20,000

As can be seen, the effect of purchasing a motor van is to decrease the balance at the bank by £5,000 and to introduce a new asset – a motor van – to the balance sheet. The total assets remain unchanged. It is only the 'mix' of assets that will change. The claims against the business will remain the same because there has been no change in the funding arrangements for the business.

The balance sheet as at 3 March, following the purchase of stock, will be as follows:

Balance sheet as at 3 March

Assets	£	Claims	£
Cash at bank	15,000	Capital	6,000
Motor van	5,000	Liabilities – loan	14,000
Stock	3,000	– trade creditor	3,000
	23,000		23,000

The effect of purchasing stock has been to introduce another new asset (stock) to the balance sheet. In addition, the fact that the goods have not yet been paid for means that the claims against the business will be increased by the £3,000 owed to the supplier who is referred to as a 'trade creditor' on the balance sheet.

Activity 2.4

Try drawing up a balance sheet for Jerry and Co. as at 4 March.

The balance sheet as at 4 March, following the repayment of part of the loan, will be as follows:

Balance sheet as at 4 March

Assets	£	Claims	£
Cash at bank	13,000	Capital	6,000
Motor van	5,000	Liabilities – loan	12,000
Stock	3,000	– trade creditor	3,000
	21,000		21,000

The repayment of £2,000 of the loan will result in a decrease in the balance at the bank of £2,000 and a decrease in the loan claim against the business by the same amount.

Activity 2.5

Try drawing up a balance sheet as at 6 March for Jerry and Co.

The balance sheet as at 6 March, following the introduction of more funds, will be as follows:

Balance sheet as at 6 March

Assets	£	Claims	£
Cash at bank	17,000	Capital	10,000
Motor van	5,000	Liabilities – loan	12,000
Stock	3,000	– trade creditor	3,000
	25,000		25,000

The introduction of more funds by the owner will result in an increase in the capital of £4,000 and an increase in the cash at the bank by the same amount.

Example 2.3 illustrates the point that the balance sheet equation (Assets = Capital + Liabilities) will always hold true. This is because the equation is based on the fact that, if a business wishes to acquire assets, it must raise funds equal to the cost of those assets. These funds must be provided by the owners (capital), or other outside parties (liabilities), or both. Hence, the total cost of assets acquired should always equal the total capital plus liabilities.

It is worth pointing out that a business would not draw up a balance sheet after each day of transactions as shown in the example above. Such an approach is likely to be impractical given even a relatively small number of transactions each day. A balance sheet for the business is usually prepared at the end of a defined reporting period. Determining the length of the reporting interval will involve weighing up the costs of producing the information against the perceived benefits of the information for decision-making purposes. In practice, the reporting interval will vary between businesses and could be monthly, quarterly, half-yearly or annually. For external reporting purposes, an annual reporting cycle is the norm (although certain businesses, typically larger ones, report more frequently than this). However, for internal reporting purposes, many businesses produce monthly financial statements.

The effect of trading operations on the balance sheet

In Example 2.3 we dealt with the effect on the balance sheet of a number of different types of transactions that a business might undertake. These transactions covered the purchase of assets for cash and on credit, the repayment of a loan, and the injection of capital. However, one form of transaction – trading – has not yet been considered. In order to deal with the effect of trading transactions on the balance sheet let us look at Example 2.4.

Example 2.4

Let us return to the balance sheet that we drew up for Jerry and Co. as at 6 March. The balance sheet at that date was as follows:

Balance sheet as at 6 March

Assets	£	Claims	£
Cash at bank	17,000	Capital	10,000
Motor van	5,000	Liabilities – loan	12,000
Stock	3,000	– trade creditor	3,000
	25,000		25,000

Let us assume that, on 7 March, the business managed to sell all of the stock for £5,000 and received a cheque immediately from the customer for this amount. The balance sheet on 7 March, after this transaction has taken place, will be as follows:

Balance sheet as at 7 March

Assets	£	Claims	£
Cash at bank	22,000	Capital [10,000 + (5,000 – 3,000)]	12,000
Motor van	5,000	Liabilities – loan	12,000
		– trade creditor	3,000
	27,000		27,000

We can see that the stock (£3,000) has now disappeared from the balance sheet but the cash at bank has increased by the selling price of the stock (£5,000). The net effect has therefore been to increase assets by £2,000 (£5,000 – £3,000). This increase represents the net increase in wealth (the profit) that has arisen from trading. Also note that the capital of the business has increased by £2,000 in line with the increase in assets. This increase in capital reflects the fact that increases in wealth as a result of trading or other operations will be to the benefit of the owner and will increase his/her stake in the business.

| Activity 2.6 | What would have been the effect on Jerry and Co.'s balance sheet if the stock had been sold on 7 March for £1,000 rather that £5,000? |

The balance sheet on 7 March would be as follows:

Balance sheet as at 7 March

	£		£
Assets		**Claims**	
Cash at bank	18,000	Capital [10,000	
		+ (1,000 – 3,000)]	8,000
Motor van	5,000	Liabilities – loan	12,000
		– trade creditor	3,000
	23,000		23,000

As we can see, the stock (£3,000) will disappear from the balance sheet but the cash at bank will rise by only £1,000. This will mean a net reduction in assets of £2,000. This reduction represents a loss arising from trading and will be reflected in a reduction in the capital of the owner.

Thus, we can see from Activity 2.6 that any decrease in wealth (loss) arising from trading or other transactions will lead to a reduction in the owner's stake in the business. If the business wished to maintain the level of assets as at 6 March, it would be necessary to obtain further funds from the owner or outside parties, or both.

What we have just seen means that the balance sheet equation can be extended as follows:

Assets = Capital +(–) Profit(Loss) + Liabilties

The profit for the period is usually shown separately in the balance sheet as an addition to capital. Any funds introduced or withdrawn by the owner for living expenses or other reasons are also shown separately. Thus, if we assume that the above business sold the stock for £5,000, as in the earlier example, and further assume that the owner withdrew £1,500 of the profit for his or her own use, the capital of the owner would appear as follows on the balance sheet:

	£
Capital	
Opening balance	10,000
Add Profit	2,000
	12,000
Less Drawings	(1,500)
Closing balance	10,500

If the drawings were in cash, then the balance of cash would decrease by £1,500 and this would be reflected in the balance sheet.

Note that, like all balance sheet items, the amount of capital is cumulative. This means that any profit made that is not taken out as drawings by the owner(s) remains in the business. These 'retained earnings' have the effect of expanding the business.

The classification of assets

To help users of financial information to locate easily items of interest on the balance sheet, it is customary to group assets and claims into categories. Assets are normally categorised as being either fixed or current.

➡ **Fixed assets** are defined primarily according to the purpose for which they are held. Fixed assets are held with the intention of being used to generate wealth rather than being held for resale (although they may be sold by the business when there is no further use for the asset). They can be seen as the tools of the business. Fixed assets are normally held by the business on a continuing basis. The minimum period for which a fixed asset is expected to be held is not precisely defined, although one year is sometimes quoted.

Activity 2.7	Can you think of two examples of assets that may be classified as fixed assets within a particular business?

Examples of assets that often meet the definition of fixed assets include:

■ Freehold premises
■ Plant and machinery
■ Motor vehicles
■ Patents
■ Copyrights

This is not an exhaustive list. You may have thought of others.

➡ **Current assets** are assets that are not held on a continuing basis. They include cash itself and other assets that are expected to be converted to cash at some future point in time in the normal course of trading. Current assets are normally held as part of the day-to-day trading activity of the business. The most common current assets are stock, trade debtors (that is, customers who owe money for goods or services supplied on credit) and cash itself. The current assets mentioned are interrelated and circulate within a business, as shown in Figure 2.2. We can see that the cash can be used to purchase stock, which is then sold on credit. When the debtors pay, the business receives an injection of cash, and so on.

It is important to appreciate that the classification of an asset as fixed or current may vary according to the nature of the business being carried out. This is because the *purpose* for which a particular type of business holds a certain asset may vary. For example, a motor-vehicle manufacturer will normally hold the motor vehicles produced for resale and would therefore classify them as stock in trade (a current asset). On the other hand, a business that uses motor vehicles for transportation purposes would classify them as fixed assets.

Figure 2.2

The circulating nature of current assets

The figure shows how stock may be sold on credit to customers. When the customers pay, the trade debtors will be converted into cash which can then be used to purchase more stocks, and so the cycle begins again.

Activity 2.8

The assets of Poplilova and Co., a large metalworking business, are shown below:

- Cash at bank
- Fixtures and fittings
- Office equipment
- Motor vehicles
- Freehold factory premises
- Goodwill purchased from business taken over
- Plant and machinery
- Computer equipment
- Stock of work in progress (that is, partly-completed products)
- Short-term investments

Which of the above do you think should be defined as fixed assets and which should be defined as current assets?

Your answer to the above activity should be as follows:

Fixed assets	Current assets
Fixtures and fittings	Cash at bank
Office equipment	Stock of work-in-progress
Motor vehicles	Short-term investments
Freehold factory premises	
Goodwill purchased	
Plant and machinery	
Computer equipment	

The item 'goodwill purchased' in the list of fixed assets in Activity 2.8 requires some explanation. When a business takes over another business, the amount that is paid for the business taken over will often exceed the total value of the individual assets that have been acquired. This additional amount represents a payment for goodwill that arises from such factors as the quality of products sold, the skill of the workforce and the relationship with customers.

We saw earlier that these qualitative items are normally excluded from the balance sheet as they are difficult to measure. However, when they have been acquired by a business at an agreed price, the amount paid provides an objective basis for measurement. Hence, goodwill purchased can be regarded as an asset and included on the balance sheet. Goodwill is regarded as a fixed asset as it is not held primarily for resale and will be held on a continuing basis. We shall discuss some of the issues surrounding goodwill later in this chapter and also in Chapter 3.

The classification of claims

As we have already seen, claims are normally classified into capital (owners' claims) and liabilities (claims of outsiders). Liabilities are further classified into two groups:

➡ ■ **Long-term liabilities** represent those amounts due to other parties that are not liable for repayment within the twelve-month period following the balance sheet date.

➡ ■ **Current liabilities** represent amounts due for repayment to outside parties within 12 months of the balance sheet date.

Unlike assets, the purpose for which the liabilities are held is not an issue. It is only the period for which the liability is outstanding that is important. Thus, a long-term liability will turn into a current liability when the settlement date comes within twelve months of the balance sheet date.

Activity 2.9	**Can you think of an example of a long-term liability and a current liability?**
	One example of a long-term liability would be a long-term loan. Two examples of a current liability would be trade creditors (that is, amounts owing to suppliers for goods supplied on credit) and a bank overdraft (a form of bank borrowing that is repayable on demand).

Balance sheet formats

Now that we have considered the classification of assets and liabilities, it is possible to consider the format of the balance sheet. Although there is an almost infinite number of ways in which the same balance sheet information could be presented, there are, in practice, two basic formats. The first of these follows the style we adopted with Jerry and Co. earlier. A more comprehensive example of this style is shown in Example 2.5.

Example 2.5

Brie Manufacturing
Balance sheet as at 31 December 2001

	£	£		£
Fixed assets			**Capital**	
Freehold premises		45,000	Opening balance	50,000
Plant and machinery		30,000	*Add* Profit	14,000
Motor vans		19,000		64,000
		94,000	*Less* Drawings	4,000
				60,000
			Long-term liabilities	
			Loan	50,000
Current assets			**Current liabilities**	
Stock in trade	23,000		Trade creditors	37,000
Trade debtors	18,000			
Cash at bank	12,000			
		53,000		
		147,000		147,000

Note that, within each category of asset (fixed and current) shown in Example 2.5, the items are listed with the least liquid (furthest from cash) first, going down to the most liquid last. This is a standard practice that is followed irrespective of the format used. Note also that the current assets are listed individually in the first column and a subtotal of current assets (£53,000) is carried out to the second column to be added to the subtotal of fixed assets (£94,000). This convention is designed to make the balance sheet easier to read.

An obvious change in the format shown in Example 2.5 from the format of Example 2.4, is to show claims on the left and assets on the right. Some people prefer this approach because the claims can be seen as the source of finance for the business and the assets show how that finance has been deployed. It could be seen as more logical to show sources first and uses second.

The format shown above is sometimes referred to as the **horizontal layout**. However, in recent years, a more common form of layout for the balance sheet is the **narrative** or **vertical form** of layout. This format is based on a rearrangement of the balance sheet equation. With the horizontal format above, the balance sheet equation is set out as:

$$FA + CA = C + LTL + CL$$

where   FA = fixed assets
         CA = current assets
           C = capital
      LTL = long-term loans
       CL = current liabilities

The vertical format merely rearranges this to:

$$FA + (CA - CL) - LTL = C$$

This rearranged equation is expressed in the format depicted in Figure 2.3.

We can now rearrange the balance sheet layout of Brie Manufacturing as shown in Example 2.6.

Figure 2.3

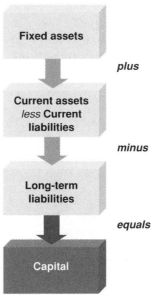

The vertical layout for a balance sheet

Fixed assets

plus

Current assets
less Current
liabilities

minus

Long-term
liabilities

equals

Capital

The figure sets out the vertical format for the balance sheet.

Example 2.6

Brie Manufacturing
Balance sheet as at 31 December 2001

	£	£
Fixed assets		
Freehold premises		45,000
Plant and machinery		30,000
Motor vans		19,000
		94,000
Current assets		
Stock in trade	23,000	
Trade debtors	18,000	
Cash at bank	12,000	
	53,000	
Current liabilities		
Trade creditors	(37,000)	
		16,000
Total assets less current liabilities		110,000
Long-term liabilities		
Loan		(50,000)
Net assets		60,000
Capital		
Opening balance		50,000
Add Profit		14,000
		64,000
Less Drawings		(4,000)
		60,000

Some people find the vertical format of Example 2.6 easier to read than the horizontal format. It usefully highlights the relationship between current assets and current liabilities. We shall consider shortly why this relationship is an important one. The figure derived from deducting current liabilities from current assets (a net amount of £16,000 for Brie Manufacturing) is sometimes referred to as **net current assets** or **working capital**.

Activity 2.10

The following information relates to the Simonson Engineering Company as at 30 September 2001:

	£
Plant and machinery	25,000
Trade creditors	18,000
Bank overdraft	26,000
Stock in trade	45,000
Freehold premises	72,000
Long-term loans	51,000
Capital at 1 October 2000	117,500
Trade debtors	48,000
Cash in hand	1,500
Motor vehicles	15,000
Fixtures and fittings	9,000
Profit for the year to 30 September 2001	18,000
Drawings for the year to 30 September 2001	15,000

Prepare a balance sheet in narrative form.

The balance sheet you prepare should be set out as follows:

Simonson Engineering Company
Balance sheet as at 30 September 2001

	£	£	£
Fixed assets			
Freehold premises			72,000
Plant and machinery			25,000
Motor vehicles			15,000
Fixtures and fittings			9,000
			121,000
Current assets			
Stock in trade		45,000	
Trade debtors		48,000	
Cash in hand		1,500	
		94,500	
Current liabilities			
Trade creditors	18,000		
Bank overdraft	26,000		
		(44,000)	
			50,500
Total assets less current liabilities			171,500

Long-term liabilities	£	£	£
Loan			(51,000)
Net assets			120,500
Capital			
Opening balance			117,500
Add Profit			18,000
			135,500
Less Drawings			(15,000)
			120,500

The balance sheet as a position at a point in time

The balance sheet is a statement of the financial position of a business at a specified point in time. The balance sheet has been compared with a photograph. A photograph 'freezes' a particular moment in time and will only represent the position at that moment; events may be quite different immediately before and immediately after. So it is with a balance sheet. When examining a balance sheet, therefore, it is important to establish the date at which it was drawn up. This information should be prominently displayed in the balance sheet heading, as is shown in the above examples. The more current the balance sheet date the better when you are trying to assess a current financial position.

A business will normally prepare a balance sheet as at the close of business on the last day of its accounting year. In the UK, businesses are free to choose their accounting year. When making a decision on which year-end date to choose, commercial convenience can often be a deciding factor. Thus a business operating in the retail trade may choose to have a year-end date early in the calendar year (for example 31 January) because trade tends to be slack during that period and more staff time is available to help with the tasks involved with the preparation of the annual accounting statements (such as checking the amount of stock held). Since trade is slack, it is also a time when the amount of stock held by the business is likely to be low as compared with other times of the year. Thus the balance sheet, though showing a fair view of what it purports to show, may not show a picture of what is more typically the position of the business over the year.

Accounting conventions and the balance sheet

Accounting is based on a number of rules, or conventions, that have evolved over time. They have evolved in order to deal with practical problems experienced by preparers and users rather than to reflect some theoretical ideal. When preparing balance sheets in this book, we have adhered to various accounting conventions though these have not been explicitly mentioned. Here we identify and discuss the major conventions that have been employed.

Money measurement convention

Accounting normally deals with only those items that are capable of being expressed in monetary terms. Money has the advantage that it is a useful common denominator with which to express the wide variety of resources held by a business. However, not all such resources are capable of being measured in monetary terms and so will be excluded from a balance sheet. The **money measurement convention**, therefore, limits the scope of accounting reports.

Activity 2.11	**Can you think of resources held by a business that are not normally included on the balance sheet because they cannot be quantified in monetary terms?**

You may have thought of the following:

- The quality of the workforce
- The reputation of the business's products
- The location of the business
- The relationship with customers
- The quality of management

Although normally excluded from the balance sheet, the items listed in Activity 2.11 may be seen as forming part of the goodwill of a business. As explained earlier, a business that purchases goodwill, by taking over another business, can show the amount paid on the balance sheet. Whilst the valuation process may be highly subjective, the amount actually paid represents an amount that can be objectively measured.

Accounting is a developing subject and the boundaries of financial measurement can change. In recent years, attempts have been made to measure particular resources of a business that have been previously excluded from the balance sheet. For example, we have seen the development of human resource accounting, which attempts to measure the value of the employees of a business. It is often claimed that employees are the most valuable 'assets' to a business. By measuring these assets and putting the amount on the balance sheet, it is sometimes argued that we have a more complete picture of financial position. For similar reasons, we have also seen attempts by certain large businesses to measure the value of product brand names that they hold (to be discussed later in the chapter). However, some of the measurement methods proposed have been controversial and often conflict with other accounting conventions. There are mixed views as to whether extending the boundaries of financial measurement will succeed in making the balance sheet a more useful representation of the financial position of a business.

Another approach to overcoming some of the limitations of money measurement is to publish a narrative financial statement. Rather than trying to 'quantify the unquantifiable', a narrative financial statement could be published to help users to assess financial health. Thus, in order to give a more complete picture of a financial position, a narrative statement might incorporate a discussion of such matters as investment policy, financial structure, liquidity and of valuable resources that have not been quantified. Many large businesses now produce such a statement, which is referred to as a 'financial review'. We shall consider this statement in more detail in Chapter 5.

Historic cost convention

➡ Assets are shown on the balance sheet at a value that is based on their **historic cost** (that is, acquisition cost). This method of measuring asset value has been adopted by accountants in preference to methods based on some form of current value. Many commentators find this particular convention difficult to support as outdated historic costs are unlikely to help in the assessment of current financial position. It is often argued that recording assets at their current value would provide a more realistic view of financial position and would be relevant for a wide range of decisions. However, a system of measurement based on current values can present a number of problems.

Activity 2.12	Can you think of reasons why current value accounting may pose problems for both preparers and users of financial statements?

The term 'current value' can be defined in a number of ways. For example, it can be defined broadly as either the current replacement cost or the current realisable value (selling price) of an item. These two types of valuation may result in quite different figures being produced to represent the current value of an item. (Think, for example, of second-hand car values; there is often quite a difference between buying and selling prices.) In addition, the broad terms 'replacement cost' and 'realisable value' can be defined in different ways. We must therefore be clear about what kind of current value accounting we wish to use. There are also practical problems associated with attempts to implement any system of current value accounting. For example, current values, however defined, are often difficult to establish with any real degree of objectivity. This may mean that the figures produced are heavily dependent on the opinion of managers. Unless the current value figures are capable of some form of independent verification, there is a danger that the financial statements will lose their credibility among users.

By reporting assets at their historic cost, it is argued that more reliable information is produced. Reporting in this way reduces the need for subjective opinion as the amount paid for a particular asset is usually a matter of demonstrable fact. However, information based on past costs may not always be relevant to the needs of users.

Later in the chapter we will consider the valuation of assets in the balance sheet in more detail. We will see that the historic cost convention is not always rigidly adhered to and that departures from this convention often occur.

Going concern convention

➡ The **going concern convention** holds that a business will continue operations for the foreseeable future. In other words, there is no intention or need to sell off the

Refer to the balance sheet for the Simonson Engineering Company shown in the answer to Activity 2.10. What would be the effect on the balance sheet of revaluing the freehold land to a figure of £110,000?

The effect on the balance sheet would be to increase the freehold land to £110,000 and the gain on revaluation (£110,000 − £72,000 = £38,000) would be added to the capital of the owner as it is the owner who will benefit from the gain. The revised balance sheet would therefore be as follows:

Balance sheet as at 30 September 2001

	£	£	£
Fixed assets			
Freehold premises (at valuation)			110,000
Plant and machinery			25,000
Motor vehicles			15,000
Fixtures and fittings			9,000
			159,000
Current assets			
Stock in trade		45,000	
Trade debtors		48,000	
Cash in hand		1,500	
		94,500	
Current liabilities			
Trade creditors	18,000		
Bank overdraft	26,000		
		(44,000)	
			50,500
Total assets less current liabilities			209,500
Long-term liabilities			
Loan			(51,000)
Net assets			158,500
Capital			
Opening balance			117,500
Add Revaluation gain			38,000
Profit			18,000
			173,500
Less Drawings			15,000
			158,500

In practice, the revaluation of land and buildings often has a significant effect on the size of the balance sheet figures for tangible fixed assets. In past years, this effect has usually been beneficial as property has risen in value throughout much of the past four decades. However, during the early 1990s there was not only a fall in property values but also some reluctance among those businesses who revalued their land and buildings upwards in earlier years, to make downward revaluations in recessionary years. A common reason cited was that the fall in value was considered to be only temporary.

Prudence convention

➡ The **prudence convention** holds that financial statements should err on the side of caution. The convention evolved to counteract the excessive optimism of some managers and owners, which resulted, in the past, in an overstatement of financial position. Operation of the prudence convention results in the recording of both actual and anticipated losses in full, whereas profits are not recognised until they are realised (that is, there is reasonable certainty that the profit will be received). When the prudence convention conflicts with another convention, it is prudence that will normally prevail. We shall see an example of this when we consider the valuation of current assets later in the chapter.

Activity 2.14	Can you think of a situation where certain users might find a cautious view of the financial position of a business can work to their disadvantage?

Applying the prudence convention can result in an understatement of financial position, because unrealised profits are not recognised whereas anticipated losses are recognised in full. This may result in owners selling their stake in the business at a price that is lower than they would have done had a more realistic approach to valuation been employed. The amount of this bias towards understatement may be difficult to judge. It is likely to vary according to the views of the individual carrying out the valuation.

Stable monetary unit convention

➡ The **stable monetary unit convention** holds that money, which is the unit of measurement in accounting, will not change in value over time. However, in the UK and throughout much of the world, inflation has been a persistent problem over the years and this has meant that the value of money has declined in relation to other assets. In past years, high rates of inflation have resulted in balance sheets, which are drawn up on a cost basis, reflecting figures for assets that were much lower than if current values were employed. The value of freehold land and buildings, in particular, increased rapidly during much of the 1970s, 1980s and 1990s, at least partly as a result of a reduction in the value of each £1. Where land and buildings were held for some time by a business, there was often a significant difference between their original cost and their current market value. This led to the criticism that balance sheet values were seriously understated and, as a result, some businesses broke away from the use of historic cost as the basis for valuing this particular asset. Instead, freehold land is periodically revalued in order to provide a more realistic statement of financial position. Although this represents a departure from accounting convention, it is a practice that has become increasingly common.

Activity 2.15

Refer to the balance sheet for the Simonson Engineering Company shown in the answer to Activity 2.10. What would be the effect on the balance sheet of revaluing the freehold land to a figure of £110,000?

The effect on the balance sheet would be to increase the freehold land to £110,000 and the gain on revaluation (£110,000 − £72,000 = £38,000) would be added to the capital of the owner as it is the owner who will benefit from the gain. The revised balance sheet would therefore be as follows:

Balance sheet as at 30 September 2001

Fixed assets	£	£	£
Freehold premises (at valuation)			110,000
Plant and machinery			25,000
Motor vehicles			15,000
Fixtures and fittings			9,000
			159,000
Current assets			
Stock in trade		45,000	
Trade debtors		48,000	
Cash in hand		1,500	
		94,500	
Current liabilities			
Trade creditors	18,000		
Bank overdraft	26,000		
		(44,000)	
			50,500
Total assets less current liabilities			209,500
Long-term liabilities			
Loan			(51,000)
Net assets			158,500
Capital			
Opening balance			117,500
Add Revaluation gain			38,000
Profit			18,000
			173,500
Less Drawings			15,000
			158,500

In practice, the revaluation of land and buildings often has a significant effect on the size of the balance sheet figures for tangible fixed assets. In past years, this effect has usually been beneficial as property has risen in value throughout much of the past four decades. However, during the early 1990s there was not only a fall in property values but also some reluctance among those businesses who revalued their land and buildings upwards in earlier years, to make downward revaluations in recessionary years. A common reason cited was that the fall in value was considered to be only temporary.

resources that have not been quantified. Many large businesses now produce such a statement, which is referred to as a 'financial review'. We shall consider this statement in more detail in Chapter 5.

Historic cost convention

➡ Assets are shown on the balance sheet at a value that is based on their **historic cost** (that is, acquisition cost). This method of measuring asset value has been adopted by accountants in preference to methods based on some form of current value. Many commentators find this particular convention difficult to support as outdated historic costs are unlikely to help in the assessment of current financial position. It is often argued that recording assets at their current value would provide a more realistic view of financial position and would be relevant for a wide range of decisions. However, a system of measurement based on current values can present a number of problems.

Activity 2.12	Can you think of reasons why current value accounting may pose problems for both preparers and users of financial statements?

The term 'current value' can be defined in a number of ways. For example, it can be defined broadly as either the current replacement cost or the current realisable value (selling price) of an item. These two types of valuation may result in quite different figures being produced to represent the current value of an item. (Think, for example, of second-hand car values; there is often quite a difference between buying and selling prices.) In addition, the broad terms 'replacement cost' and 'realisable value' can be defined in different ways. We must therefore be clear about what kind of current value accounting we wish to use. There are also practical problems associated with attempts to implement any system of current value accounting. For example, current values, however defined, are often difficult to establish with any real degree of objectivity. This may mean that the figures produced are heavily dependent on the opinion of managers. Unless the current value figures are capable of some form of independent verification, there is a danger that the financial statements will lose their credibility among users.

By reporting assets at their historic cost, it is argued that more reliable information is produced. Reporting in this way reduces the need for subjective opinion as the amount paid for a particular asset is usually a matter of demonstrable fact. However, information based on past costs may not always be relevant to the needs of users.

Later in the chapter we will consider the valuation of assets in the balance sheet in more detail. We will see that the historic cost convention is not always rigidly adhered to and that departures from this convention often occur.

Going concern convention

➡ The **going concern convention** holds that a business will continue operations for the foreseeable future. In other words, there is no intention or need to sell off the assets of the business. Such a sale may arise when the business is in financial difficulties and it needs cash to pay the creditors. This convention is important because the value of fixed assets on sale is often low in relation to the recorded values, and an expectation of having to sell off the assets would mean that anticipated losses on sale should be fully recorded. However, where there is no expectation of the need to sell off the assets, the value of fixed assets can continue to be shown at their recorded values (that is, based on historic cost). This convention, therefore, provides support for the historic cost convention under normal circumstances.

Business entity convention

For accounting purposes, the business and its owner(s) are treated as quite separate and distinct. This is why owners are treated as being claimants against their own business in respect of their investment in the business. The **business entity convention** must be distinguished from the legal position that may exist between businesses and their owners. For sole proprietorships and partnerships, the law does not make any distinction between the business and its owner(s). For limited companies, on the other hand, there is a clear legal distinction between the business and its owners. (Indeed, as Chapter 4 explains, the limited company is regarded as having a separate legal existence.) For accounting purposes, these legal distinctions are irrelevant and the business entity convention applies to all businesses.

Dual aspect convention

Each transaction has two aspects, both of which will affect the balance sheet. Thus, the purchase of a motor car for cash results in an increase in one asset (motor car) and a decrease in another (cash). The repayment of a loan results in the decrease in a liability (loan) and the decrease in an asset (cash/bank).

Activity 2.13	What are the two aspects of each of the following transactions?

- Purchase £1,000 stock on credit.
- Owner withdraws £2,000 in cash.
- Sale of stock (purchased for £1,000) for £2,000 cash.

Your answer should be as follows:

- Stock increases by £1,000; creditors increase by £1,000.
- Capital reduces by £2,000; cash reduces by £2,000.
- Assets show net increase of £1,000 (cash + £2,000; stock – £1,000); profit increases by £1,000.

Recording the **dual aspect** of each transaction ensures that the balance sheet will continue to balance.

Objectivity convention

➡ The **objectivity convention** seeks to reduce personal bias in financial statements. As far as possible, financial statements should be based on objective, verifiable evidence rather than matters of opinion.

Activity 2.16	Which of the above conventions does the objectivity convention support and with which does it conflict?

The objectivity convention provides further support (along with the going concern convention) for the use of historic cost as a basis of valuation. It can conflict, however, with the prudence convention which requires the use of judgement in determining values.

The basis of valuation of assets on the balance sheet

It was mentioned earlier that, when preparing a balance sheet, the historic cost convention is normally applied for the reporting of assets. However, this point requires further elaboration as, in practice, it is not simply a matter of recording each asset on the balance sheet at its original cost. Below, we consider the valuation procedures used for both current assets and fixed assets.

Current assets

Where the net realisable value (that is, selling price less any selling costs) of current assets falls below the cost of the assets, the former will be used as the basis of valuation instead. This reflects the influence of the prudence convention on the balance sheet. Current assets are short-term assets that are expected to be liquidated in the near future, and so any loss arising from a fall in value below their original cost is reflected in the balance sheet. The accounting policies of companies regarding their current assets will normally be shown as a note to the annual accounts that are published for external users (see Exhibit 2.1).

Exhibit 2.1	The published accounts for 2000 of J. D. Wetherspoon plc, which manages a large number of public houses throughout the UK, contains the following note:

Stocks
Stocks are held for resale and are stated at the lower of invoiced cost and net realisable value.

Tangible fixed assets

Many tangible fixed assets, such as plant and machinery, motor vehicles, computer equipment and buildings, have a limited useful life. Ultimately, these assets will be used up as a result of wear and tear, obsolescence and so on. The amount of a particular asset that has been used up over time by a business is referred to as *depreciation*. Depreciation is an expense of running the business and the amount involved each year appears in the profit and loss account. The total depreciation relating to a fixed asset, since the business first acquired it will normally be deducted from the cost of the asset on the balance sheet. This procedure is not really a contravention of the historic cost convention; it is simply recognition of the fact that a proportion of the fixed asset has been consumed in the process of generating benefits for the business. There are, however, examples where the cost convention is contravened. We shall look at depreciation in more detail in Chapter 3.

We saw earlier that some assets *appreciate* in value over time. Freehold property was mentioned as an example. As a result of this appreciation, it has become widespread practice to revalue freehold property by using current market values rather than historic cost. This practice not only contravenes the cost convention but it also contravenes the objectivity convention. This is because an opinion of what is the current market value is substituted for a cost figure (which is usually a matter of verifiable fact).

Once assets are revalued, the frequency of revaluation then becomes an important issue as assets recorded at out-of-date values can mislead users. It has been argued that using out-of-date revaluations on the balance sheet is the worst of both worlds as it lacks the objectivity and verifiability of historic cost and also lacks the realism of current values. Ideally revaluations should take place on an annual basis particularly if it is likely that a significant change in value has occurred. However, in practice, revaluations tend to be less frequent.

| Exhibit 2.2 | The revaluation policies of House of Fraser plc, which owns and manages a number of department stores throughout the UK, are shown in its accounts for the year ended 29 January 2000 as follows: |

Properties

Freehold and long leasehold properties are stated at cost or valuation on the basis of existing use. Independent professsional valuations are performed on a regular basis with directors' valuation in the intervening years. New store developments are carried at cost for a maximum of five years until the trading pattern is sufficiently established for a valuation to be carried out. Short leasehold properties and all other fixed assets are stated at cost.

This note reveals who carries out the revaluations. The fact that external valuers are involved periodically in the revaluations should give greater credibility to the values derived.

Intangible fixed assets

Some intangible assets are similar to tangible assets in so far as they have a separate identity, the rights to the assets can be clearly established and the cost of the assets can be determined. Patents, trademarks, copyright and licences would normally fall into this category. For such assets, the balance sheet treatment used for tangible fixed assets can be applied. That is, they can be recorded at their purchase cost and depreciated (or 'amortised' as it is usually termed in this context) over their useful life.

Exhibit 2.3

The following is an extract from the annual report of Manchester United plc for 2000.

Intangible fixed assets

Group	£'000
Cost of players' registrations	
At 1 August 1999	54,608
Additions	19,697
Disposals	(6,013)
At 31 July 2000	**68,292**
Amortisation of players' registration	
At 1 August 1999	24,483
Charge for year	13,092
Disposals	(1,598)
At 31 July 2000	**35,977**
Net Book Value of players' registration	
At 31 July 2000	**32,315**

The figures show how the club depreciated (or amortised) the value of the transfer fees paid for players over the life of each player's contract with the club. This provides a relatively rare example of a business's human assets being reflected on the balance sheet. The treatment is typical of how football clubs deal with transfer fees.

The logic of football clubs treating their human assets in this way is that when they pay a transfer fee for a player there is a 'past transaction', 'capable of measurement in monetary terms' – features that are normal requirements of the accounting definition of an asset (earlier in this chapter). Players brought on by the club and not, therefore, the subject of a transfer fee (David Beckham and Paul Scholes, for example) are not reflected in the Manchester United balance sheet.

At the beginning of the financial year (1 August 1999) the club had players for whom it had paid a total of £54,608,000. During the year it bought further players for £19,697,000 and players for whom the club had paid, at some stage, £6,013,000 left the club.

Of the £54,608,000, £24,483,000 had been treated as an expense by the start of the year. During the year a further £13,092,000 was treated as an expense as players' contract periods shortened by a year. Players who left the club during the year had already had £1,598,000 of their transfer value treated as an expense (depreciation or amortisation).

Some intangible assets, however, are quite different in nature from tangible fixed assets. They lack a clear and separate identity as they are really a hotch-potch of attributes that form part of the essence of the business. We saw earlier, for example, that 'goodwill' is a term used to cover the benefits arising from such factors as the quality of the products, the skill of the workforce and the relationship with customers. We also saw that goodwill is normally excluded from the balance sheet unless it has been acquired at an agreed price. The amount paid to purchase the goodwill would then provide the appropriate balance sheet value. However, the issue as to whether purchased goodwill should be shown at cost, or at cost less some measure of depreciation (or 'amortised' as it is usually termed in this context) is not straightforward. As we shall see in Chapter 3, there are different ways in which purchased goodwill can be treated.

The value of product brands is often regarded as part of the goodwill of a business. It can be argued that product brands are also a hotch-potch of attributes, which include the brand image, the quality of the product, the trademark and so on. In recent years, however, some large businesses (for example Cadbury Schweppes plc) have attempted to give their brands a separate identity and place a value on them. There is no doubt that product brands may be very valuable to a business because they can generate customer loyalty that, in turn, can lead to increased sales. This brand loyalty is often built up through many years of promotional and advertising expenditure. However, such expenditure may be difficult to trace and so some form of current valuation is often used as the basis for including brand names on the balance sheet. (It should be said that including internally generated brands on the balance sheet remains a controversial issue in accounting because of the measurement issues mentioned earlier in the chapter.)

The table below shows how assets may be categorised according to whether they are tangible or intangible. Furthermore, intangible assets can be categorised according to our ability to separate them from other assets. Although tangible assets are usually separable we can see that not all intangible assets are.

	Intangible fixed assets	
Tangible fixed assets	Separable	Non-separable
Plant and machinery	Patents	Goodwill
Computer equipment	Trademarks	Product brands
Fixtures and fittings	Copyright	
Freehold buildings	Licences	
Motor vehicles	Magazine titles	

We can see that there are exceptions to the rule that assets are recorded at their historic cost. Moreover, the list of exceptions appears to be growing. In recent years, the balance sheets of many businesses have increasingly reflected a mixture of valuation approaches. This trend is a matter of concern for the accountancy profession as users are unlikely to find a variety of valuation methods very helpful when trying to assess financial position.

Interpreting the balance sheet

We have seen that the conventional balance sheet has a number of limitations. This has led some users of financial information to conclude that the balance sheet has little to offer in the way of useful information. However, this is not necessarily the case. The balance sheet can provide useful insights to the financing and investing activities of a business. In particular, the following aspects of financial position can be examined:

■ *The liquidity of the business.* This is the ability of the business to meet its short-term obligations (current liabilities) from its liquid (cash and near-cash) assets. One of the reasons that the vertical format for the balance sheet is preferred by many users of accounts is the fact that it highlights the liquidity of the business: the current assets are directly compared to the current liabilities. Liquidity is particularly important because business failures occur when the business cannot meet its maturing obligations, whatever the root cause of that inability may be.

■ *The mix of assets held by the business.*   The relationship between fixed assets and current assets is important. Businesses with too much of their funds tied up in fixed assets could be vulnerable to financial failure. This is because fixed assets are typically not easy to turn into cash in order to meet short-term obligations. Converting many fixed assets into cash may well lead to substantial losses for the business because such assets are not always worth on the open market what they are worth to the business. For example, a specialised piece of equipment may have little value to any other business yet it could be worth a great deal to the owners. Businesses with too little of their funds invested in fixed assets, however, may also face problems. Underinvestment in fixed assets may limit output and this, in turn, is likely to have an adverse effect on the profitability of the business.

■ *The financial structure of the business.*   The relative proportion of total finance contributed by the owners and outsiders can be calculated to see whether the business is heavily dependent on outside financing. Heavy borrowing can bring with it a commitment to pay large interest charges and make large capital repayments at regular intervals. These are legally enforceable obligations that can be a real burden as they have to be paid irrespective of the financial position of the business. Funds raised from the owners of the business, on the other hand, do not impose such obligations on the business.

The interpretation of the balance sheet will be considered in more detail in Chapter 7.

? Self-assessment question 2.1

Consider the following balance sheet of a manufacturing business:

Kunalan Manufacturing Company
Balance sheet as at 30 April 2002

	£	£	£
Fixed assets			
Freehold premises			88,000
Plant and machinery			46,000
Motor vehicles			13,000
Fixtures and fittings			14,000
			161,000
Current assets			
Stock in trade		48,000	
Trade debtors		44,000	
Cash in hand		12,000	
		104,000	
Current liabilities			
Trade creditors	24,000		
Bank overdraft	18,000		
		(42,000)	

? REVIEW QUESTIONS

2.1 An accountant prepared a balance sheet for a business using the horizontal layout. In the balance sheet, the capital of Mr Dimitrov, the owner, was shown next to the liabilities. This confused Mr Dimitrov, who argued, 'My capital is my major asset and so should be shown as an asset on the balance sheet.' How would you explain this misunderstanding to Mr Dimitrov?

2.2 'The balance sheet shows how much a business is worth.' Do you agree with this statement? Discuss.

2.3 Can you think of a more appropriate name for the balance sheet?

2.4 In recent years there have been attempts to place a value on the 'human assets' of a business in order to derive a figure that can be included on the balance sheet. Do you think humans should be treated as assets? Would 'human assets' meet the conventional definition of an asset for inclusion on the balance sheet?

? EXERCISES

Exercises 2.5–2.8 are more advanced than 2.1–2.4. Those with coloured numbers have answers at the back of the book.

2.1 On the fourth day of his business venture, Paul the street trader in wrapping-paper (see earlier in the chapter), purchased more stock for £53 cash. During the day he sold stock that had cost £33 for a total of £47.

Required:
Draw up the three financial statements for Day 4 of Paul's business venture.

2.2 The 'total business wealth' belongs to Paul because he is the sole owner of the business. Can you explain how the figure for total business wealth at the end of day 4 has arisen? You will need to look back at the events of days 1, 2 and 3 (in this chapter) to do this.

2.3 Whilst on holiday in Bridlington, Helen had her credit cards and purse stolen from the beach while she was swimming. She was left with only £40, which she had kept in her hotel room; but she had three days of her holiday remaining. She was determined to continue her holiday and decided to make some money in order to be able to do so. She decided to sell orange juice to holidaymakers using the local beach. On day 1 she purchased 80 cartons of orange juice at £0.50 each for cash and sold 70 of these at £0.80 each. On the following day she purchased 60 cartons for cash and sold 65 at £0.80 each. On the third and final day she purchased another 60 cartons for cash. However, it rained and, as a result, business was poor. She managed to sell 20 at £0.80 each but sold off the rest of her stock at £0.40 each.

Required:
Prepare a profit and loss account and cash flow statement for each day's trading and prepare a balance sheet at the end of each day's trading.

business cannot meet its maturing obligations, whatever the root cause of that inability may be.

■ *The mix of assets held by the business.*   The relationship between fixed assets and current assets is important. Businesses with too much of their funds tied up in fixed assets could be vulnerable to financial failure. This is because fixed assets are typically not easy to turn into cash in order to meet short-term obligations. Converting many fixed assets into cash may well lead to substantial losses for the business because such assets are not always worth on the open market what they are worth to the business. For example, a specialised piece of equipment may have little value to any other business yet it could be worth a great deal to the owners. Businesses with too little of their funds invested in fixed assets, however, may also face problems. Underinvestment in fixed assets may limit output and this, in turn, is likely to have an adverse effect on the profitability of the business.

■ *The financial structure of the business.*   The relative proportion of total finance contributed by the owners and outsiders can be calculated to see whether the business is heavily dependent on outside financing. Heavy borrowing can bring with it a commitment to pay large interest charges and make large capital repayments at regular intervals. These are legally enforceable obligations that can be a real burden as they have to be paid irrespective of the financial position of the business. Funds raised from the owners of the business, on the other hand, do not impose such obligations on the business.

The interpretation of the balance sheet will be considered in more detail in Chapter 7.

? **Self-assessment question 2.1**

Consider the following balance sheet of a manufacturing business:

Kunalan Manufacturing Company
Balance sheet as at 30 April 2002

	£	£	£
Fixed assets			
Freehold premises			88,000
Plant and machinery			46,000
Motor vehicles			13,000
Fixtures and fittings			14,000
			161,000
Current assets			
Stock in trade		48,000	
Trade debtors		44,000	
Cash in hand		12,000	
		104,000	
Current liabilities			
Trade creditors	24,000		
Bank overdraft	18,000		
		(42,000)	

	£	£	£
Net current assets			62,000
Total assets less current liabilities			223,000
Long-term liabilities			
Loan			160,000
Net assets			63,000
Capital			
Opening balance			42,000
Add Profit			32,000
			74,000
Less Drawings			11,000
			63,000

Required:

What can you deduce about the financial position of the business from the information contained in its balance sheet?

Summary

This chapter began with an overview of the three major financial statements. We saw how each statement has a part to play in providing a picture of the financial position and performance of the business. We then went on to examine one of these financial statements – the balance sheet – in some detail. We saw that this statement shows the assets of the business and the claims against those assets at a particular moment in time. It is a statement of financial position, although it can be argued that it is not a complete statement of financial position; there are certain valuable resources held by the business that cannot be accommodated easily within conventional accounting definitions and measurement methods. We examined the conventions of accounting that underpin the balance sheet and saw how these place limits on the usefulness of the balance sheet in assessing current financial position.

→ **Key terms**

Cash flow statement   p. 19
Profit and loss account   p. 19
Balance sheet   p. 19
Final accounts   p. 23
Asset   p. 24
Claim   p. 24
Tangible assets   p. 26
Intangible assets   p. 26
Capital   p. 26
Liabilities   p. 26
Fixed asset   p. 31

Current asset   p. 31
Long-term liabilities   p. 33
Current liabilities   p. 33
Money measurement convention   p. 38
Historic cost convention   p. 39
Going concern convention   p. 39
Business entity convention   p. 40
Dual aspect convention   p. 40
Prudence convention   p. 41
Stable monetary unit convention   p. 41
Objectivity convention   p. 43

Further reading

If you would like to explore the topics covered in this chapter in more depth, we recommend the following books:

Financial Reporting, *Alexander, D.* and *Britton, A.*, 6th edn, International Thompson Business Press, 2001, chapter 3.

Accounting Principles, *Anthony, R.* and *Reece, J.*, 7th edn, Richard D Irwin, 1995, chapters 2 and 3.

Accounting Theory: Text and readings, *Schroeder, R.* and *Clark, M.*, 5th edn, Wiley, 1995, chapter 5.

Accounting Theory and Practice, *Glautier, M.* and *Underdown, B.*, 7th edn, Pitman Publishing, 2001, chapter 12.

? REVIEW QUESTIONS

2.1 An accountant prepared a balance sheet for a business using the horizontal layout. In the balance sheet, the capital of Mr Dimitrov, the owner, was shown next to the liabilities. This confused Mr Dimitrov, who argued, 'My capital is my major asset and so should be shown as an asset on the balance sheet.' How would you explain this misunderstanding to Mr Dimitrov?

2.2 'The balance sheet shows how much a business is worth.' Do you agree with this statement? Discuss.

2.3 Can you think of a more appropriate name for the balance sheet?

2.4 In recent years there have been attempts to place a value on the 'human assets' of a business in order to derive a figure that can be included on the balance sheet. Do you think humans should be treated as assets? Would 'human assets' meet the conventional definition of an asset for inclusion on the balance sheet?

? EXERCISES

Exercises 2.5–2.8 are more advanced than 2.1–2.4. Those with coloured numbers have answers at the back of the book.

2.1 On the fourth day of his business venture, Paul the street trader in wrapping-paper (see earlier in the chapter), purchased more stock for £53 cash. During the day he sold stock that had cost £33 for a total of £47.

Required:
Draw up the three financial statements for Day 4 of Paul's business venture.

2.2 The 'total business wealth' belongs to Paul because he is the sole owner of the business. Can you explain how the figure for total business wealth at the end of day 4 has arisen? You will need to look back at the events of days 1, 2 and 3 (in this chapter) to do this.

2.3 Whilst on holiday in Bridlington, Helen had her credit cards and purse stolen from the beach while she was swimming. She was left with only £40, which she had kept in her hotel room; but she had three days of her holiday remaining. She was determined to continue her holiday and decided to make some money in order to be able to do so. She decided to sell orange juice to holidaymakers using the local beach. On day 1 she purchased 80 cartons of orange juice at £0.50 each for cash and sold 70 of these at £0.80 each. On the following day she purchased 60 cartons for cash and sold 65 at £0.80 each. On the third and final day she purchased another 60 cartons for cash. However, it rained and, as a result, business was poor. She managed to sell 20 at £0.80 each but sold off the rest of her stock at £0.40 each.

Required:
Prepare a profit and loss account and cash flow statement for each day's trading and prepare a balance sheet at the end of each day's trading.

2.4 On 1 March, Joe Conday started a new business. During March he carried out the following transactions:

1 March   Deposited £20,000 in a bank account
2 March   Purchased fixtures and fittings for £6,000 cash, and stock £8,000 on credit
3 March   Borrowed £5,000 from a relative and deposited it in the bank
4 March   Purchased a motor car for £7,000 cash and withdrew £200 for own use
5 March   A further motor car costing £9,000 was purchased. The motor car purchased on 4 March was given in part exchange at a value of £6,500. The balance of purchase price for the new car was paid in cash
6 March   Conday won £2,000 in a lottery and paid the amount into the business bank account. He also repaid £1,000 of the loan

Required:
Draw up a balance sheet for the business at the end of each day.

2.5 The following is a list of the assets and claims of Crafty Engineering Ltd at 30 June 2001:

	£000
Creditors	86
Motor vehicles	38
Loan from Industrial Finance Co.	260
Machinery and tools	207
Bank overdraft	116
Stock in trade	153
Freehold premises	320
Debtors	185

Required:
(a) Prepare the balance sheet of the business as at 30 June 2001 from the above information using the vertical format. *Hint*: There is a missing item that needs to be deduced and inserted.
(b) Discuss the significant features revealed by this financial statement.

2.6 The balance sheet of a business at the start of the week is as follows:

Assets	£	Claims	£
Freehold premises	145,000	Capital	203,000
Furniture and fittings	63,000	Bank overdraft	43,000
Stock in trade	28,000	Trade creditors	23,000
Trade debtors	33,000		
	269,000		269,000

During the week the following transactions take place:

(a) Stock sold for £11,000 cash; this stock had cost £8,000.
(b) Sold stock for £23,000 on credit; this stock had cost £17,000.
(c) Received cash from trade debtors totalling £18,000.
(d) The owners of the business introduced £100,000 of their own money, which was placed in the business bank account.
(e) The owners brought a motor van, valued at £10,000, into the business.

(f) Bought stock in trade on credit for £14,000.
(g) Paid trade creditors £13,000.

Required:
Show the balance sheet after all of these transactions have been reflected.

2.7 The following is a list of assets and claims of a manufacturing business at a particular point in time:

	£
Bank overdraft	22,000
Freehold land and buildings	245,000
Stock of raw materials	18,000
Trade creditors	23,000
Plant and machinery	127,000
Loan from Industrial Finance Co.	100,000
Stock of finished goods	28,000
Delivery vans	54,000
Trade debtors	34,000

Required:
Write out a balance sheet in the standard vertical form incorporating these figures. *Hint*: There is a missing item that needs to be deduced and inserted.

2.8 You have been talking to someone who had read the first chapter of an accounting text some years ago. During your conversation the person made the following statements:

(a) The profit and loss account shows how much cash has come into and left the business during the accounting period and the resulting balance at the end of the period.
(b) In order to be included in the balance sheet as an asset, an item needs to be worth something in the market, that is all.
(c) The balance sheet equation is:

Assets + Capital = Liabilities

(d) An expense is an event that reduces capital; so when the owner of the business withdraws some capital, the business has incurred an expense.
(e) Fixed assets are things that cannot be moved.
(f) Current assets are things that stay in the business for less than twelve months.
(g) Working capital is the name given to the sum of the current assets.

Required:
Comment critically on each of the above statements, going into as much detail as you can.

CHAPTER 3

Measuring and reporting financial performance

Introduction

In this chapter the profit and loss account will be examined. We shall see how this statement is prepared and what insights it provides concerning financial performance. We shall also consider some of the key measurement problems to be faced when preparing this statement.

When you have completed this chapter you should be able to:

■ Discuss the nature and purpose of the profit and loss account.
■ Prepare a profit and loss account from relevant financial information and interpret the results.
■ Discuss the main measurement issues that must be considered when preparing the profit and loss account.
■ Explain the main accounting conventions underpinning the profit and loss account.

The profit and loss account (income statement)

In the previous chapter, we examined the nature and purpose of the balance sheet. We saw that this statement was concerned with setting out the financial position of a business at a particular moment in time. However, it is not usually enough for users to have information relating only to the amount of wealth held by the business at one moment in time; businesses exist for the primary purpose of generating wealth, or profit, and it is the profit generated *during a period* that is the primary concern of many users. Although the amount of profit generated is of particular interest to owners of the business, other groups such as managers, employees and suppliers will also have an interest in the profit-making ability of the business. The purpose of the profit and loss (P and L) account – or income

➡ statement, as it is sometimes called – is to measure and report how much **profit** (wealth) the business has generated over a period.

The measurement of profit requires that the total revenues of the business, gen-
➡ erated during a particular period, be calculated. **Revenue** is simply a measure of the inflow of assets (for example, cash or amounts owed to a business by debtors)

that arise as a result of trading operations. Different forms of business enterprise will generate different forms of revenue. Some examples of the different forms which revenue can take are:

- Sales of goods (for example, of a manufacturer)
- Fees for services (for example, of a solicitor)
- Subscriptions (for example, of a club)
- Interest received (for example, of an investment fund).

Activity 3.1

The following represent different forms of business enterprise:

(a) Accountancy practice
(b) Squash club
(c) Bus company
(d) Newspaper
(e) Finance company
(f) Songwriter
(g) Retailer
(h) Magazine publisher

Can you identify the major source(s) of revenue for each type of business enterprise?

Your answer to this activity should be along the following lines:

Type of business	Main source(s) of revenue
(a) Accountancy practice	Fees for services
(b) Squash club	Subscriptions, court fees
(c) Bus company	Ticket sales, advertising
(d) Newspaper	Newspaper sales, advertising
(e) Finance company	Interest received on loans
(f) Songwriter	Royalties, commission fees
(g) Retailer	Sale of goods
(h) Magazine publisher	Magazine sales and advertising

As you can see, it is possible for a business to have more than one form of revenue.

The total expenses relating to each accounting period must also be calculated. An **expense** represents the outflow of assets incurred as a result of generating, or attempting to generate, revenues. The nature of the business will again determine the types of expense that will be incurred. Examples of some of the more common types of expense are:

- The cost of buying goods that are subsequently sold – known as 'cost of sales' or 'cost of goods sold'
- Salaries and wages
- Rent and rates
- Motor vehicle running expenses
- Insurances
- Printing and stationery
- Heat and light
- Telephone and postage

The P and L account for a period simply shows the total revenue generated during a particular period and deducts from this the total expenses incurred in generating that revenue. The difference between the total revenue and total expenses will represent either profit (if revenues exceed expenses) or loss (if expenses exceed revenues). Thus, we have:

Profit(loss) for the period = Total revenue − Total expenses incurred in generating the revenue

Relationship between the P and L account and the balance sheet

The P and L account and the balance sheet should not be viewed as substitutes for one another. Rather, they should be seen as performing different functions. The balance sheet is, as stated earlier, a statement of the financial position of a business at a single moment in time – a 'snapshot' of the stock of wealth held by the business. The P and L account, on the other hand, is concerned with the *flow* of wealth over a period of time. The two statements are closely related. The profit and loss account can be viewed as linking the balance sheet at the beginning of a period with the balance sheet at the end of that period. Thus, at the commencement of business, a balance sheet could be produced to reveal the opening financial position. After an appropriate period, a P and L account will be prepared to show the wealth generated over the period. A balance sheet will also be prepared to reveal the new financial position at the end of the period covered by the P and L account. This balance sheet will incorporate the changes in wealth that have occurred since the previous balance sheet was drawn up.

We saw in the previous chapter that the effect, on the balance sheet, of making a profit (or loss) means that the balance sheet equation can be extended as follows:

Assets = Capital + (−) Profit(loss) + Liabilities

The amount of profit or loss for the period is shown separately in the balance sheet as an adjustment to capital. The above equation can then be further extended to:

Assets = Capital + (Revenues − Expenses) + Liabilities

In theory, it would be possible to calculate profit and loss for the period by making all adjustments for revenues and expenses through the capital account. However, this would be rather cumbersome. A better solution is to have an 'appendix' to the capital account in the form of a P and L account. By deducting expenses from the revenues for the period, the P and L account derives the profit (loss) for adjustment in the capital account. This figure represents the net effect of operations for the period. Providing this appendix means that a detailed and more informative view of performance is presented to users.

The format of the P and L account

The format of the P and L account will vary according to the type of business to which it relates. In order to illustrate a P and L account, let us consider the case of a retail business (that is, a business that purchases goods in their completed state and resells them). This type of business usually has straightforward operations and, as a result, the P and L account is easy to understand. Example 3.1 sets out a typical format for the P and L account of a retail business.

Example 3.1

Hi-Price Stores
Trading and P and L account for the year ended 31 October 2001

	£	£
Sales		232,000
Less Cost of sales		154,000
Gross profit		78,000
Interest received from investments		2,000
		80,000
Less		
Salaries and wages	24,500	
Rent and rates	14,200	
Heat and light	7,500	
Telephone and postage	1,200	
Insurance	1,000	
Motor vehicle running expenses	3,400	
Loan interest	1,100	
Depreciation – fixtures and fittings	1,000	
motor van	600	
		(54,500)
Net profit		25,500

The first part of the statement in Example 3.1 is concerned with calculating the ➡ **gross profit** for the period. The trading revenue, which arises from selling the goods, is the first item that appears. Deducted from this item is the trading expense, which is the cost of acquiring the goods sold during the period. The difference between the trading revenue and trading expense is referred to as 'gross profit'. This represents the profit from simply buying and selling goods without taking into account any other expenses or revenues associated with the business. This first part of the statement, which is concerned with the calculation of gross profit, is referred to as the **trading account** or **trading section**. The remainder of the statement is referred to as the P and L account. Hence, the head- ➡ ing of **trading and P and L account**, which is shown in Example 3.1. (You may often find, however, that the term 'P and L account' is used to describe the whole of this income statement.)

Having calculated the gross profit, any additional revenues of the business are then added to this figure. In Example 3.1, interest from investments represents an additional revenue. (Presumably, the business has some cash on deposit or similar.) From this subtotal of gross profit and additional revenues, the other expenses (overheads) that have to be incurred in order to operate the business (salaries, wages, rent, rates and so on) are deducted. The final figure derived is the ➡ **net profit** for the period. This figure represents the wealth generated during the period that is attributable to the owner(s) of the business and that will be added to their capital in the balance sheet. As can be seen, net profit is a residual – that is, the amount left over after deducting all expenses incurred in generating the sales for the period.

The P and L account – some further aspects

Having set out the main principles involved in preparing a profit and loss account, some further points need to be considered.

Cost of sales

➡ The approach taken to identifying the **cost of sales** figure can vary between businesses. In some businesses, the cost of sales is identified at the time each sale is made. For example, the more sophisticated supermarkets tend to have point-of-sale (checkout) devices that not only record each sale but that simultaneously pick up the cost of the particular sale. Businesses that sell a relatively small number of high-value items (for example an engineering business that produces custom-made equipment) also tend to match each sale with the cost of the goods sold at the time of the sale. However, some businesses (for example small retailers) do not usually find it practical to match each sale to a particular cost-of-sale figure as the accounting period progresses; they find it easier to identify the figure at the end of the accounting period.

To understand how this is done, it is important to recognise that the cost of sales figure represents the cost of goods that were *sold* during the period rather than the cost of goods that were *purchased* in the period. Goods purchased during a period may be held in stock to be sold during a later period. In order to derive the cost of sales for a period, it is necessary to know the amounts of opening and closing stocks for the period and the cost of goods purchased during the period.

The opening stocks for the period *plus* the goods purchased during the period will represent the total goods available for resale. The closing stocks will represent that portion of the total goods available for resale that remains unsold at the end of the period. Thus, the cost of goods sold during the period must be the cost associated with the total goods available for resale *less* the stocks remaining at the end of the period. Example 3.2 sets out how this calculation is sometimes shown on the face of the trading account. (The trading account in Example 3.2 is simply an expanded version of the earlier trading account for Hi-Price Stores (Example 3.1) using additional information concerning stock balances and purchases for the year.)

Example 3.2		£	£
	Sales		232,000
	Less Cost of sales		
	Opening stock	40,000	
	Add Goods purchased	189,000	
		229,000	
	Less Closing stock	75,000	154,000
	Gross profit		78,000

Classification of expenses

The classifications for the revenue and expense items, as with the classification of various assets and claims in the balance sheet, is often a matter of judgement by those who design the accounting system. In the P and L account in Example 3.1, for instance, the insurance expense could have been included with telephone and postage under a single heading – say general expenses. Such decisions are normally based on how useful a particular classification will be to users. However, for businesses that trade as limited companies, there are statutory rules dictating the classification of various items appearing in the accounts for external reporting purposes. These rules will be discussed in Chapter 4.

Activity 3.2

The following information relates to the activities of H&S Retailers for the year ended 30 April 2001:

	£
Motor vehicle running expenses	1,200
Rent received from subletting	2,000
Closing stock	3,000
Rent and rates payable	5,000
Motor vans	6,300
Annual depreciation – motor vans	1,500
Heat and light	900
Telephone and postage	450
Sales	97,400
Goods purchased	68,350
Insurance	750
Loan interest payable	620
Balance at bank	4,780
Salaries and wages	10,400
Opening stock	4,000

Prepare a trading and P and L account for the year ended 30 April 2001.
Hint: Not all items shown above should appear on this statement.

Your answer to this activity should be as follows:

Trading and P and L account for the year ended 30 April 2001

	£	£
Sales		97,400
Less Cost of sales		
Opening stock	4,000	
Purchases	68,350	
	72,350	
Closing stock	(3,000)	(69,350)
Gross profit		28,050
Rent received		2,000
		30,050

Less	£	£
Salaries and wages	10,400	
Rent and rates	5,000	
Heat and light	900	
Telephone and postage	450	
Insurance	750	
Motor vehicle running expenses	1,200	
Loan interest	620	
Depreciation – motor van	1,500	
		(20,820)
Net profit		9,230

In the case of the balance sheet, we saw that the information could be presented in either a horizontal format or a vertical format. This is also true of the trading and P and L account. Where a horizontal format is used, expenses are listed on the left-hand side and revenues on the right, the difference being either net profit or net loss. The vertical format has been used in Activity 3.2 as it is easier to understand and is now almost always used.

The reporting period

We have seen already that, for reporting to those outside the business, a financial reporting cycle of one year is the norm. However, some large businesses will provide a half-yearly, or 'interim', financial statement to give more frequent feedback on progress. For those who manage a business, it is important to have much more frequent feedback on performance. Thus, it is quite common for P and L accounts to be prepared on a quarterly or monthly basis to show the progress (or otherwise) being made during the year.

Profit measurement and the recognition of revenue

A key issue in the measurement of profit concerns the point at which revenue is recognised. It is possible to recognise revenue at different points in the production/selling cycle and the particular point chosen could have a significant effect on the total revenues reported for the period.

Activity 3.3

A manufacturing business sells goods on credit (that is, the customer is allowed to pay some time after the goods have been received). Below are four points in the production/selling cycle at which revenue might be recognised by the business:

(1) When the goods are produced.
(2) When an order is received from a customer.
(3) When the goods are delivered to, and accepted by, the customer.
(4) When the cash is received from the customer.

A substantial amount of time may elapse between these different points. At what point do you think the business should recognise revenue?

Although you may have come to a different conclusion, the point at which we normally recognise revenue is (3) above. The reasons for this are explained in the text.

➡ The **realisation convention** in accounting is designed to solve the revenue recognition problem (or at least to provide some consistency). This convention states that revenue should only be recognised when it has been 'realised'. Normally, realisation is considered to have occurred when:

■ The activities necessary to generate the revenue (for example, delivery of goods, carrying out of repairs) are substantially complete.
■ The amount of revenue generated can be objectively determined.
■ There is reasonable certainty that the amounts owing from the activities will be received.

These criteria will probably be fulfilled when the goods are passed to the customers and are accepted by them. This is the normal point of recognition when goods are sold on credit. It is also the point at which there is a legally enforceable contract between the parties.

The realisation convention in accounting means that a sale on credit is usually recognised *before* the cash is received. Thus, the total sales figure shown in the profit and loss account may include sales transactions for which the cash has yet to be received. The total sales figure in the P and L account will, therefore, be different from the total cash received from sales.

Not all businesses will wait to recognise revenue until all of the work necessary to generate the revenue is complete. A construction business, for example, which is engaged in a long-term project such as building a dam, will not usually wait until the contract is complete; doing so could mean that no revenue would be recognised by the business until several years after the work commenced. Instead, the business will normally recognise a proportion of the total value of such a contract when an agreed stage of the contract has been completed. This approach to revenue recognition is really a more practical interpretation of the realisation convention rather than a deviation from it.

Profit measurement and the recognition of expenses

Having decided on the point at which revenue is recognised, we must now turn
➡ to the issue of the recognition of expenses. The **matching convention** in accounting is designed to provide guidance concerning the recognition of expenses. This convention states that expenses should be matched to the revenues that they helped to generate. In other words, expenses must be taken into account in the same P and L account in which the associated sale is recognised.

Applying this convention may mean that a particular expense reported in the P and L account for a period may not be the same as the cash paid in respect of that item during the period – indeed, the expense reported may be either more or less than the cash paid during the period. Examples 3.3 to 3.5 illustrate this point.

When the expense for the period is more than the cash paid during the period

| Example 3.3 | Suppose that sales staff are paid a commission of 2 per cent of sales generated and that total sales during the period amounted to £300,000. This will mean that the commission to be paid in respect of the sales for the period will be £6,000. Let us say, however, that by the end of the period the sales commission paid to staff was £5,000. If the business included only the amount paid in the P and L account, it will mean that this statement will not reflect the full expense for the year. This will contravene the matching convention because not all of the expenses associated with the revenues of the period will have been matched in the P and L account. This will be remedied as follows:

■ Sales commission expense in the P and L account will include the amount paid *plus* the amount outstanding (£6,000 = £5,000 + £1,000).
■ The cash paid (£5,000) will appear in the cash flow statement and will reduce the cash balance.
■ The amount outstanding (£1,000) represents an outstanding liability at the balance sheet date and will be included under the heading 'Accruals' or **Accrued expenses** in the balance sheet. As this item will probably have to be paid within twelve months of the balance sheet date, it will be treated as a current liability.

These points are illustrated in Figure 3.1.

Figure 3.1

Accounting for sales commission

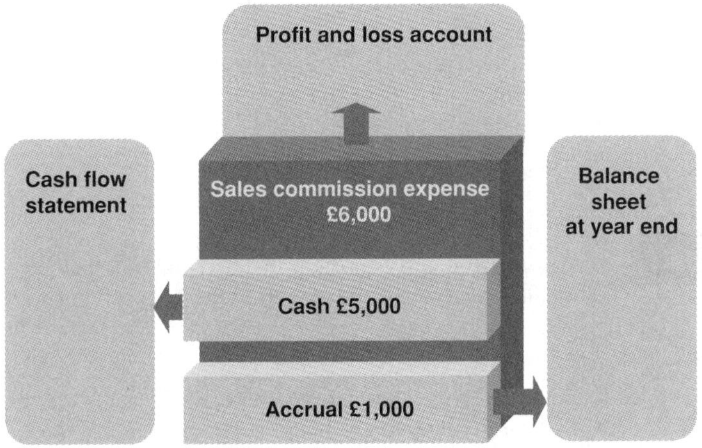

Profit and loss account

Cash flow statement

Sales commission expense £6,000

Balance sheet at year end

Cash £5,000

Accrual £1,000

The figure illustrates the main points of Example 3.3. We can see that the sales commission expense of £6,000 (which appears in the profit and loss account) is made up of a cash element £5,000 and an accrued element £1,000. The cash element appears in the cash flow statement and the accruals element will appear as a year-end liability in the balance sheet.

Ideally, all expenses should be matched to the period in which the sales to which they relate are reported. However, it is often difficult to match closely certain expenses to sales in the same way that we have matched sales commission to sales. It is unlikely, for example, that electricity charges incurred can be linked directly to particular sales in this way. Thus, as an expedient, the electricity charges incurred will normally be matched to the *period* to which they relate, as Example 3.4 illustrates.

Example 3.4

Suppose a business has reached the end of its accounting year and it has only been charged electricity for the first three quarters of the year (amounting to £1,900), simply because the electricity company has yet to send out bills for the quarter that ends on the same date as the business's year end. Where this situation exists, an estimate should be made of the electricity expense outstanding (that is, the bill for the last three months of the year is estimated). This figure (let us say the estimate is £500) is dealt with as follows:

- Electricity expense in the P and L account will include the amount paid *plus* the amount of the estimate (£1,900 + £500 = £2,400) to cover the whole year.
- The cash paid (£1,900) will appear in the cash flow statement and will reduce the cash balance.
- The amount of the estimate (£500) represents an outstanding liability at the balance sheet date and will be included under the heading 'Accruals' or 'Accrued expenses' in the balance sheet. As this item will have to be paid within 12 months of the balance sheet date, it will be treated as a current liability.

The above treatment will have the desired effect of increasing the electricity expense to the 'correct' figure for the year in the profit and loss account, assuming that the estimate is reasonably accurate. It will also have the effect of showing that, at the end of the accounting year, the business owed the amount of the last quarter's electricity bill. Dealing with the outstanding amount in this way reflects the dual aspect of the item and will ensure the balance sheet equation is maintained.

Activity 3.4

Let us say that the estimate for outstanding electricity in Example 3.4 was correct. How will the payment of the electricity bill be dealt with?

When the electricity bill is eventually paid, it will be dealt with as follows:

- Reduce cash by the amount of the bill.
- Reduce the amount of the accrued expense as shown on the balance sheet.

If there is a slight error in the estimate, a small adjustment (either negative or positive, depending on the direction of the error) can be made to the following year's expense. Dealing with the estimation error in this way is not strictly correct, but the amount is likely to be insignificant.

Activity 3.5	Can you think of other expenses that cannot be linked directly to sales and where matching will, therefore, normally be done on a time basis?

You may have thought of the following examples:

- Rent and rates
- Insurance
- Interest payments
- Licences

This is not an exhaustive list. You may have thought of others.

When the amount paid during the year is more than the full expense for the period

Example 3.5	Suppose a business pays rent for its premises quarterly in advance (on 1 January, 1 March, 1 June and 1 September) and that, on the last day of the accounting year (31 December), it pays the next quarter's rent to the following 31 March (£400) which is a day earlier than required. This would mean that a total of five quarters' rent was paid during the year. If the business reports the cash paid in the P and L account, this would be more than the full expense for the year. This treatment would also contravene the matching convention because a higher figure than the expenses associated with the revenues of the year appears in the profit and loss account.

The problem is overcome by dealing with the rental payment as follows:

- Show the rent for four quarters as the appropriate expense in the P and L account (4 × £400 = £1,600).
- Reduce the cash balance to reflect the full amount of the rent paid during the year (5 × £400 = £2,000).
- Show the quarter's rent paid in advance (£400) as a **prepaid expense** (that is, an outlay that relates to an expense for a future period) on the asset side of the balance sheet. (The prepaid expense will appear as a current asset in the balance sheet, under the heading 'Prepayments'.)

In the next period, this prepayment will cease to be an asset and become an expense in the profit and loss account of that period. This is because the rent prepaid relates to the next period and will be 'used up' during it.

In practice, the treatment of accruals and prepayments will be subject to the **materiality convention** in accounting. This convention states that, where the amounts involved are immaterial, we should consider only what is expedient. This may mean that an item will be treated as an expense in the period in which it is paid rather than being strictly matched to the revenues to which it relates. For example, a business may find that, at the end of an accounting period, there is a bill of £5 owing for stationery that has been used during the year. The time and effort involved in recording this as an accrual would have little effect on the measurement of profit or financial position for a business of any size, and so it would be ignored when preparing the P and L account for the period. The bill would, presumably, be paid in the following period and, therefore, treated as an expense of that period.

Profit and cash

The foregoing sections on revenues and expenses reveal that revenues do not usually represent cash received, and expenses are not the same as cash paid. As a result, the net profit figure (that is, total revenue minus total expenses) will not normally represent the net cash generated during a period. It is therefore important to distingish between profit and liquidity. Profit is a measure of achievement, or productive effort, rather than a measure of cash generated. Although making a profit will increase wealth, we have already seen in the previous chapter that cash is only one form in which that wealth may be held.

Profit measurement and the calculation of depreciation

➡ The expense of **depreciation** that appeared in the P and L account in Example 3.1 requires further explanation. Fixed assets (with the exception of freehold land) do not have a perpetual existence. They are eventually used up in the process of generating revenues for the business. In essence, depreciation is an attempt to measure that portion of the cost of a fixed asset that has been 'used up' in generating the revenues recognised during a particular period. The depreciation charge is considered to be an expense of the period to which it relates.

To calculate a depreciation charge for a period, four factors have to be considered. These are:

■ The cost of the asset
■ The useful life of the asset
■ Residual value
■ Depreciation method

The cost of an asset

This will include all costs incurred by the business to bring the asset to its required location and to make it ready for use. Thus, in addition to the costs of acquiring the asset, any delivery costs, installation costs (for example, for plant) and legal costs incurred in the transfer of legal title (for example, for freehold property) will be included as part of the total cost of the asset. Similarly, any costs incurred in improving or altering an asset in order to make it suitable for its intended use within the business will also be included as part of the total cost.

Activity 3.6

Andrew Wu (Engineering) Ltd purchased a new motor car for its marketing director. The invoice received from the motor car supplier revealed the following:

	£	£
New BMW 325i		26,350
Delivery charge	80	
Alloy wheels	660	
Sun-roof	200	
Petrol	30	
Number plates	130	
Road fund licence	155	1,255
		27,605
Part exchange – Reliant Robin		(1,000)
Amount outstanding		26,605

What is the total cost of the new car?

The cost of the new car will be as follows:

	£	£
New BMW 325i		26,350
Delivery charge	80	
Alloy wheels	660	
Sun-roof	200	
Number plates	130	1,070
		27,420

These costs include delivery costs and number plates as they are a necessary and integral part of the asset. Improvements (alloy wheels and sun roof) are also regarded as part of the total cost of the motor car. The petrol costs and road fund licence represent a cost of operating the asset rather than a part of the total cost of acquiring the asset and making it ready for use; hence these amounts will be charged as an expense in the period incurred (though part of the cost of the licence may be regarded as a prepaid expense) in the period incurred.

The part-exchange figure shown is part payment of the total amount outstanding and is not relevant to a consideration of the total cost.

There has been an increasing tendency for businesses to add to the cost of fixed assets being produced any interest charges incurred in financing the production of the asset. For example, some supermarket chains have used this approach when funds have been borrowed to build new stores. This practice is referred to as 'capitalising' interest payments. The argument in favour of this approach is that interest payments incurred before a particular store opens represent part of the total cost of development and should, therefore, be included as part of the cost of the asset. The interest capitalised will then normally be written off (that is, treated as an expense) over the asset's useful life. Exhibit 3.1 describes how one business capitalises its interest charges.

The following extract has been taken from the 2000 annual report of J. Sainsbury plc, a large supermarket business.

Capitalisation of interest

Interest incurred on borrowings for the financing of specific property developments is capitalised.

The amount of interest capitalised by the business for the year to 1 April 2000 was £10 million. As the profit for the financial year was £349 million, the capitalisation of interest (rather than charging it to the profit and loss account for 2000) did not have a significant effect on the reported profit.

The useful life of an asset

An asset has both a physical life and an economic life. The physical life of an asset will be exhausted through the effects of wear and tear and/or the passage of time, although it is possible for the physical life to be extended considerably through careful maintenance, improvements and so on. The economic life of an asset is determined by the effects of technological progress and changes in demand. After a while, the benefits of using the asset may be less than the costs involved. This may be because the asset is unable to compete with newer assets or because it is no longer relevant to the needs of the business. The economic life of an asset may be much shorter than its physical life. For example, a computer may have a physical life of eight years and an economic life of three years.

It is the economic life of an asset that will determine the expected useful life for the purpose of calculating depreciation. Forecasting the economic life of an asset, however, may be extremely difficult in practice. Both the rate at which technology progresses and shifts in consumer tastes can be swift and unpredictable.

Residual value (disposal value)

When a business disposes of a fixed asset that may still be of value to others, some payment may be received. This payment will represent the **residual value** or 'disposal value' of the asset. To calculate the total amount to be depreciated with regard to an asset, the residual value must be deducted from the cost of the asset. The likely amount to be received on disposal is, once again, often difficult to predict.

Depreciation method

Once the amount to be depreciated (that is, the cost less any residual value) has been estimated, the business must select a method of allocating this depreciable amount over the useful life of the fixed asset. Although there are various ways in which the total depreciation may be allocated and a depreciation charge for a period derived, there are really only two methods that are commonly used in practice.

The first of these is known as the **straight-line method** (see Example 3.6). This method simply allocates the amount to be depreciated evenly over the useful life of the asset. In other words, an equal amount of depreciation will be charged for each year the asset is held.

Example 3.6

To illustrate the straight-line method, consider the following information:

Cost of machine	£40,000
Estimated residual value at the end of its useful life	£1,024
Estimated useful life	4 years

To calculate the depreciation charge for each year, the total amount to be depreciated must be calculated. This will be the total cost *less* the estimated residual value, that is £40,000 − £1,024 = £38,976. Having done this, the annual depreciation charge can be derived by dividing the amount to be depreciated by the estimated useful life of the asset of four years. The calculation is therefore:

$$\frac{£38,976}{4} = £9,744$$

Thus, the annual depreciation charge that appears in the P and L account in relation to this asset will be £9,744 for each of the four years of the asset's life.

The amount of depreciation relating to the asset will be accumulated for as long as the asset continues to be owned by the business. This accumulated depreciation figure will increase each year as a result of the annual depreciation amount charged to the P and L account, the accumulated amount being deducted from the cost of the asset on the balance sheet. Thus, for example, at the end of the second year the accumulated depreciation will be £9,744 × 2 = £19,488 and the asset details will appear on the balance sheet as follows:

	£	£
Machine at cost	40,000	
Less Accumulated depreciation	(19,488)	
		20,512

The balance of £20,512 is referred to as the **written-down value** or **net book value** of the asset. It represents that portion of the cost of the asset that has not been treated as an expense. It must be emphasised that this figure does *not* represent the current market value, which may be quite different.

The straight-line method derives its name from the fact that the written-down value of the asset at the end of each year, when plotted on a graph against time, will result in a straight line, as shown in Figure 3.2.

The second popular approach to calculating depreciation for a period is referred to as the **reducing-balance method**. This method applies a fixed percentage rate of depreciation to the written-down value of an asset each year. The effect of this will be high annual depreciation charges in the early years and lower charges in the later years. To illustrate this method, let us take the same information used in Example 3.6 and use a fixed percentage (60 per cent) of the written-down value to determine the annual depreciation charge. The calculations will be:

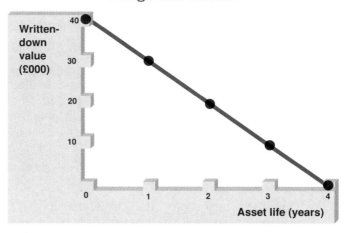

| | Figure 3.2 | **Graph of written-down value against time using the straight-line method** |

The figure shows that the written-down value of the asset declines by a constant amount each year. This is because the straight-line method provides a constant depreciation charge each year. The result, when plotted on a graph, is a straight line.

	£
Cost of machine	40,000
Year 1 Depreciation charge (60% of cost – see formula below)	(24,000)
Written-down value (WDV)	16,000
Year 2 Depreciation charge (60% WDV)	(9,600)
Written-down value	6,400
Year 3 Depreciation charge (60% WDV)	(3,840)
Written-down value	2,560
Year 4 Depreciation charge (60% WDV)	(1,536)
Residual value	1,024

Deriving the fixed percentage to be applied requires the use of the following formula:

$$P = (1 - \sqrt[n]{R/C}) \times 100\%$$

where

P = the depreciation percentage,
n = the useful life of the asset (in years),
R = the residual value of the asset, and
C = the cost of the asset.

We can see that the pattern of depreciation is quite different for the two methods. Figure 3.3 plots the written-down value of the asset, which has been derived using the reducing balance method, against time.

Figure 3.3

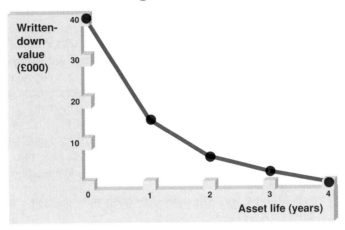

Graph of written-down value against time using the reducing-balance method

The figure shows that, under the reducing-balance method, the written-down value of an asset falls by a larger amount in the earlier years than in the later years. This is because the depreciation charge is based on a fixed percentage of the written-down value.

Activity 3.7

Assume that the machine used in Example 3.6 was owned by a business that made a profit *before* depreciation of £20,000 for each of the four years in which the asset was held. Calculate the net profit for the business for each year under each depreciation method and comment on your findings.

Your answer should be as follows:

Straight-line method

	Profit before depr'n £	Depr'n £	Net profit £
Year 1	20,000	9,744	10,256
Year 2	20,000	9,744	10,256
Year 3	20,000	9,744	10,256
Year 4	20,000	9,744	10,256

Reducing-balance method

	Profit before depr'n £	Depr'n £	Net profit (loss) £
Year 1	20,000	24,000	(4,000)
Year 2	20,000	9,600	10,400
Year 3	20,000	3,840	16,160
Year 4	20,000	1,536	18,464

The above calculations reveal that the straight-line method of depreciation results in a constant net profit figure over the four-year period. This is because both the profit before depreciation and the depreciation charge are constant over the period.

The reducing-balance method, however, results in a changing profit figure over time. In the first year a net loss is reported, and thereafter a rising net profit.

Although the *pattern* of net profit over the period will be quite different, depending on the depreciation method used, the *total* net profit for the period will remain the same. This is because both methods of depreciating will allocate the same amount of total depreciation (£38,976) over the whole period. It is only the amount allocated between years that will differ.

In practice, the effects of using different depreciation methods may not have such a dramatic effect on profits as suggested by Activity 3.7. Where a business replaces some of its assets each year, the total depreciation charge calculated under the reducing-balance method will reflect a range of charges (from high through to low) as assets will be at different points in the replacement cycle. This could mean that the total depreciation charge may not be significantly different from the total depreciation charge that would be derived under the straight-line method.

Figure 3.4 sets out the main steps in calculating an annual depreciation charge for a fixed asset.

Activity 3.8

Assume that a business purchases a machine (as described in Example 3.6) each year and that each machine is replaced at the end of its useful life of four years. Assume that this policy has been operating for several years and that the business owns four machines. What is the total depreciation charge for a year under:

(a) the straight-line method?
(b) the reducing-balance method?

Your answer should be as follows:

(a) Depreciation charges under the straight-line method will be:

£9,744 × 4 = £38,976 (At any point in time, four machines are held)

(b) Depreciation charges under the reducing-balance method will be:

		£	
Machine	1	24,000	(Depr'n yr 1)
	2	9,600	(Depr'n yr 2)
	3	3,840	(Depr'n yr 3)
	4	1,536	(Depr'n yr 4)
		38,976	

In this case, the total depreciation charges under each method will be identical. (In practice, however, it would be unusual for both methods to give exactly the same total depreciation charge for a group of machines at different points in the replacement cycle.)

Figure 3.4

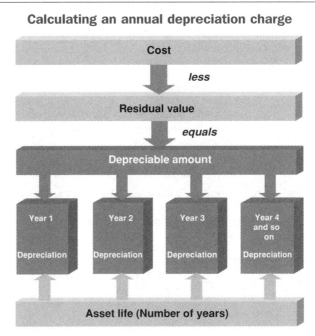

Calculating an annual depreciation charge

The figure shows how the annual depreciation charge is calculated. The depreciable amount (cost less residual value) is allocated over the life of the fixed asset using an appropriate depreciation method.

Selecting a depreciation method

How does a business choose which depreciation method to use for a particular asset? The most appropriate method should be the one that best matches the depreciation expense to the revenues that it helped generate. The business may, therefore, decide to undertake an examination of the pattern of benefits flowing from the asset. Where the benefits are likely to remain fairly constant over time (for example, from buildings), the straight-line method may be considered appropriate. Where assets lose their efficiency over time and the benefits decline as a result (for example, with certain types of machinery), the reducing-balance method may be considered more appropriate. However, other approaches to selecting a depreciation method are also used.

The accountancy profession has developed an accounting standard to deal with the problem of depreciation. As we shall see in Chapter 5, the purpose of accounting standards is to narrow the areas of difference in accounting between businesses by producing statements on best accounting practice. The standard for handling depreciation endorses the view that the depreciation method chosen should reflect the economic benefits flowing from the asset. The standard also requires that limited companies disclose, in their financial statements, the methods of depreciation used, the total depreciation for the period, and either the depreciation rates applied or the useful lives of the assets. An example of the type of disclosure required concerning depreciation policies is provided in Exhibit 3.2.

Exhibit 3.2

This extract from the 1999 published accounts of Rolls-Royce plc, a business that builds engines for aircraft, ships and other purposes, describes how the business calculates its depreciation charge.

Depreciation

(i) **Land and buildings.**
Depreciation is provided on the original cost of purchases since 1996 and on the valuation of properties adopted at December 31, 1996 and is calculated on the straight-line basis at rates sufficient to reduce them to their estimated residual value. Estimated lives, as advised by the Group's professional valuers, are:

(a) Freehold buildings – five to 45 years (average 23 years).
(b) Leasehold land and buildings – lower valuer's esitmates or period of lease.

No depreciation is provided in respect of freehold land.

(ii) **Plant and equipment.**
Depreciation is provided on the original cost of plant and equipment and is calculated on a straight-line basis at rates sufficient to reduce them to their estimated residual value. Estimated lives are in the range five to 25 years (average 17 years).

(iii) **Aircraft and engines.**
Depreciation is provided on the original cost of aircraft and engines and is calculated on a straight-line basis at rates sufficient to reduce them to their estimated residual value. Estimated lives are in the range ten to 25 years (average 18 years).

(iv) **In course of construction.**
No depreciation is provided on assets in the course of construction.

It is clear from what we have considered that making different judgements on depreciation can lead to vastly different profit figures being recorded by businesses. Exhibit 3.3 provides an example of this and how it could have led to a particular business decision being made.

Exhibit 3.3

BMW, the German car manufacturer, had owned Rover, one of the UK's car manufacturers since 1994. Early in 2000, BMW announced its decision to close the UK business because it was losing BMW £2 million a day. It transpired that this was true using German accounting standards when deriving Rover's annual depreciation expense but, when UK standards were applied, the depreciation charge was £0.44 million a day less. This still left a very large loss, but significantly less than was stated by BMW.

Source: Based on an article appearing in *Accounting Age*, 4 May 2000.

In the case of certain intangible fixed assets, such as purchased goodwill and research and development expenditure, determining the period over which the benefits extend may be extremely difficult to judge. In practice, different approaches to dealing with this problem arise. Some businesses adopt a prudent view and write off such assets immediately, whereas others may write off the assets over time (see Exhibit 3.4).

| Exhibit 3.4 | In a study of the accounting treatment of intangible assets of companies operating in the food and drink industry, it was found that where intangible assets were capitalised a wide variety of depreciation (amortisation) policies were being applied. The table below sets out the various write-off periods that are applied to different types of intangible assets in the industry. |

	Patents	Brands	Goodwill	Devel. cost	Other	No. of occurrences
10 yrs only		1	2	1		4
10–25 yrs	1		2	1		4
25–40 yrs			1			1
40 yrs	1		2			3
Not stated	3			1		4
No amortisation	1	5	1		1	8
						24

Source: Ong, A., 'The problems of accounting for intangible assets in the food and drink industry', in *Issues in Accounting and Finance*, P. Atrill and L. Lindley (eds), Ashgate Publishers, 1997, p. 184.

It is possible to avoid making a depreciation charge for a fixed asset on the grounds that it has an infinite economic life (for example freehold land) or that the estimated residual value of the fixed asset will be more or less the same as the cost or valuation figure shown in the balance sheet and, therefore, any depreciation charge would be insignificant. This latter situation will usually arise where the business provides a high standard of maintenance for its assets. Large retail chains and breweries, in particular, often argue that any depreciation charge for the freehold properties they own, such as stores and public houses, would be immaterial (see Exhibit 3.5).

| Exhibit 3.5 | The 2000 accounts of Next plc, a large fashion-clothing retail chain, show that the company considers that the depreciation charge to its freehold properties is immaterial. In its statement of accounting policies, the company argues: |

> Freehold and long leasehold properties for use in the high street retailing business are maintained to a standard whereby the estimated residual values (based on prices prevailing at the date of acquisition or revaluation) and lives of these properties are such that any depreciation would not be significant. For all other fixed assets, depreciation is provided to write down the cost less residual value of the asset over its remaining useful life by equal annual instalments.

The non-depreciation of fixed assets can be justified for the reasons stated above. However, it is not usually possible for a business to maintain the value of its fixed assets for an infinite period simply through regular maintenance and refurbishment.

Depreciation and the replacement of fixed assets

There seems to be a misunderstanding in the mind of some people that the purpose of depreciation is to provide for the replacement of an asset when it reaches the end of its useful life. However, this is *not* the purpose of depreciation as conventionally defined. It was mentioned earlier that depreciation represents an attempt to allocate the cost (less any residual value) of an asset over its expected useful life. The resulting depreciation charge in each period represents an expense, which is then used in the calculation of net profit for the period. Calculating the depreciation charge for a period is, therefore, necessary for the proper measurement of financial performance and must be calculated whether or not the business intends to replace the asset in the future.

If there is an intention to replace the asset, the depreciation charge in the profit and loss account will not ensure that liquid funds are set aside by the business specifically for this purpose. Although the effect of a depreciation charge is to reduce net profit and, therefore, to reduce the amount available for distribution to owners, the amounts retained within the business as a result may be invested in ways that are unrelated to the replacement of the specific assets.

Activity 3.9	Suppose that a business sets aside liquid funds, equivalent to the depreciation charge each year, with the intention of using this to replace the asset at the end of its useful life. Will this ensure that there will be sufficient funds available for this purpose?
	No. Even if funds are set aside each year that are equal to the depreciation charge for the year, the total amount accumulated at the end of the asset's useful life may be insufficient for replacement purposes. This may be because inflation or technological advances have resulted in an increase in the replacement cost.

Depreciation – some further issues

It is possible for certain fixed assets to appreciate in value over the short term and yet still be used up over time in the process of generating revenue. An example of such an asset is leasehold buildings. Leasehold buildings have a fixed life and will eventually be worthless to the leaseholder even though the value of the leasehold may rise at certain points during the period of the lease.

It was mentioned in the previous chapter that some businesses depart from the historic cost convention and revalue such assets periodically in order to reflect their current value on the balance sheet. When revaluation occurs, it is still appropriate to depreciate the asset, because the benefits flowing from the asset will eventually be exhausted. However, the depreciation charge should be based on the revalued amount rather than on the original cost of the asset. This will usually result in a higher depreciation charge for the asset, but it will represent a more realistic measure of the economic cost of using the asset.

When reading this section on depreciation it may have struck you that accounting is not so precise and objective as is sometimes suggested. There are areas where subjective judgement is required and depreciation provides a good illustration of this.

Activity 3.10

What kinds of judgement must be made to calculate a depreciation charge for a period?

In answering this activity, you may have thought of the following:

- The cost of the asset (for example, deciding whether to include interest charges or not)
- The expected residual or disposal value of the asset
- The expected useful life of the asset
- The choice of depreciation method

The effect of making different judgements on these matters would result in a different pattern of depreciation charges over the life of the asset and, therefore, a different pattern of reported profits. However, under- or overestimations will be adjusted for in the final year of an asset's life so that the total depreciation charge (and total profit) over the asset's life will not be affected by estimation errors.

Activity 3.11

Sally Dalton (Packaging) Ltd purchased a machine for £40,000. At the end of its useful life of four years, the amount received on sale was £4,000. When the asset was purchased the business received two estimates of the likely residual value of the asset, which were: (a) £8,000, and (b) zero.

Show the pattern of annual depreciation charges over the four years and the total depreciation charges for the asset under each of the two estimates. The straight-line method should be used to calculate the annual depreciation charges.

The depreciation charge, assuming estimate (a), will be £8,000 per year ((£40,000 − £8,000)/4). The depreciation charge, assuming estimate (b), will be £10,000 per year (£40,000/4). As the actual residual value is £4,000, estimate (a) will lead to under-depreciation of £4,000 (£8,000 − £4,000) over the life of the asset, and estimate (b) will lead to overdepreciation of £4,000 (£0 − £4,000). These under- and overestimations will be dealt with in year 4.

The pattern of depreciation and total depreciation charges will therefore be:

		Estimate (a) £	Estimate (b) £
Year			
1	Annual depreciation	8,000	10,000
2	Annual depreciation	8,000	10,000
3	Annual depreciation	8,000	10,000
4	Annual depreciation	8,000	10,000
		32,000	40,000
4	Under/(over)depreciation	4,000	(4,000)
	Total depreciation	36,000	36,000

The final adjustment for underdepreciation of an asset is often referred to as 'loss on sale of fixed asset', as the amount actually received is less than the residual value. Similarly, the adjustment for overdepreciation is often referred to as 'profit on sale of fixed asset'.

Profit measurement and the valuation of stocks

The way in which we measure the value of stock is important, because the amount of stock sold during a period will affect the calculation of net profit and the remaining stock held at the end of the period will affect the portrayal of the financial position. In Chapter 2 we saw that historical cost is the basis for valuing assets, and so you may think that stock valuation should not be a difficult issue. However, where there is a period of changing prices, the valuation of stock can be a problem.

A business must determine the cost of the stock sold during the period and the cost of the stock remaining at the end of the period. To do this the cost, of both the stock sold during the period and that remining at the end of the period, is calculated as if it had been physically handled in a particular assumed manner. The assumption made has nothing to do with how the stock is *actually* handled; it is concerned only with which assumption is likely to lead to the most useful accounting information.

The two most common assumptions used are:

➡ ■ **First in, first out (FIFO)** – the earlier stocks held are the first to be sold.
➡ ■ **Last in, first out (LIFO)** – the latest stocks held are the first to be sold.

➡ Another approach to deriving the cost of stocks is to assume that stocks entering the business lose their separate identity and any issues of stock reflect the average cost of the stocks that are held. This is the **weighted average cost (AVCO)** method, where the weights used in deriving the average cost figure are the quantities of each batch of stock purchased.

Let us now use the information contained in Example 3.7 to calculate the cost of goods sold and closing stock figures for the business using these three methods.

Example 3.7	A business that supplies coal to factories has the following transactions during a period:

		Tonnes	*Cost/tonne*
1 May	Opening stock	1,000	£10
2 May	Purchased	5,000	£11
3 May	Purchased	8,000	£12
		14,000	
6 May	Sold	(9,000)	
	Closing stock	5,000	

First in, first out (FIFO)

Using the first in, first out approach, the first 9,000 tonnes of coal are assumed to be those that are sold and the remainder will comprise the closing stock. Thus we have:

	Cost of sales			Closing stock		
	Tonnes	Cost/tonne £	Total £000	Tonnes	Cost/tonne £	Total £000
1 May	1,000	10	10.0			
2 May	5,000	11	55.0			
3 May	3,000	12	36.0	5,000	12	60.0
Cost of sales			101.0	Closing stock		60.0

Last in, first out (LIFO)

Using the last in, first out approach, the later purchases will be the first to be sold and the earlier purchases will comprise the closing stock. Thus we have:

	Cost of sales			Closing stock		
	Tonnes	Cost/tonne £	Total £000	Tonnes	Cost/tonne £	Total £000
3 May	8,000	12	96.0			
2 May	1,000	11	11.0	4,000	11	44.0
1 May				1,000	10	10.0
Cost of sales			107.0	Closing stock		54.0

Weighted average cost (AVCO)

Using this approach, a weighted average cost will be determined that will be used to derive both the cost of goods sold and the cost of the remaining stocks held. Thus we have:

	Purchases		
	Tonnes	Cost/tonne £	Total £000
1 May	1,000	10	10.0
2 May	5,000	11	55.0
3 May	8,000	12	96.0
	14,000		161.0

Average cost = £161,000/14,000 = £11.5 per tonne.

Cost of sales			Closing stock		
Tonnes	Cost/tonne £	Total £000	Tonnes	Cost/tonne £000	Total £000
9,000	11.5	103.5	5,000	11.5	57.5

Activity 3.12

Suppose the 9,000 tonnes of stock in Example 3.7 were sold for £15 per tonne.

(a) Calculate the gross profit for the period under each of the three methods.
(b) What observations concerning the portrayal of financial position and perform-ance can you make about each method when prices are rising?

Your answer should be along the following lines:

(a) Gross profit calculation:

	FIFO £000	LIFO £000	AVCO £000
Sales	135.0	135.0	135.0
Cost of sales	101.0	107.0	103.5
Gross profit	34.0	28.0	31.5
	£000	£000	£000
Closing stock figure	60.0	54.0	57.5

(b) The above figures reveal that FIFO will give the highest gross profit during a period of rising prices. This is because sales are matched with the earlier (and cheaper) purchases. LIFO will give the lowest gross profit because sales are matched against the more recent (and dearer) purchases. The AVCO method will normally give a figure that is between these two extremes.

The closing stock figure in the balance sheet will be highest with the FIFO method. This is because the cost of goods still held will be based on the more recent (and dearer) pur-chases. LIFO will give the lowest closing stock figure as the goods held in stock will be based on the earlier (and cheaper) stocks purchased. Once again, the AVCO method will normally give a figure that is between these two extremes.

Activity 3.13

Assume that prices in Activity 3.12 are falling rather than rising. How would your observations concerning the portrayal of financial performance and position be dif-ferent for the various stock valuation methods?

When prices are falling, the position of FIFO and LIFO is reversed. FIFO will give the lowest gross profit as sales are matched against the earlier (and dearer) goods pur-chased. LIFO will give the highest gross profit as sales are matched against the more recent (and cheaper) goods purchased. AVCO will give a cost of sales figure between these two extremes. The closing stock figure in the balance sheet will be lowest under FIFO as the cost of stock will be based on the more recent (and cheaper) stocks pur-chased. LIFO will provide the highest closing stock figure and AVCO will provide a figure between the two extremes.

It is important to recognise that the different stock-valuation methods will only have an effect on the reported profit *from one year to the next*. The figure derived for closing stock will be carried forward and matched with sales in a later period. Thus, if the cheaper purchases of stocks are matched to sales in the current period, it will mean that the dearer purchases will be matched to sales in a later period. Over the life of the business, therefore, the total profit will be the same whichever valuation method has been used.

Stock valuation – some further issues

Determining the cost of stock held by a manufacturing business can be more of a problem than for other types of business. This is because manufacturing businesses will normally hold three different categories of stock:

■ Raw materials
■ Work in progress (that is, partly finished goods)
■ Finished goods

The general principle to be applied when determining the cost of the stocks held is that any amounts incurred in bringing the goods to their current condition and location should be included. This will mean that, for raw materials, the cost of purchasing will include amounts incurred for transportation, handling and import duties. For work in progress and finished goods, the costs of converting the raw materials to products should be included. These costs of conversion will typically include such things as labour costs, production overheads and subcontractors' costs. However, in practice, there may be various items of expenditure that are really a matter of judgement as to whether or not they are included in the cost figure.

We saw in Chapter 2 that the closing stock figure will appear as part of the current assets of the business and that the convention of prudence requires current assets to be valued at the lower of cost and net realisable value. (The net realisable value of stocks is the estimated selling price less any further costs that may be necessary to complete the goods and any costs involved in selling and distributing the goods.) This rule may mean that the valuation method applied to stock will switch each year depending on which of cost and net realisable value is the lower. In practice, however, the cost of the stock held is usually below the current net realisable value – particularly during a period of rising prices. It is, therefore, the cost figure that will normally appear in the balance sheet.

Activity 3.14

Can you think of any circumstances where the net realisable value will be lower than the cost of stocks held, even during a period of generally rising prices?

The net realisable value may be lower where:

■ Goods have deteriorated or become obsolete.
■ There has been a fall in the market price of the goods.
■ The goods are being used as a 'loss leader'.
■ Bad purchasing decisions have been made.

The accountancy profession has produced an accounting standard to deal with the issue of stock valuation. This standard supports the lower of cost and net realisable value rule and states that, when comparing the cost with the net realisable value, each item of stock should be compared separately. If this is not practical, categories of similar stock should be grouped together. The standard also identifies a number of methods of arriving at the cost of stock that are acceptable. Although FIFO and AVCO are regarded as acceptable, the LIFO approach is not. The LIFO approach is also unacceptable to the Inland Revenue for taxation purposes. As a result, LIFO is rarely used in the UK, although it is in widespread use in the United States. The policies of one company with respect to its stock holdings are set out in Exhibit 3.6.

Exhibit 3.6	The following extract has been taken from the 2000 published accounts of Tate and Lyle plc, the sugar and other starch-based food processor, which sets out the accounting policy adopted with respect to stocks:
	Stock valued at the lower of direct cost together with attributable overheads and net realisable value and is transferred to the profit and loss account on a 'first in, first out' basis.

➡ Stock valuation and depreciation provide two examples where the **consistency convention** must be applied. This convention holds that when a particular method of accounting is selected to deal with a transaction, this method should be applied consistently over time. Thus, it would not be acceptable to switch from, say, FIFO to AVCO between periods (unless there are exceptional circumstances that make this appropriate). The purpose of this convention is to try to ensure that users are able to make valid comparisons between periods.

Activity 3.15	Stock valuation provides a further example of where subjective judgement is required to derive the figures for inclusion in the financial statements. Can you identify the main areas where judgement is required?

The main areas are:

■ The choice of cost method (FIFO, LIFO, AVCO).
■ Deciding which items should be included in the cost of stocks (particularly for work in progress and the finished goods of a manufacturing business).
■ Deriving the net realisable value figure for stocks held.

Profit measurement and the problem of bad and doubtful debts

Many businesses sell goods on credit. When credit sales are made, the revenue is usually recognised as soon as the goods are passed to, and accepted by, the customer. Recording the dual aspect of a credit sale will involve:

■ increasing the sales;
■ increasing debtors by the amount of the credit sale.

However, with this type of sale there is always the risk that the customer will not pay the amount due, however reliable the customer might have appeared to be at the time of the sale. When it becomes reasonably certain that the customer will never pay, the debt is considered to be 'bad' and this must be taken into account when preparing the financial statements.

Activity 3.16	What would be the effect of not taking into account the fact that a debt is bad, when preparing the financial statements, on the profit and the balance sheet?

The effect would be to overstate the assets (debtors) on the balance sheet and to overstate profit in the P and L account, as the sale (which has been recognised) will not result in any future benefit arising.

To provide a more realistic picture of financial performance and position, the **bad debt** must be 'written off'. This will involve:

■ reducing the debtors;
■ increasing expenses (by creating an expense known as 'bad debts written off') by the amount of the bad debt.

The matching convention requires that the bad debt is written off in the same period as the sale that gave rise to the debt is recognised.

Note that, when a debt is bad, the accounting response is not simply to cancel the original sale. If this were done, the P and L account would not be so informative. Reporting the bad debts as an expense can be extremely useful in the evaluation of management performance.

At the end of the accounting period, it may not be possible to identify with reasonable certainty all the bad debts that have been incurred during the period. It may be that some debts appear doubtful, but only at some later point in time will the true position become clear. The uncertainty that exists does not mean that, when preparing the financial statements, we should ignore the possibility that some of the debtors outstanding will eventually prove to be bad. It would not be prudent to do so, nor would it comply with the need to match expenses to the period in which the associated sale is recognised. As a result, the business will normally try to identify all those debts that, at the end of the period, can be classified as doubtful (that is, there is a possibility that they may eventually prove to be bad). This can be done by examining individual accounts of debtors or by taking a proportion of the total debtors outstanding based on past experience.

Once a figure has been derived, a **provision for doubtful debts** can be created. This provision will be:

■ Shown as an expense in the profit and loss account, and
■ Deducted from the total debtors figure in the balance sheet.

By doing this, full account is taken, in the appropriate accounting period, of those debts where there is a risk of non-payment. This accounting treatment of doubtful debts will be in addition to the treatment of bad debts described above.

Example 3.8 illustrates the reporting of bad and doubtful debts.

Example 3.8

Desai Enterprises has debtors of £350,000 at the end of the accounting year to 30 June 2001. Investigation of these debtors revealed that £10,000 was likely to prove irrecoverable and that a further £30,000 was doubtful.

Extracts from the P and L account would have been as follows:

Profit and loss account (extracts) for the year ended 30 June 2001

	£
Bad debts written off	10,000
Provision for doubtful debts	30,000

Balance sheet (extracts) as at 30 June 2001

	£
Debtors	340,000[a]
Less Provision for doubtful debts	30,000
	310,000

[a] (that is, £350,000 – £10,000 irrecoverable debts)

The provision for doubtful debts is, of course, an estimate, and it is quite likely that the actual amount of debts that prove to be bad will be different from the estimate. Let us say that, during the next accounting period, it was discovered that £26,000 of the doubtful debts in fact proved to be irrecoverable. These debts must now be written off as follows:

- Reduce debtors by £26,000, and
- Reduce provision for doubtful debts by £26,000.

However, a provision for doubtful debts of £4,000 will remain. This amount represents an overestimate made when creating the provision in the P and L account for the year to 30 June 2001. As the provision is no longer needed, it should be eliminated. Remember that the provision was made by creating an expense in the P and L account for the year to 30 June 2001. As the expense was too high, the amount of the overestimate should be 'written back' in the next accounting period. In other words, it will be treated as revenue for the year to 30 June 2002. This will mean:

- Reducing the provision for doubtful debts by £4,000, and
- Increasing revenues by £4,000.

Ideally, of course, the amount should be written back to the 2001 P and L account; however, it is too late to do this. At the end of 2002, not only will 2001's over-provision be written back but a new provision should be created to allow for the debts; arising from 2002's sales, that seem doubtful.

Activity 3.17

Clayton Conglomerates had debts of £870,000 outstanding at the end of the accounting year to 31 March 2002. The chief accountant believed that £40,000 of those debts were irrecoverable and that a further £60,000 were doubtful. In the subsequent year, it was found that an overoptimistic estimate had been made and that a further £45,000 of debts had actually proved to be bad.

Show the relevant extracts in the profit and loss account for both 2002 and 2003 to report the bad debts written off and the provision for doubtful debts. Also show the relevant balance sheet extract as at 31 March 2002.

Your answer should be as follows:

P and L account (extracts) for the year ended 31 March 2002

	£
Bad debts written off	40,000
Provision for doubtful debts	60,000

P and L account (extracts) for the year ended 31 March 2003

	£
Provision for doubtful debts written back (revenue)	15,000

Note: This figure will usually be netted off against any provision created for doubtful debts in respect of 2003.

Balance sheet (extracts) as at 31 March 2002

	£
Debtors	830,000
Less Provision for doubtful debts	(60,000)
	770,000

Activity 3.18

Bad and doubtful debts represent further areas where judgement is required in deriving expenses figures for a particular period. What will be the effect of different judgements concerning the amount of bad and doubtful debts on the profit for a particular period and on the total profit reported over the life of the business?

Judgement is often required in order to derive a figure for bad debts incurred during a period. There may be situations where views will differ concerning whether or not a debt is irrecoverable. The decision concerning whether or not to write off a bad debt will have an effect on the expenses for the period and, hence, the reported profit. However, over the life of the business, the total reported profit will not be affected as incorrect judgements in one period will be adjusted for in a later period.

Suppose, for example, that a debt of £100 was written off in a period and that, in a later period, the amount owing was actually received. The increase in expenses of £100 in the period in which the bad debt was written off would be compensated for by an increase in revenues of £100 when the amount outstanding was finally received (bad debt recoverable). If, on the other hand, the amount owing of £100 was never written off in the first place, the profit for the two periods would not be affected by the bad debt adjustment and would, therefore, be different – but the total profit for the two periods would be the same.

A similar situation would apply where there are differences in judgements concerning doubtful debts.

Self-assessment question 3.1 brings together some of the points that have been raised in this chapter.

? **Self-assessment question 3.1**

TT Limited is a new business that started trading on 1 January 2000. The following is a summary of transactions that occurred during the first year of trading:

1. The owners introduced £50,000 of capital, which was paid into a bank account opened in the name of the business.
2. Premises were rented from 1 January 2000 at an annual rental of £20,000. During the year, rent of £25,000 was paid to the owner of the premises.
3. Rates on the premises were paid during the year as follows:

   ■ For the period 1 January 2000 to 31 March 2000: £500
   ■ For the period 1 April 2000 to 31 March 2001: £1,200

4. A delivery van was bought on 1 January 2000 for £12,000. This is expected to be used in the business for four years and then to be sold for £2,000.
5. Wages totalling £33,500 were paid during the year. At the end of the year, the business owed £630 of wages for the last week of the year.
6. Electricity bills for the first three quarters of the year were paid, totalling £1,650. After 31 December 2000 but before the accounts had been finalised for the year, the bill for the last quarter arrived showing a charge of £620.
7. Stock in trade totalling £143,000 was bought on credit.
8. Stock in trade totalling £12,000 was bought for cash.
9. Sales on credit totalled £152,000 (cost £74,000).
10. Cash sales totalled £35,000 (cost £16,000).
11. Receipts from trade debtors totalled £132,000.
12. Payments to trade creditors totalled £121,000.
13. Van running expenses paid totalled £9,400.
14. At the end of the year it was clear that a trade debtor who owed £400 would not be able to pay any part of the debt.

The business uses the straight-line method for depreciating fixed asets.

Required:
Prepare a balance sheet as at 31 December 2000 and a P and L account for the year to that date.

Interpreting the P and L account

When a P and L account is presented to users, it is sometimes the case that the only item that will concern them will be the final net profit figure or 'bottom line'. Although the net profit figure is a primary measure of performance and its importance is difficult to overstate, the P and L account contains other information which should be of interest. In order to evaluate business performance effectively, it is important to find out how the final net profit figure was derived. Thus, the level of sales, the nature and amount of expenses incurred and the profit in relation to sales are important factors in understanding the performance of the business over a period. The analysis and interpretation of financial statements is considered in detail in Chapter 7; however, it may be useful at this point to consider some of the ways in which the information contained within the P and L account will be used. We shall take the profit and loss account set out in Example 3.9 as our basis.

Example 3.9			

Patel Wholesalers
Trading and P and L account for the year ended 31 March 2001

	£	£
Sales		460,500
Less Cost of sales		345,800
Gross profit		114,700
Less		
Salaries and wages	45,900	
Rent and rates	15,300	
Telephone and postage	1,400	
Motor vehicle expenses	3,900	
Loan interest	4,800	
Depreciation – Motor van	2,300	
– Fixtures and fittings	2,200	
		(75,800)
Net profit		38,900

To evaluate performance the following points might be considered:

■ The sales figure represents an important measure of output and can be compared with the sales figure of earlier periods and the planned sales figure for the current period in order to assess the achievement of the business.
■ The gross profit figure can be related to the sales figure in order to find out the profitability of the goods being sold. In the statement shown above, we can see that the gross profit is about 25 per cent of the sales figure or, to put it another way, for every £1 of sales generated the gross profit is 25p. This level of profitability may be compared with that of past periods, with planned levels of profitability or with comparable figures of similar businesses.
■ The expenses of the businesses may be examined and compared with those of past periods (and so on) in order to evaluate operating efficiency. Individual expenses can be related to sales to assess whether the level of expenses is appropriate. Thus, in Example 3.9 the salaries and wages represent almost 10 per cent of sales or, for every £1 of sales generated, 10p is absorbed by employee costs.
■ Net profit can also be related to sales. In the statement shown above, net profit is about 8 per cent of sales. Thus, for every £1 of sales, the owners of the business benefit by 8p. Whether or not this is acceptable will again depend on making the kinds of comparison referred to above. Net profit as a percentage of sales can vary substantially between different types of business. There is

usually a trade-off to be made between profitability and sales volume. Some businesses are prepared to accept a low net profit percentage in return for generating a high volume of sales. At the other extreme, some businesses may prefer to have a high net profit percentage but accept a relatively low volume of sales. For example, a supermarket may fall into the former category and a trader in luxury cars may fall into the latter.

Activity 3.19			

Chan Exporters
Trading and P and L account for the year ended 31 May 2002

	£	£
Sales		840,000
Less Cost of sales		620,000
Gross profit		220,000
Less		
Salaries and wages	92,000	
Selling and distribution costs	44,000	
Rent and rates	30,000	
Bad debts written off	86,000	
Telephone and postage	4,000	
Insurance	2,000	
Motor vehicle expenses	8,000	
Loan interest	5,000	
Depreciation – Motor van	3,000	
– Fixtures and fittings	4,000	
		(278,000)
Net profit (loss)		(58,000)

In the previous year to 31 May 2001, sales were £710,000. The gross profit was £200,000 and the net profit was £37,000.

Analyse the performance of the business for the year to 31 May 2002 in so far as the information allows.

Sales increased by nearly 18 per cent over the previous year but the 'bottom line' fell from a net profit of £37,000 to a loss of £58,000. The rapid expansion of the business has clearly brought problems in its wake. In the previous period, the business was making a gross profit of more than 28p for every £1 of sales made. This reduced in the year to 31 May 2002 to around 26p for every £1 of sales made. This seems to suggest that the rapid expansion was partly fuelled by a reduction in prices.

The gross profit increased in absolute terms by £20,000; however, there was a drastic decline in net profits during the period. In the previous period, the business was making a net profit of nearly 5p for every £1 of sales whereas, for the year to 31 May 2002, this reduced to a loss of nearly 7p for every £1 of sales made. This means that overhead expenses have increased considerably. Some increase in overhead expenses may be expected in order to service the increased level of activity. However, the increase appears to be exceptional. If we look at the list of overhead expenses we can see that the bad debts written off seem very high (more than 10 per cent of total sales). This may be a further effect of the rapid expansion that has taken place. In order to generate sales, insufficient regard may have been paid to the creditworthiness of customers. A comparison of overhead expenses with those of the previous period would be useful.

Summary

In this chapter we have considered the P and L account. We have examined the main principles underpinning this statement and we have looked at various measurement issues connected with the determination of profit. We have seen that the profit and loss account seeks to measure *accomplishment* during a period rather than the cash generated. Thus, revenues and expenses are not the same as cash received and cash paid, and net profit does not normally reflect the net cash flows for the period. Although cash flows are important to the assessment of business performance, these are dealt with in a separate financial statement.

Although accountants try to be objective when measuring profit, there are certain areas where they have to rely on subjective judgement. Three of these areas – depreciation, stock valuation and bad debts – were examined in some detail. We saw that different judgements can lead to quite different calculations of profit between years.

In this chapter and in the previous chapter, we have considered a number of accounting conventions. These have been summarised as an Appendix to this chapter to help consolidate your knowledge.

 Key terms

Profit   p. 53
Revenue   p. 53
Expense   p. 54
Gross profit   p. 56
Trading and P and L account   p. 56
Net profit   p. 56
Cost of sales   p. 57
Realisation convention   p. 60
Matching convention   p. 60
Accrued expense   p. 61
Prepaid expense   p. 63
Materiality convention   p. 63

Depreciation   p. 64
Residual value   p. 66
Straight-line method   p. 66
Written-down value   p. 66
Reducing-balance method   p. 66
First in, first out (FIFO)   p. 76
Last in, first out (LIFO)   p. 76
Weighted average cost (AVCO)   p. 76
Consistency convention   p. 80
Bad debt   p. 81
Provision for doubtful debts   p. 81

Further reading

If you would like to explore the topics covered in this chapter in more depth, we recommend the following books:

Financial Reporting, *Alexander*, A. and *Britton*, A., 5th edn, International Business Thomson Press, 2001, chapter 4.

Accounting Principles, *Anthony*, R. and *Reece*, J., 7th edn, Irwin, 1995, chapters 5, 6 and 7.

Accounting Theory and Practice, *Glautier*, M. and *Underdown*, B. 7th edn, Pitman Publishing, 2001, chapters 10 and 11.

Financial Accounting and Reporting, *Elliott*, B. and *Elliott*, J. 5th edn, Financial Times, Prentice Hall, 2001, chapters 14 and 17.

❓ REVIEW QUESTIONS

3.1 'Although the P and L account is a record of past achievement, the calculations required for certain expenses involve estimates of the future.' What is meant by this statement? Can you think of examples where estimates of the future are used?

3.2 'Depreciation is a process of allocation and not valuation.' What do you think is meant by this statement?

3.3 What is the convention of consistency? Does this convention help users in making more valid comparisons *between* businesses?

3.4 Explain the relationship between an asset and an expense. Use the two possible treatments of interest charges dealt with in the chapter to illustrate this relationship.

❓ EXERCISES

Exercises 3.6–3.8 are more advanced than 3.1–3.5. Those with coloured numbers have answers at the back of the book.

3.1 You have heard the following statements made. Comment critically on them.
  (a) 'Capital only increases or decreases as a result of the owners putting more cash into the business or taking some out.'
  (b) 'An accrued expense is one that relates to next year.'
  (c) 'Unless we depreciate this asset we will be unable to provide for its replacement.'
  (d) 'There is no point in depreciating the factory building. It is appreciating in value each year.'

3.2 Singh Enterprises has an accounting year to 31 December. On 1 January 1999 the business purchased a machine for £10,000. The machine had an expected life of four years and an estimated residual value of £2,000. On 1 January 2000 the business purchased another machine for £15,000. This machine had an expected useful life of five years and an estimated residual value of £2,500. On 31 December 2001, the business sold the first machine purchased for £3,000.
  The business employs the straight-line method of depreciation for machinery.

Required:
Show the relevant P and L account extracts and balance sheet extracts for 1999, 2000 and 2001.

3.3 The owner of a business is confused and comes to you for help. The financial statements for his business, prepared by an accountant, for the last accounting period reveal an increase in profit of £50,000. However, during the accounting period the bank balance declined by £30,000. What reasons might explain this apparent discrepancy?

3.4 Spratley Ltd is a builders merchant. On 1 September the business had 20 tonnes of sand in stock at a cost of £18 per tonne and thus at a total cost of £360. During the first week in September, the business purchased the following amounts of sand:

	Tonnes	Cost/tonne
2 September	48	20
3 September	30	22
4 September	15	24
6 September	10	25

On 7 September, the business sold 60 tonnes of sand to a local builder.

Required:

Calculate the cost of goods sold and the closing stock figures from the above information using the following stock costing methods:

(a) First in, first out
(b) Last in, first out
(c) Weighted average cost

3.5 Fill in the values (a) to (f) in the following table on the assumption that there were no opening balances involved:

	Relating to period		At end of period	
	Paid/ received	Expense/ revenue for period	Prepaid	Accruals/ deferred revenues
	£	£	£	£
Rent payable	10,000	a	1,000	
Rates and insurance	5,000	b		1,000
General expenses	c	6,000	1,000	
Loan interest payable	3,000	2,500	d	
Salaries	e	9,000		3,000
Rent receivable	f	1,500		1,500

3.6 The following is the balance sheet of TT Limited at the end of its first year of trading (from Self-assessment question 3.1):

Balance sheet as at 31 December 2000

	£	£	£
Fixed assets			
Motor van – Cost			12,000
– Depreciation			2,500
			9,500
Current assets			
Stock in trade	65,000		
Trade debtors	19,600		
Prepaid expenses[a]	5,300		
Cash	750		
		90,650	
Less **Current liabilities**			
Trade creditors	22,000		
Accrued expenses[b]	1,250		
		23,250	
			67,400
			76,900
Capital			
Original			50,000
Retained profit			26,900
			76,900

Notes:
[a] The prepaid expenses consisted of rates (£300) and rent (£5,000).
[b] The accrued expenses consisted of wages (£630) and electricity (£620).

During 2001, the following transactions took place:

1. The owners withdrew capital in the form of cash of £20,000.
2. Premises continued to be rented at an annual rental of £20,000. During the year, rent of £15,000 was paid to the owner of the premises.
3. Rates on the premises were paid during the year for the period 1 April 2001 to 31 March 2002 and amounted to £1,300.
4. A second delivery van was bought on 1 January for £13,000. This is expected to be used in the business for four years and then to be sold for £3,000.
5. Wages totalling £36,700 were paid during the year. At the end of the year, the business owed £860 of wages for the last week of the year.
6. Electricity bills for the first three quarters of the year and £620 for the last quarter of the previous year were paid, totalling £1,820. After 31 December 2001 but before the accounts had been finalised for the year, the bill for the last quarter arrived showing a charge of £690.
7. Stock in trade totalling £67,000 was bought on credit.
8. Stock in trade totalling £8,000 was bought for cash.
9. Sales on credit totalled £179,000 (cost £89,000).
10. Cash sales totalled £54,000 (cost £25,000).
11. Receipts from trade debtors totalled £178,000.
12. Payments to trade creditors totalled £71,000.
13. Van running expenses paid totalled £16,200.

The business uses the straight-line method for depreciating fixed assets.

Required:
Prepare a balance sheet as at 31 December 2001 and a P and L account for the year to that date.

3.7 The following is the balance sheet of WW, Limited as at 31 December 2000:

Balance sheet as at 31 December 2000

	£	£	£
Fixed assets			
Machinery			25,300
Current assets			
Stock in trade	12,200		
Trade debtors	21,300		
Prepaid expenses (rates)	400		
Cash	8,300		
		42,200	
Less **Current liabilities**			
Trade creditors	16,900		
Accrued expenses (wages)	1,700		
		18,600	
			23,600
			48,900
Capital			
Original			25,000
Retained profit			23,900
			48,900

During 2001 the following transactions took place:

1. The owners withdrew capital in the form of cash of £23,000.
2. Premises were rented at an annual rental of £20,000. During the year, rent of £25,000 was paid to the owner of the premises.
3. Rates on the premises were paid during the year for the period 1 April 2001 to 31 March 2002 and amounted to £2,000.
4. Some machinery, which was bought on 1 January 2000 for £13,000, has proved to be unsatisfactory. It was part-exchanged for some new machinery on 1 January 2001, and WW Limited paid a cash amount of £6,000. The new machinery would have cost £15,000 had the business bought it without the trade-in.
5. Wages totalling £23,800 were paid during the year. At the end of the year, the business owed £860 of wages.
6. Electricity bills for the four quarters of the year were paid totalling £2,700.
7. Stock in trade totalling £143,000 was bought on credit.
8. Stock in trade totalling £12,000 was bought for cash.
9. Sales on credit totalled £211,000 (cost £127,000).
10. Cash sales totalled £42,000 (cost £25,000).
11. Receipts from trade debtors totalled £198,000.
12. Payments to trade creditors totalled £156,000.
13. Van running expenses paid totalled £17,500.

The business uses the reducing-balance method of depreciation for fixed assets at the rate of 30 per cent each year.

Required:
Prepare a balance sheet as at 31 December 2001 and a P and L account for the year to that date.

3.8 The following is the trading and profit and loss account for Nikov and Co. for the year ended 31 December 2001 along with information relating to the preceding year.

Trading and profit and loss account for the year ended 31 December

	2000		2001	
	£000	£000	£000	£000
Sales		382.5		420.2
Less Cost of sales		114.8		126.1
Gross profit		267.7		294.1
Less				
Salaries and wages	86.4		92.6	
Selling and distribution costs	75.4		98.9	
Rent and rates	22.0		22.0	
Bad debts written off	4.0		19.7	
Telephone and postage	4.4		4.8	
Insurance	2.8		2.9	
Motor vehicle expenses	8.6		10.3	
Loan interest	5.4		4.6	
Depreciation – Motor van	3.3		3.1	
– Fixtures and fittings	4.5		4.3	
		216.8		263.2
Net profit (loss)		50.9		30.9

Required:
Analyse the performance of the business for the year to 31 December 2001 in so far as the information allows.

Summary of the major accounting conventions

The major accounting conventions that have been covered in Chapters 2 and 3 may be summarised as follows:

■ **Money measurement.** Accounting only deals with those items that are capable of being expressed in monetary terms.

■ **Historical cost.** Items should be recorded at their historical (acquisition) cost.

■ **Going concern.** The business will continue in operation for the foreseeable future; there is no intention to liquidate the business.

■ **Business entity.** For accounting purposes, the business and its owner(s) are treated as separate and distinct.

■ **Dual aspect.** Each transaction has two aspects and each aspect must be reflected in the financial statements.

■ **Prudence.** Financial statements should err on the side of caution.

■ **Stable monetary unit.** Money, which is the unit of measurement, is assumed to have the same purchasing power over time.

■ **Objectivity.** As far as possible, financial statements should be prepared on the basis of objective, verifiable evidence.

■ **Realisation.** Revenue should only be recognised when it is realised.

■ **Matching.** When measuring income, expenses should be matched to the revenues they helped to generate. In other words, they should appear in the same accounting period as that in which those revenues were realised.

■ **Materiality.** Where the amounts involved are immaterial, only what is expedient should be considered.

■ **Consistency.** Where a particular method is selected to deal with a transaction, this method should be applied consistently over time.

CHAPTER 4

Accounting for limited companies (1)

Introduction

In the UK, most businesses, except the very smallest, trade in the form of limited companies. In this chapter we shall examine the nature of limited companies and see how they differ in practical terms from sole proprietorships. This will involve our considering the ways in which finance is provided by the owners. It will also require us to consider the ways in which companies' financial statements (the balance sheet and the profit and loss account) differ from those of sole proprietors.

OBJECTIVES When you have completed this chapter you should be able to:

- Discuss the nature of the limited company.
- Explain the role of directors of limited companies.
- Outline and explain the particular features and restrictions of the owners' claim, in the context of limited companies.
- Prepare a profit and loss account and balance sheet for a limited company.

Generating wealth through limited companies

The nature of limited companies

A limited company is an artificial legal person. This means that a company has many of the rights and obligations that 'real' people have. With the rare exceptions of those that are created by Act of Parliament or by royal charter, all UK companies are created as a result of the Registrar of Companies entering the name of the new company on the Registry of Companies (having accepting that the necessary formalities have been met). The Registrar of Companies is an officer of the Department of Trade and Industry. The necessary formalities are the simple matters of filling in a few form and paying a modest registration fee. Thus, in the UK, companies can be formed easily and cheaply (for about £100).

Normally, companies are owned by at least two people. The owners of a limited company are usually known as 'members' or 'shareholders'. The ownership of a company is normally divided into a number – frequently a large – number, of shares each of equal size. Each shareholder owns one or more shares in the company.

A limited company is legally separate from those who own and manage it. This fact leads to the important features of the limited company: perpetual life and limited liability, as described next.

Perpetual life

The life of the company is not related to the life of the individuals who own or manage it. Shares may be sold by an existing shareholder to another person who wishes to become a shareholder. When an owner of part of the shares of the company dies, that person's shares pass to the beneficiary of his or her estate.

Limited liability

Since the company is a legal person in its own right, it must take responsibility for its own debts and losses. This means that once the shareholders have paid what they have agreed to pay for the shares, their obligation to the company, and to the company's creditors, is satisfied. Thus shareholders can limit their losses to the amount that they have paid or agreed to pay for their shares. This is of great practical importance to potential shareholders, since they know that what they can lose, as part-owners of the business, is limited.

Contrast this with the position of sole proprietors or partners (that is, the owners or part-owners of unincorporated businesses). Here, there is not the opportunity that shareholders have to 'ring-fence' the assets that they choose not to put into the business. If a sole proprietorship business finds itself in a position where liabilities exceed the business assets, the law gives unsatisfied creditors the right to demand payment out of what the sole proprietor had regarded as 'non-business' assets. Thus the sole proprietor could lose everything – house, car, the lot. This is because the law sees Jill, the sole proprietor, as being the same as Jill the private individual. The shareholder, by contrast, can lose only the amount invested in that company. Legally, a business operating as a limited company, in which Jack owns shares, is not the same as Jack himself. This is true even where Jack owns all of the shares in the company.

Activity 4.1	We have just said that the fact that shareholders can limit their losses to the amount that they have paid or have agreed to pay for their shares is of great practical importance to potential shareholders. Can you think of any practical benefit to a private-sector economy, in general, of this ability of shareholders to limit losses?

Business is a risky venture, and in some cases a very risky one. People with money to invest will tend to be more content to do so where they know the limit of their liability. This means that more businesses will tend to be formed and that existing ones will find it easier to raise additional finance from existing and/or additional part-owners. This is good for the private-sector economy, since businesses will tend to form and expand more readily. Thus the wants of society are more likely to be met, and choice offered, where limited liability exists.

➡ Though **limited liability** has this advantage to the providers of capital, namely the shareholders, it is not necessarily to the advantage of all others who have a stake in a business. Limited liability is attractive to shareholders because they can, in effect, walk away from the unpaid debts of the company if the contribution of the shareholders has not been sufficient to meet those debts. This is likely to make any individual or another business, contemplating advancing credit, wary of dealing with the limited company. This can be a real problem for smaller, less-established companies. For example, suppliers may insist on cash payment before delivery. Alternatively, the bank may require a personal guarantee from a major shareholder that debts will be paid, before allowing a company trade credit. In the latter case the supplier of credit will circumvent the company's limited liability status by establishing the personal liability of an individual. Larger, more established companies, on the other hand, tend to have built up the confidence of suppliers.

It is mainly to warn those contemplating dealing with a limited company that the liability of the owners is limited, and that this fact must be indicated in the name of the company. As we shall see later in this chapter, there are other safeguards for those dealing with a limited company in that the extent to which shareholders may withdraw their investment from the company is restricted.

Another important safeguard for those dealing with a limited company is that all limited companies must produce annual accounts (including a profit and loss account and a balance sheet) and, in effect, make these available to the public. The rules surrounding the accounts of limited companies will be discussed in Chapter 5.

Public and private companies

When a company is registered with the Registrar of Companies, it must be registered either as a public or as a private company. The main practical difference
➡ between these is that a **public company** can offer its shares for sale to the general
➡ public, but a **private company** is restricted from doing so. A public limited company must signal its status to all interested parties by having the words 'public limited company', or its abbreviation 'plc' in its name. For a private limited company, the word 'limited' or 'Ltd' must appear as part of its name.

Private limited companies tend to be smaller businesses where the ownership is divided among relatively few shareholders who are usually fairly close to one another – for example, a family company. Numerically, there are vastly more private limited companies in the UK than there are public ones. Since the public ones tend to be individually larger, they probably represent a much more important group economically. Many private limited companies are no more than the vehicle through which businesses, which are little more than sole proprietorships, operate.

Regarding accounting requirements, there is no distinction made between private and public companies.

Transferring share ownership – the role of the Stock Exchange

Shares in a company may be transferred from one owner to another without this change of share ownership having any direct impact on that company's business, or on the shareholders not involved with the particular transfer. With major companies, the desire of some existing shareholders to sell their shares, coupled with the desire of others to buy those shares, has led to the existence of a formal market in which the shares can be bought and sold. The Stock Exchange (of the UK and the Republic of Ireland), and similar organisations around the world, are simply marketplaces in which shares in major companies are bought and sold. Prices are determined by the law of supply and demand. Supply and demand are themselves determined by investors' perceptions of the future economic prospects of the companies concerned.

Activity 4.2	If, as has been pointed out, the change in ownership of the shares of a particular company does not directly affect that company, why would a particular company welcome the fact that the shares are traded in a recognised market?

The main reason is that investors are generally reluctant to pledge their money unless they can see some way in which they can turn their investment back into cash. In theory, the shares of a particular company may be very valuable as a result of the company having a very bright economic future; but unless this value is capable of being realised in cash, the benefit to the shareholders is doubtful. After all, you cannot spend shares; you generally need cash.

This means that potential shareholders are much more likely to be prepared to buy new shares from a company (thus providing the company with new finance) when they can see a way of liquidating their investment (turning it into cash) as and when they need to. The Stock Exchanges provide such a means of liquidation.

Though the buying and selling of 'second-hand' shares does not provide a company with cash, the fact that the buying and selling facility exists will make it easier for the company to raise new share capital as and when it wishes to do so.

Taxation

Another consequence of the legal separation of the limited company from its owners is the fact that companies must be accountable to the Inland Revenue for tax on their profits and gains. This introduces the effects of tax into the accounting statements of limited companies. The charge for tax is shown in the profit and loss account. Since only 50 per cent of a company's tax liability is due for payment during the year concerned, the other 50 per cent will appear on the end-of-year balance sheet as a short-term liability. This will be illustrated a little later in the chapter. The tax position of companies contrasts with that of the sole proprietorship or partnership, where tax is levied not on the business but on the owner(s). Thus tax does not impact on the accounts of unincorporated businesses, but is an individual matter between the owner(s) and the Inland Revenue.

Companies are charged **corporation tax** on their profits and gains. The percentage rates of tax tend to vary from year to year, but have recently been in the low thirties for larger companies and in the low twenties for smaller companies. These rates of tax are levied on the company's taxable profit, which is not necessarily the same as the profit shown on the profit and loss account. This is because tax law does not, in every respect, follow the normal accounting rules. Generally, however, the taxable profit and the company's accounting profit are pretty close to one another.

Managing a company – corporate governance and the role of directors

A limited company may have legal personality but it is not a human being capable of making decisions and plans about the business and exercising control over it. These management tasks must be undertaken by people. The most senior level of management of a company is the board of directors.

➡   The shareholders elect **directors** (by law there must be at least one director) to manage the company on a day-to-day basis on behalf of those shareholders. In a small company, the board may be the only level of management and consist of all of the shareholders. In larger companies, the board may consist of ten or so directors out of many thousands of shareholders. Indeed directors are not required even to be shareholders. Below the board of directors could be several layers of management comprising thousands of people.

➡   In recent years, the issue of **corporate governance** has generated much debate. The term is used to describe the ways in which companies are directed and controlled. The issue of corporate governance is important because, in companies of any size, those who own the company (that is, the shareholders) are usually divorced from the day-to-day control of the business. The directors are employed by the shareholders to manage the company on behalf of the shareholders. Given this position, it may seem safe to assume that the directors' decisions will be guided by the interests of shareholders. However, in practice this does not always occur. The directors may be more concerned with pursuing their own interests, such as increasing their pay and 'perks' (such as expensive motor cars, overseas visits and so on) and improving their job security and status. As a result, a conflict can occur between the interests of shareholders and the interests of directors.

Where directors pursue their own interests at the expense of the shareholders, it is clearly a problem for the shareholders. However, it may also be a problem for society as a whole. If shareholders feel their funds are likely to be mismanaged, they will be reluctant to invest. A shortage of funds will mean fewer investments can be made and the costs of funds will increase as businesses compete for what funds are available. Thus, a lack of concern for shareholders can have a profound effect on the performance of the economy. To avoid these problems, most competitive market economies have a framework of rules to help monitor and control the behaviour of directors.

These rules are usually based around three guiding principles:

■ *Disclosure*. This lies at the heart of good corporate governance. An OECD report (see the reference at the end of the chapter for details) summed up the benefits of disclosure as follows:

> 'Adequate and timely information about corporate performance enables investors to make informed buy-and-sell decisions and thereby helps the market reflect the value of a corporation under present management. If the market determines that

present management is not performing, a decrease in stock (share) price will sanction management's failure and open the way to management change.'

■ *Accountability.* This involves defining the roles and duties of the directors and establishing an adequate monitoring process. In the United Kingdom, company law requires that directors of a business act in the best interests of shareholders. This means, among other things, that they must not try to use their position and knowledge to make gains at the expense of the shareholders. The law also requires larger companies to have their annual accounts independently audited. The purpose of an independent audit is to lend credibility to the accounts prepared by the directors.

■ *Fairness.* Directors should not be able to benefit from access to 'inside' information that is not available to shareholders. As a result, both the law and the Stock Exchange place restrictions on the ability of directors to deal in the shares of the business. One example of these restrictions is that the directors cannot buy or sell shares immediately before the announcement of the final results of the business or before the announcement of a significant event such as a planned merger or the loss of the chief executive.

Strengthening the framework of rules

The number of rules designed to safeguard shareholders has increased considerably over the years. This has been in response to weaknesses in corporate governance procedures, which have been exposed through well-publicised business failures and frauds, large pay increases to directors of privatised businesses, and evidence that some financial reports were being 'massaged' so as to mislead shareholders. However, some believe that the shareholders must shoulder some of the blame for any weaknesses. It is often argued that large institutional shareholders (which own around 80 per cent, by market value, of the shares quoted on the UK Stock Exchange) are not very active in corporate governance matters, and so there has been little monitoring of directors. However, things are changing.

During the 1990s there was a real effort by the accountancy profession and the London Stock Exchange to address the problems mentioned above. The Cadbury Committee was formed in 1991 to consider the problems relating to financial reporting and accountability, and in 1992 the committee produced a code of Best Practice on Corporate Governance. Following that Committee, the Greenbury Committee was set up to consider the issue of directors' pay in more detail. In 1995, this committee also issued a code of practice. Soon after, the Hampel Committee was formed and, in 1998, produced a report that sought to 'fine-tune' the recommendations of the two earlier committees. The Hampel Committee also set out the principles of good practice that embraced the work of all three committees. The **Combined Code** was thereby created which has received the backing of the London Stock Exchange. This means that companies listed on the London Stock Exchange are expected to comply with the requirements of the Code or must give their shareholders good reason why they do not.

The Combined Code sets out a number principles relating to such matters as the role of the directors, their relations with shareholders, and their accountability. Exhibit 4.1 outlines some of the more important of these.

Exhibit 4.1

The combined code

Some of the key elements of the Combined Code are as follows:

- Every listed company should have a board of directors to lead and control the company.
- There should be a clear division of responsibilities between the chairman and the chief executive officer of the company to ensure that a single person does not have unbridled power.
- There should be a balance between executive and non-executive (who are often part-time and independent) members of the board, to ensure that small groups of individuals cannot dominate proceedings.
- The board should receive timely information that is of sufficient quality to enable them to carry out their duties.
- Appointments to the board should be the subject of formal and transparent procedures. All directors should submit themselves for re-election by the shareholders within a maximum period of three years.
- Boards should use the Annual General Meeting to communicate with private investors and to encourage their participation.
- The board should publish a balanced and understandable assessment of the company's position and performance.
- Internal controls should be in place to protect the shareholders' wealth.
- The board should set up an audit committee of non-executive directors to oversee the internal controls and financial reporting principles that are being applied, and to liaise with the external auditors.

Strengthening the framework of rules has improved the quality of information available to shareholders, resulted in better checks on the powers of directors, and provided greater transparency in corporate affairs. However, rules can only be a partial answer. A balance must be struck between the need to protect shareholders and the need to encourage the entrepreneurial spirit of directors – which could be stifled under a welter of rules. This implies that rules should not be too tight and so unscrupulous directors may still find ways around them.

Activity 4.3

Can you think of ways in which the shareholders themselves may try to ensure that the directors act on their behalf?

Two ways are commonly used in practice:

- The shareholders may insist on monitoring closely the actions of the directors and the way in which they use the resources of the company.
- The shareholders may introduce incentive plans for managers that link their pay to the share performance of the company. In this way, the interests of the directors and shareholders will become more closely aligned.

Exhibit 4.2 shows an extract from the statement on corporate governance made by the directors of Kingfisher plc, the retail business that owns Woolworths, Superdrug, B & Q, Comet and a number of other chains, including some in France.

Exhibit 4.2

The following extract from the 2000 annual accounts of Kingfisher plc starts with a general statement that the directors have complied with the Combined Code during the year in question. It then goes on to detail how they complied in the specific context of board meetings and the establishment of committees to deal with sensitive issues.

Corporate governance – combined code statement

Kingfisher recognises the importance of, and is committed to, high standards of corporate governance. The principles of good governance adopted by the Group have been applied in the following way:

Directors

The Kingfisher Board currently comprises the Chairman, the Chief Executive, five other executive directors and six non-executive directors. Their biographies appear on pages 30 and 31 and illustrate the directors' range of experience, which ensures an effective board to lead and control the Group. All directors have access to the Company Secretary and may take independent professional advice at the Group's expense. Non-executive directors are appointed for an initial term of three years and each director receives appropriate training on appointment and subsequently as necessary.

The Board meets not less than 11 times a year and has adopted a schedule of matters reserved for its decision. It is primarily responsible for the strategic direction of the Group. All directors have full and timely access to information. Continuing the process started last year, the Board has again undertaken a review of its effectiveness, under the leadership of the Chairman.

The Board has established five standing committees with defined terms of reference as follows:

■ The Audit Committee, chaired by John Bullock comprises not less than three independent non-executive directors and currently has five non-executive directors. This committee is responsible for providing an independent oversight of the Group's systems of internal control and financial reporting processes. Each of our UK major operating businesses is a substantial size and each has its own audit committee, which is attended by both Kingfisher's internal auditor and the external auditors.

■ The Nomination Committee comprises the Chairman, Chief Executive and three other non-executive directors and is responsible for the consideration of and recommendation for the appointment of new directors.

■ The Remuneration Committee comprises the Chairman and three other independent non-executive directors and advises the Board on the Company's executive remuneration policy and its costs and, on behalf of the Board, the application of this policy to the remuneration and benefits of executive directors and certain senior executives. The Remuneration Report on pages 37 to 42 contains a more detailed description of the Group's policy and procedures in relation to directors' and officers' remuneration.

■ The Finance Committee comprises the Chief Executive and three executive directors and is responsible for the approval and authorisation of financing documents within its terms of reference and the authority limits laid down by the Board. On behalf of the Board, it reviews borrowing arrangements and other financial transactions, and makes appropriate recommendations. It also allots new shares in the Company to Group employees following the exercise of share options.

■ The Social Responsibility Committee comprises representatives of the operating companies and at least one executive director and one non-executive director. This committee is responsible for discussing and developing a general policy relating to environmental, community and equal opportunities matters. Sir Geoffrey Mulcahy is chairman of this committee and the main board director with overall responsibility for environmental matters.

Financing a limited company

Capital (owners' claim) of limited companies

The owner's claim of a sole proprietorship is normally encompassed in one figure on the balance sheet, usually labelled 'capital'. With companies, this is usually a little more complicated, though in essence the same broad principles apply. With a company, the owners' claim is divided between shares – for example, the original investment – on the one hand and reserves – that is, profits and gains subsequently made – on the other. There is also the possibility that there will be shares of more than one type and reserves of more than one type. Thus, within the basic divisions of share capital and reserves, there might well be further subdivisions. This might seem quite complicated, but later we shall consider the reasons for these subdivisions and try to make things clear.

The basic division

When a company is first formed, those who take steps to form it, usually known as the promoters of the company, will decide how much needs to be raised by the potential shareholders to set up the company with the necessary assets to operate. Example 4.1 acts as a basis for illustration.

Example 4.1	Let us imagine that several people get together and decide to form a company to operate a particular business. They estimate that the company will need £50,000 to obtain the necessary assets to operate. Between them, they raise the cash which they use to buy shares in the company, on 31 March 2001 with a **nominal (or par) value** of £1 each.

At this point the balance sheet of the company would be:

Balance sheet as at 31 March 2001

	£
Net assets (all in cash)	50,000
Capital and reserves	
Share capital	
50,000 shares of £1 each	50,000

The company now buys the necessary fixed assets and stock in trade and starts to trade. During the first year, the company makes a profit of £10,000. This, by definition, means that the owners' claim expands by £10,000. During the year; the shareholders (owners) make no drawings of their capital, so at the end of the year the summarised balance sheet looks like this:

Balance sheet as at 31 March 2002

	£
Net assets (various assets less liabilities)	60,000
Capital and reserves	
Share capital	
50,000 shares of £1 each	50,000
Reserves (revenue reserve)	10,000
	60,000

➡ The profit is shown in a reserve, known as a **revenue reserve**, because it arises from generating revenues through sales. Note that we do not simply add the profit to the share capital: we must keep the two amounts separate (to satisfy company law). The reason for this is that there is a legal restriction on the max-
➡ imum drawings of capital (or payment of a **dividend**) that the owners can make. This is defined by the amount of revenue reserves, and so it is helpful to show these separately. We shall look at why there is this restriction, and how it works, later in this chapter.

Share capital

Shares represent the basic units of ownership of a business. All companies issue
➡ **ordinary shares**. The ordinary shares of a company are often referred to collect-
➡ ively as the **equity** of the company. The nominal value of such shares is at the discretion of the people that start up the company. For example, if the initial cap- ital is to be £50,000, this could be two shares of £25,000 each, 5 million shares of one penny each or any other combination that gives a total of £50,000. Each share must have the same value.

Activity 4.4	The initial capital requirement for a new company is £50,000. There are to be two equal shareholders. Would you advise them to issue two shares of £25,000? Why?

Such large denomination shares tend to be unwieldy. Suppose that one of the share- holders wanted to sell his or her shares. S/he would have to find one buyer. If there were shares of smaller denomination, it would be possible to sell part of the shareholding to various potential buyers. Similarly, it would be possible to sell just part of the holding and retain a part.

In practice, £1 is the normal maximum nominal value for shares. Shares of 25 pence each and 50 pence each are probably the most common.
➡ Some companies also issue other classes of shares, **preference shares** being the most common. Preference shares guarantee that *if a dividend is paid*, the prefer- ence shareholders will be entitled to the first part of it up to a maximum value. This maximum is normally defined as a fixed percentage of the nominal value of the preference shares. If, for example, a company issues 10,000 preference shares of £1 each with a dividend rate of 6 per cent, this means that the preference shareholders are entitled to receive the first £600 (that is, 6 per cent of £10,000) of any dividend that is paid by the company for a year. The excess over £600 goes to the ordinary shareholders. Normally, any undistributed profits and gains accrue to the ordinary shareholders. Thus the ordinary shareholders are the primary risk-takers, and their potential rewards reflect this risk. Power normally resides in the hands of the ordinary shareholders. Usually, only the ordinary shareholders are able to vote on issues that affect the company, such as who the directors should be.

It is open to the company to issue shares of various classes – perhaps with some having unusual and exotic conditions – but in practice it is rare to find other than straightforward ordinary and preference shares.

Though a company may have different classes of shares whose holders have different rights, within each class all shares must be treated equally. The rights of the various classes of shareholders, as well as other matters relating to a particular company, are contained in that company's set of rules, known as the 'articles and memorandum of association'. A copy of these rules is, in effect, available to the public because one must be lodged with the Registrar of Companies so as to be available for access by the general public.

Reserves

➡ **Reserves** are profits and gains that have been made by a company and that still form part of the shareholders' (owners') claim because they have not been paid out to the shareholders. Profits and gains tend to lead to cash flowing into the company.

It is worth mentioning that retained profits represent overwhelmingly the largest source of new finance for UK companies – amounting for most companies to more than share issues and borrowings combined. These ploughed-back profits create most of a typical company's reserves. As well as reserves, the shareholders' claim consists of share capital.

Activity 4.5	Are reserves amounts of cash? Can you think of a reason why this is an odd question?
	To deal with the second point first, it is an odd question because reserves are a claim, or part of one, on the assets of the company, whereas cash is an asset. So reserves cannot be cash.

Reserves are classified as either revenue reserves or capital reserves. As we have already seen, revenue reserves arise from trading profit. They also arise from gains made on the disposal of fixed assets.

➡ **Capital reserves** arise for two main reasons: issuing shares at above their nominal value (for example issuing £1 shares at £1.50) and revaluing (upwards) fixed assets. Where a company issues shares at above their nominal value, UK law requires that the excess of the issue price over the nominal value is shown separately.

Activity 4.6	Can you think why shares might be issued at above their nominal value? *Hint*: this would not usually happen when a company is first formed and the initial shares are being issued.
	Once a company has traded and has been successful, the shares would normally be worth more than the nominal value at which they were issued. If additional shares are to be issued to new shareholders to raise finance for further expansion, unless they are issued at a value higher than the nominal value, the new shareholders will be gaining at the expense of the original ones.

Now let us consider another example.

Example 4.2	Based on future prospects, the net assets of a company are worth £1.5 million. There are currently 1 million ordinary shares in the company. The company wishes to raise an additional £0.6 million of cash for expansion and has decided to raise it by issuing new shares. If the shares are issued for £1 each, that is 600,000 shares, the number of shares will increase to 1.6 million and their total value will be £2.1 million (£1.5 million + £0.6 million). This means that the value of the shares after the new issue will be £1.3125 each (£2.1 ÷ 1.6). So the original shareholders will have lost £0.1875 per share (£1.5 − £1.3125) and the new shareholders will have gained £0.3125 per share. The new shareholders will, no doubt, be delighted with this, the original ones will be less ecstatic.

Things could be made fair between the two sets of shareholders described in Example 4.2 by issuing the new shares at £1.50 each. In this case the £1 per share nominal value will be included with share capital in the balance sheet. The £0.50 per share premium will be shown as a capital reserve known as the **share premium account**. It is not clear why UK company law insists on the distinction between nominal share values and the premium. Certainly, other countries with a similar set of laws governing the corporate sector (for example, the United States) do not see the necessity to distinguish between share capital and share premium, but instead show the total value at which shares are issued as one comprehensive figure on the company balance sheet.

Altering the nominal value of shares

The point has already been made that the people who start up a new company may make their own choice of the nominal or par value of the shares. This value need not be permanent. At a later date the shareholders can decide to change it.

For example, a company has at issue 1 million ordinary shares of £1 each. A decision is made to change the nominal value of the shares from £1 to £0.50, in other words to halve the value. As a result, the company would issue each shareholder with a new share certificate (the shareholders' evidence of ownership of their shareholding) for exactly twice as many shares, each with half the nominal value. This would leave each shareholder with a holding of the same total nominal value. This process is known, not unnaturally, as splitting the shares. The opposite, reducing the number of shares and increasing the nominal value per share to compensate, is known as **consolidating**.

Since each shareholder would be left, after a split or consolidation, with exactly the same proportion of ownership of the company's assets as before, the process should not increase the value of the total shares held.

Activity 4.7	Why might the shareholders want to split their shares in the manner described above?
	The answer is probably to avoid individual shares becoming too valuable and making them a bit unwieldy, in the way discussed in the answer to Activity 4.4. If a company trades successfully, the value of each share is likely to rise, and in time could increase to a level that is considered unwieldy. Splitting would solve this problem.

Exhibit 4.3

Photo-Me has a share split

In October 1999, Photo-Me International plc split its ordinary shares nominal value of 2.5p per share to 0.5p per share. This meant that each ordinary shareholder became the owner of five times as many new shares, with each share having a market value of one fifth of each of the old ones. In the business's report and accounts for 2000, the chairman (Dan David) said that the split 'was undertaken to improve the liquidity of the company's shares'.

Photo-Me provides many of the coin-operated photobooths that are found in bus and train stations and elsewhere.

Bonus shares

It is always open to a company to take reserves of any kind (capital or revenue) and turn them into share capital. The new shares arising from such a conversion are known as **bonus shares**. Issues of bonus shares are quite frequently encountered in practice. Example 4.3 illustrates this aspect of share issues.

Example 4.3

The summary balance sheet of a company is as follows:

Balance sheet as at 31 March 2002

	£
Net assets (various assets less liabilities)	128,000
Capital and reserves	
Share capital	
50,000 shares of £1 each	50,000
Reserves	78,000
	128,000

The company decides that it will issue to existing shareholders one new share for every share owned by each shareholder. The balance sheet immediately following this will appear as follows:

Balance sheet as at 31 March 2002

	£
Net assets (various assets less liabilities)	128,000
Capital and reserves	
Share capital	
100,000 shares of £1 each (50,000 + 50,000)	100,000
Reserves (78,000 − 50,000)	28,000
	128,000

Activity 4.8	A shareholder of the company in Example 4.3 owned 100 shares before the bonus issue. How will things change for this shareholder as regards the number of shares owned and the value of the shareholding?

The answer should be that the number of shares will double from 100 to 200. Now the shareholder owns 1/500 of the company (200/100,000). Before the bonus issue, the shareholder also owned 1/500 of the company (100/50,000). The company's assets and liabilities have not changed as a result of the bonus issue and so, logically, 1/500 of the value of the company should be identical to what it was before. Thus each share is worth half as much.

➡ A **bonus issue** simply takes one part of the owners' claim (part of a reserve) and puts it into another part of the owners' claim (share capital). Note that this is not the same as a share split, where the reserves are not affected.

Activity 4.9	Can you think of any reasons why a company might want to make a bonus issue if it has no economic consequence?

We think that there are three possible reasons:

■ To lower the value of each share without reducing the shareholders' collective or individual wealth. This is the same effect as splitting and may be seen as an alternative to splitting.

■ To provide the shareholders with a 'feel-good factor'. It is believed that shareholders like bonus issues because it seems to make them better off, though in practice it should not affect their wealth.

■ Where reserves arising from operating profits and/or realised gains on the sale of fixed assets are used to make the bonus issue, it has the effect of taking part of that portion of the owners' claim that could be drawn by the shareholders, as drawings (or dividends), and locking it up. We shall see, a little later in this chapter, that there are severe restrictions on the extent to which shareholders may make drawings from their capital. An individual or organisation contemplating lending money to the company may insist that the dividend payment possibilities are restricted as a condition of making the loan. This point will be explained later.

Rights issues

➡ **Rights issues** are made when companies that have been established for some time seek to raise additional share capital for expansion, or even to solve a liquidity problem (cash shortage) by issuing additional shares for cash. Company law gives existing shareholders the first right of refusal on these new shares. So the new shares would be offered to shareholders in proportion to their existing holding. Thus existing shareholders are each given the right to buy some new shares. Only where the existing shareholders agree to waive their right would the shares be offered to the investing public generally.

The company (that is, the existing shareholders) would typically prefer that the shares are bought by existing shareholders, irrespective of the legal position. This is for two reasons:

- The ownership (and, therefore, control) of the company remains in the same hands.
- The costs of making the issue (advertising, complying with various company law requirements) tend to be less if the shares are to be offered to existing shareholders.

To encourage existing shareholders to take up their 'rights' to buy some new shares, those shares are virtually always offered at a price below the current market price of the existing ones.

Activity 4.10	Earlier, in Example 4.2, the point was illustrated that issuing new shares at below their current worth was to the advantage of the new shareholders at the expense of the old ones. In view of this, does it matter that rights issues are almost always made at below the current value of the shares?

The answer is that it does not matter *in these particular circumstances*. This is because, in a rights issue, the existing shareholders and the new shareholders are exactly the same people. Not only this, but the new shares will be held by the shareholders in the same proportion as they held the existing shares. Thus, a particular shareholder will be gaining on the new shares exactly as much as he or she is losing on the existing ones: in the end, no one is better or worse off as a result of the rights issue being made at a discount.

You should be clear that a rights issue is a totally different notion from a bonus issue. Rights issues result in an asset (cash) being transferred from shareholders to the company. Bonus issues involve no transfer of assets in either direction.

Share capital – some expressions used in company law

Before leaving our detailed discussion of share capital, it might be helpful to clarify some of the jargon used in company accounts.

When a company is first formed, the shareholders give the directors an upper limit on the amount of nominal value of the shares that can be issued. This is known as the *authorised share capital*. This value can easily be revised upwards, but only if the shareholders agree.

That part of the authorised share capital that has been issued to shareholders is the **issued (or allotted) share capital**.

Sometimes, but not very commonly, a company may not require shareholders to pay all of the price of the shares issued at the time of issue. This would normally be where the company does not need the money all at once. Some money would normally be paid at the time of issue and the company would 'call' for further instalments until the shares were **fully paid**. That part of the total issue price that has been 'called' is known as the **called-up share capital**. That part that has been called and paid is known as the **paid-up share capital**.

Exhibit 4.4 shows equity capital and reserves of J. N. Nichols (Vimto) plc, the business that manufactures a range of foods and drinks, including the Vimto softdrink.

| Exhibit 4.4 | The following extract shows the equity capital and reserves section of the balance sheet of Nichols plc as at 31 December 1999. Note that the company has just one class of shares and three types of reserve. |

	1999
Share capital	**£'000**
Authorised 52,000,000 (1988 – 52,000,000) ordinary 10p shares	**5,200**
Allotted, issued and fully paid 36,968,772 (1998 – 36,960,645)	
ordinary 10p shares	**3,697**

During the year the company purchased and cancelled 1,900,000 shares at an average price, including cost of 134p per share. 1,908,127 shares were issued for part consideration of the purchase of Balmoral Trading Limited.

Reserves	Share premium account (Group) £000	Capital redemption reserve (Group) £000	Profit and loss account (Group) £000
At 1 January 1999	746	1,019	24,557
Retained profit for the year	–	–	3,004
Ordinary shares issued	2,509	–	–
Ordinary shares cancelled	–	190	(2,548)
At 31 December 1999	**3,255**	**1,209**	**25,013**

Long-term loans and other sources of finance

While we are looking at the role of the company's owners in financing the company, it is worth briefly considering other sources of finance used by companies. Many companies borrow money on a long-term basis, perhaps on a ten-year contract. Lenders may be banks and other professional providers of loan finance. Many companies raise loan finance in such a way that small investors, including private individuals, are able to lend small amounts. This method is particularly favoured by the larger, Stock Exchange-listed, companies and involves their making a **loan stock** or **debenture** issue, which, though large in total, can be taken up in small slices by individual investors, both private individuals and investing institutions, such as pension funds and insurance companies. In some cases, these slices of loans can be bought and sold through the Stock Exchange. This means that investors do not have to wait the full term of the loan to obtain repayment, but can sell their slice of the loan to another would-be lender at intermediate points in the term of the loan.

Some of the features of loan financing, particularly the possibility that loan stock may be marketable on the Stock Exchange, can lead to a confusion that loan stock are shares by another name. You should be clear that this is not the case. It is the shareholders who own the company and therefore who share in its losses and profits. Loan stock holders lend money to the company under a legally binding contract that normally specifies the rate of interest, the interest payment dates and the date of repayment of the loan itself. Usually, long-term loans are secured on assets of the company.

Long-term financing of companies can be depicted as in Figure 4.1.

Figure 4.1

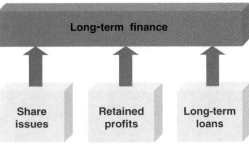

Sources of long-term finance for a typical limited company

Long-term finance

Share issues   **Retained profits**   **Long-term loans**

Companies derive their long-term financing needs from three sources: new share issues, retained profit and long-term borrowings. For a typical company, the sum of the first two (jointly known as 'equity finance') exceeds the third. Retained profit usually exceeds either of the other two in terms of the amount of finance raised in most years.

Companies may also borrow finance on a short-term basis, perhaps from a bank as an overdraft. Most companies buy goods and services on a month or two's credit, as is normal in business-to-business transactions. This is, in effect, an interest-free loan.

It is important to the prosperity and stability of a company that it strikes a suitable balance between finance provided by the shareholders (equity) and loan financing. This topic will be explored in Chapter 7.

Exhibit 4.5 shows the long-term borrowings of Rolls-Royce plc, the engine-building business, at 31 December 2000. Note the large number of sources from which the company borrows. This is typical of most large companies and probably reflects a desire to exploit all available means of raising finance, each of which may have some advantages and disadvantages. 'Secured' in this context means that the lender would have the right, should Rolls-Royce fail to meet its interest and/or capital repayment obligations, to seize a specified asset of the business (probably some land) and use it to raise the sums involved. Normally, a lender would accept a lower rate of interest where the loan is secured in this way as there is less risk involved. It should be said that whether a loan to a company like Rolls-Royce is secured or unsecured is usually pretty academic. It is unlikely that such a large and profitable company would fail to meet its obligations.

'Finance leases' are, in effect, arrangements where Rolls-Royce needs the use of a fixed asset and, instead of buying the asset itself, it arranges for a financier to buy the asset and then to lease it to the business, probably for the entire economic life of the asset. Though legally it is the financier who owns the asset, from an accounting point of view the essence of the arrangement is that, in effect, Rolls-Royce has borrowed cash from the financier to buy the asset. Thus, the asset appears among the business's fixed assets and the financial obligation to the financier is shown here as a long-term loan. This is a good example of how accounting tries to report the economic *substance* of a transaction, rather than its strict legal *form*. Finance leasing is a fairly popular means of raising long-term funds.

Exhibit 4.5	The following extract from the annual accounts of Rolls-Royce plc sets out the sources of the company's long-term borrowing as at 31 December 1999.

Borrowings – amount falling due after one year

	1999 £m
Unsecured	
Bank loans	734
$7\frac{1}{8}$% Notes 2003[1]	199
$4\frac{1}{2}$% Notes 2005[2]	177
Other loans 2001–2009 (interest rates nil)	5
Secured	
Obligations under finance leases payable;[3]	
Between one and two years	8
Between two and five years	45
After five years	44
Zero-coupon bonds 2005/2007 (including 9.0% interest accretion)[4]	33
Bank loans 2001 (interest rates 5.8% to 6.8%)[4]	26
	1,271
Repayable	
Between one and two years – by instalments	26
– otherwise	408
Between two and five years – by instalments	48
– otherwise	497
After five years – by instalments	82
– otherwise	210
	1,271

Restriction on the right of shareholders to make drawings of capital

Limited companies are required by law to distinguish between that part of their capital (shareholders' claim) that may be withdrawn by the shareholders and that part which may not.

The withdrawable part is that which has arisen from trading profits and from realised profits on the disposal of fixed assets (to the extent that tax payments on these profits and gains, as well as previous drawings, have not extinguished this part of the capital). This withdrawable element of the capital is *revenue reserves*.

The non-withdrawable part normally consists of that which has risen from funds injected by shareholders buying shares in the company and that which came from upward revaluations of company assets that still remain in the company – that is, *share capital and capital reserves*.

The law does not specify how large the non-withdrawable part of a particular company's capital should be, but simply that anyone dealing with the company should be able to tell from looking at the company's balance sheet how large it is. In the light of this, a particular prospective lender, or supplier of goods or services on credit, can make a commercial judgement as to whether to deal with the company or not.

Activity 4.11	Can you think of the reason why limited companies are required to distinguish different parts of their capital, whereas sole proprietorship businesses are not required to do so?

The reason for this situation is the limited liability, which company shareholders enjoy but which owners of unincorporated businesses do not. If a sole proprietor withdraws all of the owner's claim, or even an amount in excess of this, the position of the creditors of the business is not weakened since they can legally enforce their claims against the sole proprietor as an individual. With a limited company, where the business and the owners are legally separated, such a legal right to enforce claims against individuals does not exist. However, to protect the company's creditors, the law insists that a specific part of the capital of a company cannot legally be withdrawn by the shareholders.

Let us now look at another example.

Example 4.4	The summary balance sheet of a company at a particular date is as follows:

Balance sheet

	£
Total assets less current liabilities	43,000
Capital and reserves	
Share capital	
20,000 shares of £1 each	20,000
Reserves (revenue)	23,000
	43,000

A bank has been asked to make a £25,000 long-term loan to the company. If the loan were to be made, the balance sheet immediately following would appear as follows:

Balance sheet (after the loan)

	£
Total assets less current liabilities	
(£43,000 + £25,000))	68,000
Less **Long-term liabilities**	
Long-term loan	25,000
	43,000
Capital and reserves	
Share capital	
20,000 shares of £1 each	20,000
Reserves (revenue)	23,000
	43,000

As things stand in our company in Example 4.4, there are total assets less current liabilities to a total balance sheet value of £68,000 to meet the bank's claim of £25,000. It would be possible, however, for the company to pay perfectly legally a dividend (which is a cash return to shareholders) of £23,000. The balance sheet would then appear as follows:

Balance sheet (after dividend)

	£
Total assets less current liabilities	
(£68,000 − £23,000)	45,000
Less **Long-term liabilities**	
Long-term loan	25,000
	20,000
Capital and reserves	
Share capital	
20,000 shares of £1 each	20,000
Reserves (revenue (£23,000 − £23,000))	–
	20,000

This leaves the bank in a very much weaker position, in that there are now total assets less current liabilities with a balance sheet value of £45,000 to meet a claim of £25,000. Note that the difference between the amount of the bank loan and the total assets less current liabilities always equals the capital and reserves total. Thus, the capital and reserves represent a *margin of safety* for creditors. The larger the amount of the owners' claim withdrawable by the shareholders, the smaller is the potential margin of safety for creditors.

It is important to recognise that company law says nothing about how large the margin of safety must be. It is left as a matter of commercial judgement of the company concerned as to what is desirable. The larger it is, the easier will the company find it to persuade potential lenders to lend and suppliers to supply goods and services on credit. Put another way, a large margin of safety would normally enhance creditor confidence and increase the abilty of the business to borrow, if required.

Activity 4.12

Would you expect a company to pay all of its revenue reserves as a dividend? What factors might be involved with a dividend decision?

It would be rare for a company to pay all of its revenue reserves as a dividend: a legal right to do so does not necessarily make it a good idea. Most companies see ploughed-back profits as a major – usually the major – source of new finance.

The factors that influence the dividend decision are likely to include:

- The availability of cash to pay a dividend. It would not be illegal to borrow to pay a dividend, but it would be unusual and, possibly, imprudent.
- The needs of the business for finance for investment.
- Possibly a need for the directors to create good relations with investors, who may regard a dividend as a positive feature.

You might have thought of others.

| Figure 4.2 | **Availability for dividends of various parts of the shareholders' claim** |

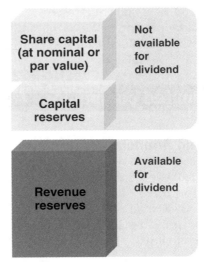

Total equity finance of limited companies consists of share capital, capital reserves and revenue reserves. Only the revenue reserves (which arise from realised profits and gains) can be used to fund a dividend. In other words, the maximum legal dividend is the amount of the revenue reserves.

The law is adamant, however, that it is illegal, under normal circumstances, for shareholders to withdraw that part of their claim that is represented by shares and capital reserves. This means that potential creditors of the company know the maximum amount of the shareholders' claim that can be drawn by the shareholders. Figure 4.2 shows the important division between that part of the shareholders' claim that can be withdrawn as a dividend and that part that cannot.

Earlier in this chapter, the point was made that a potential creditor may insist that some revenue reserves are converted to bonus shares (or capitalised) in order to increase the margin of safety, as a condition of granting the loan.

Perhaps it is worth pointing out, as a practical footnote to Example 4.4, that most potential long-term lenders would seek to have their loan secured against a particular asset of the company – particularly an asset like freehold property. This would give them the right to seize the asset concerned, sell it and satisfy their claim, should the company default. Lenders often place restrictions or *covenants* on the borrowing company's freedom of action, as a condition of granting the loan. The covenants typically restrict the level of risk to which the company, and the lender's asset, is exposed.

| Activity 4.13 | Can you think of any circumstances where the non-withdrawable part of a company's capital could be reduced, without contravening the law? |

It can be reduced, but only as a result of the company sustaining trading losses or losses on disposal of fixed assets, that exceed the amount of the withdrawable portion of the company's capital. It cannot be reduced by shareholders making drawings.

Drawings are usually made in the form of a dividend paid by the company to the shareholders, in proportion to the number of shares owned by each one.

If we refer back to Exhibit 4.4, we can see that J. N. Nichols (Vimto) plc could legally have paid a dividend of £25.013 million on 31 December 1999, which is the amount of its revenue reserves. For several reasons, including the fact that this would represent well over half of the balance sheet value of the company's net assets, no such dividend was paid.

Accounting for limited companies

The main financial statements

As we might expect, the financial statements of a limited company are, in essence, identical to those of a sole proprietor. There are, however, some differences of detail, and we shall now consider these.

Set out in Example 4.5 are the profit and loss account and balance sheet of a limited company:

Example 4.5

Da Silva plc
Profit and loss account for the year ended 31 December 2001

	£m	£m
Sales		840
Less Cost of sales		520
Gross profit		320
Less Operating expenses		
Wages and salaries	98	
Heat and light	18	
Rent and rates	24	
Motor vehicle expenses	20	
Insurance	4	
Printing and stationery	12	
Depreciation	45	
Audit fee	4	
		225
Operating profit		95
Less Interest payable		10
Profit before tax		85
Tax on profit		24
Profit after tax		61
Less Transfer to general reserve	20	
Proposed dividend	25	
		45
Unappropriated profit carried forward		16

Balance sheet as at 31 December 2001

	£m	£m
Fixed assets		
Land and buildings		132
Plant and machinery		<u>171</u>
		303
Current assets		
Stock	65	
Debtors	112	
Cash	<u>36</u>	
	<u>213</u>	
Less Creditors: amounts		
falling due within 12 months		
Creditors	74	
Corporation tax	12	
Proposed dividend	<u>25</u>	
	<u>111</u>	
Net current assets (working capital)		<u>102</u>
Total assets less current liabilities		405
Less Creditors: amounts		
falling due in more than 12 months		
10% debentures		<u>100</u>
Net assets		<u>305</u>
Share capital		
Ordinary shares of £0.50 each		200
Reserves		
Share premium account	30	
General reserve	50	
Profit and loss account	<u>25</u>	
		<u>105</u>
		<u>305</u>

You may well feel that the most striking thing about these statements is the extent to which they look exactly the same as those that you have been used to with sole proprietors. This is correct; the differences are small. Let us go through and pick up these differences.

The profit and loss account

There is a number of features in the P and L account that need consideration:

- *Layout*. The profit from trading activities, before interest payable (or receivable), is separately identified as **operating profit**. Interest is then deducted to find the profit for the year. The statement does not end there as it would were this the profit and loss account of a sole proprietor. The statement goes on to show how the profit has been appropriated between funds set aside to meet the tax on the profit, to pay a dividend to shareholders, and to make a transfer to a general (revenue) reserve. This last part of the statement is known as the **appropriation account**.

- *Audit fees.* As we shall see later in this chapter, companies are normally required to have their financial statements audited by an independent firm of auditors, for which they are charged a fee. Though it is open to all sole proprietors to have their accounts audited, very few do so. This is therefore an expense that will normally be present in the P and L account of a company but not that of a sole proprietor.

- *Tax.* As separate legal entities, companies are required to be responsible for their own tax on profit. The calculation of the tax (known as corporation tax) would be based on the profit for the year.

- *Dividend.* This is the amount of dividend that will be paid to the shareholders. This is in the nature of drawings of capital by the owners of the company. The fact that the dividend is 'proposed' means that the cash had not yet been paid at 31 December 2001 (the year-end). Sometimes shareholders receive a dividend before the end of the year. With many companies, they receive an 'interim' dividend part-way through the year, and a 'final' one shortly after the year end.

- *Transfer to general reserve.* What is left over of the year's profit, after tax and dividends have been accounted for, is retained, normally to be reinvested ('ploughed back') into the operations of the company. For this company, the amount left is £36 million (that is, £61 million – £25 million). This could all have gone to increasing the profit and loss balance in the balance sheet. As is quite common in practice, however, an amount (£20 million for this company) has been transferred to a general reserve.

It is not totally clear why directors decide to make transfers to general reserve, since the funds concerned remain part of the revenue reserves, still available for dividend. The most plausible explanation seems to be that directors feel that taking funds out of the profit and loss account and placing them in a 'reserve' indicates an intention to retain the funds permanently in the company and not to use them to pay a dividend. Of course, the balance on the profit and loss account is also a reserve, but that fact is not indicated in its title.

The balance sheet

For the balance sheet certain items need special consideration:

- *Terminology.* Two terms used in the balance sheet are 'Creditors: amounts falling due within 12 months' and 'Creditors: amounts falling due in more than 12 months'. These terms refer to current liabilities and long-term liabilities respectively. As we shall see in the next chapter, the law requires that these new terms be used when reporting to external users.

- *Corporation tax.* The amount that appears in short-term liabilities represents 50 per cent of the tax on the profit of the year [2001]. It is half of the tax charge that appears in the profit and loss account; the other 50 per cent will already have been paid. The unpaid 50 per cent will be paid shortly following the balance sheet date. These payment dates are set down by law.

- *Dividend.* The dividend that was proposed in the profit and loss account also appears under short-term liabilities once more, to be paid early in the new accounting year.
- *Share capital and reserves.* We have already discussed this area at length earlier in the chapter. Before the year end, the general reserve balance must have stood at £30 million, to be enhanced to its final level by the transferred appropriation of the year [2001] profit. Similarly, the P and L account balance must have been £9 million, just before the year end. As was mentioned above, the general reserve and the profit and loss account balance are identical in all respects; they both arise from retained profits, and are both available for dividend.

? Self-assessment question 4.1

The summarised balance sheet of Dev Ltd is as follows:

Balance sheet as at 31 December 2001

	£
Net assets (various assets less liabilities)	235,000
Capital and reserves	
Share capital: 100,000 shares @ £1	100,000
Share premium account	30,000
Revaluation reserve	37,000
Profit and loss account balance	68,000
	235,000

Required:
(a) Without any other transactions occurring at the same time, the company made a one-for-five rights share issue at £2 per share payable in cash (all shareholders taking up their rights) and, immediately afterwards, made a one-for-two bonus issue. Show the balance sheet immediately following the bonus issue, assuming that the directors wanted to retain the maximum dividend payment potential for the future.
(b) Explain what external influence might cause the directors to choose not to retain the maximum dividend payment possibilities.
(c) Show the balance sheet immediately following the bonus issue, assuming that the directors wanted to retain the *minimum* dividend payment potential for the future.
(d) What is the maximum dividend that could be paid before and after the events described in (a) if the minimum dividend payment potential is achieved?
(e) Lee owns 100 shares in Dev Ltd before the events described in (a). Assuming that the net assets of the company have a value equal to their balance sheet value, show how these events will affect Lee's wealth.
(f) Looking at the original balance sheet of Dev Ltd, shown above, what four things do we know about the company's status and history that are not specifically stated on the balance sheet?

Summary

This chapter has reviewed the position of limited companies, particularly in the context of accounting. Limited companies have their own legal status as 'people', which leads to many of their peculiarities, including the close attention that the law pays to company accounting. The owners' claim on limited companies is made up of share capital and reserves. Each share represents a part of the ownership of the company. There are strict limits on the extent to which companies are allowed to make payments to their owners (the shareholders) as 'drawings' of capital.

The accounts of companies are, in essence, very similar to those of sole-proprietorship businesses but there are some important differences. These differences were discussed in the chapter.

→ Key terms

Limited liabilities p. 95	Reserves p. 103
Public company p. 95	Capital reserves p. 103
Private company p. 95	Share premium account p. 104
Corporation tax p. 96	Consolidating p. 104
Director p. 97	Bonus shares p. 105
Corporate governance p. 97	Bonus issue p. 106
Combined Code p. 98	Rights issues p. 106
Nominal value p. 101	Issued (allotted) share capital p. 107
Revenue reserve p. 102	Fully paid shares p. 107
Dividend p. 102	Called-up share capital p. 107
Ordinary shares p. 102	Paid-up share capital p. 107
Equity p. 102	Debenture p. 108
Preference shares p. 102	

Further reading

If you would like to explore the topics covered in this chapter in more depth, we recommend the following books:

Financial Reporting, *Alexander, D.* and *Britton, A.*, 6th edn, International Thomson Business Press, 2001, chapter 12.

Financial Accounting and Reporting, *Elliott, B.* and *Elliott, J.*, 5th edn, Financial Times Prentice Hall, 2001, chapters 10 and 19.

Accounting Theory and Practice, *Glautier, M.* and *Underdown, B.*, 7th edn, Pitman Publishing, 2001, chapter 13.

Reference

'Corporate Governance: Improving competitiveness and access to capital in global markets', an OECD report by Business Sector Advisory Group on Corporate Governance, Organisation for Economic Co-operation and Development, 1988, p. 14.

? REVIEW QUESTIONS

4.1 How does the liability of a limited company differ from the liability of a real person in respect of amounts owed to others?

4.2 Some people are about to form a company as a vehicle through which to run a new business. What are the advantages to them of forming a private limited company rather than a public one?

4.3 What is a reserve, in the context of the owners' claim on a limited company?

4.4 What is called-up share capital?

? EXERCISES

Exercises 4.6–4.8 are more advanced than 4.1–4.5. Those with coloured numbers have answers at the back of the book.

4.1 Comment on the following quotation:

Limited companies can set a limit on the amount of debts which they will meet. They tend to have reserves of cash, as well as share capital and they can use these reserves to pay dividends to the shareholders. Many companies have preference as well as ordinary shares. The preference shares give a guaranteed dividend. The shares of many companies can be bought and sold on the Stock Exchange, and a shareholder selling his or her shares can represent a useful source of new capital to the company.

4.2 Comment on the following quotes:

(a) 'Bonus shares increase the shareholders' wealth because, after the issue, they have more shares, but each one of the same nominal value as they had before. Share splits, on the other hand, do not make the shareholders richer, because the total nominal value of their shareholding is the same before the issue as after it.'
(b) 'By law, once shares have been issued at a particular nominal value, they must always be issued at that value in any future share issues.'
(c) 'By law, companies can pay as much as they like by way of dividends on their shares, provided that they have sufficient cash to do so.'
(d) 'Companies do not have to pay tax on their profits because the shareholders have to pay tax on their dividends.'

4.3 Briefly explain each of the following expressions that you have seen in the accounts of a limited company:

(a) Dividend
(b) Debenture
(c) Share premium account

4.4 Iqbal Ltd started trading on 1 January 1998. During the first five years of trading, the following occurred:

Year ended 31 December	Trading profit (loss)	Profit (loss) on sale of fixed assets	Upward revaluation of fixed assets
	£	£	£
1998	(15,000)	–	–
1999	8,000	–	10,000
2000	15,000	5,000	–
2001	20,000	(6,000)	–
2002	22,000	–	–

Required
Assuming that the company paid the maximum legal dividend each year, how much would each year's dividend be?

4.5 Da Silva plc's outline balance sheet as at a particular date was as follows:

	£m
Sundry net assets	72
£1 ordinary shares	40
General reserve	32
	72

The directors made a one-for-four bonus issue, immediately followed by a one-for-four rights issue at a price of £1.80 per share.

Required:
Show the balance sheet of Da Silva plc immediately following the two share issues.

4.6 Presented below is a draft set of simplified accounts for Pear Limited for the year ended 30 September 2001.

Profit and loss account for the year ended 30 September 2001

	£000	£000
Turnover		1,456
Costs of sales		(768)
Gross profit		688
Less Expenses:		
Salaries	220	
Depreciation	249	
Other operating costs	131	(600)
Operating profit		88
Interest payable		(15)
Profit before taxation		73
Taxation at 30%		(22)
Profit after taxation		51

Balance sheet as at 30 September 2001

	£000	£000
Fixed assets		
Cost	1,570	
Depreciation	(690)	880
Current assets		
Stocks	207	
Debtors	182	
Cash at bank	21	
	410	
Less **Creditors: amounts due within one year**		
Trade creditors	88	
Other creditors	20	
Taxation	22	
Bank overdraft	105	
	235	
Net current assets		175
		1,055
Less **Creditors: amounts due after more than one year** 10% debenture – repayable 2008		(300)
		755
Capital and reserves		
Share capital		300
Share premium account	300	
Retained profit at beginning of year	104	
Profit for year	51	455
		755

The following information is available:

(i)   Depreciation has not been charged on office equipment with a written-down value of £100,000. This class of assets is depreciated at 12 per cent per annum using the reducing-balance method.

(ii)   A new machine was purchased, on credit, for £30,000 and delivered on 29 September but has not been included in the financial statements.

(iii) A sales invoice to the value of £18,000 for September has been omitted from the accounts. (The cost of sales is stated correctly.)

(iv)   A dividend has been proposed of £25,000.

(v)   The interest payable on the debenture for the second half-year has not been included in the accounts.

(vi)   A general provision against bad debts is to be made at the level of 2 per cent of debtors.

(vii) An invoice for electricity to the value of £2,000 for the quarter ended 30 September 2001 arrived on 4 October and has not been included in the accounts.

(viii) The charge for taxation will have to be amended to take account of the above information. Make the simplifying assumption that tax is payable shortly after the end of the year, at the rate of 30 per cent.

Required:
Prepare a revised set of financial statements for the year ended 30 September 2001 incorporating the additional information in (i)–(viii) above. Note: work to the nearest £1,000.

4.7 Presented below is a draft set of financial statements for Chips Limited.

Chips Limited
Profit and loss account for the year ended 30 June 2001

	£000	£000
Turnover		1,850
Cost of sales		(1,040)
Gross profit		810
Less Depreciation	(220)	
Other operating costs	(375)	(595)
Operating profit		215
Interest payable		(35)
Profit before taxation		180
Taxation		(60)
Profit after taxation		120

Balance sheet as at 30 June 2001

Fixed assets	Cost	Depreciation	
	£000	£000	£000
Buildings	800	112	688
Plant and equipment	650	367	283
Motor vehicles	102	53	49
	1,552	532	1,020

Current assets		
Stock		950
Debtors		420
Cash at bank		16
		1,386

Less Creditors due within one year		
Trade creditors		(361)
Other creditors		(117)
Taxation		(60)
		(538)

Net current assets		848
Less Creditors due after more than one year		
Secured 10% loan		(700)
		1,168

Capital and reserves		
Ordinary shares of £1, fully paid		500
6% preference shares of £1		300
Reserves at 1 July 2000	248	
Profit for year	120	368
		1,168

The following additional information is available:

(i) Purchase invoices for goods received on 29 June 2001 amounting to £23,000 have not been included.

(ii) A motor vehicle costing £8,000 with depreciation amounting to £5,000 was sold on 30 June 2001 for £2,100, paid by cheque. This transaction has not been included in the company's records.

(iii) No depreciation on motor vehicles has been charged. The annual rate is 20 per cent of cost at the year end.

(iv) A sale on credit for £16,000 made on 1 July 2001 has been included in the accounts in error.

(v) A half-yearly payment of interest on the secured loan due on 30 June 2001 has not been paid.

(vi) The tax charge should be 30 per cent of the reported profit before taxation. Assume that it is payable, in full, shortly after the year end.

(vii) A dividend will be proposed by the directors of 2p per ordinary share; the preference dividend has not been incorporated.

Required:
Prepare a revised set of financial statements incorporating the additional information in (i)–(vii) above. Note: work to the nearest £1,000.

4.8 Rose Limited operates a small chain of retail shops that sell high-quality teas and coffees. Approximately half of sales are on credit. Abbreviated and unaudited accounts are given below:

Profit and loss account for the year ended 31 March 2001

	£000	£000
Sales		12,080
Cost of sales		6,282
Gross profit		5,798
Labour costs	2,658	
Depreciation	625	
Other operating costs	1,003	
		4,286
Net profit before interest		1,512
Interest payable		66
Net profit before tax		1,446
Tax payable		434
Net profit after tax		1,012
Dividend payable		300
Retained profit for year		712
Retained profit brought forward		756
Retained profit carried forward		1,468

Balance sheet as at 31 March 2001

	£000	£000
Fixed assets		2,728
Current assets		
Stocks	1,583	
Debtors	996	
Cash	26	
	2,605	
Creditors: amounts due within one year		
Trade creditors	1,118	
Other creditors	417	
Tax	434	
Dividends	300	
Overdraft	296	
	2,565	
Net current assets		40
Creditors: amounts due after more than one year		
Secured loan (2010)		(300)
		2,468
Share capital		
(50p shares, fully paid)		750
Share premium		250
Retained profit		1,468
		2,468

Since the unaudited accounts for Rose Limited were prepared, the following information has become available:

(i) An additional £74,000 of depreciation should have been charged on fixtures and fittings.

(ii) Invoices for credit sales on 31 March 2001 amounting to £34,000 have not been included; costs of sales is not affected.

(iii) Bad debts should be provided at a level of 2 per cent of debtors at the year end.

(iv) Stocks, which had been purchased for £2,000, have been damaged and are unsaleable.

(v) Fixtures and fittings to the value of £16,000 were delivered just before 31 March 2001, but these assets were not included in the accounts and the purchase invoice had not been processed.

(vi) Wages for Saturday-only staff, amounting to £1,000, have not been paid for the final Saturday of the year.

(vii) Tax is payable at 30 per cent of net profit after tax. Assume that it is payable shortly after the year end.

Required:

Prepare a balance sheet and profit and loss account for Rose Limited for the year ended 31 March 2001, incorporating the information in (i)–(vii) above. Note: work to the nearest £1,000.

CHAPTER 5

Accounting for limited companies (2)

Introduction

In this chapter we continue our examination of the accounts of limited companies. We begin by considering the regulatory framework of limited company accounts. We identify the legal responsibilities of directors and auditors and discuss the main sources of accounting rules that govern the published accounts of limited companies. Although a detailed consideration of these accounting rules is beyond the scope of this text, we discuss the ways in which accounting regulations shape the form and content of the profit and loss account and balance sheet that are published for external use.

The degree of accounting regulation affecting limited companies has increased significantly over the past two decades and this has inevitably produced a reaction. It has been argued that such regulation is costly and unnecessary. In this chapter we review the case for and against accounting regulation. One important criticism of the accounting rules that have been developed is that they lack a clear framework of principles. In this chapter we consider the attempts that have been made by the accounting profession to deal with this problem.

The increasing complexity of business and the increasing demands for information by users have led to the publication of a number of additional financial statements. In this chapter we consider two of the more important, namely the segmental financial report and the operating and financial review. The aim of both these reports is to provide users with a more complete picture of financial performance and position.

OBJECTIVES

When you have completed this chapter, you should be able to:

- Describe the legal responsibilities of directors and auditors concerning the annual accounts provided to external users.
- Identify the main sources of regulation affecting the accounts of limited companies and discuss the case for and against regulation.
- Discuss the progress made in developing a framework of principles for accounting.
- Prepare a profit and loss account and balance sheet for a limited company in accordance with an acceptable legal format.
- Explain the purpose of segmental reports and the operating and financial review and discuss the contents of these reports.

The directors' duty to account – the role of company law

It is not usually possible for all of the shareholders to be involved in the general management of the company, nor do most of them wish to be involved, and so they elect directors to act on their behalf. It is both logical and required by company law that directors are accountable for their actions in respect of their stewardship (management) of the company's assets. In this context, directors are required by law:

■ To maintain appropriate accounting records.
■ To prepare an annual profit and loss account, a balance sheet that shows a 'true and fair' view of events, as well as a directors' report, and to make these available to all shareholders and to the public at large.

Exhibit 5.1 is an extract from the 2000 annual accounts of Pizza Express plc, the high street restaurant chain. This statement sets out what the directors regard as their responsibilities for the annual accounts.

Exhibit 5.1

The following extract is from the 2000 annual report of Pizza Express plc:

Statement of Directors' Responsibilities
Company law requires the directors to prepare financial statements for each financial year which give a true and fair view of the state of affairs of the Company and the Group and of the profit or loss of the Group for that period. In preparing those financial statements, the directors are required to:

■ select suitable accounting policies and then apply them consistently;
■ make judgements and estimates that are reasonable and prudent;
■ state whether applicable accounting standards have been followed, subject to any material departures disclosed and explained in the financial statements;
■ prepare the financial statements on the going concern basis unless it is inappropriate to presume that the Group will continue in business.

The directors confirm that the financial statements comply with the above requirements.

The directors are responsible for keeping proper accounting records which disclose with reasonable accuracy at any time the financial position of the Company and the Group and which enable them to ensure that the financial statements comply with the Companies Act 1985. They are also responsible for safeguarding the assets of the Group and hence for taking reasonable steps for the prevention and detection of fraud and other irregularities.

The relevant rules on director's duties are embodied in the Companies Acts 1985 and 1989. Company law goes quite a long way in prescribing the form and content of the accounting statements that directors must publish. A copy of each year's accounts must be made available to all of the company's shareholders and debenture holders. The accounts must also be made available to the general public. This is achieved by the company submitting a copy to the Registrar of Companies (Department of Trade and Industry), which allows anyone who wishes to do so to inspect these accounts.

Activity 5.1	Can you think of any reasons why various parliaments have decreed that companies must account, and have set up rules as to how they should do this? We think there are broadly three reasons.

We thought of the following:

- *To inform and protect shareholders*   If shareholders feel that they are not getting a reasonable supply of reliable information from their company, they have no means of assessing their investment and how well it is being managed. In these circumstances, they would be reluctant to provide risk (equity) finance. As a result, the corporate sector could not function effectively, if at all. Any society with a significant private sector needs to encourage equity investment.
- *To inform and protect suppliers of labour, goods, services and finance, particularly those supplying credit (loans) or goods and services on credit*   People and organisations may be reluctant to engage in commercial relationships with a company, including being employed by it and lending it money, where they have no information about the company's likely future viability. This is likely to be more so when the company has limited liability, so that unsatisfied claims against the company cannot be pursued against the shareholders' other assets. Again, if people are reluctant to deal commercially with companies, the private sector cannot flourish.
- *To inform and protect society more generally*   Some companies exercise enormous power and influence in society generally, particularly on a geographically local basis. For example, a particular company may be the dominant employer and purchaser of commercial goods and services in a particular town or city. The legislators have tended to take the view that society generally has the right to information about the company and its activities.

True and fair

The legislation uses the expression 'true and fair view' in stating what the published accounts of companies should show, although the expression is not defined in the legislation. It is probably reasonable to say that accounts show a true and fair view when they seem unlikely to mislead a user into gaining a false impression of the company. The requirement for accounts to show a true and fair view tends to override any other requirements.

Activity 5.2	Why, in your opinion, does the legislation not require that accounts show a 'correct' or an 'accurate' view? *Hint*: Think of depreciation of fixed assets.

Financial accounting can never really be said to be 'correct' or 'accurate' in that these words imply that there is just one value that any asset, claim, revenue or expense could have. This is simply not true in many, if not most, cases. Depreciation provides a good example. The annual depreciation expense, and in turn the balance sheet values of depreciating fixed assets, are based on judgements about the future.

How long is the economic life of an asset? What will its residual value be at the end of that life? How should the depreciation, over the economic life of the asset, best be matched against the revenues that it helps to generate? All these are matters of judgement. Someone who has a reasonable understanding of business and accounting could probably say whether or not the judgements are reasonable, given all the circumstances. If the judgements are reasonable, then they are likely to lead to accounts that show a true and fair view.

The profit and loss account

Company law offers companies the choice of four formats in which they may publish their profit and loss account. Each company must choose just one and is encouraged to continue to use that format. The objective of allowing companies to use one of only four formats is an attempt to standardise presentation, so as to make comparison of one company's accounts with those of another one somewhat easier.

Format 1 seems to be the most popular in practice. We shall concern ourselves only with this one. Not surprisingly, the four formats are quite similar in principle and provide more or less identical information. Example 5.1 shows a profit and loss account that has been set out according to Format 1.

Example 5.1			
	Jhamna plc		
	Profit and loss account for the year ended 31 December 2001		
		£000	£000
	Turnover		576
	Cost of sales		307
	Gross profit		269
	Distribution costs	65	
	Administrative expenses	26	91
			178
	Other operating income		21
			199
	Income from other fixed-asset investments	5	
	Other interest receivable and similar income	12	17
			216
	Interest payable and similar charges		23
			193
	Tax on profit or loss on ordinary activities		46
	Profit on ordinary activities after taxation		147
	Retained profit brought forward from last year		56
			203
	Transfer to general reserve	60	
	Proposed dividend on ordinary shares	50	110
	Retained profit carried forward		93

The legislation requires that comparative figures for the previous year are also given for each entry in the profit and loss account. Note that tax is included in the format. This is because companies, as independent legal entities, are responsible for their own tax. As we saw in the last chapter, companies are subject to corporation tax on their profits. This fact will tend to be reflected in both the profit and loss account and the balance sheet.

Though not mentioned in any of the formats, there is also a requirement to include the last part shown in Example 5.1 – the part that starts after 'Profit on ordinary activities after taxation'. This section shows how the sum of the current year's after-tax profit and any unappropriated (retained) profit accumulated from previous years has been appropriated. In the example, the current year's after-tax profit is £147,000. To this is added £56,000 that was unappropriated from previous years, giving £203,000 that could be appropriated. Of this, £60,000 has been transferred to general reserve and £50,000 earmarked for the payment of a dividend, probably within a few weeks of the accounting year-end. The remaining £93,000 is carried forward until next year, when it will be entered as 'retained profit brought forward from last year'. This figure is a reserve; it is part of the shareholders' claim, but it is not share capital. The transfer of the £60,000 to general reserve has no legal significance. It tends to be seen as a statement by the directors that they do not see this amount as available for payment of a dividend. This does not preclude the directors reversing this transfer at a later date.

Most of the items in the profit and loss account are self-explanatory, but there are four that are not defined in the legislation. They are generally interpreted as follows:

- *Cost of sales.* This includes all of the expenses of producing the goods or services that were sold during the period. This would include materials, production labour, depreciation of production facilities and so on. For a company that does not manufacture – for example, a retailer – the cost of sales would simply be the cost of the stock that was sold during the year.
- *Distribution costs.* The expenses concerned with selling and delivering goods or services sold during the year.
- *Administrative expenses.* Virtually any other expenses of running the company during the year that are not included in cost of sales, distribution costs or any other expense categories appearing in Format 1.
- *Other operating income.* All income (revenues) of the company for the year that are not specified elsewhere in Format 1.

The balance sheet

There are two formats available for the balance sheet. Format 1 is the one most used in practice, and so we shall concentrate on it here. As with the profit and loss account, the other format gives exactly the same basic information but is set out differently. Again, as with the profit and loss account, comparative figures from the previous year are required and a category of asset or claim need not be mentioned if it does not exist as far as a particular company is concerned.

Jhamna plc's balance sheet, set out in Format 1 style, is shown in Example 5.2.

Example 5.2	**Jhamna plc** **Balance sheet as at 31 December 2001**			
		£000	£000	£000
	Fixed assets:			
	Intangible assets:			
	Patents and trade marks		37	
	Tangible assets:			
	Land and buildings	310		
	Plant and machinery	125		
	Fixtures, fittings, tools and equipment	<u>163</u>	<u>598</u>	635

	£000	£000	£000
Current assets:			
Stocks:			
Raw materials and consumables	8		
Work-in-progress	11		
Finished goods and goods for resale	22	41	
Debtors:			
Trade debtors	123		
Prepayments and accrued income	16	139	
Cash at bank and in hand		17	
		197	
Creditors: amounts falling due within one year			
Trade creditors	36		
Other creditors including taxation and social security	101		
Accruals and deferred income	15	152	
Net current assets			45
Total assets less current liabilities			680
Creditors: amounts falling due after more than one year			
Debenture loans		250	
Provisions for liabilities and charges			
Pensions		33	283
			397
Capital and reserves			
Called-up share capital			150
Share premium account			50
Revaluation reserve			34
General reserves			70
Profit and loss account			93
			397

You may recall from Chapter 4 that 'Creditors: amounts falling due within one year' are usually known as **current liabilities**. 'Creditors: amounts falling due after more than one year' are usually known as **long-term liabilities**. It is not obvious why the legislators introduced these new expressions, except to make clear to readers of the accounts the time periods involved. 'Current' and 'long-term' remain the adjectives used by most people when referring to liabilities.

Notes to the accounts

As well as providing the information set out in the profit and loss account and balance sheet, additional information must also be made public. This information is usually contained in the notes to the accounts and is mainly concerned with directors' and highly paid employees' salaries and with fixed assets movements.

Directors' report

Company law requires the directors to prepare an annual report to shareholders and other interested parties. This report contains information of both a financial and a non-financial nature and goes beyond that which is contained in the profit and loss account and balance sheet. The information disclosed falls under the following categories:

- *Business activities.* This covers such matters as the main activities carried out by the company during the year and any significant changes that may have occurred. It will also include the disclosure of any events affecting the company since the end of the financial year and a discussion of any likely future developments.
- *Share ownership.* This includes disclosure of the purchase by the company of its own shares and details of shareholders that hold more than 3 per cent of the nominal share capital of the company.
- *Dividend policy.* This deals with the dividend that the directors' propose for the year.
- *Asset values.* Any significant difference between the market value of land and buildings held and the current market value must be stated.
- *Details of directors.* The names of the directors of the company must be disclosed. In addition, details of any directors' interest in shares or debentures of the company or any contract in which a director has a significant interest must be disclosed.
- *Social and employee matters.* This rather broad category deals with a variety of matters, including disclosure of charitable and political donations made by the company. It also deals with the disclosure of the creditor payment policy and employment policies relating to such matters as employment of diasabled persons, health and safety at work, and the involvement of employees in the management of the company.

The auditors do not carry out an audit of the **directors' report**. However, they will check to see that the information in the report is consistent with that contained within the audited accounts.

Smaller companies

The reduced economic impact and the rather more close-knit structure of share ownership of smaller companies, plus the proportionately higher costs of complying with the requirements, has led to the legislators reducing the amount of information disclosure required of smaller companies. The criteria for being classified as a small company are concerned with size of turnover, total assets and workforce. Relaxation of information disclosure requirements is allowed to companies that can meet two of the following three criteria:

- Total assets (balance sheet figures) less than £5.6 million.
- Annual turnover (sales) less than £11.2 million.
- Number of employees less than 250.

Further relaxations in the rules are available for even smaller companies.

Summary financial statements

Though directors of all companies are required to make a set of the company accounts available to each shareholder, these accounts can be a summarised version of the full version that follows the complete legal requirements. The reasons for not requiring that the full version be sent to all shareholders are broadly that:

■ Many shareholders do not wish to receive the full version, because they may not have the time, interest or skill necessary to be able to gain much from it.
■ Directors could improve their communication with their shareholders by providing something closer to the needs of many shareholders.
■ Reproducing and posting copies of the full version is expensive and a waste of resources where particular shareholders do not wish to receive it.

➡ Many companies send all of their private shareholders a copy of the **summary financial statements**, with a clear message that the full versions are available on request. Each full version is, however, required for filing with the Registrar of Companies.

Exhibit 5.2 is the summarised group balance sheet for 1999 of Glaxo Wellcome plc, the UK-based pharmaceutical business that now forms part of GlaxcoSmith Kline plc. This is much briefer than the full balance sheet that the company would make available on request.

Exhibit 5.2

The following extract is the summarised group balance sheet of Glaxco Wellcome plc as at 31 December 1999.

Summary Accounts for the year to 31st December 1999

	1999 £m	1998 £m
Summary Group balance sheet		
Net operating assets	4,306	3,934
Long-term investments	58	87
Own shares	425	11
Net debt	(1,596)	(1,264)
Net assets	3,193	2,768
Shareholders' funds	3,142	2,702
Minority interests	51	66
Financing of net assets	3,193	2,768
Fixed assets	*4,347*	*3,837*
Current assets	*6,080*	*5,509*
Current liabilities: due within one year	*(5,263)*	*(4,145)*
Current assets less current liabilities	*817*	*1,364*
Total assets less current liabilities	*5,164*	*5,201*
Liabilities: due after one year	*(1,376)*	*(1,965)*
Provisions for liabilities and charges	*(595)*	*(468)*
Net assets	*3,193*	*2,768*

Role of accounting standards in company accounting

➔ **Accounting standards** (sometimes called **financial reporting standards**) are rules established by the UK accounting profession that should be followed by preparers of the annual accounts of companies. Though they do not have the same status as company law, the standards define what is meant by a true and fair view, in various contexts and circumstances. Since company law requires that accounting statements show a true and fair view, this gives accounting standards an important place in company accounts preparation.

When UK accounting standards were introduced in the 1970s, the committee responsible for developing them saw the role of the standards as being to 'narrow the difference and variety of accounting practice by publishing authoritative statements on best practice – which will, whenever possible, be definitive'. This continues to reflect the role of accounting standards.

Exhibit 5.3	The following list of the accounting standards currently in force in the UK will give an idea of the range of topics involved:		

SSAP 4	Accounting for government grants	1992
SSAP 5	Accounting for value added tax	1974
SSAP 8	The treatment of taxation under the imputation system in the accounts of companies	1992
SSAP 9	Stocks and long-term contracts	1988
SSAP 13	Accounting for research and development	1989
SSAP 17	Accounting for post balance sheet events	1980
SSAP 19	Accounting for investment properties	1994
SSAP 20	Foreign currency translation	1983
SSAP 21	Accounting for leases and hire purchase contracts	1997
SSAP 24	Accounting for pension costs	1992
SSAP 25	Segmental reporting	1990
FRS 1	Cash flow statements	1996
FRS 2	Accounting for subsidiary undertakings	1992
FRS 3	Reporting financial performance	1993
FRS 4	Capital instruments	1993
FRS 5	Reporting the substance of transactions	1998
FRS 6	Acquisitions and mergers	1994
FRS 7	Fair values in acquisition accounting	1994
FRS 8	Related party disclosures	1995
FRS 9	Associates and joint ventures	1997
FRS 10	Goodwill and intangible assets	1997
FRS 11	Impairment of fixed assets and goodwill	1998
FRS 12	Provisions contingent liabilities and contingent assets	1998
FRS 13	Derivatives and other financial instruments	1998
FRS 14	Earnings per share	1998
FRS 15	Tangible fixed assets	1999
FRS 16	Current tax	1999
FRS 17	Retirement benefits	2000
FRS 18	Accounting policies	2000
FRS 19	Deferred tax	2000

Key:
SSAP = Statement of Standard Accounting Practice
FRS   = Financial Reporting Standard

Several standards have been issued and subsequently withdrawn, which explains the gaps in the numerical sequence. In addition, many of them have been revised and reissued. The dates given are the reissue dates, where relevant. This explains why they are not listed in chronological order.

Accounting standards can be seen as being of four types:

- Those that deal with *describing* how a particular item has been treated in the accounts, without seeking to prescribe how it should be treated. For example FRS 15 requires that relevant assets should be depreciated and that the accounts should reveal how assets have been depreciated.
- Those that are concerned with *presenting* information in accounts. SSAP 5 is of this type in that it sets out how the incidence of value added tax should be reflected in the accounts of companies.
- Those that set out rules on *disclosing* information in the accounts above and beyond that which is prescribed by company law. FRS 1, which requires most companies to produce a cash flow statement, in addition to the other statements required by law, is of this type.
- Those that give guidance on *valuing* assets and *measuring* profit. SSAP 9 is of this type in that it sets out rules on how to value stocks, which has a direct effect on the profit figure.

We have already met some of the rules set out in accounting standards. For example, the rules that we use to value stocks and to charge depreciation were discussed in Chapter 3. Another of them we shall meet in the next chapter (FRS 1 in Chapter 6). Some of the others are rather specialised and, for most companies, of no great importance. This leaves a couple that we shall look at now.

FRS 18: Accounting policies

This standard is concerned with the way in which a company should approach the selection, application and disclosure of its accounting policies. The purpose of the standard is threefold. First, it seeks to ensure that each company selects accounting policies that are most suitable to its particular circumstances. When selecting a policy, the standard requires that the key characteristics of relevance, reliability, comparability and understandability (which we considered in Chapter 1) should be used as the appropriate benchmarks. Second, it seeks to ensure that the accounting policies that have been adopted are reviewed on a regular basis. Where existing policies are no longer considered to be appropriate, they should be replaced by new policies. Finally, the standard seeks to ensure that users of financial reports are properly informed about the particular accounting policies that have been adopted, as well as any changes to those policies. This means that there must be adequate disclosure in the accounts.

FRS 3: Reporting financial performance

This standard is concerned with trying to give users of the accounts greater insights to the company's performance for the period to which the accounts relate and, through this, enable them to make more informed judgements about the future prospects for the company. To achieve this objective, the standard requires that all companies should provide the following items as part of their accounts:

- *An analysis of the turnover, cost of sales, operating expenses and resultant profit (before interest).*   These amounts should be analysed between continuing operations and discontinued operations:

  - *continuing operations*, that is, those parts of the company's business that will continue to exist in the year following the one being reported on in the accounts. Continuing operations should further be analysed between those that were acquired during the year (for example, as a result of a takeover of another company) and those that were existing operations of the company at the start of the year being reported on;
  - *discontinued operations*, that is, those operations of the company that were sold or terminated during the year being reported on.

  This analysis should aid users of the accounts in assessing the extent to which a company's reported performance has been affected by acquiring new operations and/or abandoning others.

- *Information on exceptional items.*   An exceptional item is a revenue or expense that, though part of the company's normal operations, is large or remarkable enough to require special mention if users of the accounts are to gain a true and fair view of the company's operations. An example of an exceptional item could be a particularly large loss suffered by a civil engineering company on a major contract. It is part of normal operations, but unless users of the accounts are provided with information about the loss, they are lacking information that might help them to gain a true and fair impression of the company's operations.

  Information on exceptional items should be disclosed by way of a note. The items should be included in the accounts as if they were unexceptional.

- *Information on extraordinary items.*   These are items that are material in size and that fall outside the ordinary activities of the company. Like exceptional items, failure to give information on them could mislead a user of the accounts. An example of an extraordinary item might be the sales proceeds, less the book value, of a painting on the wall of an office that was subsequently discovered to have been by a well-known artist and was, therefore, very valuable. The company is not in the business of selling its fixed assets at a profit, and so this transaction is deemed extraordinary.

  Extraordinary items should be disclosed by showing them separately in the profit and loss account. They should be shown after 'profit or loss on ordinary activities after tax'. The tax on the extraordinary item should be shown as deducted from the item itself. The item should be described, either on the face of the profit and loss account or in a separate note, in enough detail to enable users of the accounts to understand its nature. The objective of this treatment is to enable users to see the results of trading operations, ignoring the extraordinary item, but also to see the effect of the item.

- *A* **statement of recognised gains and losses**.   This is a statement that summarises all of the profits (and losses) that have been recognised in the year being reported on. This statement is deemed to be necessary because not all of the profits and losses will appear in the profit and loss account. For example, it is common practice for companies to revalue (upwards) certain of their fixed assets, particularly land and buildings. These increases in value are not shown on the profit and loss account – reasonably enough, because they are not revenues arising from trading operations. The amount of the revaluation is added to a revaluation reserve.

Company law permits companies to charge the administrative costs of making a share issue direct to the share premium account, where one exists, and to the extent that there is a sufficiently large balance, as an alternative to charging these costs to the profit and loss account. The net effect on the shareholder is the same whichever way it is done. If the amount is charged to the share premium account, that balance diminishes; if it is charged to the profit and loss account, the retained profit (the balance on the profit and loss account) diminishes by the same amount.

The objective of the statement of recognised gains and losses is to give users of the accounts a summary of the overall change in the shareholders funds, other than as a result of injections (new share issues) and withdrawals (dividends) of capital by the shareholders.

Note that the statement of recognised gains and losses is now regarded as a 'primary financial statement' and so takes its place alongside the balance sheet, the profit and loss account and the cash flow statement.

Exhibit 5.4 is the statement of recognised gains and losses for Anglia Water plc, the water utility business.

| **Exhibit 5.4** | The following extract from the annual accounts of Anglia Water plc shows the statement of total recognised gains and losses for the year ended 31 March 2000. Note that, apart from the normal trading profit (which also appears in the company's profit and loss account), the only other gains (losses) arose from a difference, on translating the value of some overseas assets, between the start of the year and the end. |

**Statement of total recognised gains and losses
for the year ended 31 March**

	Group	
	2000	1999
	£m	£m
Profit for the financial year	164.8	223.7
Currency translation differences on foreign currency net investments	(5.0)	(0.1)
Total recognised gains and losses	159.8	223.6

| **Activity 5.3** | **Why does company law not deal with all of the detailed rules? Why do we also need accounting standards?** |

Probably the main reason is that circumstance and commercial practices alter at a faster rate than Parliament is prepared to legislate on accounting rules for companies. The law, therefore, sets out the broad framework and leaves it, in effect, to the accounting profession to flesh it out. The accounting standard setters are able to respond relatively quickly to fresh needs and, perhaps as important, have a more direct interest in doing so.

International accounting standards

The internationalisation of business has led to a need for some degree of international harmonisation of accounting rules. It can no longer be assumed that the potential users of the accounts of a company whose head office is in the UK are familiar with UK accounting standards. Whichever user group we care to think of – employees, suppliers, customers, shareholders – some members of that group are likely to be residents of another country. It seems likely, too, that the trend towards internationalisation of business will increase.

These facts have led to the need for international accounting standards and the creation of the International Accounting Standards Committee (IASC). The IASC has issued a number of standards, but there is a problem: it is difficult to reconcile international differences on accounting procedures, which has tended to mean that the international standards have been slow to emerge. They have also tended to be fairly permissive of variations in practice. However, it is likely that international accounting standards will take on increasing importance in the future.

Role of the London Stock Exchange in company accounting

The London Stock Exchange extends the accounting rules for those companies that are listed as being eligible to have their shares traded there. These extensions include the following requirements:

- Summarised interim (half-year) accounts in addition to the annual accounts required by statute law.
- A geographical analysis of turnover.
- Details of holdings of more than 20 per cent of the shares of other companies.

Figure 5.1 illustrates the sources of accounting rules with which larger UK companies must comply.

Figure 5.1

Sources of external accounting rules for a UK limited company listed on the London Stock Exchange

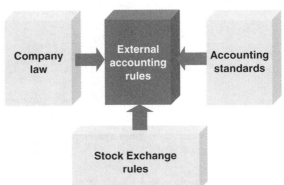

Company law provides the basic framework of company accounting regulation. This is augmented by the accounting standards, which have virtually the force of law. The London Stock Exchange has its own additional rules for companies listed by it.

Auditors

→ Shareholders are required to elect a qualified and independent person or, more usually, a firm to act as **auditor**. The auditor's main duty is to make a report as to whether, in his or her opinion, the statements do what they are supposed to do, namely show a true and fair view and comply with statutory and accounting-standard requirements. To be in a position to make such a statement, auditors must scrutinise both the annual accounting statements prepared by the directors and the evidence on which they are based. The auditors' opinion must be included with the accounting statements that are sent to the shareholders and to the Registrar of Companies.

The relationship between the shareholders, the directors and the auditors is illustrated in Figure 5.2. This shows that the shareholders elect the directors to act on their behalf, in the day-to-day running of the company. The directors are required to 'account' to the shareholders on the performance, position and cash flows of the company, on an annual basis. The shareholders also elect auditors, whose role it is to give the shareholders an impression of the extent to which they can regard as reliable the accounting statements prepared by the directors.

Exhibit 5.5 is the auditors' report for National Express Group plc, the business that operates various bus and train services in the UK, the US and Australia. The statement appeared with the annual accounts of the business for the year ended 31 December 1999. Note how the auditors, in their report, try to tell the reader exactly what they have done and the standards that they applied in doing so.

Figure 5.2

The relationship between the shareholders, the directors and the auditors

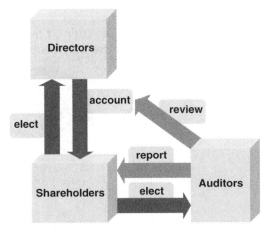

The directors are appointed by the shareholders to manage the company on the shareholders' behalf. The directors are required to report each year to the shareholders, principally by means of accounting statements, on the company's performance and position. To give greater confidence in the reports, the shareholders also appoint auditors to investigate the reports and express an opinion on their reliability.

Exhibit 5.5

Report of the Auditors

To the shareholders of National Express Group plc
We have audited the accounts on pages 46 to 74 which have been prepared under the historical cost convention, as modified by the revaluation of certain fixed assets and the accounting policies set out on pages 50 to 52.

Respective responsibilities of Directors and Auditors
The Directors are responsible for preparing the Annual Report. As described on page 44, this includes responsibility for preparing the accounts in accordance with applicable United Kingdom law and accounting standards. Our responsibilities, as independent auditors, are established in the United Kingdom by statute, the Auditing Practices Board, the Listing Rules of the London Stock Exchange and by our profession's ethical guidance.

We report to you our opinion as to whether the accounts give a true and fair view and are properly prepared in accordance with the Companies Act. We also report to you if, in our opinion, the Directors' report is not consistent with the accounts, if the Company has not kept proper accounting records, if we have not received all the information and explanations we require for our audit, or if the information specified by law or the Listing Rules regarding Directors' remuneration and transactions with the Company is not disclosed.

We review whether the corporate governance statement on pages 39 to 40 reflects the Company's compliance with the seven provisions of the Combined Code specified for our review by the Stock Exchange, and we report if they do not. We are not required to consider whether the Board's statements on internal control cover all risks and controls, or form an opinion on the effectiveness of either the Group's corporate governance procedures or its risk and control procedures.

We read the other information contained in the Annual Report, including the corporate governance statement, and consider whether it is consistent with the audited accounts. We consider the implications for our report if we become aware of any apparent misstatements or material inconsistencies with the accounts.

Basis of audit opinion
We conducted our audit in accordance with Auditing Standards issued by the Auditing Practices Board. An audit includes examination, on a test basis, of evidence relevant to the amounts and disclosures in the accounts. It also includes an assessment of the significant estimates and judgements made by the Directors in the preparation of the accounts, and of whether the accounting policies are appropriate to the Group's circumstances, consistently applied and adequately disclosed.

We planned and performed our audit so as to obtain all the information and explanations which we considered necessary in order to provide us with sufficient evidence to give reasonable assurance that the accounts are free from material misstatement, whether caused by fraud or other irregularity or error. In forming our opinion we also evaluated the overall adequacy of the presentation of information in the accounts.

Opinion
In our opinion the accounts give a true and fair view of the state of affairs of the Company and the Group as at 31 December 1999 and of the profit of the Group for the year then ended and have been properly prepared in accordance with the Companies Act 1985.

Ernst & Young *Registered Auditor*
London
14 March 2000

National Express Group's auditors are Ernst & Young, one of the world's leading firms of accountants. According to the 1999 accounts of National Express Group, they were charged a fee of £600,000 for this audit work, but to put that into perspective, the National Express Group made a pre-tax profit of £89.6 million during that year.

The case against accounting regulation

So far in this chapter we have treated the existence of a body of company law and accounting standards as being a good thing. However, not everyone accepts that the development of accounting rules is really a form of progress. It is, therefore, worth reciting the main arguments for and against accounting regulation.

Let us begin with the case for regulation. It seems that there are really four major arguments in favour of regulation:

- *To protect investors.* A lack of regulation increases the risk that unscrupulous directors will introduce 'unacceptable' accounting practices that will portray a different view of company performance than is actually warranted. This, it is argued, may mislead investors and, in turn, may result in them making losses.

Activity 5.4

Is there any way that we could test whether or not a lack of regulation will result in unacceptable accounting practices?

One way of examining this argument is to look back at the state of affairs that existed when the regulatory framework was in its infancy.

There is evidence from both the UK and the US to support the view that manipulation and concealment have been a real problem in the past. Indeed, the development of accounting standards is really a response to various financial scandals that have been unearthed over the years.

- *To improve the functioning of financial markets.* Where there is no accounting regulation, investors are likely to find it difficult to judge the relative performance of different businesses. The introduction of regulation, so it is argued, will help bring greater uniformity of practice – which, in turn, should help investors distinguish between the efficient and less-efficient businesses and so ensure that funds are allocated in the most profitable way.

- *To maintain the credibility of the accounts.* Where there is no accounting regulation, there will be greater flexibility in accounting practice. Thus, it is argued, it would be possible for two accountants, each using the same basic financial information relating to a business, to prepare accounts showing quite different profits earned during a period and quite different financial positions at the end of that period. The differences between each set of accounts prepared would simply reflect the particular accounting practices adopted (for example, the use of FIFO rather than LIFO for stock valuation). Through regulation we can reduce the areas of difference and bring about greater uniformity, and this should lend greater credibility to the accounts among readers.

Activity 5.5

Could the use of rules to provide greater uniformity 'backfire' on accountants? Is there a risk that attempts to achieve greater uniformity will not satisfy the readers of accounts?

Some argue that we run the risk that the expectations of readers concerning the accuracy and comparability of the accounts will be increased beyond what can be achieved.

Accounting is not a precise science, as we have already seen, and it will always be necessary for judgements and estimates to be made. In addition, there may be valid reasons for different companies to adopt different accounting methods in certain circumstances (for example, the use of the straight-line method and reducing-balance methods of depreciation are appropriate to different circumstances). Thus, readers must recognise that comparing the performance of different companies can only yield limited benefits.

■ *To reduce pressures on auditors and preparers of accounts.* Company directors may put their auditors and accounting staff under considerable pressure to agree to particular accounting practices that will provide the particular story that the directors wish to tell the readers of accounts rather than what is, in the accountants' and auditors' opinion, a true and fair view of performance and position. It is argued that where there are accounting rules in place, there is a source of external support to resist this kind of pressure.

Although the arguments above have some force, let us now consider the case against regulation. There are five main arguments against accounting regulation:

■ *Ossifying accounting practice.* There is a danger that regulation tends to discourage the natural development of better approaches to financial reporting. Accountants may be discouraged from finding a better approach because it is recognised that any new approach would not be permitted under the rules. Although changes to the rules can occur, it may be difficult to persuade the regulators that a particular new approach is an improvement. They may feel that the matter was resolved when the existing rules were developed, and so dissent may not be tolerated.

■ *Slowness of reaction.* Even when the need for change is accepted, policy makers are often slow to react. The development of new law tends to be very slow because of the length of the law-making process and the competing pressures on legislators' time. Accounting standards, which are developed by the accounting profession, can change more quickly although even these can lag behind events. As a result, there is a danger that the accounting rules become increasingly irrelevant to the changing environment.

■ *False uniformity.* There is a risk that accounting regulations may be imposed on businesses in such a rigid manner that a false uniformity will result that obscures the real differences between businesses. However, this risk may not be as great as is sometimes suggested. It is worth remembering that company law requires that the accounts must show a *true and fair view* of performance and position. This requirement overrides any requirement for particular accounting rules to be followed, and so there is always room to exercise judgement and thereby avoid this problem.

■ *The myth of 'best practice'.* Accounting rules are designed to reflect 'best practice'. However, some would argue that there is often wide disagreement about what constitutes best practice. There has been much criticism over the years that accounting rules lack any underpinning body of theory or principles to guide accounting rule-makers. The accounting profession has recognised this problem and in recent years there have been efforts to develop a body of accounting principles to underpin the development of rules. This topic will be considered in more detail in the following section.

■ *The political nature of accounting rules.* Some argue (see, for instance, reference (1) at the end of the chapter) that setting regulations is, in essence, a political process and that the rules developed will often reflect the requirements of particular interest groups (such as large companies that must implement the rules) that have lobbied for a particular solution rather than the technically 'correct' solution. The effect of successful lobbying can result in bad accounting practices being imposed and can undermine the credibility of accounting rules. Although there have been suggestions that, in both the US and the UK, accounting policy makers have yielded to lobbying pressure, there is no real evidence that this is a major problem.

The debate for and against regulation rumbles on and is unlikely to be resolved in the near future. A major problem preventing early resolution is that the costs of developing, monitoring and complying with the rules have not been properly identified or measured, and the benefits of accounting rules are even more vague. Until the costs of regulation can be weighed against the benefits, the debate will remain inconclusive. In the meantime, however, the number of accounting rules continues to increase.

In search of principles

In the early chapters of this book, we came across various accounting conventions such as prudence, historic cost, going concern, and so on. These conventions were developed as a practical response to particular problems that were confronted when preparing accounts. Nowadays, they help to guide the preparers of accounting information when deciding which items should be reported and *how* they should be reported. These conventions have stood the test of time and are still of value to preparers today. However, they do not provide, and were never designed to provide, accounting with a framework for the development of accounting reports. As we grapple with increasingly complex financial reporting problems, it becomes very clear indeed that we need to have a sound understanding of *why* we account for things in a particular way. Knowing *why* we account rather than simply *how* we account is very important if we are to identify best practice and move the discipline of accounting forward.

In recent years, much effort has been expended in various countries, including the UK, to develop a clear framework of principles that will guide us in the development of accounting. Such a framework should provide clear answers to such fundamental questions as:

■ What is the purpose of financial reports?
■ Who are the main users of accounting information?
■ What qualities should accounting information possess?
■ What kind of accounting reports should be prepared?
■ What should accounting reports include?
■ How should items be included in the accounting reports?

If we can answer these questions, accounting rule makers will be in a stronger position to identify best practice and to develop rules based on rigorous logic, which should increase the credibility of financial reports in the eyes of users. It may even help reduce the possible number of rules, because some issues may be resolved by reference to the application of general principles rather than the generation of further rules.

The Statement of Principles

The quest for accounting principles began in earnest in the 1970s when the Financial Accounting Standards Board (FASB) in the United States devoted a very large amount of time and resources to developing a framework of principles for financial reports. In the UK, this development was watched with considerable interest and in the 1990s a draft Statement of Principles (see reference (2) at the end of the chapter) was developed by the Accounting Standards Board (ASB) that draws upon much of the early work of the FASB. This draft Statement begins by identifying the objectives of financial statements as being:

> to provide information about the reporting entity's financial performance and financial position that is useful to a wide range of users for assessing the stewardship of management and for making economic decisions.

This objective is consistent with other recent attempts to define the purpose of accounting or the purpose of financial statements. For this reason, perhaps, it has not generated any real debate.

The draft Statement of Principles then goes on to identify those groups potentially interested in financial statements and these are:

- Investors
- Lenders
- Suppliers and other trade creditors
- Employees
- Customers
- Government and their agencies
- The public

This again is uncontentious ground: it reflects mainstream opinion and is similar to other lists that have been compiled over recent years. Interestingly, the draft, Statement assumes that financial statements should focus on the interests of investors as all other users are likely to share the investors' concern for such matters as cash generation and financial adaptability. This implies that information that is not needed by investors will not need to be included in the financial reports. Where the assumption of 'what is good for investors is good for everyone' is not valid, there is no reason in principle why the needs of others should not be accommodated.

Activity 5.6 Can you think of situations where this assumption may not be valid?

There is likely to be a number of situations where the needs of investors and those of other groups do not coincide. For example, employees may require more information concerning the profitability of particular manufacturing plants in order to establish the future prospects within those plants. However, investors may not be concerned with this issue provided that the impact on overall profitability is not significant.

The draft Statement of Principles continues by setting out:

■ How the entities that should prepare and publish financial statements are identified

■ The qualitative characteristics of financial information (relevance, reliability, comparability, understandability, materiality)

These aspects of the draft Statement have also created little debate. The qualitive characteristics identified are those set out in the first chapter and have achieved a wide degree of acceptance.

So far, so good. However, the draft Statement then ventures into more dangerous territory by considering:

■ The main elements of financial statements (including the definition of assets, liabilities, owners' interests and contributions, gains and losses)

■ The way in which transactions or events are recognised in the main elements of financial statements

■ The measurement process and how a choice is made between measurement bases that are available

■ The presentation of financial information (including what constitutes good presentation)

■ Accounting for interest in other entities (including consolidated financial statements)

The first three topics in the above list, in particular, have proved to be very contentious. The first draft of the Statement of Principles, published in 1995, generated heated debate and the ASB received much criticism for it. It is beyond the scope of this text to consider the criticisms in detail; however, the main charges against the draft Statement are that it favours the balance sheet at the expense of the profit and loss account, it favours current values rather than historic cost, and that the importance of the matching convention is not recognised. Ernest & Young, a major international firm of accountants, is a strong critic and has argued in a paper (reference (3) at the end of chapter) that the draft Statement of Principles is 'fundamentally misguided. It strives for a model that we do not believe is desirable based on principles that we do not consider workable'. This provoked a response from the chairman of the ASB (reference (4)) that the paper in question 'had all the vision of a mole and the elequence of a whoopee cushion'.

It seems safe to conclude from this exchange that it will be some time before a consensus will emerge! Developing a single framework of principles that will satisfy the views of users, preparers, and assorted commentators on accounting is a difficult task. However, it is also difficult to see what other choices exist for the ASB. If we accept the need for accounting rules, we must also accept the need for a clear framework of principles that will give these rules coherence. The goal of an agreed framework of principles will, therefore, continue to be pursued.

Segmental financial reports

Most large businesses do not undertake a single type of activity; they are usually diverse entities that are engaged in a number of different business activities. Each type of activity undertaken will involve the supply of different products or services and will have different levels of risk, growth and profitability. The problem for users of financial statements is that the profit and loss account, balance sheet and so on will normally aggregate the information relating to each type of business activity in order to provide an overall picture of financial performance and position. For the purposes of analysis and interpretation, however, these aggregate figures are not particularly useful. It is very difficult to evaluate the performance of a business that has diverse interests from the aggregated financial information, because comparisons cannot easily be made. The various activities undertaken by the business are likely to differ in range and/or scale by comparison with other businesses.

Where a business operates in different geographical markets, the same kind of arguments apply. The markets of different countries may well have different levels of risk, profitability and growth associated with them, and aggregation will obscure these differences. It will not be possible, for example, to assess the impact on a business of political changes, or changes in inflation or exchange rates occurring in relation to a particular country or geographical region unless the degree of exposure to the country/region is known.

To undertake any meaningful analysis of financial performance and position, it is usually necessary to disaggregate the information contained within the conventional financial statements. By breaking down the financial information according to business activities and/or geographical markets, we can evaluate the relative risks and profitability of each segment and make useful comparisons with other businesses or other business segments. We can also see the trend of performance for each segment over time and so determine more accurately the likely growth prospects for the business as a whole. We should also be able to assess more easily the impact on the overall business of changes in market conditions relating to particular activities.

Disclosure of the performance of each segment should also be useful in improving the efficiency of the business and of its managers. Information concerning business segments that are performing poorly will be revealed to shareholders, and this may in turn put pressure on managers to take corrective action. Where a particular business segment has been sold, the shareholders will be better placed to assess the wisdom of the managers' decision from the segmental information provided.

Activity 5.7

Shareholders are unlikely to be the only user group interested in the disclosure of segmental information. How might the following groups find segmental information useful?

(a) Employees
(b) Consumers
(c) Government

(a) Employees may find the information relating to profitability and turnover in the area in which they work useful when they are assessing pay and job prospects.
(b) Consumers may be interested to find out the profits arising from particular business activities in order to assess whether the business is making excessive returns.
(c) A government may wish to assess the level of investment, profitability and market presence of a large business operating within the economy. This may be useful when making a range of policy decisions relating to industry grants, subsidies and pricing regulations.

Segmental reporting: regulations and practice

In the UK, an accounting standard (SSAP 25) requires that large companies normally disclose segmental information according to each class of business *and* to each geographical region. Both forms of segmentation are regarded as important to users. A 'class of business', for the purposes of the standard, is a part of the overall business that can be identified as providing a separate product or service, or group of related products or services. A geographical segment may comprise an individual country or a group of countries in which the business operates.

Where a business is involved in two or more classes of business activity or two or more geographical segments, there should normally be separate disclosure for each segment. Each segment should normally include the following key items:

- Turnover, distinguishing between turnover from external customers and turnover from other segments of the business.
- Profit (loss) before taxation, minority interests and extraordinary items.
- Net assets.

Turnover for each geographical segment is according to origin. However, if the destination of the goods or services is substantially different from the geographical region from which they were supplied, the geographical segmentation of turnover according to the *destination* of the goods and services should also be shown.

→   Example 5.3 shows a simple **segmental financial report** for a company with two classes of business. A similar layout can be used to show geographical segments.

Example 5.3		Segment X £m	Segment Y £m	Total £m
	Turnover			
	Total sales	150	200	350
	Intersegment sales	(20)	–	(20)
	Sales to third parties	130	200	330
	Profit before taxation			
	Segment profit	15	19	34
	Less Common costs			16
				18
	Net assets			
	Segment net assets	74	86	160
	Unallocated assets			32
				192

Note: Common costs are those costs that relate to more than one business segment. They may include such items as head office costs, research and development costs, and marketing and advertising costs. You will note that they have not been apportioned between the two segments but have been deducted from the total profit. The treatment of common costs is discussed further below.

Unallocated assets are those assets that are not used in the operations of a particular segment (for example, the head office buildings).

Problems of segmental reporting

A number of problems arise concerning the publication of segmental reports. Some directors are reluctant to disclose this type of information for fear that it may damage the competitive position of the business. This may be a particularly sensitive issue where the main competitors of the business are based abroad and do not have to disclose segmental information. The accounting standard on segmental reporting recognises this problem and states that companies do not have to comply with the disclosure requirements if the directors feel that publication would seriously prejudice the interests of the business.

Activity 5.8	**Can you think of any reasons why it may not be a good idea to allow directors discretion regarding disclosure of segmental information?**

There is a risk that directors of a company will use the opt-out clause for reasons for which it was not designed. For example, disclosure of segmental information might be opposed by directors because it would expose managerial inefficiency in certain areas or because it would reveal that excessive profits are being made in particular areas of activity.

An interesting point to note is that a diverse company can keep its various activities obscured from close scrutiny if it so wishes. However, a business operating a single class of business is not able to do this. Information concerning turnover, profits and so on relating to that particular class of business must be disclosed whatever the effect on competitive position.

Some have questioned the usefulness of segmental data. It is sometimes argued that shareholders invest in the business as a whole, and therefore it is the overall results that are relevant to this end. It is also argued that unsophisticated shareholders may be confused by the segmental reports and may not be able 'to see the wood for the trees'. Both of these arguments, however, may be challenged.

Activity 5.9	**Can you think what counterarguments may be used in order to defend segmental reporting?**

It can be argued that segmental reports help in arriving at a better understanding of the overall performance and position of a business. By breaking down the business into its constituent parts, it is possible to see more readily the various sources of profit, turnover, growth and so on, and therefore obtain a better understanding of the overall results. It should also be borne in mind that the segmental information is a supplement to the overall results, and so shareholders are not denied the aggregated results. We should also remember that shareholders are not the only users of financial information. We saw earlier that other users may have good reason to examine the segmental information provided by a business.

The point concerning unsophisticated users raises the question as to who the financial reports are really for. Many would argue that it is the sophisticated users who need to understand company results, because their decisions will enable a fair price to be set for the shares of the company. If the unsophisticated user cannot understand the accounts, then he/she should either obtain expert advice or study accountancy.

In addition to issues of principle, there are certain technical problems that relate to segmental reports. To begin with, there is the problem of what exactly constitutes a segment for reporting purposes. Unfortunately, the relevant standard does not identify the particular characteristics that determine a class of business or a geographical region. Identifying a set of characteristics that could be applied to each type of business is probably an impossible task. As a result, the issue of what constitutes a segment for reporting purposes is left largely to the judgement of the directors of companies. Although this may be the only sensible course of action, it does mean that comparisons between businesses may be difficult owing to different definitions of a class of business or geographical segment being applied.

Having established a segment for reporting purposes, the next problem is how to deal with common transactions and costs. It is unlikely that each segment will operate in a completely independent manner. There may be, for example, a significant amount of sales of goods or services between segments. If this is the case, the **transfer price** of the goods or services between segments can have a substantial impact on the reported profits of each segment. Indeed, it may be possible to manipulate profit figures for each segment through the use of particular transfer pricing policies. Although the standard requires that turnover be divided between external sales and intersegment sales, the effect of the latter on the results will be difficult to determine because details of transfer pricing policies are not required by the standard and so are not normally disclosed.

There is also the problem of **common costs** – that is, costs that relate to more than one of the business segments. These may include such items as head office costs, research and development costs and marketing costs. Common costs may be apportioned between the segments in some way or simply deducted from the total of the segment results, as shown in Example 5.3 (above). There are no clear-cut rules concerning how such costs should be treated and so, once again, the solution to this problem is left to the directors of companies to determine. This can lead to variations in practice, which will therefore hinder comparisons.

? Self-assessment question 5.1

Segmental information relating to J. Sainsbury plc (a retailer with four separate store chains, a bank and a property development activity) for the year to 1 April 2000 is shown below, together with the equivalent information for the preceding year.

	Turnover (excluding taxes)		Profit (before exceptional items)		Net assets	
	2000 £m	1999 £m	2000 £m	1999 £m	2000 £m	1999 £m
Food retailing (UK)	12,353	13,074	509	731	4,750	4,554
Food retailing (USA)	2,376	1,970	79	55	796	505
Do it yourself retailing (UK)	1,217	1,187	55	65	522	442
Banking (UK)	136	158	3	(6)(loss)	113	101
Property development (UK)	165	32	16	9	123	130

Required:
Analyse the performance of each of the business segments over the two-year period and comment on your results.

Operating and financial review

Businesses have become more complex over time and, as a result, their financial statements have become more difficult to understand. The way in which businesses organise, the nature of their financing and investing activities and the types of trading relationships entered into can make it difficult for users to analyse and interpret the figures set out in annual reports. This has led to growing support for the inclusion of a narrative report from the directors, within the annual reports, that discusses the main points concerning the performance and position of the company.

To some extent, information in narrative form is already available to users through the chairman's report and the directors' report, and various studies have shown that private investors find these reports very useful. However, there are wide variations in practice. In particular, the content of the chairman's report (which is a voluntary form of disclosure) can vary considerably between companies. As a result, many believe there is a need for a separate report that sets out, in a systematic fashion, the key points and issues that affect the business.

The Accounting Standards Board (ASB) has recognised the need for such a report and has recommended that large companies prepare an **operating and financial review** (OFR) each year, which will contain a discussion and interpretation of the business activities and the main factors that affect it. Although the report is meant to be a review of the past year rather than a forecast of the future, it should help users to identify those factors that are useful in assessing future trends and prospects.

The review should be clear and succinct in its style and therefore easy for users to understand. It should also be balanced and objective. There is always a risk with such reports that the directors will seek to emphasise positive aspects of performance and play down or ignore negative ones. It is recommended that the OFR should also try to distinguish between those factors that have affected the results of the business during the current year but are not expected to continue and those that are likely to affect performance in future years. This distinction should help users to form a view of the future, particularly as the business will not normally publish a profit forecast. Where individual aspects of a business are discussed within the review, they should be placed within the context of the overall business.

The operating review

The recommended format of the OFR consists of two elements: the operating review and the financial review. The operating review is designed to help explain to the user the main influences on the various lines of the business. It also discusses the main factors that underlie the business and any changes that have occurred, or are likely to occur, to these factors. The following areas have been identified by the ASB as providing a framework for the operating review.

Operating results for the period

This section should discuss the significant features of the operating perform-ance of the various business segments, as well as the business as a whole (see Exhibit 5.6). It should also discuss any significant changes within the industry or in the environment, such as changes in market conditions, new products, fluctu-ations in exchange rates, and so on.

Exhibit 5.6	Monsoon plc operates a high-street women's fashion business. The company's operating review for the year ended 27 May 2000 includes a trading summary from which the following extracts have been taken: During the year to 27 May 2000, profit before tax was up 13% to £23.0m. The group increased operating profit before exceptionals from £20.8m to £22.9m, an increase of 10%. Turnover increased by 17%, from £132.0m to £154.5m. UK operating profits rose as a result of an increase in total UK sales of 18%, including a like-for-like sales increase of 6% and an improvement in gross margin of 0.34 percentage points.

Dynamics of the business

This section should include a discussion of the main factors that are likely to influence future results. It will also consider the main risks and uncertainties relating to the various lines of business and how they are managed (see Exhibit 5.7). These risks and uncertainties may cover a wide range of matters and could include inflation, skills shortages, product liability, scarcity of raw materials, and so on.

Exhibit 5.7	Monsoon plc includes in its operating review for 2000 a section concerning its assess-ment of the best strategy for overseas operations. The following extracts have been taken from this section: Over the medium and long term we believe that significant opportunities exist to expand overseas. We currently have operations in fifteen countries, of which ten are franchise partnerships or dis-tributorships. We are convinced that franchise partnerships with good local operators are the best strategy. The risks to the group are minimised, as we have no property or employee obligations and no funding requirements for capital expenditure. Our return from these franchise partnerships, although not as high as from our own UK stores, is still good. We believe that the key to the success of these ventures lies in choosing the right partners and in aligning our interests closely together. As a result of this strategy we are looking to convert our existing wholly owned overseas stores to partnership arrangements.

Investment in the future

This section should include a discussion of current and planned levels of capital expenditure. In addition, other forms of investment, such as marketing and advertising campaigns, training programmes and research and development pro-grammes, should be discussed (see Exhibit 5.8). The likely future benefits from the various forms of investment should also be considered.

Exhibit 5.8	The issue of investment can be dealt with in various ways by a business. In its operating review for 2000, Monsoon plc includes sections that discuss the enhancement of its brand and its stores: We continued to invest in the brand through the restructuring of the Design and Buying teams and have recruited additional specialist resource. We introduced our new store design into three of five existing stores that we re-sited into larger and more prominent locations during the year. We have continued to enhance this new design and with our latest opening we believe we have created a store environment that reflects the core values of the brand and also makes the shopping experience more pleasurable.

Profit for the year

The OFR should discuss the returns to shareholders in terms of dividends, earnings per share, and changes in shareholders' funds. It should also comment on any significant gains and losses that are shown in the statement of total gains and losses.

Accounting policies

The directors are often required to make judgements concerning accounting policies (for example, the choice of depreciation method). Where the financial results are sensitive to the particular policies adopted, the directors should explain and discuss the choices made.

The financial review

The second part of the OFR, the financial review, is concerned with explaining the capital structure of the business, its treasury policy and the influences on its financial position. The following areas have been identified as providing a framework for the review.

Capital structure and treasury policy

This should involve a discussion of the capital structure (that is, the mix of share capital, reserves and long-term borrowing) of the business along with any relevant ratios. **Treasury policy** is concerned with such matters as managing cash and credit, obtaining finance, managing relationships with financial institutions, and dividend payments to shareholders. Possible areas for discussion in the financial review are interest and foreign-exchange risk, and the maturity of loans (see Exhibit 5.9).

Exhibit 5.9	Monsoon plc included the following statement on foreign exchange risk in its 2000 operating and financial review: A substantial proportion of the group's product offering is imported and the group currently holds deposits in key trading currencies. In addition, from time to time, when there is clear justification for so doing, the group uses forward currency contracts to give greater certainty to future costs, although no such contracts were used during the period under review. The group has several overseas subsidiaries, whose revenues and expenses are denominated in local currencies. None of these operations is sufficiently substantial in group terms for adverse exchange rate fluctuations to affect materially the outcome of group results; therefore, no hedging of these exchange rates is made.

Taxation

The OFR should contain a discussion of any difference between the normal tax rate applied to corporate profits and the actual rate applied.

Funds from operating activities and other sources of cash

This section should include a discussion of the cash flows either from operations or other sources and the special factors, if any, that influenced these (see Exhibit 5.10).

Exhibit 5.10	Monsoon plc included the following statement on cash flows and financing in its 2000 operating and financial review: The group has not, to date, borrowed funds to fund the expansion of the business. The cash requirements of the business are carefully monitored and there are no current plans to arrange bank facilities. The cash flows for the period are shown in the consolidated cash flow statement on page 16. At the end of the period net funds totalled £16.2m compared with £9.2m the previous year.

Current liquidity

The liquidity at the end of the accounting period should be discussed, along with comment on the level of borrowing at the end of the period. Any loan conditions or restrictions on the ability to transfer funds within the business should be mentioned.

Going concern and balance sheet values

The OFR should contain a confirmation, if appropriate, that the business is a going concern and should comment on the strengths and resources of the business where the value of these items are not reflected in the balance sheet.

Activity 5.10	**What resources might not be reflected in the balance sheet?** These may include, among others: ■ Brand names ■ Goodwill ■ Quality of employees

We can see from the list of headings above that the OFR can be quite a long report – often between five and ten pages in length. However, for many companies, the OFR is really an incremental rather than a radical change in reporting practice. The OFR builds on best practice, as many of the topics identified are already contained within the chairman's report or directors' report of progressive companies.

It should be emphasised that the headings above might not always be relevant to particular companies. The OFR of a particular company may therefore contain different, but nevertheless valid, information for users. There is some survey evidence to suggest there are wide variations in the content of OFRs, which may hinder comparisons between businesses. The fact that the OFR is a voluntary report is likely to increase the degree of variation in content. It may also increase the risk that a business will emphasise the positive aspects of performance and obscure the shortcomings.

Summary

In this chapter we discussed the legal aspects of limited company accounts. We began by considering the responsibilities of the directors and auditors of a company. We saw that it is the responsibility of the directors of the company to prepare the annual accounts for external users and to ensure that these accounts show a true and fair view of the company's performance and position: it is the responsibility of the auditors to report on whether the directors have fulfilled their statutory duty. We also saw that company law sets out fairly precise rules that must be followed concerning the form and content of the annual accounts. These statutory rules are augmented by accounting standards and Stock Exchange rules.

We reviewed the case for and against accounting regulation. We saw that accounting rules are not universally regarded as a valuable step towards better accounting practice. However, there are powerful arguments in favour of accounting regulation that, so far and throughout the world, have won the day. We also reviewed the progress that has been made to date in providing a framework of principles for accounting rules. We saw that, although some progress has been made, there is likely to be much more heated debate before an agreed framework is developed.

Finally, we considered two additional financial statements that companies often prepare. It was argued that as companies grow larger and more diverse, the basic financial statements become less useful to users. This is because the aggregated information they contain tends to obscure the results of the various activities or geographical markets in which the company is engaged. As a result, large companies produce segmental reports that disaggregate the financial data so that the risk, profitability and growth of the separate aspects of the business can be more readily understood. The second additional financial statement examined was the operating and financial review (OFR). The complexity of modern business has led to a need for a report that discusses and intereprets the performance and position of a business. The OFR is designed to do just this. We considered the various elements that an OFR might include and that could provide the basis for a report to users. A further important financial statement, the cash flow statement, will be considered in detail in the following chapter.

Key terms

Directors' report   p. 131
Summary financial statement   p. 132
Accounting (financial reporting)
    standards   p. 133
Statement of recognised gains and
    losses   p. 135

Auditor   p. 138
Segmental financial report   p. 146
Transfer price   p. 148
Common costs   p. 148
Operating and financial review
    (OFR)   p. 149

Further reading

If you would like to explore the topics covered in this chapter in more depth, we recommend the following books:

Statement of Principles for Financial Reporting, Revised Exposure Draft, Accounting Standards Board, 1999.

Students' Guide to Accounting and Financial Reporting Standards, *Black, G.*, 7th edn, Financial Times Prentice Hall, 2000, chapters 1, 2 and 10.

Financial Accounting and Reporting, *Elliott, B.* and *Elliott, J.*, 5th edn, Financial Times Prentice Hall, 2001, chapters 6–8.

Accountants without Standards, *Myddleton, D.*, Institute of Economic Affairs, 1995.

Advanced Financial Accounting, *Lewis, R.* and *Pendrill, D.*, 6th edn, Financial Times Prentice Hall, 2000, chapters 1, 2 and 11.

References

1. **Accountants without standards**, *Myddleton, D.*, Institute of Economic Affairs, 1995.
2. **Statement of Principles for Financial Reporting: Revised Exposure Draft**, Accounting Standards Board, 1999.
3. **The ASB's Framework – Time to Decide**, Ernst & Young, 1996. Quoted in 'The ASB's statement of principles – blueprint or blind alley?', Sir Julian Hodge Lecture by R. Paterson, The University of Wales, February 1998, p. 3.
4. *Financial Times*, 26 February 1996. Quoted in Paterson, 1998 (see ref. (3)).

? REVIEW QUESTIONS

5.1 'Searching for an agreed framework of principles for accounting rules is likely to be a journey without an ending'. Discuss.

5.2 The size of annual financial reports published by limited companies has increased steadily over the years. Can you think of any reasons, apart from the increasing volume of accounting regulation, why this has occurred?

5.3 What problems does a user of segmental financial statements face when seeking to make comparisons between businesses?

5.4 'An OFR should not be prepared by accountants but should be prepared by the board of directors.' Why should this be the case?

? EXERCISES

Exercises 5.6–5.8 are more advanced than 5.1–5.5. Those with coloured numbers have answers at the back of the book.

5.1 It has been suggested that too much information might be as bad as too little information for users of annual reports. Explain.

5.2 What problems are likely to be encountered when preparing summary financial statements for shareholders?

5.3 The following information was extracted from the accounts of I. Ching (Booksellers) plc for the year to 31 December:

	£m
Interest payable	40
Retained profit brought forward from previous year	285
Cost of sales	460
Distribution costs	110
Income from fixed asset investments	42
Turnover	943
Other operating income	86
Administration expenses	314
Other interest receivable	25

Note:
1. Corporation tax is calculated at 25 per cent of the profit on ordinary activities.
2. The directors wish to transfer £100(m) to general reserve at the end of the year.
3. Dividends proposed on ordinary shares for the year will be 30 per cent of the profit on ordinary activities after tax (to nearest £m)

Required:
Prepare a profit and loss account for the year ended 31 December that is set out in accordance with the requirements of Format 1 of the UK's Companies Acts.

5.4 The following items appeared in the accounts of G. Stavros and Co. plc at the end of the current financial period:

	£m
Raw materials and consumables stock	120
Land and buildings at written down values	165
Trade creditors	75
Debenture loans	230
Pension liabilities	54
Share premium account	30
Taxation and social security creditors	23
General reserve	163
Motor vehicles at written down values	22
Trade debtors	86
Plant and machinery at written down values	143
Retained profit carried forward	75
Accruals and deferred income	47
Work-in-progress	18
Cash at bank and in hand	12
Revaluation reserve	100
Finished goods	96
Patents and trade marks	170
Prepayments	15

Required:
Prepare a balance sheet for the business as at the end of the current financial period in accordance with the requirements of Format 1 of the UK's Companies Acts. (One figure is missing from the list of balances and must be deduced.)

5.5 Professor Myddleton argues that accounting standards should be limited to disclosure requirements and should not impose rules on companies as to how to measure particular items in the financial statements. He states: 'The volume of accounting instructions is already high. If things go on like this, where will we be in 20 or 30 years time? On balance I conclude we would be better off without any standards on accounting measurement. There could still be some disclosure requirements for listed companies, though probably less than now.' Do you agree with this idea? Discuss.

5.6 The following information has been extracted from the accounts of a major retailer.

	Current year £m	Previous year £m
Turnover		
United Kingdom and Europe		
Retailing		
Books	390.3	368.3
Music	333.1	310.8
News	182.5	171.5
Greeting cards and stationery	175.7	168.7
Video	126.4	109.8
Other	140.3	157.9
	1,348.3	1,287.0

	Current year £m	Previous year £m
Distribution		
News and books	863.4	825.9
Office supplies	153.9	135.1
	1,017.3	961.0
Do-it-yourself	192.2	194.4
	2,557.8	2,442.4
USA		
Retailing		
Books	16.6	12.4
Music	104.4	91.5
News	17.2	15.7
Gifts and other	85.1	81.0
	223.3	200.6
Total turnover	2,781.1	2,643.0
Analysed as:		
Group companies	2,441.6	2,311.8
Intragroup	89.6	82.6
Share of associated undertakings	249.9	248.6
	2,781.1	2,643.0

Note: Turnover by destination is not significantly different from turnover by origin.

Operating profit including associated undertakings

	Before exceptional items £m	Exceptional items £m	Total Current year £m	Total Previous year £m
Retailing				
UK and Europe	93.8	(6.0)	87.8	86.0
USA	11.8	–	11.8	11.0
Distribution	37.7	–	37.7	33.2
Do-it-yourself	(10.5)	(36.6)	(47.1)	(14.3)
Operating profit inc. associated undertakings	132.8	(42.6)	90.2	115.9
Analysed as:				
Group companies	141.1	(6.0)	135.1	130.3
Share of results of associated undertakings	(8.3)	(36.6)	(44.9)	(14.4)
	132.8	(42.6)	90.2	115.9
Total net assets				
Retailing				
UK and Europe			496.6	490.7
USA			65.3	51.1
Distribution			41.3	20.7
Do-it-yourself			34.9	64.7
Net operating assets			638.1	627.2
Net unallocated liabilities			(66.8)	(65.2)
Net borrowings			(95.1)	(86.0)
Total net assets			476.2	476.0

Required:

(a) Compare the turnover of the UK and European operations with those of the USA operations of the retailer in the following retailing areas:

    (i)   Books

    (ii) Music

    (iii) News

(b) Compare the profitability of the UK and European operations with those of the USA operations in the area of retailing.

5.7 Obtain a copy of an operating and financial review of two companies within the same industry. Compare the usefulness of each. In answering this question, you should consider the extent to which the OFRs incorporate the recommendations made by the Accounting Standards Board.

5.8 Segmental information for an electricity distribution business is as follows:

Notes to the accounts for the year ended 31 March 2002

Segmental information
(a) Turnover and operating profit

	Turnover		Operating profit	
	2002 £m	2001 £m	2002 £m	2001 £m
Distribution	363.8	337.7	149.4	138.7
Supply	1,215.6	1,210.7	16.1	13.5
Retail	187.0	139.1	7.1	6.0
Other	48.6	33.5	0.9	(2.8)
Inter-business adjustments	(344.4)	(307.5)	–	–
	1,470.6	1,413.5	173.5	155.4

(b) Net assets by class of business

	2002 £m	2001 £m
Distribution	496.1	451.5
Supply	(88.3)	20.8
Retail	141.6	88.0
Other	255.2	197.2
Inter-business adjustments	(18.6)	(63.6)
	786.0	693.9
Unsecured bonds	(153.0)	(153.0)
	633.0	540.9

Operating assets and liabilities are allocated or apportioned to the business to which they relate. All cash, investments, borrowings, dividends receivable and payable and taxation items have not been allocated and are included in 'Other'.

Required:

(a) Analyse the performance of each of the *three* major business segments over the two-year period for which information is available.

(b) Do you think the information contained in the segmental reports could be presented in a more informative way? Discuss.

CHAPTER 6

Measuring and reporting cash flows

Introduction

Despite the undoubted value of the P and L account as a means of assessing the effect on a business's wealth of its trading activities, it has increasingly been recognised that the approach taken in preparing the P and L account can mask problems, or potential problems, of cash shortages. This is because in the P and L account we concern ourselves not with cash receipts and payments, but with revenues and expenses. This is principally because large expenditures on such things as fixed assets and stocks do not necessarily have an immediate effect on the P and L account. You may recall from Chapter 2, when we were considering the business of Paul, the wrapping-paper seller, that the P and L account and the cash flow statement showed quite different information.

Cash is important because, without it, no business can operate. Companies are required to produce a cash flow statement as well as the more traditional P and L account and balance sheet. In this chapter we consider the deficiencies of these traditional statements, in the context of assessing cash flow issues. We go on to consider how the cash flow statement is prepared and how it may be interpreted.

OBJECTIVES When you have completed this chapter you should be able to:

- Discuss the crucial importance of cash to a business.
- Explain the nature of the cash flow statement and discuss how it can be helpful in identifying cash flow problems.
- Prepare a cash flow statement.
- Interpret a cash flow statement.

The importance of cash and cash flow

Some simple organisations, such as small clubs and other not-for-profit associations, limit their accounting activities to a record of cash receipts and cash payments. Periodically (normally annually), a summary of all cash transactions – the **cash flow** – for the period is produced for the members. The summary would show one single figure for each category of payment or receipt, for example membership subscriptions. This summary is usually the basis of decision making for a club and the main means of its management committee fulfilling its moral duty to account to the club members. This is usually found to be sufficient for such organisations.

Activity 6.1	Most organisations, including most businesses and many not-for-profit organisations, do not simply rely on a summary of cash receipts and payments but also produce a profit-and-loss type of statement. Can you remember the difference between a cash receipts and payments statement and an 'accruals-based' profit and loss account? Can you think why simple organisations do not feel the need for a profit-and-loss type of statement?

The difference between the two is that while a receipts and payments summary confines itself to cash movements, an accruals-based (that is, profit-and-loss type of statement) is concerned with movements in wealth.

Increases and decreases in wealth do not necessarily involve cash. A business making a sale (generating revenue) increases its wealth; but if the sale is made on credit, no cash changes hands – not at the time of the sale, at least. Here the increase in wealth is reflected in another asset: an increase in trade debtors. If an item of stock is the subject of the sale, the business incurs an expense in order to make the sale – wealth is lost to the business through the reduction in stock. Here, an expense has been incurred but no cash has changed hands. There is also the important distinction for profit-seeking organisations that the participants are going to be very concerned with *wealth* generation, not just with cash generation.

For an organisation with any real level of complexity, a cash receipts and payments summary would not tell the participants all that they would want to know. An 'accruals-based' statement is necessary.

A simple organisation may just collect subscriptions from its members, perhaps raise further cash from activities, and spend cash on pursuing the purposes of the club, for example making payments to charity. Here everything which accounting is capable of reflecting is reflected in a simple cash receipts and payments statement. The club has no stock. There are no fixed assets. All transactions are for cash, rather than on credit.

Clearly, organisations that are more complicated than simple clubs need to produce a P and L account that reflects movements in wealth, and the net increase (profit) or decrease (loss) for the period concerned. Until the mid-1970s, in the UK, there was not generally felt to be any need for businesses to produce more than a P and L account and balance sheet. It seemed to be believed that all that shareholders and other interested parties needed to know, in accounting terms, about a business could be taken more or less directly from those two statements. This view seemed to be based partly on the implicit belief that if a business was profitable, then automatically it would have plenty of cash. Though in the very long run this is likely to be true, it is not necessarily true in the short-to-medium term.

Activity 6.2	The following is a list of business/accounting events. In each case, state the effect (increase, decrease or no effect) on both cash and profit:

	Effect on profit	Effect on cash
1. Repayment of a loan		
2. Making a sale on credit		
3. Buying a fixed asset for cash		
4. Receiving cash from a trade debtor		
5. Depreciating a fixed asset		
6. Buying some stock for cash		
7. Making a share issue for cash		

You should have come up with the following:

	Effect on profit	Effect on cash
1. Repayment of a loan	none	decrease
2. Making a sale on credit	increase	none
3. Buying a fixed asset for cash	none	decrease
4. Receiving cash from a trade debtor	none	increase
5. Depreciating a fixed asset	decrease	none
6. Buying some stock for cash	none	decrease
7. Making a share issue for cash	none	increase

The reasons for this are as follows:

1. Repaying the loan requires that cash is paid to creditors. Thus, two figures in the balance sheet will be affected, but not the P and L account.
2. Making a sale on credit will increase the sales figure and probably profit (unless the sale was made for a price that precisely equalled the expenses involved). No cash will change hands, however, at this point.
3. Buying a fixed asset for cash obviously reduces the cash balance of the business, but its profit figure is not affected.
4. Receiving cash from a debtor increases the cash balance and reduces the debtors' balance. Both of these figures are on the balance sheet. The P and L account is unaffected.
5. Depreciating a fixed asset means that an expense is recognised. This causes the value of the asset, as it is recorded on the balance sheet, to fall by an amount equal to the amount of the expense.
6. Buying some stock for cash means that the value of the stock will increase and the cash balance will decrease by a similar amount. Profit is not affected.
7. Making a share issue for cash increases the owners' claim and increases the cash balance; profit is unaffected.

In 1991, a financial reporting standard, FRS 1, emerged that required all but the smallest companies to produce and publish, in addition to the P and L account and balance sheet, a statement that reflects movements in cash. The reason for this requirement was the increasing belief that, despite their usefulness, the P and L account and balance sheet do not concentrate sufficiently on liquidity. It was believed that the accruals-based nature of the P and L account tends to obscure the question of how and where the business is generating the cash that it needs to continue its operations. Why liquidity is viewed as being so important we shall consider next.

Why is cash so important?

To businesses that are pursuing a goal that is concerned with profit/wealth, why is cash so important? Activity 6.1 illustrated the fact that cash and profit do not go hand in hand; so why the current preoccupation with cash? After all, cash is just an asset that a business needs in order to help it to function. The same could be said of stock or fixed assets.

The reason for the importance of cash is that people and organisations will not normally accept other than cash in settlement of their claims against a business. If a business wants to employ people, it must pay them in cash. If it wants to buy a new fixed asset to exploit a business opportunity, the seller of the asset will normally insist on being paid in cash, probably after a short period of credit. When businesses fail, it is their inability to find the cash to pay claimants that really drives them under. These factors lead to cash being the pre-eminent business asset and, therefore, the one that analysts and others watch most carefully in trying to assess the ability of businesses to survive and/or to take advantage of commercial opportunities as they arise.

The cash flow statement

The cash flow statement is, in essence, a summary of the cash receipts and payments over the period concerned. All payments of a particular type – for example cash payments to acquire additional fixed assets – are added together to give just one figure that appears in the statement. The net total of the statement is the net increase or decrease of the cash of the business over the period. The statement is basically an analysis of the business's cash movements for the period. The cash flow statement is now accepted, along with the P and L account, balance sheet and statement of recognised gains and losses as a primary financial statement.

The relationship between the cash flow statement, P and L account and balance sheet is shown in Figure 6.1. The balance sheet reflects the combination of assets (including cash) and claims (including the owners' capital) of the business *at a particular point in time*. Both the cash flow statement and the P and L account explain the *changes over a period* to two of the items in the balance sheet, namely cash and owners' claim respectively. In practice, this period is typically the business's accounting year.

The standard layout of the cash flow statement is summarised in Figure 6.2. An explanation of the terms used in the figure is as follows:

➡ ■ **Net cash flow from operating activities.** This is the net inflow or outflow from trading operations. It is equal to the sum of cash receipts from trade debtors (and cash sales where relevant) less the sums paid to buy stock, to pay rent, to

Figure 6.1

The relationship between the balance sheet, the profit and loss account, and the cash flow statement

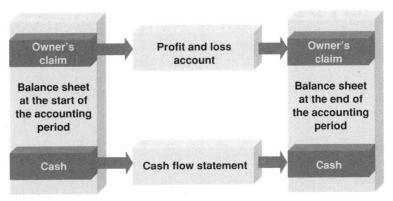

The balance sheet shows the position, at a particular point in time, of the business's assets and claims. The profit and loss account explains how, over a period between two balance sheets, the owners' claim figure in the first balance sheet has altered, as a result of trading operations, to become the figure in the second balance sheet. The cash flow statement also looks at changes over the accounting period, but this statement explains the alteration in the cash balances shown in the two consecutive balance sheets.

Figure 6.2

Standard layout of the cash flow statement

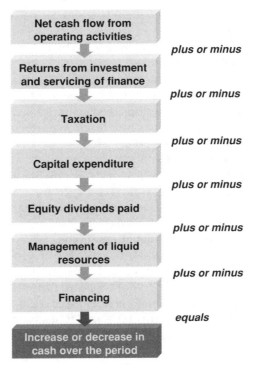

The figure sets out in diagrammatic form the standard layout for the cash flow statement as required by FRS 1, *Cash Flow Statements*.

pay wages and so on. Note that it is the amounts of cash received and paid, not the revenue and expense, that feature in the cash flow statement. It is, of course, the P and L account that deals with the expenses and revenues.

➡ ■ **Returns from investment and servicing of finance.** This category deals with payments made to suppliers of fixed-return finance to reward them for the use of their money. Fixed-return finance includes preference shares and interest-bearing loans and the rewards are preference dividends and interest, respectively. Similarly, this part of the statement deals with cash that the business receives as interest and dividends from investments (in loans and shares) that it has made. The object of distinguishing between payments and receipts arising from financing and investment outside of the business and money deriving from normal operating activities is to enable the reader of the statement to separate the cash flow arising from these different types of activity.

Note that dividends paid by a business to its ordinary shareholders are dealt with later in the statement.

Note also that the word 'servicing' in this context refers to rewarding suppliers of finance for the use of their money. If they are not rewarded, they will not normally allow their money to be used.

➡ ■ **Taxation.** This is fairly obvious, but you should be clear that the amounts shown here are payments and receipts of tax made during the period covered by the statement. Companies normally pay tax on their profits in two parts: 50 per cent during the year in which it is earned, and 50 per cent shortly after the year end. This means that the tax payment that is made this year is 50 per cent of last year's liability, *plus* 50 per cent of this year's. At the end of any year, 50 per cent of that year's tax liability remains unpaid and will appear as a creditor (current libility) in the balance sheet.

➡ ■ **Capital expenditure.** This part of the statement is concerned with cash payments made to acquire additional fixed assets and cash receipts from the disposal of fixed assets. These fixed assets could be loans made by the business, or shares in another business bought by the business, as well as the more usual fixed assets such as buildings, machinery and so on.

➡ ■ **Equity dividends paid.** This is cash dividends paid to the business's ordinary shareholders (equity holders) during the period covered by the statement. Businesses frequently declare a dividend that is shown in one year's P and L account but that is not paid until the following year, being treated as a current liability until it is paid. This means that the dividend 'for the year' is often not paid until the following year.

➡ ■ **Management of liquid resources.** This part of the statement deals with cash receipts and payments arising from the acquisition and disposal of readily disposable investments. These are investments that the business did not or does not intend to hold for any other reason than to find a profitable depository for what will probably be a short-term cash surplus. Readily disposable investments of this type will typically be investments in shares of businesses listed on a stock exchange, and government bills (short-term loans to the government).

➡ ■ **Financing.** This part of the statement is concerned with the long-term financing of the business. So we are considering borrowings (other than in the very short term) and finance from share issues. This category is concerned with repayment/redemption of finance as well as the raising of it.

■ **Increase or decrease in cash over the period.**   Naturally, the total of the statement must be the net increase or decrease in cash over the period covered by the statement. Cash here means notes and coins in hand and deposits in banks and similar institutions that are accessible to the business within 24 hours' notice without incurring a penalty for premature withdrawal.

Example 6.1 sets out a cash flow statement according to the requirements of FRS 1. The headings printed in bold type are specifically required, and are the primary categories into which cash payments and receipts for the period must be analysed.

Example 6.1

Propulsion plc
Cash flow statement for the year ended 31 December 2001

	£m	£m
Net cash inflows from operating activities		55
Returns from investment and servicing of finance		
Interest received	1	
Interest paid	(2)	
Net cash outflow from returns on investment and servicing of finance		(1)
Taxation		
Corporation tax paid	(4)	
Net cash outflow for taxation		(4)
Capital expenditure		
Payments to acquire intangible fixed assets	(6)	
Payments to acquire tangible fixed assets	(23)	
Receipts from sales of tangible fixed assets	4	
Net cash outflow for capital expenditure		(25)
		25
Equity dividends		
Dividend on ordinary shares	(10)	
Net cash outflow for equity dividends		(10)
		15
Management of liquid resources		
Disposal of treasury bills	3	
Net cash inflow from management of liquid resources		3
Financing		
Repayments of debenture stock	(6)	
Net cash outflow for financing		(6)
Increase in cash		12

Note in Example 6.1 that there is a subtotal in the statement after 'Capital expenditure'. This is to highlight the extent to which the cash flows of the period, arising from the 'normal' activities of the business (operations, servicing loans, tax and capital investment), cover the dividend on ordinary shares paid during the period.

Similarly there is a subtotal after the ordinary share dividend paid. The reason for drawing this subtotal is to highlight the extent to which the business has relied on additional external finance to support its trading and other normally-recurring operations. It is claimed that, before the requirement for businesses to produce the cash flow statement, some businesses were able to obscure the fact that they were only able to continue their operations as a result of a series of borrowings and/or share issues. It is no longer possible to obscure such actions.

The effect on a business's cash balance of its various activities is shown in Figure 6.3. The activities that affect cash are analysed in the same way as is required by FRS 1. As explained below, the arrows in the figure show the *normal* direction of cash flow for the typical healthy, profitable business in a typical year.

Normally 'operating activities' provide positive cash flow – that is, they help to increase a business's cash resources. In fact, for UK businesses, cash generated from normal trading, even after deducting tax, interest and dividends, is overwhelmingly the most important source of new finance for most businesses.

Figure 6.3

Diagrammatical representation of the cash flow statement

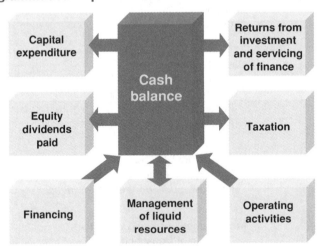

Various activities of the business each have their own effect on its cash balance, either positive (increasing the cash balance) or negative (decreasing the cash balance). The increase or reduction in the cash balance over a period will be the sum of these individual effects, taking account of the direction (cash in or cash out) of each activity's effect on cash.

Note that the direction of an arrow shows the *normal* direction of the cash flow in respect of each activity. In certain circumstances each of these arrows could be reversed in direction; for example, in some circumstances the business might be eligible to claim a repayment of tax instead of having to pay it. Only with 'management of liquid resources' will there not be a 'normal' direction of the cash flow.

Activity 6.3

Last year's cash flow statement for Angus plc showed a negative cash flow from operating activities. What could be the reason for this and should the business's management be alarmed by it? *Hint*: we think that there are two broad possible reasons for a negative cash flow.

The two reasons are:

- *The business is unprofitable.*   This leads to more cash being paid out to employees, suppliers of goods and services, and so on than is received from debtors in respect of sales. This would be particularly alarming because a major expense for most businesses is depreciation of fixed assets. Since depreciation does not lead to a cash flow, it is not considered in cash flow from operating activities. Neither would interest paid on any money borrowed by the business be included here, because it is taken into account under 'servicing of finance'. Thus, a negative operating cash flow might well indicate a very much larger negative trading profit, and a significant loss of the business's wealth.

- *The business is expanding.*   This reason might be less alarming. A business that is expanding its activities (its levels of sales) would tend to spend quite a lot of cash, relative to the amount of cash coming in from sales. This is because it will probably be expanding its stockholdings to accommodate the increased demand. In the first instance, it would not necessarily benefit, in cash flow terms, from all of the additional sales. Normally, a business may well have to have the stock in place before additional sales could be made. Even when the additional sales *are* made, the sales would normally be made on credit, with the cash inflow lagging behind the sale. This is likely to be particularly true of a new business, which would be expanding stocks and other assets from zero.

    Expansion typically causes cash flow strains for the reasons just explained. This can be a particular problem because a business's increased profitability might encourage a feeling of optimism, which could lead in turn to a lack of concern for the cash flow problem.

To continue with our consideration of the 'normal' direction of cash flow, a business would, in general, pay out more to service its loan finance than it receives from the financial investments (loans made and shares owned) that it has itself made.

Companies pay tax on profits, and so the cash flow would be from the company to the Inland Revenue when the company is profitable. When a company makes a trading loss, there would be no cash flow. However, if the loss followed a period where tax was paid on profits, the company would be entitled to set the current loss against past profits and obtain a refund of past tax paid as a result. Thus, there might be positive cash flow from taxation.

Investing activities can give rise to positive cash flows when a business sells some fixed assets. Because most types of fixed asset wear out and because businesses tend to seek to expand their asset base, the normal direction of cash in this area is out of the business, that is negative.

Financing can go in either direction, depending on the financing strategy at the time. Since businesses seek to expand, there is a general tendency for this area to lead to cash coming into the business rather than leaving it.

Deducing net cash inflows from operating activities

The first category of cash flow that appears in the cash flow statement, and the one that is typically the most important for most businesses, is the cash flow from operations. There are two methods that can be used to derive the figure for inclusion in the statement: the direct method and the indirect method.

The direct method

➡ The **direct method** involves an analysis of the cash records of the business for the period, picking out all payments and receipts relating to operating activities. These are summarised to give the net figure for inclusion in the cash flow statement. This could be a time-consuming and laborious activity, although it could be done by computer. Not many businesses adopt this approach.

The indirect method

➡ The **indirect method** is the more popular method. It relies on the fact that, broadly, sales give rise to cash inflows, and expenses give rise to outflows. Broadly, therefore, net profit will be equal in amount to the net cash inflow from operating activities. Since businesses have to produce a profit and loss account in any case, information from it can be used to deduce the cash from operating activities.

Within a particular accounting period, however, it is not strictly true that the net profit equals the net cash inflow from operating activities. We have already seen in Chapter 3 that sales revenues are not the same as cash received from sales during a particular period and expenses are not the same as cash paid for expenses during a period. Thus profit (which is the difference between revenues and expenses) will not equal operating cash flows (which is the difference between cash received from sales and cash paid for expenses).

Activity 6.4	How can we deduce the cash inflow from sales using the P and L account and balance sheet for the business?

The balance sheet will tell us how much was owed in respect of credit sales at the beginning and end of the year (trade debtors). The P and L account tells us the sales figure. If we adjust the sales figure by the increase or decrease in trade debtors over the year, we deduce the cash from sales for the year.

When sales are made on credit, the cash receipt occurs some time after the sale. This means that sales made towards the end of an accounting year will be included in that year's P and L account, but most of the cash from those sales will flow into the business, and should be included in the cash flow statement, in the following year. Fortunately, it is easy to deduce the cash received from sales if we have the relevant P and L account (see Examples 6.2 and 6.3 following).

Example 6.2

The sales figure for a business for the year is £34 million. The trade debtors were £4 million at the beginning of the year, but had increased to £5 million by the end of the year.

Basically, the debtors figure is affected by sales and cash receipts. It is increased when a sale is made and decreased when cash is received from a debtor. If, over a year, the sales and the cash receipts had been equal, the beginning-of-year and end-of-year debtors figures would have been equal. Since the debtors figure increased, it must mean that less cash was received than sales were made. Thus, the cash receipts from sales must be £33 million $(34 - (5 - 4))$.

Put slightly differently, we can say that, as a result of sales, assets of £34 million flowed into the business during the year. If £1 million of this went to increasing the asset of trade debtors, this leaves only £33 million that went to increase cash.

A similar approach to that applied in respect of sales can be applied to most expense items. However, in the case of depreciation, the charge in the P and L account may not be associated with any movement in cash during the accounting period. (This is because the cash movement will usually occur when the fixed asset is acquired.)

All of this means that if we take the operating profit (that is, the profit before interest and tax) for the year, add back the depreciation charged in arriving at that profit and adjust this total by movements in stock, debtors and creditors, we have the effect on cash.

Example 6.3

The relevant information from the accounts of Dido plc for last year is as follows:

	£m
Net operating profit	122
Depreciation charged in arriving at net operating profit	34
At the beginning of the year:	
Stock	15
Debtors	24
Creditors	18
At the end of the year:	
Stock	17
Debtors	21
Creditors	19

The cash flow from operating activities is derived as follows:

		£m
Net operating profit		122
Add Depreciation		34
Net inflow of working capital from operations		156
Less Increase in stock		(2)
		154
Add Decrease in debtors	3	
Increase in creditors	1	4
Net cash inflow from operating activities		158

> Thus, the net increase in working capital was £156 million. Of this, £2 million went into increased stocks. More cash was received from debtors than sales were made, and less cash was paid to creditors than purchases were of goods and services on credit. Both of these had a favourable effect on cash, which increased by £158 million.

The indirect method of deducing the net cash flow from operating activities is summarised in Figure 6.4.

Activity 6.5

The relevant information from the accounts of Pluto plc for last year is as follows:

	£m
Net operating profit	165
Depreciation charged in arriving at net operating profit	41
At the beginning of the year:	
Stock	22
Debtors	18
Creditors	15
At the end of the year:	
Stock	23
Debtors	21
Creditors	17

What figure should appear in the cash flow statement for 'net cash inflow from operating activities'?

Net cash flow from operating activities:

	£m	£m
Net operating profit		165
Add Depreciation		41
Net increase in working capital from operations		206
Less Increase in stock	1	
Increase in debtors	3	(4)
		202
Add Increase in creditors		2
Net cash inflow from operating activities		204

We can now go on to take a look at the preparation of a complete cash flow statement – see Example 6.4.

Figure 6.4	**The indirect method of deducing the net cash flow from the operating activities**

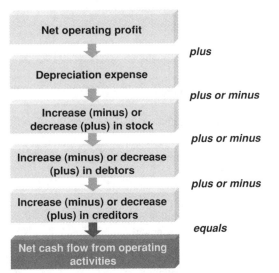

The figure sets out the indirect method of determining the net cash flows from operating activities. This involves adding back the depreciation charge to the net profit for the period and then adjusting for increases or decreases in stock, debtors and creditors.

Example 6.4	Torbryan plc's profit and loss account for the year ended 31 December 2001 and the balance sheets as at 31 December 2000 and 2001 are as follows:

Profit and loss account for the year ended 31 December 2001

	£m	£m
Turnover		576
Cost of sales		307
Gross profit		269
Distribution costs	65	
Administrative expenses	26	91
		178
Other operating income		21
		199
Interest receivable and similar income		17
		216
Interest payable and similar charges		23
		193
Tax on profit or loss on ordinary activities		46
Profit on ordinary activities after taxation		147
Retained profit brought forward from last year		26
		173
Proposed dividend on ordinary shares		(50)
Retained profit carried forward		123

Balance sheet as at 31 December 2000 and 2001

	2000 £m	2001 £m
Fixed assets		
Tangible assets:		
Land and buildings	241	241
Plant and machinery	309	325
	550	566
Current assets		
Stocks	44	41
Trade debtors	121	139
	165	180
Creditors: amounts falling due within one year		
Bank overdraft	28	6
Trade creditors	55	54
Corporation tax	16	23
Dividend proposed	40	50
	139	133
Net current assets	26	47
Total assets less current liabilities	576	613
Creditors: amounts falling due after more than one year		
Debenture loans	400	250
	176	363
Capital and reserves		
Called-up ordinary share capital	150	200
Share premium account	–	40
Profit and loss account	26	123
	176	363

During 2001, the business spent £95 million on additional plant and machinery. There were no other fixed-asset acquisitions or disposals. The cash flow statement would be as follows:

Torbryan plc
Cash flow statement for the year ended 31 December 2001

	£m	£m
Net cash inflows from operating activities (note 1)		262
Returns from investment and servicing of finance		
Interest received	17	
Interest paid	(23)	
Net cash outflow from returns on investment and servicing of finance		(6)
Taxation		
Corporation tax paid (note 2)	(39)	
Net cash outflow for taxation		(39)

Capital expenditure	£m	£m
Payments to acquire tangible fixed assets	(95)	
Net cash outflow for capital expenditure		(95)
		122
Equity dividends paid		
Dividends paid (note 3)	(40)	
Net cash outflow for dividends		(40)
		82
Management of liquid resources		–
Financing		
Repayments of debenture stock (note 4)	(150)	
Issue of ordinary shares (note 5)	90	
Net cash outflow for financing		(60)
Net increase in cash		22

To see how this relates to the cash of the business at the beginning and end of the year it is useful to show a reconciliation as follows:

Reconciliation of cash movements during the year ended 31 December 2001

	£m
Balance at 1 January 2000	(28)
Net cash inflow	22
Balance at 31 December 2001	(6)

Notes

1. Calculation of net cash inflow from operating activities

	£m	£m
Net operating profit (from the profit and loss account)		199
Add Depreciation of plant and machinery[a]		79
		278
Less Increase in debtors (139 – 121)	18	
Decrease in creditors (55 – 54)	1	19
		259
Add Decrease in stocks (44 – 41)		3
		262

[a] Since there were no disposals, the depreciation charges must be the difference between the start and end of the year's fixed asset values, adjusted by the cost of any additions.

	£m
Book value, at 1 January 2001	309
Add Additions	95
	404
Less Depreciation (balancing figure)	79
Book value, at 31 December 2001	325

2. Taxation

50 per cent of the tax due from companies is paid during the accounting year and 50 per cent in the following year. Thus the 2001 payment would have been half of the tax on the 2000 profit plus half of the 2001 tax charge; put another way, it is the figure that would have appeared in the current liabilities at the end of 2000, plus half of the 2001 tax charge (that is, $16 + (\frac{1}{2} \times 46) = 39$).

Probably the easiest way to deduce the amount paid during the year to 31 December 2001 is by following this approach:

	£m
Tax owed by the business at start of year (1.1.00)	16
Add: Tax charge for the year	46
	62
Less: Tax owed by the business at the end of the year	(23)
Tax paid during the year	39

This follows the logic that if we start with what the business owed at the beginning of the year, add on the increase in what was owed as a result of the current year's tax and then deduct what was still owed at the end, the resulting figure must be what was paid during the year. A similar approach can be taken with equity dividend payments, if the situation is at all complicated.

3. **Dividend**

Since all of the dividend for 2001 was unpaid at the end of 2001, it seems that the business pays just one final dividend each year, some time after the year end. Thus it is the 2000 dividend that will have led to a cash outflow in 2001.

4. **Debentures**

It has been assumed that the debentures were redeemed for their balance sheet value. This is not always the case, however.

5. **Shares**

The share issue raised £90 million, of which £50 million went into the share capital total on the balance sheet and £40 million into share premium.

Exhibit 6.1 shows the cash flow statement of Monsoon plc, the high-street fashion retail business, for the year ended 27 May 2000.

Exhibit 6.1 **Monsoon plc's cash flow statement for the year ended 27 May 2000**

For the 52 weeks ended 27 May 2000	2000 £000	1999 £000
Net cash inflow from operating activities	29,917	25,874
Returns on investments and servicing of finance	567	488
Taxation	(7,457)	(6,723)
Capital expenditure and financial investment	(8,616)	(10,104)
Equity dividends paid	(7,998)	(7,998)
Net cash inflow before management of liquid resources	6,413	1,537
Management of liquid resources	(2,720)	(6,262)
Increase/(decrease) in net cash in the period	3,693	(4,725)

What the cash flow statement tells us

The cash flow statement tells us how the business has generated cash during the period and where that cash has gone. Since cash is properly regarded as the lifeblood of just about any business, this is potentially very useful information.

Tracking the sources and uses of cash over several years could show financing trends that a reader of the statements could use to help to make predictions about the likely future behaviour of the business.

Looking specifically at the cash flow statement for Torbryan plc in Example 6.4, we can see the following:

- Net cash flow from operations was strong – much larger than the profit figure. This would be expected because depreciation is deducted in arriving at profit. There was a general tendency for working capital to absorb some cash. This would not be surprising had there been an expansion of activity (sales output) over the year. However, from the information supplied, we do not know whether there was an expansion or not.
- There were net outflows of cash in servicing of finance, payment of tax and increasing fixed assets.
- There seems to be a healthy figure of net cash flow after equity dividends.
- There was a fairly major outflow of cash to redeem some debt finance, partly offset by the proceeds of a share issue.
- The net effect was a rather healthier-looking cash position in 2001 than was the case in 2000.

Chapter 7 deals, in a more analytical manner, with the interpretation of cash flow statements.

? Self-assessment question 6.1

Touchstone plc's P and L accounts for the years ended 31 December 2000 and 2001, and the balance sheets as at 31 December 2000 and 2001, are as follows:

Profit and loss accounts for the years ended 2000 and 2001

	2000 £m	2001 £m
Turnover	173	207
Cost of sales	(96)	(101)
Gross profit	77	106
Distribution costs	(18)	(22)
Administrative expenses	(25)	(26)
	34	58
Other operating income	3	4
	37	62
Interest receivable and similar income	1	2
	38	64
Interest payable and similar charges	(2)	(4)
	36	60
Tax on profit or loss on ordinary activities	(8)	(16)
Profit on ordinary activities after taxation	28	44
Retained profit brought forward from last year	16	30
	44	74
Dividend (proposed and paid) on ordinary shares	(14)	(18)
Retained profit carried forward	30	56

Balance sheet as at 31 December 2000 and 2001

	2000 £m	2001 £m
Fixed assets		
Tangible assets:		
Land and buildings	94	110
Plant and machinery	53	62
	147	172
Current assets		
Stocks	25	24
Debtors	16	26
Cash at bank and in hand	4	19
	45	69
Creditors: amounts falling due within one year		
Trade creditors	26	23
Corporation tax	4	8
Dividend proposed	12	14
	42	45
Net current assets	3	24
Total assets less current liabilities	150	196
Creditors: amounts falling due after more than one year		
Debenture loans (10%)	20	40
	130	156
Capital and reserves		
Called-up ordinary share capital	100	100
Profit and loss account	30	56
	130	156

Included in 'cost of sales', 'distribution costs' and 'administration expenses', depreciation was as follows:

	2000 £m	2001 £m
Land and buildings	5	6
Plant and machinery	6	10

There were no fixed-asset disposals in either year. In both years an interim dividend was paid in the year in whose profit and loss account it was shown, and a final dividend just after the end of the year concerned.

Required:
Prepare a cash flow statement for the business for 2001.

Summary

In this chapter we have seen that users of accounting information find it of considerable benefit to have a statement that highlights how a business has generated cash, how it has used its cash, and the resultant effect on its cash resources over a period (typically one year). The cash flow statement does this. The cash flow statement contrasts with the P and L account to the extent that the former shows cash movements, whereas the latter shows changes in business wealth (not just that which is represented by cash) as a result just of trading activities. The statement used by UK businesses is of the form and content laid down by FRS 1. This standard requires that cash flows are analysed into various types of cash flows.

 Key terms

Cash flow   p. 159
Net cash flow from operating activities
   p. 162
Returns from investment and servicing
   of finance   p. 164
Taxation   p. 164
Capital expenditure   p. 164

Equity dividends paid   p. 164
Management of liquid resources
   p. 164
Financing   p. 164
Direct method   p. 168
Indirect method   p. 168

Further reading

If you would like to explore the topics covered in this chapter in more depth, we recommend the following books:

Financial Reporting, *Alexander, D.* and *Britton, A.*, 6 edn, International Thompson Business Press 2001, chapter 27.

Students' Guide to Accounting and Financial Reporting Standards, *Black, G.*, 7 edn, Financial Times Prentice Hall 2000, chapter 12.

Financial Accounting and Reporting, *Elliott, B.* and *Elliott, J.*, 5th edn, Financial Times Prentice Hall 2001, chapter 24.

Students' Manual of Accounting, *PricewaterhouseCoopers*, International Thomson Business Press 1999, chapter 30.

6.1 The typical business outside of the service sector has about 50 per cent more of its resources tied up in stock than in cash, yet there is no call for a 'stock flow statement' to be prepared. Why is cash regarded as more important than stock?

6.2 What is the difference between the direct and indirect methods of deducing cash flow from operating activities?

6.3 Taking each of the categories of the cash flow statement in turn, in which direction would you normally expect the cash flow to be?

(a) Cash flow from operations
(b) Cash flow from returns from investments and servicing of finance
(c) Cash flow from taxation
(d) Cash flow from capital expenditure
(e) Cash flow from equity dividends
(f) Cash flow from management of liquid resources
(g) Cash flow from financing.

6.4 What causes the net profit for the year not to equal the net cash inflow?

Exercises 6.3–6.8 are more advanced than 6.1 and 6.2. Those with coloured numbers have answers at the back of the book.

6.1 How will each of the following events ultimately affect the amount of cash in a business?

(a) An increase in the level of stock in trade.
(b) A rights issue of ordinary shares.
(c) A bonus issue of ordinary shares.
(d) Writing off the value of some stock in trade.
(e) The disposal of a large number of the business's shares by a major shareholder.
(f) Depreciating a fixed asset.

6.2 The following information has been taken from the accounts of Juno plc for 2000 and 2001:

	2001 £m	2000 £m
Net operating profit	187	156
Depreciation charged in arriving at net operating profit	55	47
Stock held at end of year	31	27
Debtors at end of year	23	24
Creditors at end of year	17	15

Required:
What is the 'cash flow from operations' figure for Juno plc for 2001?

6.3 Torrent plc's profit and loss account for the year ended 31 December 2001 and the balance sheets as at 31 December 2000 and 2001 are as follows:

Profit and loss account	£m	£m
Turnover		623
Cost of sales		(353)
Gross profit		270
Distribution costs	(71)	
Administrative expenses	(30)	(101)
		169
Other operating income		13
		182
Interest receivable and similar income		14
		196
Interest payable and similar charges		(26)
		170
Tax on profit on ordinary activities		(36)
Profit on ordinary activities after taxation		134
Retained profit brought forward from last year		123
		257
Proposed dividend on ordinary shares		(60)
Retained profit carried forward		197

Balance sheet as at 31 December 2000 and 2001

	2000 £m	2001 £m
Fixed assets		
Land and buildings	310	310
Plant and machinery	325	314
	635	624
Current assets		
Stocks	41	35
Trade debtors	139	145
	180	180
Creditors: amounts falling due within one year		
Bank overdraft	6	29
Trade creditors	54	41
Corporation tax	23	18
Dividend proposed	50	60
	133	148
Net current assets	47	32
Total assets less current liabilities	682	656
Creditors: amounts falling due after more than one year		
Debenture loans	250	150
	432	506
Capital and reserves		
Called-up ordinary share capital	200	300
Share premium account	40	–
Revaluation reserve	69	9
Profit and loss account	123	197
	432	506

During 2001, the business spent £67 million on additional plant and machinery. There were no other fixed asset acquisitions or disposals. There was no share issue for cash during the year.

Required:
Prepare the cash flow statement for Torrent plc for the year ended 31 December 2001.

6.4   Cheng plc's profit and loss accounts for the years ended 31 December 2000 and 2001 and balance sheets as at 31 December 2000 and 2001 are as follows:

Profit and loss account

	2000 £m	2001 £m
Turnover	207	153
Cost of sales	(101)	(76)
Gross profit	106	77
Distribution costs	(22)	(20)
Administrative expenses	(26)	(28)
	58	29
Other operating income	4	–
	62	29
Interest receivable and similar income	2	–
	64	29
Interest payable and similar charges	(4)	(4)
	60	25
Tax on profit or loss on ordinary activities	(16)	(6)
Profit on ordinary activities after taxation	44	19
Retained profit brought forward from last year	30	56
	74	75
Dividends on ordinary shares (paid and proposed)	(18)	(18)
Retained profit carried forward	56	57

Balance sheet as at 31 December 2000 and 2001

	2000 £m	2001 £m
Fixed assets		
Tangible assets:		
Land and buildings	110	130
Plant and machinery	62	56
	172	186
Current assets		
Stocks	24	25
Debtors	26	25
Cash at bank and in hand	19	–
	69	50
Creditors: amounts falling due within one year		
Bank overdraft	–	2
Trade creditors	23	20
Corporation tax	8	3
Dividend proposed	14	14
	45	39

	2000 £m	2001 £m
Net current assets	24	11
Total assets less current liabilities	196	197
Creditors: amounts falling due after more than one year		
Debenture loans (10%)	40	40
	156	157
Capital and reserves		
Called-up ordinary share capital	100	100
Profit and loss account	56	57
	156	157

Included in 'cost of sales', 'distribution costs' and 'administration expenses', depreciation was as follows:

	2000 £m	2001 £m
Land and buildings	6	10
Plant and machinery	10	12

There were no fixed asset disposals in either year. In both years, an interim dividend was paid in the year in whose profit and loss account it was shown, and a final dividend was paid just after the end of the year concerned.

Required:
Prepare a cash flow statement for the business for 2001.

6.5 The following are the accounts for Nailsea Limited for the year ended 30 June 2001 and 2002.

Profit and loss accounts for year ended 30 June

	2001 £000	2002 £000
Sales	1,230	2,280
Operating costs	(722)	(1,618)
Depreciation	(270)	(320)
Operating profit	238	342
Interest	–	(27)
Profit before tax	238	315
Tax	(110)	(140)
Profit after tax	128	175
Dividend	(80)	(85)
Retained profit for year	48	90

Balance sheets as at 30 June

	2001 £000	2001 £000	2002 £000	2002 £000
Fixed assets (see note below)		2,310		2,640
Current assets				
Stock	275		450	
Debtors	100		250	
Bank	–		83	
	375		783	

	2001		2002	
	£000	£000	£000	£000
Less **Creditors due within one year**				
Creditors	130		190	
Taxation	55		70	
Dividend	80		85	
Bank overdraft	32		–	
	297		345	
Net current assets		78		438
		2,388		3,078
Less **Creditors falling due after more than one year**				
9% debentures		–		300
		2,388		2,778
Capital and reserves				
Share capital (fully paid £1 shares)		1,400		1,600
Share premium account		200		300
Retained profits		788		878
		2,388		2,778

Note: **Schedule of fixed assets**

	Land and buildings £m	Plant and machinery £m	Total £m
Cost			
At 1 July 2001	1,500	1,350	2,850
Additions	400	250	650
At 30 June 2002	1,900	1,600	3,500
Depreciation			
At 1 July 2001	–	540	540
Charge for year at 20%	–	320	320
At 30 June 2002	–	860	860
Net book value at 30 June 2002	1,900	740	2,640

Required:
Prepare a cash flow statement for Nailsea Limited for the year ended 30 June 2002.

6.6 The following financial statements for Blackstone plc are a slightly simplified set of published accounts. Blackstone plc is an engineering firm that developed a new range of products in 2000; these now account for 60 per cent of its turnover.

Profit and loss account for the years ended 31 March

	notes	2001 £m	2002 £m
Turnover		7,003	11,205
Cost of sales		(3,748)	(5,809)
Gross profit		3,255	5,396
Operating costs	1	(2,205)	(3,087)
Operating Profit		1,050	2,309
Interest payable		(216)	(456)

	notes	2001 £m	2002 £m
Profit before taxation		834	1,853
Taxation		(210)	(390)
Profit after taxation		624	1,463
Dividends		(300)	(400)
Retained profit for the year		324	1,063
Retained profit brought forward		361	685
Retained profit carried forward		685	1,748

Balance sheets as at 31 March

	notes	2001 £m	2001 £m	2002 £m	2002 £m
Fixed assets					
Intangible assets	2	–		700	
Tangible assets	3	4,300		7,535	
			4,300		8,235
Current assets					
Stocks		1,209		2,410	
Trade debtors		941		1,573	
		2,150		3,983	
Creditors: amounts falling due within one year					
Trade creditors		731		1,507	
Taxation		105		195	
Dividends		300		400	
Overdraft		77		1,816	
		1,213		3,918	
Net current assets			937		65
Creditors: amounts falling due after more than one year					
Bank loan (repayable 2007)			(1,800)		(3,800)
			3,437		4,500
Capital and reserves					
Share capital			1,800		1,800
Share premium			600		600
Capital reserves			352		352
Retained profits			685		1,748
			3,437		4,500

Notes to the accounts

1. Operating costs include the following items:

	£m
Exceptional items	503
Depreciation	1,251
Administrative expenses	527
Marketing expenses	785

2. Intangible assets represent the amounts paid for the goodwill of another engineering business acquired during the year.

3. The movements in tangible fixed assets during the year are set out below.

	Land and buildings £m	Plant and machinery £m	Fixtures and fittings £m	Total £m
Cost				
At 1 April 2001	4,500	3,850	2,120	10,470
Additions	–	2,970	1,608	4,578
Disposals	–	(365)	(216)	(581)
At 31 March 2002	4,500	6,455	3,512	14,467
Depreciation				
At 1 April 2001	1,275	3,080	1,815	6,170
Charge for year	225	745	281	1,251
Disposals	–	(305)	(184)	(489)
At 31 March 2002	1,500	3,520	1,912	6,932
Net book value				
At 31 March 2002	3,000	2,935	1,600	7,535

Proceeds from the sale of fixed assets in the year ended 31 March 2002 amounted to £54 million.

Required:
Prepare a cash flow statement for Blackstone plc for the year ended 31 March 2002. *Hint*: a loss (deficit) on disposal of fixed assets is simply an additional amount of depreciation and should be dealt with as such in preparing the cash flow statement.

6.7 Simplified financial statements for York plc are set out below.

York plc
Profit and loss account for the year ended 30 September 2001

	£m
Turnover	290.0
Cost of sales	(215.0)
Gross profit	75.0
Less Operating expenses (note 1)	(62.0)
Operating profit	13.0
Interest paid	(3.0)
Profit before taxation	10.0
Taxation	(2.6)
Profit after taxation	7.4
Dividends	(3.5)
Retained profit	3.9

Balance sheet at 30 September

	2000		2001	
	£m	£m	£m	£m
Fixed assets (note 2)		80.0		85.0
Current assets				
Stock and debtors	119.8		122.1	
Cash at bank	9.2		16.6	
	129.0		138.7	
Current liabilities				
Trade creditors	(78.2)		(80.5)	
Dividends	(1.8)		(2.0)	
Taxation	(1.0)		(1.3)	
	(81.0)		(83.8)	
Net current assets		48.0		54.9
Long-term liabilities		(32.0)		(35.0)
		96.0		104.9
Share capital		35.0		40.0
Share premium account		30.0		30.0
Reserves		31.0		34.9
		96.0		104.9

Notes to the accounts

1. Operating expenses include depreciation of £13 million and a profit of £3.2 million on the sale of fixed assets.
2. Fixed assets costs and depreciation:

	Cost	Accumulated depreciation	Net book value
	£m	£m	£m
At 1 October 2000	120.0	40.0	80.0
Disposals	(10.0)	(8.0)	(2.0)
Additions	20.0		20.0
Depreciation		13.0	(13.0)
At 30 September 2001	130.0	45.0	85.0

Required:

Prepare a cash flow statement for York plc for the year ended 30 September 2001 using the data above.

6.8 The balance sheets of Axis plc as at 31 December 2000 and 2001 and the summary profit and loss account for the year ended 31 December 2001 were as follows:

Balance sheet as at 31 December

	2000		2001	
	£m	£m	£m	£m
Fixed assets				
Land and building at cost	130		130	
Less Accumulated depreciation	30	100	32	98
Plant and machinery at cost	70		80	
Less Accumulated depreciation	17	53	23	57
		153		155

	2000		2001	
	£m	£m	£m	£m
Current assets				
Stock	25		24	
Debtors	16		26	
Short-term investments	–		12	
Cash at bank and in hand	–		7	
	41		69	
Creditors: amounts due in less than one year				
Trade creditors	19		22	
Taxation	7		8	
Proposed dividends	12		14	
	38		44	
Net current assets		3		25
		156		180
Creditors: amounts due beyond one year				
10% debentures		20		40
		136		140
Financed by:				
Share capital		100		100
Revenue reserves		36		40
		136		140

Profit and loss account for the year ended 31 December 2001

	£m	£m
Sales		173
Less Cost of sales		(96)
Gross profit		77
Interest receivable		2
		79
Less		
Sundry expenses	24	
Interest payable	2	
Loss on sale of fixed asset	1	
Depreciation – buildings	2	
– plant	16	(45)
Net profit before tax		34
Corporation tax		(16)
Net profit after tax		18
Proposed dividend		(14)
Unappropriated profit added to revenue reserves		4

During the year, plant costing £15 million and with accumulated depreciation of £10 million was sold for £4 million.

Required:
Prepare a cash flow statement for Axis plc for the year ended 31 December 2001.

Analysing and interpreting financial statements

Introduction

In this chapter we will see how financial ratios can help in the analysis and interpretation of financial statements. We shall also consider problems that are encountered when applying this technique. Financial ratios can be used to examine various aspects of financial position and performance and are widely used for planning and control purposes. They can be used to evaluate the financial health of a business and can be utilised by management in a wide variety of decisions involving such areas as profit planning, pricing, working-capital management, financial structure and dividend policy.

OBJECTIVES When you have completed this chapter you should be able to:

- Identify the major categories of ratios that can be used for analysis purposes.
- Calculate important ratios for determining the financial performance and position of a business and explain the significance of the ratios calculated.
- Explain the nature and purpose of common-size financial statements.
- Discuss the use of ratios in helping to predict financial distress.
- Discuss the limitations of ratios as a tool of financial analysis.

Financial ratios

Financial ratios provide a quick and relatively simple means of examining the financial condition of a business. A ratio simply expresses the relation of one figure appearing in the financial statements to some other figure appearing there (for example, net profit in relation to capital employed) or perhaps to some resource of the business (for example, net profit per employee, sales per square metre of counter space).

Ratios can be very helpful when comparing the financial health of different businesses. Differences may exist between businesses in the scale of operations, and so a direct comparison of (say) the profits generated by each business may be misleading. By expressing profit in relation to some other measure (for example, sales), the problem of scale is eliminated. A business with a profit of, say, £10,000 and a sales turnover of £100,000 can be compared with a much larger business with a profit of, say, £80,000 and a sales turnover of £1,000,000 by the use of a simple ratio. The net profit to sales turnover ratio for the smaller company is 10 per cent [(10,000/100,000) × 100%] and the same ratio for the larger company is 8 per cent [(80,000/1,000,000) × 100%]. These ratios can then be directly compared, whereas comparison of the absolute profit figures would be less meaningful. The need to eliminate differences in scale through the use of ratios can also apply when comparing the performance of the same business over time.

By calculating a relatively small number of ratios, it is often possible to build up a reasonably good picture of the position and performance of a business. Thus, it is not surprising that ratios are widely used by those who have an interest in businesses and business performance. Although ratios are not difficult to calculate, they can be difficult to interpret. For example, a change in the net profit per employee of a business may be for a number of possible reasons such as:

■ A change in the number of employees without a corresponding change in the level of output.
■ A change in the level of output without a corresponding change in the number of employees.
■ A change in the mix of goods/services being offered which, in turn, changes the level of profit.

It is important to appreciate that ratios are really only the starting point for further analysis. They help to highlight the financial strengths and weaknesses of a business but they cannot, by themselves, explain why certain strengths or weaknesses exist or why certain changes have occurred. Only a detailed investigation will reveal these underlying reasons.

Ratios can be expressed in various forms, for example as a percentage, as a fraction or as a proportion. The way in which a particular ratio is presented will depend on the needs of those who will use the information. Although it is possible to calculate a large number of ratios, only a few, based on key relationships, are likely to be helpful to a user. Many ratios that could be calculated from the financial statements (for example rent payable in relation to current assets) may not be considered because there is no clear or meaningful relationship between the items.

There is no generally accepted list of ratios that can be applied to financial statements, nor is there a standard method of calculating many of them. Variations in both the choice of ratios and their precise definition will be found in the literature and in practice. However, it is important to be *consistent* in the way in which ratios are calculated for comparison purposes. The ratios discussed below are those that are widely used because many consider them to be among the more important for decision-making purposes.

Financial ratio classification

Ratios can be grouped into certain categories, each of which reflects a particular aspect of financial performance or position. The following broad categories provide a useful basis for explaining the nature of the financial ratios to be dealt with:

- *Profitability*.   Businesses come into being with the primary purpose of creating wealth for the owners. Profitability ratios provide an insight to the degree of success in achieving this purpose. They express the profits made (or figures bearing on profit, such as overheads) in relation to other key figures in the financial statements or to some business resource.
- *Efficiency*.   Ratios may be used to measure the efficiency with which certain resources have been utilised within the business. These ratios are also referred to as **activity ratios**.
- *Liquidity*.   We have seen in Chapter 2 that it is vital to the survival of a business that there be sufficient liquid resources available to meet maturing obligations. Certain ratios may be calculated that examine the relationship between liquid resources held and creditors due for payment in the near future.
- *Gearing*.   This is the relationship between the amount financed by the owners of the business and the amount contributed by outsiders, which has an important effect on the degree of risk associated with a business. Gearing is thus something that managers must consider when making financing decisions.
- *Investment*.   Certain ratios are concerned with assessing the returns and performance of shares held in a particular business.

We shall consider ratios falling into each of these categories later in this chapter.

The need for comparison

Calculating a ratio will not by itself tell you very much about the position or performance of a business. For example, if a ratio reveals that a business was generating £100 in sales per square metre of counter space, it would not be possible to deduce from this information alone whether this particular level of performance was good, bad or indifferent. It is only when you compare this ratio with some 'benchmark' that the information can be interpreted and evaluated.

Activity 7.1	Can you think of any bases that could be used to compare a ratio you have calculated from the financial statements of a particular period?

In answering this activity you may have thought of the following bases:

- *Past periods*.   By comparing the ratio you have calculated with the ratio of a previous period, it is possible to detect whether there has been an improvement or deterioration in performance. Indeed, it is often useful to track particular ratios over time (say five or ten years) in order to see whether it is possible to detect trends. However, the comparison of ratios from different time periods brings certain problems. In particular, there is always the possibility that trading conditions may have been quite different in the periods being compared. There is a further problem that when comparing the performance of a single business over time, operating inefficiencies may not be clearly exposed. For example, the fact that net profit per employee has risen by 10 per cent over the previous period may at first sight appear to be satisfactory, however, this may not be the case if similar businesses have shown an improvement of 50 per cent for the same period. Finally, there is the problem that inflation may have distorted the figures on which the ratios are based. As we shall see later, inflation can lead to an overstatement of profit and an understatement of asset values.

- *Planned performance*.　Ratios may be compared with the targets that management developed before the commencement of the period under review. The comparison of planned performance with actual performance may therefore be a useful way of revealing the level of achievement attained. However, the planned levels of performance must be based on realistic assumptions if they are to be useful for comparison purposes.
- *Similar businesses*.　In a competitive environment, a business must consider its performance in relation to those of other businesses operating in the same industry. Survival may depend on the ability to achieve comparable levels of performance. Thus, a useful basis for comparing a particular ratio is the ratio achieved by similar businesses during the same period. This basis is not, however, without its problems. Competitors may have different year-ends, and therefore trading conditions might not be identical. They may also have different accounting policies, which have a significant effect on reported profits and asset values (for example, different methods of calculating depreciation, different methods of valuing stock). Finally, it may be difficult to obtain the accounts of competitor businesses. Sole proprietorships and partnerships, for example, are not obliged to publish their financial statements. In the case of limited companies, there is a legal obligation to publish accounts; however, a diversified company may not provide a detailed breakdown of activities sufficient for analysts to compare with the activities of other businesses.

Key steps in financial ratio analysis

When employing financial ratios, a sequence of steps is carried out by an analyst. The first step involves identifying the key indicators and relationships that require examination. In order to carry out this step, the analyst must be clear *who* the target users are and *why* they need the information. Different types of users of financial information are likely to have different information needs that will, in turn, determine the ratios that they find useful. For example, shareholders are likely to be interested in their returns in relation to the level of risk associated with their investment. Thus, profitability, investment and gearing ratios will be of particular interest. Long-term lenders are concerned with the long-term viability of the business. In order to help them to assess this, the profitability ratios and gearing ratios of the business are also likely to be of particular interest. Short-term lenders, such as suppliers, may be interested in the ability of the business to repay the amounts owing in the short term. As a result, the liquidity ratios should be of interest.

The next step in the process is to calculate ratios that are considered appropriate for the particular users and the purpose for which they require the information.

The final step is interpretation and evaluation of the ratios. Interpretation involves examining the ratios in conjunction with an appropriate basis for comparison and any other information that may be relevant. The significance of the ratios calculated can then be established. Evaluation involves forming a judgement concerning the value of the information uncovered in the calculation and interpretation of the ratios. Whilst calculation is usually straightforward, and can be easily carried out by computer, the interpretation and evaluation are more difficult and often require high levels of skill. This skill can only really be acquired through much practice. The three steps described are shown in Figure 7.1.

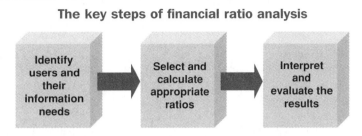

Figure 7.1

The key steps of financial ratio analysis

Identify users and their information needs → Select and calculate appropriate ratios → Interpret and evaluate the results

The three steps involve: firstly, identifying for whom and for what purpose the analysis and interpretation is required; secondly, selecting appropriate ratios and calculating them; and, finally, forming a judgement on the information produced.

The ratios calculated

Probably the best way to explain financial ratios is to work through an example. Example 7.1 provides a set of financial statements from which we can calculate important ratios in the subsequent sections.

Example 7.1

The following financial statements relate to Alexis plc, which owns a small chain of wholesale/retail carpet stores.

Balance sheets as at 31 March

	2001		2002	
	£000	£000	£000	£000
Fixed assets				
Freehold land and buildings at cost	451.2		451.2	
Less Accumulated depreciation	70.0	381.2	75.0	376.2
Fixtures and fittings at cost	129.0		160.4	
Less Accumulated depreciation	64.4	64.6	97.2	63.2
		445.8		439.4
Current assets				
Stock at cost	300.0		370.8	
Trade debtors	240.8		210.2	
Bank	3.4		3.0	
	544.2		584.0	
Creditors due within one year				
Trade creditors	(221.4)		(228.8)	
Dividends proposed	(40.2)		(60.0)	
Corporation tax due	(30.1)		(38.0)	
	(291.7)	252.5	(326.8)	257.2
		698.3		696.6
Creditors due beyond one year				
12% debentures (secured)		200.0		60.0
		498.3		636.6
Capital and reserves				
£0.50 ordinary shares		300.0		334.1
General reserve		26.5		40.0
Retained profit		171.8		262.5
		498.3		636.6

Profit and loss accounts for the year ended 31 March

	2001		2002	
	£000	£000	£000	£000
Sales		2,240.8		2,681.2
Less Cost of sales				
Opening stock	241.0		300.0	
Purchases	1,804.4		2,142.8	
	2,045.4		2,442.8	
Less closing stock	300.0	1,745.4	370.8	2,072.0
Gross profit		495.4		609.2
Wages and salaries	137.8		195.0	
Directors' salaries	48.0		80.6	
Rates	12.2		12.4	
Heat and light	8.4		13.6	
Insurance	4.6		7.0	
Postage and telephone	3.4		7.4	
Audit fees	5.6		9.0	
Depreciation:				
Freehold buildings	5.0		5.0	
Fixtures and fittings	27.0	252.0	32.8	362.8
Net profit before interest and tax		243.4		246.4
Less Interest payable		24.0		6.2
Net profit before tax		219.4		240.2
Less Corporation tax		60.2		76.0
Net profit after tax		159.2		164.2
Add Retained profit brought forward		52.8		171.8
		212.0		336.0
Less Transfer to general reserve		–		(13.5)
Dividends proposed		(40.2)		(60.0)
Retained profit carried forward		171.8		262.5

Cash flow statement for the year ended 31 March

	2001		2002	
	£000	£000	£000	£000
Net cash inflow from operating activities		231.0		251.4
Returns on investments and servicing of finance				
Interest paid	(24.0)		(6.2)	
Net cash inflow (outflow) from returns on investments and servicing of finance		(24.0)		(6.2)
Taxation				
Corporation tax paid	(46.4)		(68.1)	
Tax paid		(46.4)		(68.1)
Capital expenditure				
Purchase of fixed assets	(121.2)		(31.4)	
Net cash inflow (outflow) from capital expenditure		(121.2)		(31.4)
Equity dividends				
Dividend on ordinary shares	(32.0)		(40.2)	
Net cash outflow for equity dividends		(32.0)		(40.2)

	2001		2002	
	£000	£000	£000	£000
Management of liquid resources		–		–
Financing				
Issue of ordinary shares	20.0		34.1	
Repayment of loan capital	–	20.0	(140.0)	(105.9)
Increase (decrease) in cash and				
cash equivalents		27.4		(0.4)

The company has employed 14 staff in 2001 and 18 in 2002. All sales and purchases are made on credit. The market value of the shares of the company at the end of each year was £2.50 and £3.50 respectively. The issue of equity shares during the year ended 31 March 2002 occurred at the beginning of the year.

Profitability ratios

Ratios used to evaluate the profitability of a business include the following: return on ordinary shareholders' funds; return on capital employed; net profit margin; and gross profit margin. We shall look at all of these in turn.

Return on ordinary shareholders' funds (ROSF)

The **return on ordinary shareholders' funds** compares the amount of profit for the period available to the ordinary shareholders with the ordinary shareholders' stake in the business. For a limited company, the ratio (which is normally expressed in percentage terms) is as follows:

$$\text{ROSF} = \frac{\text{Net profit after taxation and preference dividend (if any)}}{\text{Ordinary share capital plus reserves}} \times 100\%$$

The net profit after taxation and any preference dividend is used in calculating the ratio, because this figure represents the amount of profit available to the ordinary shareholders.

In the case of Alexis plc, the ratio for the year ended 31 March 2001 is:

$$\text{ROSF} = \frac{159.2}{498.3} \times 100\%$$

$$= 31.9\%$$

Activity 7.2

Calculate the return on ordinary shareholders' funds for Alexis plc for the year to 31 March 2002.

The return on ordinary shareholders' funds for the year to 31 March 2002 will be:

$$\text{ROSF} = \frac{164.2}{636.6} \times 100\%$$

$$= 25.8\%$$

Note that in calculating the ROSF, the figure for ordinary shareholders' funds as at the end of the year has been used. However, it can be argued that it is preferable to use an average figure for the year as this would be more representative of the amount invested by ordinary shareholders during the period. The easiest approach to calculating the average ordinary shareholder investment would be to take a simple average based on the opening and closing figures for the year. However, where these figures are not available, it is usually acceptable to use the year-end figures, provided that this approach is consistently applied.

Return on capital employed (ROCE)

→ The **return on capital employed** is a fundamental measure of business performance. This ratio expresses the relationship between the net profit generated by the business and the long-term capital invested in the business. The ratio is expressed in percentage terms and is as follows:

$$\text{ROCE} = \frac{\text{Net profit before interest and taxation}}{\text{Share capital + Reserves + Long-term loans}} \times 100\%$$

Note, in this case, that the profit figure used in the ratio is the net profit *before* interest and taxation. This figure is used because the ratio attempts to measure the returns to all suppliers of long-term finance before any deductions for interest payable to lenders or payments of dividends to shareholders are made.

For the year to 31 March 2001, the ratio for Alexis plc is:

$$\text{ROCE} = \frac{243.4}{698.3} \times 100\%$$
$$= 34.9\%$$

Activity 7.3

Calculate the return on capital employed for Alexis plc for the year to 31 March 2002.

For the year ended 31 March 2002, the ratio is:

$$\text{ROCE} = \frac{246.4}{696.6} \times 100\%$$
$$= 35.4\%$$

ROCE is considered by many to be a primary measure of profitability. It compares inputs (capital invested) with outputs (profit). This comparison is of vital importance in assessing the effectiveness with which funds have been deployed. Once again, an average figure for capital employed may be used where the information is available.

It is important to be clear about the distinction between ROSF and ROCE. Although both ROSF and ROCE measure returns on capital invested, ROSF is concerned with measuring the returns achieved by ordinary shareholders, whereas ROCE is concerned with measuring returns achieved from all the long-term capital invested.

Net profit margin

➡ The **net profit margin** ratio relates the net profit for a period to the sales during that period. The ratio is expressed as:

$$\text{Net profit margin} = \frac{\text{Net profit before interest and taxation}}{\text{Sales}} \times 100\%$$

The net profit before interest and taxation is used in this ratio as it represents the profit from trading operations before any costs of servicing long-term finance are taken into account. This is often regarded as the most appropriate measure of operational performance for comparison purposes, because differences arising from the way in which a particular business is financed will not influence this measure. However, this is not the only way in which this ratio may be calculated in practice. The net profit after taxation is also used, on occasions, as the numerator (the top part of the fraction). The purpose for which the ratio is required will determine which form of calculation is appropriate.

For the year ended 31 March 2001, the net profit margin of Alexis plc (based on the net profit before interest and taxation) is:

$$\text{Net profit margin} = \frac{243.4}{2{,}240.8} \times 100\%$$
$$= 10.9\%$$

This ratio compares one output of the business (profit) with another output (sales). The ratio can vary considerably between types of business. For example, a supermarket will often operate on low prices and, therefore, low profit margins in order to stimulate sales and thereby increase the total amount of profit generated. A jeweller, on the other hand, may have a high net profit margin but have a much lower level of sales volume. Factors such as the degree of competition, the type of customer, the economic climate and industry characteristics (such as the level of risk) will influence the net profit margin of a business.

Activity 7.4   Calculate the net profit margin for Alexis plc for the year to 31 March 2002.

The net profit margin for the year to 31 March 2002 will be:

$$\text{Net profit margin} = \frac{246.4}{2{,}681.2} \times 100\%$$
$$= 9.2\%$$

Gross profit margin

➡ The **gross profit margin** ratio relates the gross profit of the business to the sales generated for the same period. Gross profit represents the difference between sales value and the cost of sales. The ratio is therefore a measure of profitability in buying (or producing) and selling goods before any other expenses are taken into account. As cost of sales represents a major expense for retailing, wholesaling and manufacturing businesses, a change in this ratio can have a significant effect on the **bottom line** (that is, the net profit for the year). The gross profit ratio is calculated as follows:

$$\text{Gross profit margin} = \frac{\text{Gross profit}}{\text{Sales}} \times 100\%$$

For the year to 31 March 2001, the ratio for Alexis plc is:

$$\text{Gross profit margin} = \frac{495.4}{2,240.8} \times 100\%$$

$$= 22.1\%$$

Activity 7.5

Calculate the gross profit margin for Alexis plc for the year to 31 March 2002.

The gross profit margin for the year to 31 March 2002 is:

$$\text{Gross profit margin} = \frac{609.2}{2,681.2} \times 100\%$$

$$= 22.7\%$$

Thus the profitability ratios for Alexis plc over the two years can be set out as follows:

	2001	2002
ROSF	31.9%	25.8%
ROCE	34.9%	35.4%
Net profit margin	10.9%	9.2%
Gross profit margin	22.1%	22.7%

Activity 7.6

What do you deduce from a comparison of the profitability ratios of Alexis plc over the two years?

The gross profit margin shows a slight increase in 2002 over the previous year. This may be for a number of reasons, such as an increase in selling prices or a decrease in the cost of sales. However, the net profit margin has shown a slight decline over the period. This means that operating expenses (wages, rates, insurance and so on) are absorbing a greater proportion of sales income in 2002 than in the previous year.

   The net profit available to ordinary shareholders has risen only slightly over the period, whereas the share capital and reserves of the company have increased considerably (see the financial statements). The effect of this has been to reduce the return on ordinary shareholders' funds. The return on capital employed has improved slightly in 2002. The slight decrease in long-term capital over the period and increase in net profit before interest and tax has resulted in a better return.

Efficiency ratios

Ratios used to examine the efficiency with which various resources of the business are managed include the following: average stock turnover period; average settlement period for debtors; average settlement period for creditors; sales to capital employed; and sales per employee. We shall look at all of these in turn.

Average stock turnover period

Stocks often represent a significant investment for a business. For some types of business (for example manufacturers), stocks may account for a substantial proportion of the total assets held. The **average stock turnover period** measures the average number of days for which stocks are being held. The ratio is calculated thus:

$$\text{Stock turnover period} = \frac{\text{Average stock held}}{\text{Cost of sales}} \times 365 \text{ days}$$

The average stock for the period can be calculated as a simple average of the opening and closing stock levels for the year. However, in the case of a highly seasonal business, where stock levels may vary considerably over the year, a monthly average may be more appropriate.

In the case of Alexis plc, the stock turnover period for the year ended 31 March 2001 is:

$$\text{Stock turnover period} = \frac{(241 + 300)/2}{1,745.4} \times 365 \text{ days}$$

$$= 57 \text{ days} \quad \text{(to nearest day)}$$

This means that, on average, the stock held is being 'turned over' every 57 days.

A business will normally prefer a low stock turnover period to a high period as funds tied up in stocks cannot be used for other profitable purposes. In judging the amount of stocks to carry, a business must consider such things as the likely future demand, the possibility of future shortages, the likelihood of future price rises, the amount of storage space available, and the perishability of the product.

The stock turnover period is sometimes expressed in terms of months rather than days. Multiplying by 12 rather than 365 will achieve this.

Activity 7.7

Calculate the average stock turnover period for Alexis plc for the year ended 31 March 2002.

The stock turnover period for the year to 31 March 2002 will be:

$$\text{Stock turnover period} = \frac{(300 + 370.8)/2}{2,072} \times 365 \text{ days}$$

$$= 59 \text{ days}$$

Average settlement period for debtors

A business will usually be concerned with how long it takes for customers to pay the amounts owing. The speed of payment can have a significant effect on the cash flows of the business. The **average settlement period for debtors** calculates how long, on average, credit customers take to pay the amounts they owe to the business. The ratio is as follows:

$$\text{Average settlement period} = \frac{\text{Trade debtors}}{\text{Credit sales}} \times 365 \text{ days}$$

We are told that all sales made by Alexis plc are on credit and so the average settlement period for debtors for the year ended 31 March 2001 is:

$$\text{Average settlement period} = \frac{240.8}{2,240.8} \times 365 \text{ days}$$

$$= 39 \text{ days}$$

As no figures for opening debtors are available, the year-end debtors figure only is used. This is common practice.

Activity 7.8

Calculate the average settlement period for debtors for Alexis plc for the year ended 31 March 2002. (For the sake of consistency, use the year-end debtors figure rather than an average figure.)

The average settlement period for the year to 2002 is:

$$\text{Average settlement period} = \frac{210.2}{2,681.2} \times 365 \text{ days}$$

$$= 29 \text{ days}$$

A business will normally prefer a shorter average settlement period to a longer one as, once again, funds are being tied up that may be used for more profitable purposes. Although this ratio can be useful, it is important to remember that it produces an *average* figure for the number of days that debts are outstanding. This average may be badly distorted by, for example, a few large customers who are very slow payers.

Average settlement period for creditors

The **average settlement period for creditors** tells us how long, on average, the business takes to pay its trade creditors. The ratio is calculated as follows:

$$\text{Average settlement period} = \frac{\text{Trade creditors}}{\text{Credit purchases}} \times 365 \text{ days}$$

For the year ended 31 March 2001, the average settlement period for Alexis plc is:

$$\text{Average settlement period} = \frac{221.4}{1,804.4} \times 365 \text{ days}$$

$$= 45 \text{ days}$$

Once again, the year-end figure rather than an average figure for creditors has been employed in the calculations.

Activity 7.9

Calculate the average settlement period for creditors for Alexis plc for the year ended 31 March 2002. (For the sake of consistency, use a year-end figure for creditors.)

The average settlement period for creditors is:

$$\text{Average settlement period} = \frac{228.8}{2{,}142.8} \times 365 \text{ days}$$

$$= 39 \text{ days}$$

This ratio provides an average figure, which, like the average settlement period for debtors ratio, can be distorted by the time taken to pay one or two large suppliers.

As trade creditors provide a free source of finance for the business, it is perhaps not surprising that some businesses attempt to increase their average settlement period for trade creditors. However, such a policy can be taken too far and can result in a loss of goodwill by suppliers.

Sales to capital employed

The **sales to capital employed** ratio examines how effective the long-term capital employed of the business has been in generating sales revenue. It is calculated as follows:

$$\text{Sales to capital employed} = \frac{\text{Sales}}{\text{Long-term capital employed (that is, Shareholders' funds + Long-term loans)}}$$

For the year ended 31 March 2001, this ratio for Alexis plc is as follows:

$$\text{Sales to capital employed} = \frac{2{,}240.8}{(498.3 + 200.0)}$$

$$= 3.2 \text{ times}$$

Once again, year-end figures have been used, although an average figure for long-term capital employed could also be used if sufficient information was available.

Activity 7.10

Calculate the sales to long-term capital employed ratio for Alexis plc for the year ended 31 March 2002. (For the sake of consistency, use a year-end figure for capital employed.)

The sales to long-term capital employed ratio for the year ended 31 March 2002 will be:

$$\text{Sales to capital employed} = \frac{2{,}681.2}{(636.6 + 60.0)}$$

$$= 3.8 \text{ times}$$

Generally speaking, a higher ratio for sales to capital employed is preferred to a lower one. A higher ratio will normally suggest that the capital (as represented by the total assets less current liabilities) is being used more productively in the generation of revenue. However, a *very* high ratio may suggest that the business is undercapitalised – that is, it has insufficient long-term capital to support the level of sales achieved. When comparing this ratio between businesses, such factors as the age and condition of assets held, the valuation bases for assets, and whether assets are rented or purchased outright can affect the calculation of the capital employed figure (as represented by total assets less current liabilities) and can complicate interpretation.

A variation of this formula is to use the total assets less current liabilities (which is equivalent to long-term capital employed) in the denominator (the lower part of the fraction) – the identical result is obtained. This variation is sometimes referred to as the **net asset turnover ratio**.

Sales per employee

The **sales per employee** ratio relates sales generated to a particular business resource. It provides a measure of the productivity of the workforce. The ratio is:

$$\text{Sales per employee} = \frac{\text{Sales}}{\text{Number of employees}}$$

For the year ended 31 March 2001, the ratio for Alexis plc is:

$$\text{Sales per employee} = \frac{£2,240,800}{14}$$
$$= £160,057$$

It would also be possible to use other ratios, such as sales per square metre of floorspace or sales per member of the sales staff, in order to help assess productivity.

Activity 7.11	Calculate the sales per employee for Alexis plc for the year ended 31 March 2002.

The ratio for the year ended 31 March 2002 is:

$$\text{Sales per employee} = \frac{£2,681,200}{18}$$
$$= £148,956$$

Thus the activity ratios for Alexis plc may be summarised as follows:

	2001	2002
Stock turnover period	57 days	59 days
Average settlement period for debtors	39 days	29 days
Average settlement period for creditors	45 days	39 days
Sales to capital employed	3.2 times	3.8 times
Sales per employee	£160,057	£148,956

Activity 7.12

What do you deduce from a comparison of the efficiency ratios of Alexis plc over the two years?

A comparison of the efficiency ratios between years provides a mixed picture. The average settlement period for both debtors and creditors has reduced. The reduction may have been the result of deliberate policy decisions – for example tighter credit control for debtors, or paying creditors promptly in order to maintain goodwill or to take advantage of discounts. However, it must always be remembered that these ratios are *average* figures and therefore may be distorted by a few exceptional amounts owed to, or owed by, a company.

The stock turnover period has shown a slight increase over the period but this may not be significant. Overall, there has been an increase in the sales to capital employed ratio, which means that the sales have increased by a greater proportion than the capital employed by the company. Sales per employee, however, have declined and the reasons for this should be investigated.

Relationship between profitability and efficiency

In our earlier discussions concerning profitability ratios, you will recall that return on capital employed (ROCE) is regarded as a key ratio by many businesses. The ratio is:

$$\text{ROCE} = \frac{\text{Net profit before interest and taxation}}{\text{Long-term capital employed}} \times 100\%$$

(where long-term capital employed comprises share capital plus reserves plus long-term loans). This ratio can be broken down into two elements, as shown in Figure 7.2.

Figure 7.2

The main elements comprising the ROCE ratio

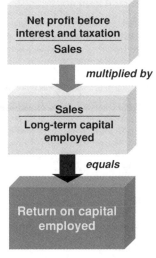

The ROCE ratio can be divided into two main elements: net profit to sales and sales to capital employed. By analysing ROCE in this way, we can see the influence of both profitability and efficiency on this important ratio.

The first ratio is, of course the net profit margin ratio and the second ratio is the sales to capital employed ratio that we discussed earlier. By breaking down the ROCE ratio in this manner, we highlight the fact that the overall return on funds employed within the business will be determined both by the profitability of sales and by the efficiency in the use of capital.

Example 7.2

Consider the following information concerning two different businesses, A and B, operating in the same industry:

	Business	
	A	B
Profit before interest and tax	£20m	£15m
Long-term capital employed	£100m	£75m
Sales	£200m	£300m

The ROCE for each business is identical (20 per cent). However, the manner in which the return was achieved by each business was quite different. In the case of business A, the net profit margin is 10 per cent and the sales to capital employed is 2 times (hence ROCE = [10% × 2] = 20%). In the case of business B, the net profit margin is 5 per cent and the sales to capital employed ratio is 4 times (hence, ROCE = [5% × 4] = 20%).

Example 7.2 demonstrates that a relatively low net profit margin can be compensated for by a relatively high sales to capital employed ratio, and a relatively low sales to capital employed ratio can be compensated for by a relatively high net profit margin. In many areas of retail and distribution (for example supermarkets and delivery services) the net profit margins are quite low but the ROCE can be high, provided that the capital employed is used productively.

Liquidity ratios

There is a number of liquidity ratios, each of which is described further below: the current ratio; the acid test ratio; and the operating cash flows to maturing obligations ratio.

Current ratio

The **current ratio** compares the 'liquid' assets (cash and those assets held that will soon be turned into cash) of a business with the current liabilities (creditors due within one year). The ratio is calculated as follows:

$$\text{Current ratio} = \frac{\text{Current assets}}{\text{Current liabilities (creditors due within one year)}}$$

For the year ended 31 March 2001, the current ratio of Alexis plc is:

$$\text{Current ratio} = \frac{544.2}{291.7}$$

$$= 1.9 \text{ times}$$

The ratio reveals that the current assets cover the current liabilities by 1.9 times.

In some texts the notion of an 'ideal' current ratio (usually 2 times) is suggested for businesses. However, this fails to take into account the fact that different types of business require different current ratios. For example, a manufacturing business will often have a relatively high current ratio because it is necessary to hold stocks of finished goods, raw materials and work in progress. It will also normally sell goods on credit, thereby incurring debtors. A supermarket chain, on the other hand, will have a relatively low current ratio as it will hold only fast-moving stocks of finished goods and will generate mostly cash sales (see Exhibit 7.1).

The higher the ratio, the more liquid the business is considered to be. As liquidity is vital to the survival of a business, a higher current ratio is normally preferred to a lower one. However, if a business has a *very* high ratio, this might suggest that funds are being tied up in cash or other liquid assets and are not being used as productively as they might otherwise be.

Activity 7.13	Calculate the current ratio for Alexis plc for the year ended 31 March 2002.

The current ratio for the year ended 31 March 2002 is:

$$\text{Current ratio} = \frac{584.0}{326.8}$$

$$= 1.8 \text{ times}$$

Acid-test ratio

➡ The **acid-test ratio** represents a more stringent test of liquidity. It can be argued that, for many businesses, the stock in hand cannot be converted into cash quickly. (Note that, in the case of Alexis plc, the stock turnover period was more than 50 days in both years.) As a result, it may be better to exclude this particular asset from any measure of liquidity. The acid-test ratio is based on this idea and is calculated as follows:

$$\text{Acid-test ratio} = \frac{\text{Current assets (excluding stock)}}{\text{Current liabilities (creditors due within one year)}}$$

The acid-test ratio for Alexis plc for the year ended 31 March 2001 is:

$$\text{Acid-test ratio} = \frac{(544.2 - 300)}{291.7}$$

$$= 0.8 \text{ times}$$

We can see that the 'liquid' current assets do not quite cover the current liabilities, and so the business may be experiencing some liquidity problems. In some types of business, however, where a pattern of strong positive cash flows exists, it is not unusual for the acid-test ratio to be below 1.0 without causing liquidity problems (see Exhibit 7.1).

The current and acid-test ratios of Alexis plc for 2001 can be expressed as 1.9 : 1 and 0.8 : 1 respectively, rather than as a number of times. This form can be found in some texts. The interpretation of the ratios, however, will not be affected by this difference in form.

Exhibit 7.1

The average current ratio and average acid-test ratio for UK listed companies operating in various industrial sectors is given below.

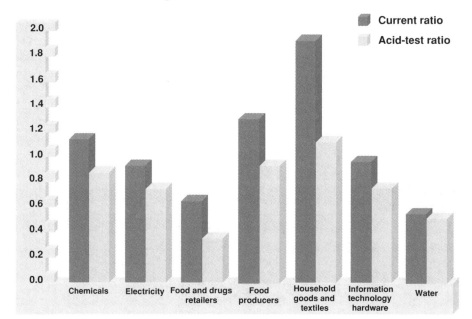

Source: Datastream data, February 2001.

It is interesting to note that nearly all of the sectors reveal an average acid-test ratio of less than 1.0 and that some sectors reveal an average current ratio of less than 1.0.

Activity 7.14

Calculate the acid-test ratio for Alexis plc for the year ended 31 March 2002.

The acid-test ratio for the year ended 31 March 2002 is:

$$\text{Acid-test ratio} = \frac{(584.0 - 370.8)}{326.8}$$

$$= 0.7 \text{ times}$$

Both the current ratio and acid-test ratio derive the relevant figures from the balance sheet. As the balance sheet is simply a 'snapshot' of the financial position of the business at a single moment in time, care must be taken when interpreting the ratios. It is possible that the balance sheet figures are not representative of the liquidity position during the year. This may be owing to exceptional factors or simply to the fact that the business is seasonal in nature and the balance sheet figures represent the cash position at just one particular point in the cycle.

Operating cash flows to maturing obligations

→ The **operating cash flows to maturing obligations** ratio compares the operating cash flows to the current liabilities of the business. It provides a further indication of the ability of the business to meet its maturing obligations. The ratio is expressed as:

$$\text{Operating cash flows to maturing obligations} = \frac{\text{Operating cash flows}}{\text{Current liabilities}}$$

The higher this ratio, the better the liquidity of the business. This ratio has the advantage that the operating cash flows for a period usually provide a more reliable guide to the liquidity of a business than the current assets held at the balance sheet date. The ratio for the year ended 31 March 2001 of Alexis plc is:

$$\text{Operating cash flows to maturing obligations} = \frac{231.0}{291.7}$$

$$= 0.8 \text{ times}$$

This ratio indicates that the operating cash flows for the period are not sufficient to cover the current liabilities at the end of the period.

Activity 7.15	Calculate the operating cash flows to maturing obligations ratio for Alexis plc for the year ended 31 March 2002.

The ratio is:

$$\text{Operating cash flow to maturing obligations} = \frac{251.4}{326.8}$$

$$= 0.8 \text{ times}$$

Thus, the liquidity ratios for Alexis plc for the two-year period may be summarised as follows:

	2001	2002
Current ratio	1.9	1.8
Acid-test ratio	0.8	0.7
Operating cash flows to maturing obligations	0.8	0.8

Activity 7.16	What do you deduce from a comparison of the liquidity ratios of Alexis plc over the two years?

The table above reveals a decrease in both the current ratio and the acid-test ratio. These changes suggest a worsening liquidity position for the business. The company must monitor its liquidity carefully and be alert to any further deterioration in these ratios. The operating cash flows to maturing obligations ratio has not changed over the period. This ratio is quite low and reveals that the cash flows for the period do not cover the maturing obligations. This ratio should give some cause for concern.

Gearing ratios

→ **Financial gearing** occurs when a business is financed, at least in part, by contributions from outside parties. The level of gearing (that is, the extent to which a business is financed by outside parties) is often an important factor in assessing risk. Where a business borrows heavily, it takes on a commitment to pay interest charges and make capital repayments. This can be a significant financial burden and can increase the risk of a business becoming insolvent. Nevertheless, it is the case that most businesses are geared to a greater or lesser extent.

Given the risks involved, you may wonder why a business would want to take on gearing. One reason may be that the owners have insufficient funds and, therefore, the only way to finance the business adequately is to borrow from others. Another reason may be that loan interest is an allowable charge against tax (whereas dividends paid to shareholders are not), and this can reduce the costs of financing the business. A third reason may be that gearing can be used to increase the returns to owners. This is possible provided that the returns generated from borrowed funds exceed the cost of paying interest. Example 7.3 can be used to illustrate this point.

Example 7.3

Two companies X Ltd and Y Ltd commence business with the following long-term capital structures:

	X Ltd £	Y Ltd £
£1 ordinary shares	100,000	200,000
10% loan	200,000	100,000
	300,000	300,000

In the first year of operations they both make a profit before interest and taxation of £50,000.

Although both companies have the same total long-term capital employed, the mix of funding is quite different. X Ltd would be considered highly geared as it has a high proportion of borrowed funds in its long-term capital structure; Y Ltd is much lower geared. The profit available to the shareholders of each company in the first year of operations will be:

	X Ltd £	Y Ltd £
Profit before interest and taxation	50,000	50,000
Interest payable	(20,000)	(10,000)
Profit before taxation	30,000	40,000
Taxation (30%)	(9,000)	(12,000)
Profit available to ordinary shareholders	21,000	28,000

The return on ordinary shareholders' funds for each company will be:

$$\text{X Ltd:} \frac{£21,000}{£100,000} \times 100\% = 21.0\%$$

$$\text{Y Ltd:} \frac{£28,000}{£200,000} \times 100\% = 14.0\%$$

We can see that X Ltd, the more highly geared company, has generated a better return on ordinary shareholders' funds than Y Ltd.

One particular effect of gearing is that returns to ordinary shareholders become more sensitive to changes in profits. For a highly geared company, a change in profits can lead to a proportionately greater change in the returns to ordinary shareholders.

Activity 7.17

Assume that the profit before interest and tax was 20 per cent higher for each company than stated above. What would be the effect of this on the return on ordinary shareholders' funds?

The revised profit available to the shareholders of each company in the first year of operations will be:

	X Ltd £	Y Ltd £
Profit before interest and taxation	60,000	60,000
Interest payable	(20,000)	(10,000)
Profit before taxation	40,000	50,000
Taxation (30%)	(12,000)	(15,000)
Profit available to ordinary shareholders	28,000	35,000

The return on ordinary shareholders' funds for each company will now be:

$$\text{X Ltd:} \frac{£28,000}{£100,000} \times 100\% = 28.0\%$$

$$\text{Y Ltd:} \frac{£35,000}{£200,000} \times 100\% = 17.5\%$$

We can see in Activity 7.17 that, for X Ltd, the higher-geared company, the returns to ordinary shareholders have increased by 33 per cent [(28.0 – 21.0)/21.0], whereas for the lower geared company the benefit of gearing is less pronounced; the increase in the returns to equity for Y Ltd has only been 25 per cent [(17.5 – 14.0)/14.0]. The effect of gearing can, of course, work in both directions. Thus, for a highly-geared company a small decline in profits may bring about a much greater decline in the returns to ordinary shareholders. This means that gearing increases the potential for greater returns to ordinary shareholders but also increases the level of risk that they must bear.

The effect of gearing is like that of two intermeshing cogs of unequal size (see Figure 7.3). The movement in the larger cog (profit before interest and tax) causes a more-than-proportionate movement in the smaller cog (returns to ordinary shareholders).

Gearing ratio

➡ The **gearing ratio** measures the contribution of long-term lenders to the long-term capital structure of a business. It is calculated as follows:

$$\text{Gearing ratio} = \frac{\text{Long-term liabilities}}{\text{Share capital} + \text{Reserves} + \text{Long-term liabilities}} \times 100\%$$

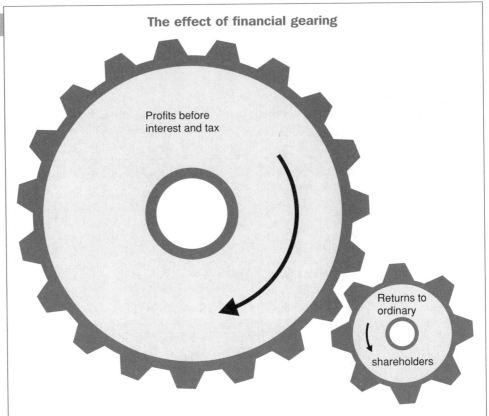

Figure 7.3

The effect of financial gearing

The two wheels are linked by the cogs, so that a relatively small movement in the large wheel (profit before interest and tax) leads to a relatively large circular movement in the small wheel (returns to ordinary shareholders).

The gearing ratio for Alexis plc for the year ended 31 March 2001 is:

$$\text{Gearing ratio} = \frac{200}{(498.3 + 200)} \times 100\%$$
$$= 28.6\%$$

This ratio reveals a level of gearing that would not normally be considered to be very high. However, in deciding what an acceptable level of gearing might be, we should consider the likely future pattern and growth of profits and cash flows. A business that has profits and cash flows that are stable or growing is likely to feel more comfortable about taking on higher levels of gearing than a business that has a volatile pattern of cash flows and profit. This is because the consequences of defaulting on payments of interest, or repayments of capital, are likely to be very serious for the business.

| Activity 7.18 | Calculate the gearing ratio of Alexis plc for the year ended 31 March 2002. |

The gearing ratio will be:

$$\text{Gearing ratio} = \frac{60}{(636.6 + 60)} \times 100\%$$
$$= 8.6\%$$

This ratio reveals (by comparison with the 2001 result above) a substantial fall in the level of gearing over the year for the company.

Interest cover ratio

➡ The **interest cover ratio** measures the amount of profit available to cover the interest payable. The ratio may be calculated as follows:

$$\text{Interest cover ratio} = \frac{\text{Profit before interest and taxation}}{\text{Interest payable}}$$

The ratio for Alexis plc for the year ended 31 March 2001 is:

$$\text{Interest cover ratio} = \frac{(219.4 + 24)}{24}$$
$$= 10.1 \text{ times}$$

This ratio shows that the level of profit is considerably higher than the level of interest payable. Thus, a significant fall in profits could occur before profit levels failed to cover interest payable. The lower the level of profit coverage, the greater the risk to lenders that interest payments will not be met.

| Activity 7.19 | Calculate the interest cover ratio of Alexis plc for the year ended 31 March 2002. |

The interest cover ratio for the year ended 31 March 2002 is:

$$\text{Interest cover ratio} = \frac{(240.2 + 6.2)}{6.2}$$
$$= 39.7 \text{ times}$$

| Activity 7.20 | What do you deduce from a comparison of the gearing ratios over the two years? |

The gearing ratios are:

	2001	2002
Gearing ratio	28.6%	8.6%
Interest cover ratio	10.1 times	39.7 times

Both the gearing ratio and interest cover ratio have improved significantly in 2002. This is owing mainly to the fact that a substantial part of the long-term loan was repaid during 2002. This repayment has had the effect of reducing the relative contribution of long-term lenders to the financing of the company and reducing the amount of interest payable.

The gearing ratio at the end of 2002 would normally be considered to be very low and may indicate that the business has some debt capacity (that is, it is capable of borrowing more if required). However, other factors such as the availability of adequate security and profitability must also be taken into account before the debt capacity of a business can be properly assessed.

Investment ratios

There are various ratios available that are designed to help investors who hold shares in a company to assess the returns on their investment. We consider some of these ratios next.

Dividend per share

➡ The **dividend per share** ratio relates the dividends announced during a period to the number of shares in issue during that period. The ratio is calculated as follows:

$$\text{Dividend per share} = \frac{\text{Dividends announced during the period}}{\text{Number of shares in issue}}$$

In essence, the ratio provides an indication of the cash return that a shareholder receives from holding shares in a company. Although it is a useful measure, it must always be remembered that the dividends received will usually only represent a partial measure of return to investors. Dividends are usually only a proportion of the total earnings generated by a company and available to shareholders. A company may decide to plough back some of its earnings into the business in order to achieve future growth. These ploughed-back profits also belong to the shareholders and should, in principle, increase the value of the shares held.

When assessing the total returns to investors, we must take account of both the cash returns received *plus* any change in the market value of the shares held.

The dividend per share for Alexis plc for the year ended 31 March 2001 is:

$$\text{Dividend per share} = \frac{40.2}{600} \quad \text{(that is, £0.50 shares and £300 share capital)}$$
$$= 6.7\text{p}$$

This ratio can be calculated for each class of share issued by a company. Alexis plc has only ordinary shares in issue and therefore only one dividend per share ratio can be calculated.

Activity 7.21

Calculate the dividend per share of Alexis plc for the year ended 31 March 2002.

The dividend per share for the year ended 31 March 2002 is:

$$\text{Dividend per share} = \frac{60.0}{668.2}$$
$$= 9.0\text{p}$$

Dividends per share can vary considerably between companies. A number of factors will influence the amount that a company is willing or able to issue in the form of dividends to shareholders. These factors include:

- The profit available for distribution to investors.
- The future expenditure commitments of the company.
- The expectations of shareholders concerning the level of dividend payment.
- The cash available for dividend distribution.

Comparing dividend per share between companies is not always useful as there may be differences between the nominal value of shares issued. However, it is often useful to monitor the trend of dividends per share for a company over a period of time.

Dividend payout ratio

The **dividend payout ratio** measures the proportion of earnings that a company pays out to shareholders in the form of dividends. The ratio is calculated as follows:

$$\text{Dividend payout ratio} = \frac{\text{Dividends announced for the year}}{\text{Earnings for the year available for dividends}} \times 100\%$$

In the case of ordinary (equity) shares, the earnings available for dividend will normally be the net profit after taxation and after any preference dividends announced during the period. This ratio is normally expressed as a percentage.

The dividend payout ratio for Alexis plc for the year ended 31 March 2001 is:

$$\text{Dividend payout ratio} = \frac{40.2}{159.2} \times 100\%$$
$$= 25.3\%$$

The information provided by this ratio is often expressed slightly differently as the **dividend cover ratio**. Here, the calculation is the inverse of the dividend payout ratio:

$$\text{Dividend cover ratio} = \frac{\text{Earnings for the year available for dividend}}{\text{Dividend announced for the year}}$$

In the case of Alexis plc, it would be (159.2/40.2) = 3.96 times. That is to say, the earnings available for dividend cover the amount announced by nearly four times.

Activity 7.22   Calculate the dividend payout ratio of Alexis plc for the year ended 31 March 2002.

The dividend payout ratio for the year ended 31 March 2002 is:

$$\text{Dividend payout ratio} = \frac{60.0}{164.2} \times 100\%$$
$$= 36.5\%$$

Dividend yield ratio

→ The **dividend yield ratio** relates the cash return from a share to its current market value. This can help investors to assess the cash return on their investment in the company. The ratio is calculated as:

$$\text{Dividend yield} = \frac{\text{Dividend per share}/(1 - t)}{\text{Market value per share}} \times 100\%$$

where t is the 'lower' rate of income tax. The numerator (the top part) of this ratio requires some explanation. In the UK, investors who receive a dividend from a company also receive a tax credit. This tax credit is equal to the amount of tax that would be payable on the dividends received by a lower-rate income-tax payer. As this tax credit can be offset against any tax liability arising from the dividends received, this means that the dividends are in effect issued net of tax to lower-rate income-tax payers.

Investors may wish to compare the returns from shares with the returns from other forms of investment. As these other forms of investment are often quoted on a 'gross' (pre-tax) basis, it is useful to 'gross up' the dividend in order to make comparison easier. This can be done by dividing the dividend per share by $(1 - t)$.

Assuming a lower rate of income tax of 10 per cent, the dividend yield for Alexis plc for the year ended 31 March 2002 is:

$$\text{Dividend yield} = \frac{£0.067^*/(1 - 0.10)}{£2.50} \times 100\%$$

$$= 3.0\%$$

$$^* \frac{\text{Dividend proposed}}{\text{Number of shares}} = \frac{£40.2}{300.0 \times 2} = £0.067 \text{ dividend per share}$$

(The 300.0 is multiplied by 2 because they are £0.50 shares.)

Activity 7.23	Calculate the dividend yield for Alexis plc for the year ended 31 March 2002.

The dividend yield for the year ended 31 March 2002 is:

$$\text{Dividend yield} = \frac{£0.09^*/(1 - 0.10)}{£3.50} \times 100\%$$

$$= 2.9\%$$

$$^* \frac{£60.0}{334.1 \times 2} = £0.09$$

Earnings per share (EPS)

→ The **earnings per share** (EPS) relates the earnings generated by the company during a period and available to shareholders to the number of shares in issue. For ordinary shareholders, the amount available will be represented by the net profit after tax (less any preference dividend where applicable). The ratio for ordinary shareholders is calculated as follows:

$$\text{Earnings per share} = \frac{\text{Earnings available to ordinary shareholders}}{\text{Number of ordinary shares in issue}}$$

In the case of Alexis plc, the earnings per share for the year ended 31 March 2001 will be as follows:

$$\text{Earnings per share} = \frac{£159.2}{600}$$

$$= 26.5p$$

The EPS is regarded by many investment analysts as a fundamental measure of share performance. The trend in earnings per share over time is used to help assess the investment potential of a company's shares.

Although it is possible to make total profits rise through ordinary shareholders investing more in a company, this will not necessarily mean that the profitability *per share* will rise as a result.

Activity 7.24

Calculate the earnings per share of Alexis plc for the year ended 31 March 2002.

The earnings per share for the year ended 31 March 2002 will be:

$$\text{Earnings per share} = \frac{£164.2}{668.2}$$

$$= 24.6p$$

In the case of Alexis plc, the new issue of shares occurred at the beginning of the financial year. Where an issue is made part-way through the year, a weighted average of the shares in issue will be taken based on the date at which the new share issue took place.

It is not usually very helpful to compare the earnings per share from one company to another. Differences in capital structures can render any such comparison meaningless. However, like dividend per share, it can be very useful to monitor the changes that occur in this ratio for a particular company over time.

Operating cash flow per share

It can be argued that, in the short run at least, operating cash flows provide a better guide to the ability of a company to pay dividends and to undertake planned expenditures than the earnings per share figure. The **operating cash flow (OCF) per ordinary share** is calculated as follows:

$$\text{OCF per ordinary share} = \frac{\text{Operating cash flows} - \text{Preference dividends (if any)}}{\text{Number of ordinary shares in issue}}$$

The ratio for Alexis plc for the year ended 31 March 2001 is as follows:

$$\text{OCF per share} = \frac{£231.0}{600.0}$$

$$= 38.5p$$

Activity 7.25

Calculate the OCF per ordinary share for Alexis plc for the year ended 31 March 2002.

The OCF per share for the year ended 31 March 2002 is:

$$\text{OCF per share} = \frac{£251.4}{668.2}$$

$$= 37.6p$$

There has been a slight decline in this ratio over the two-year period.

Note that, for both years, the operating cash flow per share for Alexis plc is higher than the earnings per share. This is not unusual. The effect of adding back depreciation in order to derive operating cash flows will often ensure that a higher figure is derived.

Price/earnings (P/E) ratio

→ The **price/earnings ratio** relates the market value of a share to the earnings per share. This ratio can be calculated as follows:

$$\text{P/E ratio} = \frac{\text{Market value per share}}{\text{Earnings per share}}$$

The EPS figure for Alexis plc was calculated earlier in this chapter for the year to 31 March 2001 as 26.5p. The P/E ratio for Alexis plc for that year can be calculated thus:

$$\text{P/E ratio} = \frac{£2.50}{£0.265}$$

$$= 9.4 \text{ times}$$

This ratio reveals that the capital value of the share is 9.4 times higher than its current level of earnings.

The ratio is, in essence, a measure of market confidence in the future of a company. The higher the P/E ratio, the greater the confidence in the future earning power of the company and, consequently, the more that investors are prepared to pay in relation to the earnings stream of the company.

Price/earnings ratios provide a useful guide to market confidence concerning the future, and therefore they can be helpful when comparing different companies. However, differences in accounting conventions between businesses can lead to different profit and earnings-per-share figures, and this can distort comparisons.

Activity 7.26

Calculate the P/E ratio of Alexis plc for the year ended 31 March 2002.

The P/E ratio for the year ended 31 March 2002 is:

$$\text{P/E ratio} = \frac{£3.50}{£0.246}$$

$$= 14.2 \text{ times}$$

Thus, the investment ratios for Alexis plc over the two-year period are as follows:

	2001	2002
Dividend per share	6.7p	9.0p
Dividend payout ratio	25.3%	36.5%
Dividend yield ratio	3.0%	2.9%
Earnings per share	26.5p	24.6p
Operating cash flow per share	38.5p	37.6p
Price/earnings ratio	9.4 times	14.2 times

Activity 7.27

What do you deduce from the investment ratios set out above?

There has been a significant increase in the dividend per share in 2002 when compared with the previous year. The dividend payout ratio reveals that this can be attributed, at least in part, to an increase in the proportion of earnings distributed to ordinary shareholders. However, the payout ratio for the year ended 31 March 2002 is still fairly low. Only about one third of earnings available for dividend is being distributed. The dividend yield has changed very little over the period and remains fairly low.

Earnings per share show a slight fall in 2002 when compared with the previous year. A slight fall also occurs in the operating cash flows per share. However, the price/earnings ratio shows a significant improvement. The market is clearly much more confident about the future prospects of the business at 31 March 2002 than it had been 12 months earlier.

Exhibit 7.2 gives some information about the shares of several large food retailers and Exhibit 7.3 shows how investment ratios can vary between different industry sectors.

Exhibit 7.2

The following shares were extracted from the *Financial Times* of 8 December 2000, relating to the previous day trading on the London Stock Exchange:

Retail food Share	Price	(+/–)	52 week High	Low	Volume 000s	Y'ld Gr's	P/E
Iceland	334	+3	$345\frac{1}{2}$	228	7,828	2.0	15.0
Safeway	300	–6	335	147	6,221	2.9	16.3
Sainsbury	394	$+11\frac{1}{4}$	438	237	6,815	3.6	22.5
Somerfield	$85\frac{1}{2}$	$-\frac{1}{2}$	$97\frac{1}{2}$	45	3,121	1.8	7.4
Tesco	$270\frac{1}{4}$	$+7\frac{1}{4}$	$292\frac{1}{2}$	$153\frac{1}{2}$	30,001	1.7	25.2

The column headings are as follows:

Price — Mid-market price (that is the price midway between buying and selling price) of the stock at the end of 7 December 2000.

(+/–) — Gain or loss (usually stated in pence) from the previous day's mid-market price.

High/Low — Highest and lowest prices reached by the share during the year (stated in pence).

Volume — The number of shares (in thousands) that were bought and sold on 7 December 2000.

Y'ld gross — Gross dividend yield, based on the most recent year's dividend and the current share price.

P/E — Price/earnings ratio, based on the most recent year's after-tax profit and the current share price.

Exhibit 7.3

Investment ratios can vary significantly between industries. To give you some indication of the variation that occurs, the average dividend yield ratio and the P/E ratio for Stock Exchange listed companies falling within twelve different industries are shown below in the charts. The relevant financial information was derived from that available in the *Financial Times* of 8 December 2000.

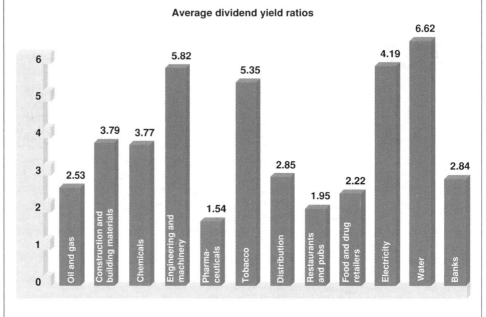

Average dividend yield ratios

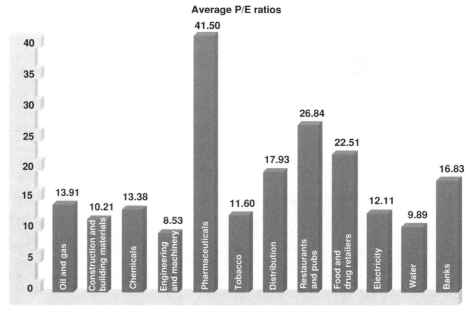

Average P/E ratios

? Self-assessment question 7.1

A plc and B plc operate electrical wholesale stores in the south of England. The accounts of each company for the year ended 30 June 2001 are as follows:

Balance sheets as at 30 June 2001

	A plc		B plc	
	£000	£000	£000	£000
Fixed assets				
Freehold land and buildings at cost	436.0		615.0	
Less Accumulated depreciation	76.0	360.0	105.0	510.0
Fixtures and fittings at cost	173.4		194.6	
Less Accumulated depreciation	86.4	87.0	103.4	91.2
		447.0		601.2
Current assets				
Stock at cost	592.0		403.0	
Debtors	176.4		321.9	
Cash at bank	84.6		91.0	
	853.0		815.9	
Creditors due within one year				
Trade creditors	(271.4)		(180.7)	
Dividends	(135.0)		(95.0)	
Corporation tax	(16.0)		(17.4)	
	(422.4)	430.6	(293.1)	523.4
		877.6		1,124.6
Creditors due beyond one year				
Debentures		(190.0)		(250.0)
		687.6		874.6
Capital and reserves				
£1 ordinary shares		320.0		250.0
General reserves		355.9		289.4
Retained profit		11.7		335.2
		687.6		874.6

Trading and profit and loss accounts for the year ended 30 June 2001

	A plc		B plc	
	£000	£000	£000	£000
Sales		1,478.1		1,790.4
Less Cost of sales				
Opening stock	480.8		372.6	
Purchases	1,129.5		1,245.3	
	1,610.3		1,617.9	
Less closing stock	592.0	1,018.3	403.0	1,214.9
Gross profit		459.8		575.5
Wages and salaries	150.4		189.2	
Directors salaries	45.4		96.2	
Rates	28.5		15.3	
Heat and light	15.8		17.2	
Insurance	18.5		26.8	
Postage and telephone	12.4		15.9	
Audit fees	11.0		12.3	

	A plc		B plc	
Depreciation:	£000	£000	£000	£000
Freehold buildings	8.8		12.9	
Fixtures and fittings	17.7	308.5	22.8	408.6
Net profit before interest and tax		151.3		166.9
Less Interest charges		19.4		27.5
Net profit before tax		131.9		139.4
Corporation tax		(32.0)		(34.8)
Net profit after taxation		99.9		104.6
Add Retained profit brought forward		46.8		325.6
		146.7		430.2
Dividends proposed		(135.0)		(95.0)
Retained profit carried forward		11.7		335.2

All purchases and sales are on credit. The market values of the shares in each company at the end of the year were £6.50 and £8.20 respectively.

Required:

For each company, calculate two ratios that are concerned with each of liquidity, gearing and investment (six ratios in total). What can you conclude from the ratios you have calculated?

Financial ratios and the problem of overtrading

➜ **Overtrading** occurs where a business is operating at a level of activity that cannot be supported by the amount of finance that has been committed. This situation usually reflects a poor level of financial control over the business. The reasons for overtrading are varied. It may occur in young, expanding businesses that fail to prepare adequately for the rapid increase in demand for its goods or services. It may also occur in businesses where the managers may have miscalculated the level of expected sales demand or have failed to control escalating project costs. It may occur as a result of a fall in the value of money (inflation), causing more finance to be committed to stock in trade and debtors, even where there is no expansion in the real volume of trade. It may occur where the owners are unable both to inject further funds into the business and to persuade others to invest in the business. Whatever the reason for overtrading, the problems that it brings must be dealt with if the business is to survive over the longer term.

Overtrading results in liquidity problems such as exceeding borrowing limits, or slow repayment of lenders and creditors. It can also result in suppliers withholding supplies, thereby making it difficult to meet customer needs. The managers of the business might be forced to direct all their efforts to dealing with immediate and pressing problems, such as finding cash to meet interest charges due or paying wages. Longer-term planning becomes difficult and managers may spend their time going from crisis to crisis. At the extreme, a business may collapse because it cannot meet its maturing obligations.

In order to deal with the overtrading problem, a business must ensure that the finance available is commensurate with the level of operations. Thus, if a business that is overtrading is unable to raise new finance, it should cut back its level of operations in line with the finance available. Although this may mean lost sales and lost profits in the short term, it may be necessary to ensure survival over the longer term.

Activity 7.28	If a business is overtrading, do you think the following ratios would be higher or lower than normally expected?

(a) Current ratio
(b) Average stock turnover period
(c) Average settlement period for debtors
(d) Average settlement period for creditors

Your answer should be as follows:

(a) The current ratio would be lower than normally expected. This is a measure of liquidity, and lack of liquidity is an important symptom of overtrading.
(b) The average stock turnover period would be lower than normally expected. Where a business is overtrading, the level of stocks held will be low because of the problems of financing stocks. In the short term, sales may not be badly affected by the low stock levels and therefore stocks will be turned over more quickly.
(c) The average settlement period for debtors may be lower than normally expected. Where a business is suffering from liquidity problems it may chase debtors more vigorously so as to improve cash flows.
(d) The average settlement period for creditors may be higher than normally expected. The business may try to delay payments to creditors because of the liquidity problems arising.

Trend analysis

It is important to see whether there are trends occurring that can be detected from the use of ratios. Thus, key ratios can be plotted on a graph to provide users with a simple visual display of changes occurring over time. The trends occurring within a company may be plotted against those occurring within the industry as a whole for comparison purposes. An example of trend analysis is shown in Figure 7.4.

Figure 7.4	**Graph plotting current ratio against time**

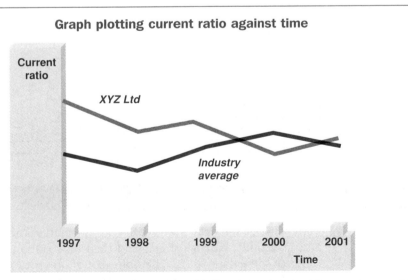

Plotting key ratios for a company over time, along with the relevant industry ratios, can be a useful way of detecting trends for a particular business and for comparing the extent to which these trends are in line with those of the industry as a whole.

Some companies publish key financial ratios as part of their annual accounts in order to help users identify important trends. Exhibit 7.4 shows ratios for a ten-year period for Tate & Lyle plc, as taken from its annual accounts.

| Exhibit 7.4 | The following ratios, covering the period 1991–2000 are included in the annual accounts of Tate & Lyle plc, the sugar (and other foods) business. |

Business Ratios

	1991	1992	1993	1994	1995	1996	1997	1998	1999	2000
Interest cover – times	6.5	5.0	5.5	6.7	7.9	6.6	3.5	4.2	3.5	**3.9**
Profit before interest less share of joint ventures' and associates' interest divided by net interest charge – excluding exceptional items	5.9	5.0	5.5	6.7	8.2	6.9	5.0	4.3	3.6	**4.5**
Gearing	81%	96%	92%	84%	75%	75%	84%	92%	84%	**64%**
Net borrowing as a percentage of net assets										
Net margin	8.8%	9.0%	7.6%	7.9%	8.7%	8.3%	5.6%	6.4%	5.9%	**7.0%**
Profit before interest and exceptional items as a percentage of turnover										
Return on net operating assets	20.5%	20.7%	16.2%	17.7%	20.4%	20.3%	13.3%	13.7%	11.9%	**13.5%**
Profit before interest and exceptional items as a percentage of average net operating assets										
Dividend cover – times	3.6	2.6	2.7	3.1	3.3	3.1	1.0	1.8	1.8	**1.1**
Earnings per share divided by dividends per share – excluding exceptional items	3.3	2.6	2.4	2.9	3.0	3.3	2.2	2.1	1.7	**1.4**

Common-size financial statements

➡ **Common-size financial statements** are normal financial statements (such as the P and L account, balance sheet, and cash flow statement), which are expressed in terms of some base figure. The objective of presenting financial statements in this way is to help make better comparisons. The detection of differences and trends is often more obvious than may be the case when examining the original statements, which are expressed in financial values.

One approach to common-size statements is to express all the figures in a particular statement in terms of one of the figures in that statement. This 'base' figure is typically one that is seen as a key figure in the statement, such as sales in a P and L account, total long-term funds in a balance sheet and the net cash flow from operating activities in the cash flow statement.

Example 7.4 is a common-size P and L account that uses sales as the base figure. Note the base figure is set at 100 and all other figures are expressed as a percentage of this.

Example 7.4

The common-size P and L account of Alexis plc (see Example 7.1 on page 191) for 2001 in abbreviated form, and using sales as the base figure, will be as follows:

Common-size P and L account for the year ended 31 March 2001

		Calculation of figures
Sales	100.0	Base figure
Cost of sales	(77.9)	$(1,745.4/2,240.8) \times 100\%$
Gross profit	22.1	$(495.4/2,240.8) \times 100\%$
Operating expenses	(11.2)	$(252.0/2,240.8) \times 100\%$
Net profit before interest and tax	10.9	$(243.4/2,240.8) \times 100\%$
Less Interest payable	1.1	$(24.0/2,240.8) \times 100\%$
Net profit before tax	9.8	$(219.4/2,240.8) \times 100\%$
Less Corporation tax	2.7	$(60.2/2,240.8) \times 100\%$
Net profit after tax	7.1	$(159.2/2,240.8) \times 100\%$

Each of the figures in the P and L account is simply the original financial figure divided by the sales figure and then expressed as a percentage.

Of course, not much can be discerned from looking at just one common-size statement. We need some benchmark for comparison, and this could be other accounting periods for the same business.

Activity 7.29

The following is a set of common-size P and L accounts for a major high street department store for five consecutive accounting periods:

	Year 1	Year 2	Year 3	Year 4	Year 5
Sales	100.0	100.0	100.0	100.0	100.0
Cost of sales	(68.9)	(68.5)	(67.2)	(66.5)	(66.3)
Gross profit	31.1	31.5	32.8	33.5	33.7
Other operating expenses	(28.1)	(28.4)	(27.6)	(29.2)	(30.2)
Operating profit	3.0	3.1	5.2	4.3	3.5
Interest	(1.1)	(1.2)	(1.6)	(2.1)	(1.3)
Profit before tax	1.9	1.9	3.6	2.2	2.2

What significant features are revealed by the common-size P and L accounts?

Operating profit, relative to sales, rose in Year 3 but fell back again in Years 4 and 5 to end the five-year period at much the same level as it had been in Years 1 and 2. Although the gross profit margin rose steadily over the five-year period, the operating expenses also rose steadily, with the exception of Year 3. Clearly, the fall in operating expenses to sales in Year 3 led to the improvement in operating profit to sales.

The common-size financial statements being compared do not have to be for the same business. They can be for different businesses. Exhibit 7.5 is a set of common-size balance sheets for five UK businesses that are either very well known by name, or whose products are everyday commodities for most of us. The figures in each of the five balance sheets are the actual financial figures, expressed as a percentage of the total long-term finance (share capital plus reserves plus long-term borrowings) in each case.

Exhibit 7.5	Business	The Boots Company plc	Rolls-Royce plc	The Go-ahead Group plc	Fuller Smith and Turner plc	Anglia Water plc
	Balance sheet date	31.3.00	31.12.99	1.7.00	25.3.00	31.3.00
		%	%	%	%	%
	Fixed assets	84	73	114	96	99
	Current assets					
	Stock	29	33	2	3	–
	Trade debtors	12	23	14	4	4
	Other debtors	6	21	23	3	2
	Cash and near cash	18	25	26	8	4
		65	102	65	18	10
	Current liabilities					
	Trade creditors	15	17	17	5	3
	Tax and dividends	14	8	13	5	–
	Other short-term liabilities	11	39	46	4	4
	Overdrafts and short-term loans	9	11	3	–	2
		49	75	79	14	9
	Working capital	16	27	(14)	4	1
	Total long-term investment	100	100	100	100	100

The businesses were randomly selected from different industries. Boots (the high-street chemist) is a manufacturer and retailer of health and personal care products. Rolls-Royce manufactures engines and electrical generating equipment. Go-Ahead provides urban public train and bus services including Thames trains. Fuller Smith and Turner manages pubs and hotels in and around London, also brewing, perhaps most famously London Pride bitter. Anglia Water supplies water and collects and treats waste water.

It is quite striking, in Exhibit 7.5, how different the make up of the balance sheet is from one business to the next. This seems particularly so for working capital. Though the percentages for current assets are generally pretty large in relation to the total long-term investment, these percentages vary considerably from one type of business to the next. Rolls-Royce is the only business that is solely engaged in manufacturing and so may be expected to have a relatively large investment in stocks. However, Boots also has manufacturing operations and also has a relatively large investment in this asset. Go-Ahead and Anglia provide a service and so hold little or no stock. Most of Anglia's sales are paid for in advance (water rates), so it has low trade debtors. Rolls-Royce makes most of its sales on credit and so has relatively high trade debtors.

So far we have been considering what is known as **vertical analysis**. That is we have been treating all of the figures in each statement as a percentage of a figure in that statement, the sales figure, in the case of the P and L account, and the total long-term investment with the balance sheet. Note that common-size statements do not have to be expressed in terms of any particular factor; it is up to the individual carrying out the analysis. It seems, however, that sales and long-term investment are popular bases for vertically analysed common-size P and L accounts and balance sheets, respectively.

Horizontal analysis is an alternative to the vertical analysis that we have seen so far. Here the figures appearing in a particular financial statement are expressed as a base figure (that is 100) and the equivalent figures appearing in similar statements are expressed as a percentage of this base figure. So, for example, the stock figure appearing in a particular balance sheet may be set as the base figure (that is, set at 100) and then the stock figures appearing in successive balance sheets could each be expressed as a percentage of this base stock figure. The 'base' statement would normally be the earliest (or latest) of a set of statements for the same business. Where the analysis was between businesses, as in Exhibit 7.5 (above), selecting which business should be the base one is not so obvious, unless one of the businesses is the one of most interest, perhaps because the objective is to compare a particular business with each of the others in turn.

Exhibit 7.6 show a horizontal analysis for the business, a department store, that was the subject of Activity 7.29.

Exhibit 7.6

The following is a set of common-size P and L accounts for a major high street department store for five consecutive accounting periods, using horizontal analysis and making Year 1 the base year:

	Year 1	Year 2	Year 3	Year 4	Year 5
Sales	100.0	104.3	108.4	106.5	108.9
Cost of sales	(100.0)	(103.7)	(105.7)	(102.9)	(104.8)
Gross profit	100.0	105.5	114.4	114.5	118.0
Other operating expenses	(100.0)	(105.4)	(106.7)	(110.4)	(117.2)
Operating profit	100.0	106.6	185.9	153.3	125.6
Interest	(100.0)	(111.9)	(157.1)	(202.4)	(127.4)
Profit before tax	100.0	103.5	202.8	124.5	124.5

Year 1 is the base year so all of the figures in the Year 1 P and L account are 100.0. All of the figures for the other years are that year's figure divided by the year 1 figure for the same item and then expressed as a percentage. For example, the Year 4 profit before tax, divided by the profit before tax for Year 1 was 124.5 or the Year 4 profit was 24.5% greater in year 4 than it had been for year 1. (By coincidence, the profits for Years 4 and 5 were identical.)

Activity 7.30	What are the significant features revealed by by the common-size P and L accounts in Exhibit 7.6?

Sales did not show much of an increase over the five years, particularly if these figures are not adjusted for inflation. Years 2 and 3 saw increases, but Years 4 and 5 were less impressive. The rate of increase in the cost of sales was less, and, therefore, the gross profit growth was greater, than the rate of increase of sales. Other operating expenses showed fairly steady growth over the years. Interest increased strongly during the first four years of the period, but then fell back significantly in Year 5.

Activity 7.31	The vertical approach to common-size financial statements has the advantage of being able to see each figure expressed in terms of the same item (sales, long-term finance and so on). What are the disadvantages of this approach and how do horizontally analysed common-sized statements overcome any problems, and what problems do they bring.

The problem with the horizontal approach is that it is not possible to see, for example, that sales are different from one year or business to the next. Normally a vertically analysed common-size P and L account shows the sales figure as 100 for all years or businesses. This is, of course, a problem of all approaches to ratio analysis.

Horizontally analysed common-sized statements overcome this problem because, say, sales figures are expressed in terms of one year or one particular business. This makes differences in sales levels crystal clear. Unfortunately, such an approach makes comparison within each year's, or within a particular business's, statement rather difficult.

Perhaps the answer is to produce two sets of common-size statements, one analysed vertically and the other horizontally.

The use of ratios in predicting financial distress

Financial ratios, based on current or past performance, are often used to help predict the future. However, both the choice of ratios and the interpretation of results are normally dependent on the judgement of the analyst. In recent years, however, attempts have been made to develop a more rigorous and systematic approach to the use of ratios for prediction purposes. In particular, researchers have shown an interest in the ability of ratios to predict financial distress in a business. This, of course, is an area with which all those connected with the business are likely to be concerned.

A number of methods and models employing ratios have now been developed that claim to predict future financial distress. Early research focused on the examination of ratios on an individual basis to see whether they were good or bad predictors of financial distress. The first research in this area was carried out by Beaver (see reference (1) at the end of the chapter) which compared the mean ratios of 79 businesses that failed over a ten-year period with a sample of 79 businesses that did not fail over this period. (The research used a matched-pair design, where each failed business was matched with a non-failed business of similar size and industry type.) Beaver found that certain mean ratios exhibited a marked difference between the failed and non-failed businesses for up to five years prior to failure (see Figure 7.5).

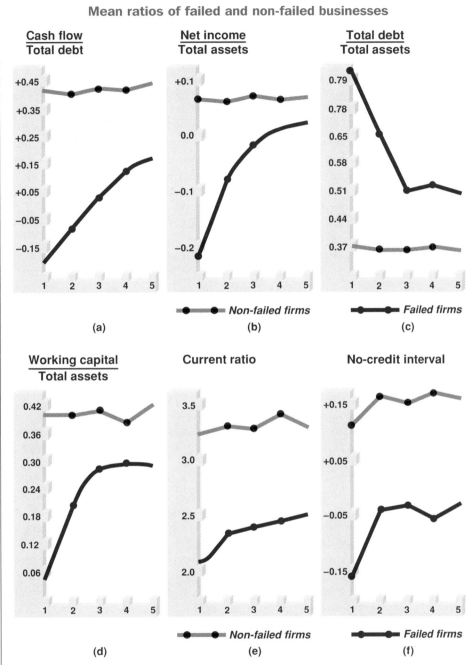

Figure 7.5

Mean ratios of failed and non-failed businesses

Each of the ratios (a)–(f) above indicates a marked difference in the average ratio between the sample of failed businesses and a matched sample of non-failed businesses. The difference between each of the average ratios can be detected five years prior to the failure of those businesses within the failed sample. (From Beaver – see ref. (1) at the end of chapter.)

Note: The no-credit interval is the same as the operating cash flows to maturing obligations ratio discussed earlier in the chapter.

Research by Zmijewski (see reference (2) at the end of the chapter) using a sample of 72 failed and 3,573 non-failed businesses over a six-year period found that failed businesses were characterised by lower rates of return, higher levels of gearing, lower levels of coverage for their fixed interest payments and more variable returns on shares. Whilst you may not find these results very surprising, it is interesting to note that Zmijewski, like a number of other researchers in this area, did not find liquidity ratios particularly useful in identifying financial distress.

The approach adopted by Beaver and Zmijewski is referred to as **univariate analysis** because it looks at one ratio at a time. Although this approach can produce interesting results, there are practical problems associated with its use. Let us say, for example, that past research has identified two ratios as being good predictors in identifying financial distress. When applied to a particular business, however, it may be found that one ratio predicts financial distress whereas the other does not. Given these conflicting signals, how should the decision maker interpret the results?

The weaknesses of univariate analysis have led researchers to develop models that combine ratios in such a way as to produce a single index that can be interpreted more clearly. One approach to model development, much favoured by researchers, employs **multiple discriminate analysis (MDA)**. This is, in essence, a statistical technique that can be used to draw a boundary between those businesses that fail and those businesses that do not. This boundary is referred to as the **discriminate function**. MDA attempts to identify those factors likely to influence a particular event (such as financial failure). However, unlike regression analysis, MDA assumes that the observations come from two different populations (for example, failed and non-failed businesses) rather than from a single population.

To illustrate this approach, let us assume that we wish to test whether two ratios (say, the current ratio and the return on capital employed) can help to predict distress. In order to do this, we can calculate these ratios first for a sample of failed businesses and then for a matched sample of non-failed businesses. From these two sets of data we can produce a scatter diagram that plots each business according to these two ratios to produce a single co-ordinate. Figure 7.6 illustrates this approach. Using the observations plotted on the diagram, we try to identify the boundary between the failed and the non-failed businesses.

We can see in Figure 7.6 that those businesses that fall to the left of the line are predominantly failed companies and those that fall to the right are predominantly non-failed companies. Note that there is some overlap between the two populations. The boundary produced is unlikely, in practice, to eliminate all errors, and so some businesses that fail may fall on the side of the boundary with non-failed companies, and vice versa. However, it will *minimise* the misclassification errors.

The boundary shown in Figure 7.6 can be expressed in the form:

$$Z = a + b \times \textbf{(current ratio)} + c \times \textbf{(ROCE)}$$

where a is a constant and b and c are weights to be attached to each ratio. A weighted average or total score (Z) is then derived. The weights given to the two ratios will depend on the slope of the line and its absolute position.

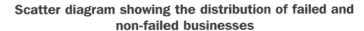

Figure 7.6

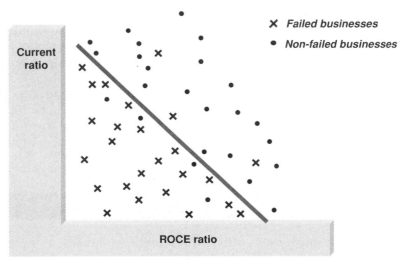

Scatter diagram showing the distribution of failed and non-failed businesses

✗ *Failed businesses*

● *Non-failed businesses*

Current ratio

ROCE ratio

The figure shows the distribution of failed and non-failed businesses based on two ratios. The line represents a boundary between the samples of failed and non-failed businesses. Although there is some crossing of the boundary, the boundary represents the line that minimises the problem of mis-classifying particular businesses.

Edward Altman (see reference (3) at the end of the chapter) in the USA was the first to develop a model using financial ratios in order to predict financial distress. His model, the *Z* score model, is based on five financial ratios and is as follows:

$$Z = 1.2a + 1.4b + 3.3c + 0.6d + 1.0e$$

where *a* = Working capital/Total assets
   b = Accumulated retained profits/Total assets
   c = Profit before interest and taxation/Total assets
   d = Market value of ordinary and preference shares/Total liabilities at book value
   e = Sales/Total assets

In order to develop this model, Altman carried out experiments using a paired sample of failed businesses and non-failed businesses and collected relevant data for each business for five years prior to failure. He found that the model shown through the formula above was able to predict failure for up to two years prior to bankruptcy. However, the predictive accuracy of the model became weaker the further the period from failure.

The ratios used in this model were identified by Altman through a process of trial and error as there is no underlying theory of financial distress to help guide researchers in their selection of appropriate ratios. According to Altman, those companies with a *Z* score of less than 1.81 failed, and the lower the score the greater the probability of failure. Those with a *Z* score greater than 2.99 did not fail. Those businesses with a *Z* score between 1.81 and 2.99 occupied a 'zone of ignorance' and were difficult to classify. However, the model was able overall to classify 95 per cent of the businesses correctly.

In recent years, this model has been updated and other models, using a similar approach, have been developed throughout the world. In the UK, Taffler (see reference (4) at the end of the chapter) has developed separate *Z* score models for different types of business.

The prediction of financial distress is not the only area where research into the predictive ability of ratios has taken place. Researchers have also developed ratio-based models that claim to assess the vulnerability of a company to takeover by another company. This is another area that is of vital importance to all those connected with the business.

Limitations of ratio analysis

Although ratios offer a quick and useful method of analysing the position and performance of a business, they are not without their limitations. Some of the more important limitations are considered below.

■ *Quality of financial statements.*   It must always be remembered that ratios are based on financial statements and that the results of ratio analysis are dependent on the quality of those underlying statements. Ratios will inherit the limitations of the financial statements on which they are based. Some of the more important points concerning the quality of financial statements are considered next.

One important issue when making comparisons between businesses is the degree of conservatism that each business adopts in the reporting of profit. Any review of the financial statements should, therefore, include an examination of the accounting policies that are being adopted. Some businesses adopt a very conservative approach, which would be reflected in particular accounting policies such as the immediate writing off of intangible assets (for example, research and development and goodwill), the use of the reducing balance method of depreciation (which favours high depreciation charges in the early years), and so on. The effect of these policies is to report profit later rather than sooner, and so when profits are reported they are often referred to as being 'of high quality'. Businesses that do not adopt conservative accounting policies would report profits more quickly. The writing off of intangible assets over a long period (or perhaps, not writing off intangible assets at all), the use of the straight-line method of depreciation, and so on will mean that profits are reported more quickly.

In addition, there are some businesses that may adopt particular accounting policies or structure particular transactions in such a way that portrays a picture of financial health that is in line with what those who prepared the financial statements would like to see rather than what is a true and fair view of financial performance and position. This practice is referred to as **creative accounting** and has been a major problem for accounting rule-makers.

Exhibit 7.7	**The thoughts of Warren Buffett**

Warren Buffett is regarded by many as the world's most successful investor and is one of the world's richest individuals. He has expressed concern about the problem of creative accounting as follows:

> A growing number of otherwise high-grade managers – CEOs [chief executive officers] you would be happy to have as spouses for your children or as trustee under your will – have come to the view that it's okay to manipulate earnings to safisfy what they believe are Wall Street's desires. Indeed, many CEOs think this kind of manipulation is not only okay, but actually their duty.

Activity 7.32	**Why might the managers of a business engage in creative accounting?**

There are many reasons and these include:

– To get around restrictions (for example, to report sufficient profit to pay a dividend)
– To avoid government action (for example, the taxation of excessive profits)
– To hide poor management decisions
– To achieve sales or profit targets, thereby ensuring that management bonuses are paid
– To attract new share capital or loan capital by showing a healthy financial position
– To satisfy the demands of major investors concerning levels of return.

When examining the financial statements of a business, a number of checks may be carried out on the financial statements to help gain a 'feel' for their reliability. These will include checks to see whether:

– the reported profits are significantly higher than the operating cash flows for the period (which may suggest profits have been overstated);
– the corporation tax charge is low in relation to reported profits (which may, again, suggest that profits are overstated, although there may be other, more innocent, explanations);
– the valuation methods used for assets held are based on historic cost or current values (and if the latter approach is used, it is important to find out why and what particular valuation approach has been adopted);
– there have been any changes in accounting policies over the period, particularly in key areas such as depreciation, stock valuation, and the reporting of doubtful debts that can have a significant impact on reported profit;
– the accounting policies adopted are in line with those adopted by the rest of the industry;
– the auditors' report gives a 'clean bill of health' to the financial statements;
– the 'small print' (that is, the notes to the accounts) is not being used to hide significant events or changes.

Although such checks are useful, they are not guaranteed to identify creative accounting practices, some of which may be very deeply seated.

Exhibit 7.8	**Look out for what is hidden under the carpet**

The following is an extract from *The Times* (29 April 1999):

> Allied Carpets admitted last summer that its store managers had been marketing a carpet as 'sold'
> as soon as an order was placed. The practice, known as 'pre-dispatching', is not illegal but
> violated company policy that sales should not be marked as completed until delivery. The scam
> flattered trading figures and led to a £3m charge against profits last year.

One consequence of this 'scam' was the firing of the Managing Director.

■ *Inflation.* A persistent problem in most Western countries is that the financial results of a business are distorted as a result of inflation. One effect of inflation is that the values of assets held for any length of time may bear little relation to current values. Generally speaking, the value of assets will be understated in current terms during a period of inflation as they are usually recorded at their original cost (less any amounts written off for depreciation). This means that comparisons, either between businesses or between periods, will be hindered. A difference in, say, return on capital employed may simply be owing to the fact that assets in one of the balance sheets being compared were acquired more recently (ignoring the effect of depreciation on the asset values). Another effect of inflation is to distort the measurement of profit. Sales revenue for a period is often matched against costs from an earlier period. This is because there is often a time lag between acquiring a particular resource and using it in the business. For example, stocks may be acquired in one period and sold in a later period. During a period of inflation, this will mean that the costs do not reflect current prices. As a result, costs will be understated in the current profit and loss account and this, in turn, means that profit will be overstated. One effect of this will be to distort the profitability ratios discussed earlier.

The problem of inflation is considered in more detail in Chapter 9.

■ *The restricted vision of ratios.* It is important not to rely on ratios exclusively and thereby lose sight of information contained in the underlying financial statements. Some items reported in these statements can be vital in assessing position and performance. For example, the total sales, capital employed and profit figures may be useful in assessing changes in absolute size that occur over time, or differences in scale between businesses. Ratios do not provide such information. In comparing one figure with another, ratios measure *relative* performance and position and therefore provide only part of the picture. Thus, when comparing two businesses, it will often be useful to assess the absolute size of profits as well as the relative profitability of each business. For example, company A may generate £1 million profit and have a ROCE of 15 per cent and company B may generate £100,000 profit and have a ROCE of 20 per cent. Although company B has a higher level of *profitability*, as measured by ROCE, it generates lower total profits.

■ *The basis for comparison.* We saw earlier that ratios require a basis for comparison in order to be useful. Moreover, it is important that the analyst compares like with like. When comparing businesses, however, no two businesses will be identical; and the greater the differences between the businesses being compared, the greater the limitations of ratio analysis. Furthermore, when comparing businesses, differences in such matters as accounting policies, financing policies and financial year-ends will add to the problems of evaluation.

- *Balance sheet ratios.* Because the balance sheet is only a 'snapshot' of the business at a particular moment in time, any ratios based on balance sheet figures, such as the liquidity ratios, may not be representative of the financial position of the business for the year as a whole. For example, it is common for a seasonal business to have a financial year-end that coincides with a low point in business activity. Thus, stocks and debtors may be low at the balance sheet date and the liquidity ratios may also be low as a result. A more representative picture of liquidity can only be gained by taking additional measurements at other points in the year.

Exhibit 7.9	**Remember it's people that really count . . .**

Lord Weinstock was an influential industrialist whose management style and philosophy helped to shape management practice in many UK businesses. During his long reign at GEC plc, a major engineering business, Lord Weinstock relied heavily on financial ratios to assess performance and to exercise control. In particular, he relied on ratios relating to sales, costs, debtors, profit margins and stock turnover. However, he was keenly aware of the limitations of ratios and recognised that, ultimately, profits are produced by people.

In a memo written to GEC managers he pointed out that ratios are an aid to, rather than a substitute for, good management. He wrote:

> The operating ratios are of great value as measures of efficiency but they are only the measures and not efficiency itself. Statistics will not design a product better, make it for a lower cost or increase sales. If ill-used, they may so guide action as to diminish resources for the sake of apparent but false signs of improvement . . .
>
> Management remains a matter of judgement, of knowledge of products and processes and of understanding and skill in dealing with people. The ratios will indicate how well all these things are being done and will show comparison with how they are done elsewhere. But they will tell us nothing about how to do them. That is what you are meant to do.

Source: Extract from **Arnold Weinstock and the making of GEC** by S. *Aris* (Arum Press 1998), published in *Sunday Times* 22 February 1998, p. 3.

Summary

In this chapter, we have seen that ratios can be used to analyse various aspects of the position and performance of a business. Used properly, they help provide a quick thumbnail sketch of a business. However, they require a sound basis for comparison and will only be as useful as the quality of the underlying financial statements permit. Though they can highlight certain strengths and weaknesses concerning financial performance and position, ratios do not identify underlying causes. This can only be done through a more detailed investigation of business practices and records.

We have also seen that ratios are being used increasingly to predict the future. Indeed we saw how certain ratios, when combined into a single index, can be used to predict financial distress.

 **Key terms**

Further reading

If you would like to explore the topics covered in this chapter in more depth, we recommend the following books:

Financial Accounting and Reporting, *Elliott, B.* and *Elliott, J.*, 5th edn, Financial Times Prentice Hall International, 2001, chapters 25 and 26.
Financial Reporting and Analysis, *Revsine, L.*, *Collins, D.* and *Bruce Johnson, W.*, Prentice Hall, 1999, chapter 4.
Financial Analysis, *Rees, B.*, 2nd edn, Prentice Hall International, 1995, chapters 1–3.
The Analysis and Use of Financial Statements, *White, G.* and *Sondhi, A.*, 2nd edn, Wiley, 1997, chapter 4.

References

1. 'Financial ratios as predictors of failure', *Beaver, W. H.*, in **Empirical Research in Accounting: Selected studies**, 1966, pp. 71–111.
2. **Predicting Corporate Bankruptcy: An empirical comparison of the extent of financial distress models**, *Zmijewski, M. E.*, Research Paper, State University of New York, 1983.
3. 'Financial ratios, discriminant analysis and the prediction of corporate bankruptcy', by *Altman, E. I.*, in **Journal of Finance**, September 1968, pp. 589–609.
4. 'The assessment of company solvency and performance using a statistical model: a comparative UK-based study', by *Taffler, R.*, in **Accounting and Business Research**, Autumn 1983, pp. 295–307.

? REVIEW QUESTIONS

7.1 Some businesses operate on a low net-profit margin (for example a supermarket chain). Does this mean that the return on capital employed from the business will also be low?

7.2 What potential problems arise from the use of balance sheet figures in the calculation of financial ratios?

7.3 In the chapter it was mentioned that ratios help to eliminate some of the problems of comparing businesses of different sizes. Does this mean that size is irrelevant when interpreting and analysing the position and performance of different businesses?

7.4 Identify and discuss three reasons why the P/E ratio of two companies operating within the same industry may differ.

? EXERCISES

Exercises 7.5–7.8 are more advanced than 7.1–7.4. Those with coloured numbers have answers at the back of the book.

7.1 Jiang (Western) Ltd has recently produced its accounts for the current year. The board of directors met to consider the accounts and, at this meeting, concern was expressed that the return on capital employed had decreased from 14 per cent last year to 12 per cent for the current year.

The following reasons were suggested as to why this reduction in ROCE had occurred:

(a) Increase in the gross profit margin.
(b) Reduction in sales.
(c) Increase in overhead expenses.
(d) Increase in amount of stock held.
(e) Repayment of a loan at the year-end.
(f) Increase in the time taken by debtors to pay.

Required:
State, with reasons, which of the above might lead to a reduction in ROCE.

7.2 Business A and Business B are both engaged in retailing, but seem to take a different approach to this trade according to the information available. This information consists of a table of ratios, shown below.

Ratio	Business A	Business B
Return on capital employed (ROCE)	20%	17%
Return on ordinary shareholders' funds (ROSF)	30%	18%
Average settlement period for debtors	63 days	21 days
Average settlement period for creditors	50 days	45 days
Gross profit percentage	40%	15%
Net profit percentage	10%	10%
Stock turnover period	52 days	25 days

Required:
(a) Explain how each ratio is calculated.
(b) Describe what this information indicates about the differences in approach between the two businesses. If one of them prides itself on personal service and one of them on competitive prices, which do you think is which and why?

7.3 Conday and Co. Ltd has been in operation for three years and produces reproduction antique furniture for the export market. The most recent set of accounts for the company is set out below:

Balance sheet as at 30 November 2001

	£000	£000	£000
Fixed assets			
Freehold land and buildings at cost			228
Plant and machinery at cost		942	
Less Accumulated depreciation		180	762
			990
Current assets			
Stocks		600	
Trade debtors		820	
		1,420	
Less **Creditors: amounts falling due within one year**			
Trade creditors	665		
Taxation	48		
Bank overdraft	432	1,145	275
			1,265
Less **Creditors: amounts falling due in more than one year**			
12% debentures (note 1)			200
			1,065
Capital and reserves			
Ordinary shares of £1 each			700
Retained profits			365
			1,065

Profit and loss account for the year ended 30 November 2001

	£000	£000
Sales		2,600
Less Cost of sales		1,620
Gross profit		980
Less Selling and distribution expenses (note 2)	408	
Administration expenses	174	
Finance expenses	78	660
Net profit before taxation		320
Less Corporation tax		95
Net profit after taxation		225
Less Proposed dividend		160
Retained profit for the year		65

Notes:
1. The debentures are secured on the freehold land and buildings.
2. Selling and distribution expenses include £170,000 in respect of bad debts.

An investor has been approached by the company to invest £200,000 by purchasing ordinary shares in the company at £6.40 each. The company wishes to use the funds to finance a programme of further expansion.

Required:
(a) Analyse the financial position and performance of the company and comment on any features you consider to be significant.
(b) State, with reasons, whether or not the investor should invest in the company on the terms outlined.

7.4 The directors of Helena Beauty Products Ltd have been presented with the following abridged accounts for the current year and the preceding year:

Helena Beauty Products Ltd
Profit and loss account for the year ended 30 September

	2000		2001	
	£000	£000	£000	£000
Sales		3,600		3,840
Less Cost of sales				
Opening stock	320		400	
Purchases	2,240		2,350	
	2,560		2,750	
Less Closing stock	400	2,160	500	2,250
Gross profit		1,440		1,590
Less Expenses		1,360		1,500
Net profit		80		90

Balance sheets as at 30 September

	2000		2001	
	£000	£000	£000	£000
Fixed assets		1,900		1,860
Current assets				
Stock	400		500	
Debtors	750		960	
Bank	8		4	
	1,158		1,464	
Less Creditors: amounts due within one year	390	768	450	1,014
		2,668		2,874
Capital and reserves				
£1 ordinary shares		1,650		1,766
Reserves		1,018		1,108
		2,668		2,874

Required:
Using six ratios, comment on the profitability and efficiency of the business as revealed by the accounts shown above.

7.5 Threads Limited manufactures nuts and bolts, which are sold to industrial users. The abbreviated accounts for 2000 and 2001 are given below.

Profit and loss account for the year ended 30 June

	2000 £000	2000 £000	2001 £000	2001 £000
Sales		1,180		1,200)
Cost of sales		(680)		(750)
Gross profit		500		450
Operating expenses	(200)		(208)	
Depreciation	(66)		(75)	
Interest	(–)		(8)	
		(266)		(291)
Profit before tax		234		159
Tax		(80)		(48)
Profit after tax		154		111
Dividend proposed		(70)		(72)
Retained profit for year		84		39

Balance sheets as at 30 June

	2000 £000	2000 £000	2001 £000	2001 £000
Fixed assets		702		687
Current assets				
Stocks	148		236	
Debtors	102		156	
Cash	3		4	
	253		396	
Creditors: amounts due within one year				
Trade creditors	(60)		(76)	
Other creditors and accruals	(18)		(16)	
Dividend	(70)		(72)	
Tax	(40)		(24)	
Bank overdraft	(11)		(50)	
	(199)		(238)	
Net current assets		54		158
		756		845
Creditors: amounts due beyond one year				
Bank loan		–		(50)
		756		795
Capital and reserves				
Ordinary share capital of £1 (fully paid)		500		500
Retained profits		256		295
		756		795

Required:

(a) Calculate the following financial statistics for both 2000 and 2001, using end-of-year figures where appropriate:

(i)   return on capital employed
(ii)   net profit margin
(iii)   gross profit margin
(iv)   current ratio
(v)   liquidity ratio (acid test ratio)
(vi)   days debtors (settlement period)
(vii)   days creditors (settlement period)
(viii) stock turnover period

(b) Comment on the performance of Threads Limited from the viewpoint of a company considering supplying a substantial amount of goods to Threads Limited on usual credit terms.

(c) What action could a supplier take to lessen the risk of not being paid should Threads Limited be in financial difficulty?

7.6 Bradbury Ltd is a family-owned clothes manufacturer based in the south-west of England. For a number of years the chairman and managing director was David Bradbury. During his period of office the company's sales turnover had grown steadily at a rate of 2 to 3 per cent each year. David Bradbury retired on 30 November 2000 and was succeeded by his son Simon. Soon after taking office, Simon decided to expand the business. Within weeks he had successfully negotiated a five-year contract with a large clothes retailer to make a range of sports and leisurewear items. The contract will result in an additional £2 million in sales during each year of the contract. In order to fulfil the contract, new equipment and premises were acquired by Bradbury Ltd.

Financial information concerning the company is given below.

Profit and loss account for the year ended 30 November

	2000 £000	2001 £000
Turnover	9,482	11,365
Profit before interest and tax	914	1,042
Interest charges	22	81
Profit before tax	892	961
Taxation	358	386
Profit after tax	534	575
Dividend	120	120
Retained profit	414	455

Balance sheet as at 30 November

	2000 £000	2000 £000	2001 £000	2001 £000
Fixed assets				
Freehold premises at cost		5,240		7,360
Plant and equipment (net)		2,375		4,057
		7,615		11,417
Current assets				
Stock	2,386		3,420	
Trade debtors	2,540		4,280	
	4,926		7,700	

	2000		2001	
	£000	£000	£000	£000
Creditors: amounts due within one year				
Trade creditors	(1,157)		(2,245)	
Taxation	(179)		(193)	
Dividends payable	(120)		(120)	
Bank overdraft	(52)		(2,616)	
	(1,508)		(5,174)	
Net current assets		3,418		2,526
		11,033		13,943
Creditors: amounts due beyond one year				
Loans		(1,220)		(3,674)
Total net assets		9,813		10,269
Capital and reserves				
Share capital		2,000		2,000
Reserves		7,813		8,269
Net worth		9,813		10,269

Required:

(a) Calculate for each year the following ratios:
   (i)   net profit margin
   (ii) return on capital employed
   (iii) current ratio
   (iv) gearing ratio
   (v)   days debtors (settlement period)
   (vi) sales to capital employed.

(b) Using the above ratios, and any other ratios or information you consider relevant, comment on the results of the expansion programme.

7.7 | The financial statements for Harridges Limited are given below for the two years ended 30 June 2001 and 2002. Harridges Limited operates a department store in the centre of a small town.

Harridges Limited
Profit and loss account for the years ended 30 June

	2001		2002	
	£000	£000	£000	£000
Sales		2,600		3,500
Cost of sales		(1,560)		(2,350)
Gross profit		1,040		1,150
Expenses: Wages and salaries	(320)		(350)	
Overheads	(260)		(200)	
Depreciation	(150)		(250)	
		(730)		(800)
Operating profit		310		350
Interest payable		(50)		(50)
Profit before taxation		260		300
Taxation		(105)		(125)
Profit after taxation		155		175
Dividend proposed		(65)		(75)
Profit retained for the year		90		100

Balance sheet as at 30 June

	2001 £000	2001 £000	2002 £000	2002 £000
Fixed assets		1,265		1,525
Current assets				
Stocks	250		400	
Debtors	105		145	
Cash at bank	380		115	
	735		660	
Creditors: amounts falling due within one year				
Trade creditors	(235)		(300)	
Dividend	(65)		(75)	
Other	(100)		(110)	
	(400)		(485)	
Net current assets		335		175
Total assets less current liabilities		1,600		1,700
Creditors: amounts falling due after more than one year				
10% loan stock		(500)		(500)
		1,100		1,200
Capital and reserves				
Share capital: £1 shares fully paid		490		490
Share premium		260		260
Profit and loss account		350		450
		1,100		1,200

Required:

(a) Choose and calculate eight ratios that would be helpful in assessing the performance of Harridges Limited. Use end-of-year values and calculate ratios for both 2002 and 2001.

(b) Using the ratios calculated in (a) and any others you consider helpful, comment on the company's performance from the viewpoint of a prospective purchaser of a majority of shares.

7.8 Genesis Ltd was incorporated in 1998 and has grown rapidly over the past three years. The rapid rate of growth has created problems for the business which the directors of the company have found difficult to deal with. Recently, a firm of management consultants has been asked to help the directors of the company overcome these problems.

In a preliminary report to the board of directors of the company, the management consultants state: 'Most of the difficulties faced by the company are symptoms of an underlying problem of overtrading.'

The most recent accounts of the business are set out below:

Balance sheet as at 31 October 2001

	£000	£000	£000
Fixed assets			
Freehold land and buildings at cost		530	
Less Accumulated depreciation		88	442
Fixtures and fittings at cost		168	
Less Accumulated depreciation		52	116
Motor vans at cost		118	
Less Accumulated depreciation		54	64
			622

	£000	£000	£000
Current assets			
Stock in trade		128	
Trade debtors		<u>104</u>	
		232	
Less Creditors: amount falling due			
within one year			
Trade creditors	184		
Proposed dividend	4		
Taxation	8		
Bank overdraft	<u>354</u>	(550)	(318)
			304
Less Creditors: amounts falling			
due beyond one year			
10% debentures (secured)			(120)
			184
Capital and reserves			
Ordinary £0.50 shares			60
General reserve			50
Retained profit			<u>74</u>
			<u>184</u>

Profit and loss account for the year ended 31 October 2001

	£000	£000
Sales		1,640
Less Cost of sales		
Opening stock	116	
Purchases	<u>1,260</u>	
	1,376	
Less Closing stock	<u>128</u>	(1,248)
Gross profit		392
Less Selling and distribution expenses	204	
Administration expenses	92	
Interest expenses	<u>44</u>	(340)
Net profit before taxation		52
Corporation tax		(16)
Net profit after taxation		36
Proposed dividend		(4)
Retained profit for the year		<u>32</u>

All purchases and sales were on credit.

Required:
(a) Explain the term 'overtrading' and state how overtrading might arise for a business.
(b) Discuss the kinds of problem that overtrading can create for a business.
(c) Calculate and discuss _five_ financial ratios that might be used to establish whether or not the business is overtrading.
(d) State the ways in which a business may overcome the problem of overtrading.

CHAPTER 8

Reporting the financial results of groups of companies

Introduction

Many larger businesses, including virtually all of those that are household names in the UK, consist not just of one single company but of a group of companies. Here one or more companies are controlled by another company, the parent company. This usually arises because the shares of some of the companies are owned by another company, usually with one parent company owning a majority of the shares of the other companies in the group.

   In this chapter we shall look at groups and, more particularly, at the accounting treatment that they usually receive. We shall also briefly consider associate companies.

OBJECTIVES On completion of this chapter you should be able to:

■ Discuss the nature of groups, and explain why they exist and how they are formed.

■ Prepare a group balance sheet and profit and loss account.

■ Explain the nature of associate company status and its accounting implications.

■ Explain and interpret the contents of a set of group accounts.

What is a group of companies?

It is quite common for one company to be able to exercise control over the activities of another. Control typically arises because the first company (the **parent company**) owns a majority of the ordinary (voting) shares of the second company (the **subsidiary company**). This means that the directors of the parent company are able to appoint the directors of the subsidiary company and, therefore, dictate the policies of the subsidiary company. Where this relationship arises, a **'group' of companies** is said to exist. Where there is a group, UK company law, and that of most countries, requires that a set of accounts is drawn up annually not only for each individual company, but also for the group taken as a whole. Before we go on to consider how the **group accounts** (that is, the final accounts of a group of companies) are prepared, we shall look at the reasons why groups exist at all and at the types of group relationships that can exist.

Why do groups exist?

Companies have subsidiaries where:

1. The parent company creates a new company to operate some part of its business, perhaps a new activity.
2. The parent company buys a majority, perhaps all, of the shares of some other existing company; that is, a '**takeover**'.

Many companies have subsidiaries as a result of both of these reasons.

Newly created companies

It is very common for large businesses to be made up of, and to operate through, a number, often a large number, of individual companies all of which are wholly owned by the parent company, sometimes known as the **'holding' company**. In some cases, the only assets of the parent company are the shares, that it owns, in the subsidiary companies. It is the subsidiary companies that strictly own the land, buildings, machinery, stocks, and so on which is used to generate profit. However, since the parent owns the subsidiaries, in effect, it owns the individual 'real' assets of those companies.

An obvious question is why do businesses operate through subsidiaries? To put it another way, why do the parent companies not own all of the assets of the business directly, instead of through the subsidiaries? The answers to these questions are probably:

- *Limited liability*. Each individual company has individual limited liability. This means that if there is a financial failure of one subsidiary, neither the assets of other subsidiaries nor of the parent could be legally demanded by any unsatisfied creditors of the failed company. Thus the group can 'ring fence' each part of the business by having separate companies, each with their own limited liability, operating each part.
- *Individual identity*. A sense of independence and autonomy may be created that may, in turn, increase levels of commitment among staff. It may also help to develop, or perpetuate, a market image of a smaller, independent business. Customers, as well as staff, may prefer to deal with, what they see as a smaller, specialist business than a division of a large diversified business.

To create a subsidiary, the would-be parent may simply form a new company in the normal way. The new company would then issue shares to the parent, in exchange for some asset or assets of the parent. Where the new subsidiary has been formed to undertake a completely new activity, the asset may well be cash. If the subsidiary is to carry on some activity, which the parent had undertaken directly up to that point, the assets are likely to be such things as the fixed and current assets associated with the particular activity.

Example 8.1

The summarised balance sheet of Baxter plc is as follows:

Balance sheet as at 31 December

	£m	£m	£m
Fixed assets (at cost less depreciation)			
Land			43
Plant			15
Vehicles			8
			66
Current assets			
Stock	15		
Debtors	23		
Cash	13		
		51	
Less **Creditors: amounts falling due within one year**			
Creditors		11	
Net current assets			40
Total assets less current liabilities			106
Less **Creditors: amounts falling due after more than one year**			
Debentures			40
			66
Capital and reserves			
Called-up share capital:			
ordinary shares of £1 each, fully paid			50
Profit and loss account			16
			66

Baxter plc has recently formed a new company, Nova Ltd, which is to undertake the work that has previously been done by the industrial fibres division of Baxter plc. The following assets are to be transferred to Nova Ltd at the values that currently are shown in the balance sheet of Baxter plc:

	£m
Land	10
Plant	5
Vehicles	3
Stock	6
Cash	3
	27

Nova Ltd is to issue £1 ordinary shares at the nominal or par value (that is, £1) to Baxter plc in exchange for these assets.

Baxter plc's balance sheet immediately after these transfers will be:

Balance sheet as at 31 December

Fixed assets (at cost less depreciation)	£m	£m	£m
Land (43 – 10)			33
Plant (15 – 5)			10
Vehicles (8 – 3)			5
Investment in 27 million ordinary			
£1 shares of Nova Ltd			27
			75
Current assets			
Stocks (15 – 6)	9		
Debtors	23		
Cash (13 – 3)	10		
		42	
Less **Creditors: amounts falling**			
due within one year			
Creditors		11	
Net current assets			31
Total assets less current liabilities			106
Less **Creditors: amounts falling**			
due after more than one year			
Debentures			40
			66
Capital and reserves			
Called-up share capital:			
ordinary shares of £1 each, fully paid			50
Profit and loss account			16
			66

As you have probably noted, the individual assets have simply been replaced by the asset, shares in Nova Ltd.

Activity 8.1	Try to prepare the balance sheet of Nova Ltd immediately following the transfers of the assets and the shares being issued.

It should look something like this:

Balance sheet as at 31 December

Fixed assets (at transfer value)	£m	£m
Land		10
Plant		5
Vehicles		3
		18
Current assets		
Stocks	6	
Cash	3	
		9
Total assets		27
Capital and reserves		
Called-up share capital: ordinary shares of £1 each, fully paid		27

Takeovers

A would-be parent company may also create a subsidiary by a takeover of an existing company. Here it buys enough of the shares of a hitherto unconnected ➡ **target company** to enable it to exercise control over the target company, thereby making the target a new subsidiary company. The shares are, of course, bought from the existing shareholders of the target company.

The shares may be bought through the Stock Exchange or an approach may be made directly to the individual shareholders of the target company. This second course is feasible because all companies are required by law to provide the names and addresses of their shareholders to any interested party. In many takeovers, the parent offers to the target company shareholders, shares in the parent as all, or part of the bid consideration. This means the target company shareholders who accept the offer will exchange shares in the target for shares in the parent. Thus, they cease to be shareholders of the target company and become shareholders in the parent.

Example 8.2

The summarised balance sheet of Adams plc is as follows:

Balance sheet as at 31 March

	£m	£m	£m
Fixed assets (at cost less depreciation)			
Land			35
Plant			21
Vehicles			12
			68
Current assets			
Stocks	25		
Debtors	28		
Cash	22		
		75	
Less **Creditors: amounts falling due within one year**			
Creditors		23	
Net current assets			52
Total assets less current liabilities			120
Less **Creditors: amounts falling due after more than one year**			
Debentures			50
			70
Capital and reserves			
Called-up share capital:			
ordinary shares of £1 each, fully paid			50
Share premium account			5
Profit and loss account			15
			70

Adams plc has recently made an offer of £1 a share for all the share capital of Beta Ltd (20 million shares of 50p each). This is to be met by issuing the appropriate number of new ordinary shares of Adams plc at an issue value of £2 a share.

All the Beta Ltd shareholders accepted the offer. This means that to meet the required consideration, Adams plc will need to issue shares to the value of £20 million (that is, 20 million × £1). Since the Adams plc shares are to be issued at £2 each, 10 million shares will need to be issued, at a share premium of £1 each.

Following the takeover, the balance sheet of Adams plc will look as follows:

Balance sheet as at 31 March

	£m	£m	£m
Fixed assets (at cost less depreciation)			
Land			35
Plant			21
Vehicles			12
Investment in Beta Ltd			20
			88
Current assets			
Stocks	25		
Debtors	28		
Cash	22		
		75	
Less **Creditors: amounts falling due within one year**			
Creditors		23	
Net current assets			52
Total assets less current liabilities			140
Less **Creditors: amounts falling due after more than one year**			
Debentures			50
			90
Capital and reserves			
Called-up share capital:			
ordinary shares of £1 each, fully paid			60
Share premium account			15
Profit and loss account			15
			90

Note that the assets have increased by £20 million and that this is balanced by the value of the shares issued (£10 million share capital and £10 million share premium).

Activity 8.2	If, instead of the consideration offered being in shares, the offer had been 50 per cent in cash and 50 per cent in Adams plc shares, what would the balance sheet of Adams plc have looked like after the takeover?

The total offer value would still be £20 million, but this would be met by paying cheques totalling £10 million and by issuing shares worth £10 million (£5 million share capital and £5 million share premium). So the balance sheet would be:

Balance sheet as at 31 March

Fixed assets (at cost less depreciation)	£m	£m	£m
Land			35
Plant			21
Vehicles			12
Investment in Beta Ltd			20
			88
Current assets			
Stocks	25		
Debtors	28		
Cash	12		
		65	
Less **Creditors: amounts falling due within one year**			
Creditors		23	
Net current assets			42
Total assets less current liabilities			130
Less **Creditors: amounts falling due after more than one year**			
Debentures			50
			80
Capital and reserves			
Called-up share capital:			
ordinary shares of £1 each, fully paid			55
Share premium account			10
Profit and loss account			15
			80

Activity 8.3	How would the takeover affect the balance sheet of Beta Ltd?

The balance sheet of Beta Ltd would not be affected at all. A change of shareholders does not affect the accounts of a company.

It is not necessary that the parent company should retain the target/subsidiary as a separate company, following the takeover. The latter could be wound up and its assets owned directly by the parent. Normally this would not happen, however, for the reasons that are given above; namely limited liability and individual identity. The latter may be particularly important in the case of a takeover. The new parent company may be very keen to retain the name and identity of its new subsidiary, where the subsidiary has a good marketing image.

Types of group relationship

So far we have considered a situation where there is the simple relationship between a parent and its subsidiary or subsidiaries which is shown in Figure 8.1. A slightly more complex relationship is shown in Figure 8.2. Here subsidiary 2 is a subsidiary by virtue of being controlled by another company (subsidiary 1) which is,

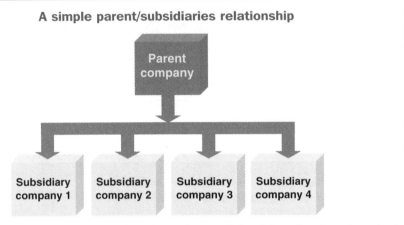

Figure 8.1

A simple parent/subsidiaries relationship

The parent company exercises control directly by owning a majority of the voting shares in each of the four subsidiaries.

Figure 8.2

A more complex parent/subsidiaries relationship

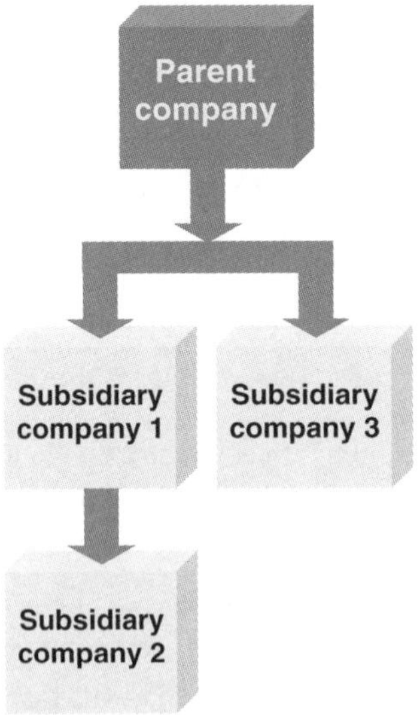

The parent company exercises control over subsidiaries 1 and 3 directly by owning a majority of the voting shares in it. The parent exercises control over subsidiary 1, but it exercises control over subsidiary 2 because subsidiary 1 has control over subsidiary 2.

in turn, a subsidiary of the parent. In these circumstances, subsidiary 2 is usually called a 'sub-subsidiary' of the parent. Subsidiary 3 is a straightforward subsidiary. The parent company here is sometimes known as the 'ultimate' parent company of subsidiary 2.

Earlier in this chapter, it was pointed out that one company is a subsidiary of another because the latter *controls* the former. This is usually as a result of the latter owning a majority of the voting shares of the other, but this does not need to be the case. Consider Figure 8.2 and suppose that the parent owns 60 per cent of the voting shares of subsidiary 1 and that subsidiary 1 owns 60 per cent of the shares of subsidiary 2. In effect, the parent only owns 36 per cent of the shares of subsidiary 2 (that is, 60 per cent of 60 per cent), yet the latter is a subsidiary of the former. This is because the parent has complete control over (though not total ownership of) subsidiary 1, which in turn has complete control over (though again not total ownership of) subsidiary 2.

Activity 8.4	Company A owns 40 per cent of the voting shares of both company B and company C. The other 60 per cent of the voting shares of company C are owned by company B.

Is company C a subsidiary of company A?

The answer is no. This is despite the fact that company A can be seen to own 64 per cent of the shares of company C; 40 per cent directly and 24 per cent (that is, 40 per cent × 60 per cent) through company B. Since A does not control B, it cannot control B's shares in C.

Though ownership and control do not necessarily go hand-in-hand, in practice this tends to be the case.

The reason that we are concerned as to whether one company is a subsidiary of another is, of course, that group accounts must be prepared where there is a parent/subsidiary relationship, but not otherwise.

Exhibit 8.1	This exhibit shows the principal subsidiaries of De La Rue plc, an international company whose main focus is security systems and security printing (for example, bank notes). We can see that it has many subsidiaries throughout the world and these are usually wholly owned. In some cases, the equity interest of De La Rue is substantial but less than 50 per cent. Where this occurs, the relevant company is not a subsidiary. It is referred to as an associated company. We shall deal with this type of company later in the chapter.

Principal subsidiaries, branches and associated companies
as at 31 March 2001

The companies and branches listed on these two pages include those which principally affect the profits and assets of the Group. A full list of subsidiary undertakings will be filed with the Company's Annual Return.

Country of incorporation and operation	Activities	De La Rue interest in ordinary shares %
EUROPE		
United Kingdom		
De La Rue Holdings plc	Holding and general commercial activities	100+
De La Rue International Limited	Security paper and printing, sale and maintenance of cash handling products and services, Identity systems, Brand protection, Holographics and Transaction Services	100
De La Rue Overseas Limited	Holding company	100
De La Rue InterClear Limited	Digital Security	100
De La Rue Investments Limited	Holding company	100
Portals Group plc	Holding company	100
Portals Property Limited	Property holding company	100
Royal Mint Services Limited	Marketing	50*
Camelot Group plc	Lottery operator	20*
Channel Islands		
The Burnhill Insurance Company Limited	Insurance	100
Belgium		
De La Rue Cash Systems NV	Distribution and marketing	100
Ireland		
De La Rue Smurfit Limited	Security printing	50
De La Rue Cash Systems Limited	Distribution and marketing	100
Italy		
De La Rue Cash Systems s.r.l.	Distribution and marketing	100
France		
De La Rue France Holdings SAS	Holding company	100
De La Rue Cash Systems SA	Distribution and marketing	100
Germany		
IMW Immobilien AG	Property company	95.67
De La Rue Cash Systems GmbH	Distribution and marketing	100
De La Rue Systems GmbH	Holding company and distribution and marketing of cash handling products for export	100
Malta		
De La Rue Currency and Security Print Limited	Security printing	100
The Netherlands		
De La Rue BV	Holding company and distribution and marketing of cash handling products	100
Portugal		
De La Rue Cash Systems	Distribution and marketing (branch)	100
Valora-Servicos de Apoio a Emissao Monitaria SA	Currency printing	25*
Spain		
De La Rue Systems S.A.	Distribution and marketing	100

Country of incorporation and operation	Activities	De La Rue interest in ordinary shares %
Sweden		
De La Rue Cash Systems AB	Manufacturer of cash handling equipment	100
De La Rue Svetsprodukter AB	Manufacturer of cash handling equipment	100
Switzerland		
Thomas De La Rue A.G.	Holding company	100
De La Rue Giori S.A.	Security printing machinery	50*
Fidink S.A.	Security ink marketing	33.33*
De La Rue Cash Systems A.G.	Distribution and marketing	100
De La Rue International Limited, Swiss Branch	Design and development centre principally for cash handling products and solutions	100
NORTH AMERICA		
United States of America		
De La Rue Inc	Holding company	100
De La Rue Security Print Inc	Security printing	100
De La Rue Cash Systems Inc	Identity systems, design, assembly, distribution and marketing	100
SOUTH AMERICA		
Brazil		
De La Rue Cash Systems Ltda	Distribution and marketing	100
Mexico		
De La Rue Mexico SA de CV	Identity Systems	100
AFRICA		
Kenya		
De La Rue Currency and Security Print Limited	Security printing	100
Nigeria		
The Nigerian Security Printing and Minting Company Limited	Security printing	25*
South Africa		
De La Rue Systems (Proprietary) Limited	Distribution and marketing	100
FAR EAST		
Australia		
De La Rue Cash Systems Pty Limited	Distribution and marketing	100
Hong Kong		
De La Rue Systems Asia Pacific Limited	Distribution and marketing	100
Malaysia		
De La Rue (Malaysia) Sdn Bhd	Identification systems	100
Singapore		
De La Rue Currency and Security Print Pte Ltd	Security printing	100
Sri Lanka		
De La Rue Lanka Currency and Security Print (Private) Limited	Security printing	60

+ Shares held by De La Rue plc   * Associated company

Preparation of a group balance sheet

➡ We are now going to look at the preparation of a **group balance sheet**. We shall do this by considering a series of examples, starting with the most simple possible case and gradually building on more and more of the complexities found in real life.

Each company within the group will prepare its own balance sheet, which considers things from the perspective of each particular company. As well as this, the parent company will produce a balance sheet that reflects the assets and claims of the group as a whole. In effect, the group balance sheet looks at the group as if the parent company owned the assets and, therefore, was responsible for the outside liabilities of all the group members. This means, among other things, that whereas the *parent company* balance sheet will include the assets of investments in the shares of the subsidiary companies, in the *group* balance sheet, this will be replaced by the net assets (assets less claims of non-group claimants). In other words, the group balance sheet looks behind the subsidiary company shares to see what they represent, in terms of assets and claims. The assets and liabilities of

➡ subsidiaries are '**consolidated**' into the balance sheet of the parent company. This point should become clearer as we look at some examples.

Example 8.3	The balance sheets of Parent plc and of Subsidiary Ltd, on the date that the former bought the shares in the latter, were as follows:

Balance sheets as at 31 May

	Parent plc		Subsidiary Ltd	
	£m	£m	£m	£m
Fixed assets (at cost less depreciation)				
Land		40		5
Plant		30		2
Vehicles		20		2
Investment in 5 million shares				
of Subsidiary Ltd		10		–
		100		9
Current assets				
Stocks	20		3	
Debtors	30		2	
Cash	10		2	
	60		7	
Less **Creditors: amounts falling due within one year**				
Creditors	20		6	
Net current assets		40		1
Total assets less current liabilities		140		10
Less **Creditors: amounts falling due after more than one year**				
Debentures		30		–
		110		10

Capital and reserves	Parent plc £m	Parent plc £m	Subsidiary Ltd £m	Subsidiary Ltd £m
Called-up share capital:				
ordinary shares of £1 each, fully paid		70		5
Share premium account		10		–
Profit and loss account		30		5
		110		10

To deduce the group balance sheet, we simply combine each of the like items by adding them together. For example, the group investment in land is £45 million, representing £40 million invested by Parent plc and £5 million invested by Subsidiary Ltd.

The only exceptions to the rule that we simply add like items together, lies with the investment in the shares of Subsidiary Ltd, in the balance sheet of Parent plc, and with the owners' claim (share capital plus reserves) in the balance sheet of Subsidiary Ltd. In effect, these are two sides of the same coin, since Parent plc is the owner of Subsidiary Ltd. For this reason, it is logical simply to add these two items together and since one is an asset and the other is a claim and they are equal in amount, they will cancel each other out.

The group balance sheet will be as follows:

Balance sheet as at 31 May

	£m	£m
Fixed assets (at cost less depreciation)		
Land (40 + 5)		45
Plant (30 + 2)		32
Vehicles (20 + 2)		22
		99
Current assets		
Stocks (20 + 3)	23	
Debtors (30 + 2)	32	
Cash (10 + 2)	12	
	67	
Less **Creditors: amounts falling due within one year**		
Creditors (20 + 6)	26	
Net current assets		41
Total assets less current liabilities		140
Less **Creditors: amounts falling due after more than one year**		
Debentures (30 + 0)		30
		110
Capital and reserves		
Called-up share capital:		
ordinary shares of £1 each, fully paid		70
Share premium account		10
Profit and loss account		30
		110

The 'capital and reserves' section of the group balance sheet is simply that of Parent plc. The £10m capital and reserves for Subsidiary Ltd cancels out with the £10m 'Investment in 5 million shares of Subsidiary Ltd' in the fixed assets section of the parent company balance sheet.

Activity 8.5

The balance sheets of Large plc and of Small plc, on the date that Large plc bought the shares in Small plc, were as follows:

Balance sheets as at 30 June

	Large plc		Small plc	
	£m	£m	£m	£m
Fixed assets (at cost less depreciation)				
Land		55		–
Plant		43		21
Vehicles		25		17
Investment in 20 million				
shares of Small plc		32		–
		155		38
Current assets				
Stocks	42		18	
Debtors	18		13	
Cash	24		13	
	84		44	
Less **Creditors: amounts falling**				
due within one year				
Creditors	25		20	
Net current assets		59		24
Total assets less current liabilities		214		62
Less **Creditors: amounts falling**				
due after more than one year				
Debentures		50		30
		164		32
Capital and reserves				
Called-up share capital:				
ordinary shares of £1 each, fully paid		100		20
Share premium account		–		5
Profit and loss account		64		7
		164		32

Have a try at deducing the group balance sheet.

The group balance sheet will be as follows:

Balance sheet as at 30 June

	£m	£m
Fixed assets (at cost less depreciation)		
Land (55 + 0)		55
Plant (43 + 21)		64
Vehicles (25 + 17)		42
		161
Current assets		
Stocks (42 + 18)	60	
Debtors (18 + 13)	31	
Cash (24 + 13)	37	
	128	

	£m	£m
Less **Creditors: amounts falling due within one year**		
Creditors (25 + 20)	45	
Net current assets		83
Total assets less current liabilities		244
Less **Creditors: amounts falling due after more than one year**		
Debentures (50 + 30)		80
		164
Capital and reserves		
Called-up share capital:		
ordinary shares of £1 each, fully paid		100
Profit and loss account		64
		164

The 'capital and reserves' section of the group balance sheet is simply that of Large plc. The £32m for the capital and reserves of Small plc cancels out with the £32m 'Investment in 20 million shares of Small plc' in the fixed assets section of the balance sheet of Large plc.

The example and the activity represent the most simple case because:

- The parent owns all of the shares of the subsidiary.
- The price paid for the shares (£10 million and £32 million) exactly equals the 'book' or balance sheet value of the net assets of the subsidiary.
- No trading has taken place since the shares were purchased.

In practice, these three 'simplifications' frequently do not all exist; often none of them exists.

We shall now go on to look at the 'complications', firstly, one by one and then all together.

Less than 100 per cent ownership of the subsidiary by the parent

The problem here is that when we come to set the asset of 'investment in subsidiary', in the balance sheet of the parent, against the 'share capital and reserves' (owners' claim) in the balance sheet of the subsidiary, they do not completely cancel one another.

Example 8.4   The balance sheets of Parent plc and of Subsidiary Ltd, on the date that the former bought the shares in the latter, are the same as in the previous example except that Parent plc owns only 4 million (of the 5 million) shares of Subsidiary Ltd. Thus the investment is only £8 million, instead of £10 million. As a result, Parent plc's cash balance is £2 million greater than in the previous example.

The two balance sheets were as follows:

Balance sheets as at 30 September

	Parent plc £m	Parent plc £m	Subsidiary Ltd £m	Subsidiary Ltd £m
Fixed assets (at cost less depreciation)				
Land		40		5
Plant		30		2
Vehicles		20		2
Investment in 4 million shares of				
Subsidiary Ltd		8		–
		98		9
Current assets				
Stocks	20		3	
Debtors	30		2	
Cash	12		2	
	62		7	
Less **Creditors: amounts falling due within one year**				
Creditors	20		6	
Net current assets		42		1
Total assets less current liabilities		140		10
Less **Creditors: amounts falling due after more than one year**				
Debentures		30		–
		110		10
Capital and reserves				
Called-up share capital:				
ordinary shares of £1 each, fully paid		70		5
Share premium account		10		–
Profit and loss account		30		5
		110		10

As before, to prepare the group balance sheet, we simply add like items together. The problem is that when we come to set the £8 million investment made by Parent plc against the £10 million owners' claim of Subsidiary Ltd, they do not cancel. There is an owners' claim of £2 million in the balance sheet of Subsidiary Ltd that has not been accounted for.

| Activity 8.6 | **Can you puzzle out what the £2 million represents?** |

It represents the extent to which Parent plc does not own all of the shares of Subsidiary Ltd. Parent plc only owns 80 per cent of the shares, and therefore others must own the rest. Since we are including all of the assets and liabilities of Subsidiary Ltd as being those of the group, the group balance sheet needs to acknowledge that there is another source of equity finance, as well as Parent plc.

➡ This £2 million owners' claim is known as '**minority interests**' or 'outsiders' interests'. It is shown in the group balance sheet as an addition to, but not part of, the capital and reserves.

The group balance sheet will be as follows:

Balance sheet as at 30 September

	£m	£m
Fixed assets (at cost less depreciation)		
Land (40 + 5)		45
Plant (30 + 2)		32
Vehicles (20 + 2)		22
		99
Current assets		
Stocks (20 + 3)	23	
Debtors (30 + 2)	32	
Cash (12 + 2)	14	
	69	
Less **Creditors: amounts falling due within one year**		
Creditors (20 + 6)	26	
Net current assets		43
Total assets less current liabilities		142
Less **Creditors: amounts falling due after more than one year**		
Debentures (30 + 0)		30
		112
Capital and reserves		
Called-up share capital: ordinary shares of £1 each, fully paid		70
Share premium account		10
Profit and loss account		30
		110
Minority or outsiders' interests		2
		112

This balance sheet can be interpreted as the group having control over net assets totalling £112 million. Of this, £110 million is financed by the shareholders of the parent company and £2 million by others.

It may have occurred to you that an alternative approach to dealing with less than 100 per cent ownership is to scale down the assets and liabilities, to reflect this, before carrying out the 'consolidation' of the two sets of accounts. Since Parent plc only owns 80 per cent of Subsidiary Ltd, we could multiply all of the figures in Subsidiary Ltd's balance sheet by 0.8 before preparing the group accounts. If we did this, the owners' claim would be reduced to £8 million, which would exactly cancel with the asset in the balance sheet of Parent plc.

Activity 8.7

Can you think of the (logical) reason why we do not 'scale down' for less than 100 per cent owned subsidiaries when preparing the group balance sheet?

The reason that all of the assets and liabilities of the subsidiary are included in the group balance sheet, in these circumstances, is that the parent company *controls* all of the subsidiaries' assets, even though it may not strictly own them all. Control is the key issue in group accounts.

Activity 8.8

The balance sheets of Large plc and of Small plc, on the date that Large plc bought the shares in Small plc, were as follows:

Balance sheets as at 30 June

	Large plc £m	Large plc £m	Small plc £m	Small plc £m
Fixed assets (at cost less depreciation)				
Land		55		–
Plant		43		21
Vehicles		25		17
Investment in 15 million				
shares of Small plc		24		–
		147		38
Current assets				
Stocks	42		18	
Debtors	18		13	
Cash	32		13	
	92		44	
Less Creditors: amounts falling				
due within one year				
Creditors	25		20	
Net current assets		67		24
Total assets less current liabilities		214		62
Less Creditors: amounts falling				
due after more than one year				
Debentures		50		30
		164		32
Capital and reserves				
Called-up share capital:				
ordinary shares of £1 each, fully paid		100		20
Share premium account		–		5
Profit and loss account		64		7
		164		32

Have a go at preparing the group balance sheet.

The group balance sheet will be as follows:

Balance sheet as at 30 June

	£m	£m
Fixed assets (at cost less depreciation)		
Land (55 + 0)		55
Plant (43 + 21)		64
Vehicles (25 + 17)		42
		161
Current assets		
Stocks (42 + 18)	60	
Debtors (18 + 13)	31	
Cash (32 + 13)	45	
	136	
Less **Creditors: amounts falling due within one year**		
Creditors (25 + 20)	45	
Net current assets		91
Total assets less current liabilities		252
Less **Creditors: amounts falling due after more than one year**		
Debentures (50 + 30)		80
		172
Capital and reserves		
Called-up share capital:		
ordinary shares of £1 each, fully paid		100
Profit and loss account		64
		164
Minority interests		8
		172

The £8 million for minority interests represents the 25 per cent of the Small plc shares owned by the 'outside' shareholders (that is, 25 per cent of £32 million).

Paying more or less than the underlying net asset value for the shares

Here the problem is that, even where the subsidiary is 100 per cent owned, the asset of 'shares in the subsidiary', in the balance sheet of the parent, will not exactly cancel against the owners' claim in the balance sheet of the subsidiary. Anything paid in excess of the underlying net asset value of the subsidiary's shares must represent an undisclosed asset which is normally referred to as '**goodwill arising on consolidation**'. Any amount paid below the underlying net asset value is normally referred to as '**capital reserve arising on consolidation**'.

For the sake of simplicity, we shall assume that the asset values reported in the balance sheet of a subsidiary reflect their fair values. We shall, however, consider the situation where this assumption is not made later in the chapter.

Example 8.5

We are returning to the original balance sheets of Parent plc and Subsidiary Ltd, on the date that the former bought the shares in the latter. So Parent plc owns all of the shares in Subsidiary Ltd, but we shall assume that they were bought for £15m rather than £10m. Parent plc's cash balance reflects the higher amount paid. The balance sheets are as follows:

Balance sheets as at 30 September

	Parent plc		Subsidiary Ltd	
	£m	£m	£m	£m
Fixed assets (at cost less depreciation)				
Land		40		5
Plant		30		2
Vehicles		20		2
Investment in 5 million shares of				
Subsidiary Ltd		15		–
		105		9
Current assets				
Stocks	20		3	
Debtors	30		2	
Cash	5		2	
	55		7	
Less **Creditors: amounts falling due within one year**				
Creditors	20		6	
Net current assets		35		1
Total assets less current liabilities		140		10
Less **Creditors: amounts falling due after more than one year**				
Debentures		30		–
		110		10
Capital and reserves				
Called-up share capital:				
ordinary shares of £1 each, fully paid		70		5
Share premium account		10		–
Profit and loss account		30		5
		110		10

The normal routine of adding like items together and cancelling the investment in Subsidiary Ltd shares against the owners' claim of that company is followed, except that the last two do not exactly cancel. The difference is, of course, goodwill arising on consolidation.

The group balance sheet will be as follows:

Balance sheet as at 30 September

	£m	£m
Fixed assets (at cost less depreciation)		
Goodwill arising on consolidation (15 – 10)		5
Land (40 + 5)		45
Plant (30 + 2)		32
Vehicles (20 + 2)		22
		104

	£m	£m
Current assets		
Stocks (20 + 3)	23	
Debtors (30 + 2)	32	
Cash (5 + 2)	<u>7</u>	
	62	
Less **Creditors: amounts falling due within one year**		
Creditors (20 + 6)	<u>26</u>	
Net current assets		<u>36</u>
Total assets less current liabilities		140
Less **Creditors: amounts falling due within one year**		
Debentures (30 + 0)		<u>30</u>
		<u>110</u>
Capital and reserves		
Called-up share capital:		
ordinary shares of £1 each, fully paid		70
Share premium account		10
Profit and loss account		<u>30</u>
		<u>110</u>

The goodwill represents the excess of what was paid by Parent plc for the shares over their underlying net asset value, according to Subsidiary Ltd's balance sheet.

Activity 8.9

The balance sheets of Large plc and of Small plc, on the date that Large plc bought the shares in Small plc, were as follows:

Balance sheets at 30 June

	Large plc		Small plc	
	£m	£m	£m	£m
Fixed assets (at cost less depreciation)				
Land		55		–
Plant		43		21
Vehicles		25		17
Investment in 20 million shares of Small plc		<u>28</u>		<u>–</u>
		151		38
Current assets				
Stocks	42		18	
Debtors	18		13	
Cash	<u>28</u>		<u>13</u>	
	88		44	

	Large plc		Small plc	
	£m	£m	£m	£m
Less **Creditors: amounts falling due within one year**				
Creditors	25		20	
Net current assets		63		24
Total assets less current liabilities		214		62
Less **Creditors: amounts falling due after more than one year**				
Debentures		50		30
		164		32
Capital and reserves				
Called-up share capital:				
ordinary shares of £1 each, fully paid		100		20
Share premium account		–		5
Profit and loss account		64		7
		164		32

Have a go at preparing the group balance sheet.

The group balance sheet will be as follows:

Balance sheet as at 30 June

	£m	£m
Fixed assets (at cost less depreciation)		
Land (55 + 0)		55
Plant (43 + 21)		64
Vehicles (25 + 17)		42
		161
Current assets		
Stocks (42 + 18)	60	
Debtors (18 + 13)	31	
Cash (28 + 13)	41	
	132	
Less **Creditors: amounts falling due within one year**		
Creditors (25 + 20)	45	
Net current assets		87
Total assets less current liabilities		248
Less **Creditors: amounts falling due after more than one year**		
Debentures (50 + 30)		80
		168
Capital and reserves		
Called-up share capital:		
ordinary shares of £1 each, fully paid		100
Capital reserve arising on consolidation (32 − 28)		4
Profit and loss account		64
		168

In effect, the capital reserve arising on consolidation represents the apparent gain that has been made by Large plc as a result of buying assets for less than they are worth (according to the fair values reflected in Small plc's balance sheet).

We shall now take a look at how we cope with a situation where the parent owns less than all of the shares of its subsidiary and it has paid more or less than the underlying net asset value of the shares.

Example 8.6

Again we shall look at Parent plc and of Subsidiary Ltd, on the date that the former bought the shares in the latter. This time we shall combine both of the 'complications' that we have already met. Thus, Parent plc now only owns 80 per cent of the shares of Subsidiary Ltd, for which it paid £3 a share, that is, £1 above their underlying net asset value.

Balance sheets as at 30 September

	Parent plc £m	Parent plc £m	Subsidiary Ltd £m	Subsidiary Ltd £m
Fixed assets (at cost less depreciation)				
Land		40		5
Plant		30		2
Vehicles		20		2
Investment in 4 million shares of				
Subsidiary Ltd		12		–
		102		9
Current assets				
Stocks	20		3	
Debtors	30		2	
Cash	8		2	
	58		7	
Less **Creditors: amounts falling due within one year**				
Creditors	20		6	
Net current assets		38		1
Total assets less current liabilities		140		10
Less **Creditors: amounts falling due after more than one year**				
Debentures		30		–
		110		10
Capital and reserves				
Called-up share capital:				
ordinary shares of £1 each, fully paid		70		5
Share premium account		10		–
Profit and loss account		30		5
		110		10

The normal routine still applies. This means adding like items together and cancelling the investment in Subsidiary Ltd shares against the owners' claim of that company. Again they will not cancel, but this time for a combination of two reasons; minority interests *and* goodwill arising on consolidation.

We need to separate out the two issues before we go on to prepare the group accounts.

To establish the minority interests element, we need simply to calculate the part of the owners' claim of Subsidiary Ltd that is not owned by Parent plc. Parent plc owns 80 per cent of the shares, so others own 20 per cent. Twenty per cent of the owners' claim of Subsidiary Ltd is £2 million (that is, 20 per cent × £10 million).

To discover the appropriate goodwill figure (or capital reserve), we need to compare what Parent plc paid and what it got, in terms of balance sheet values. It paid £12 million and got net assets with a balance sheet value of £8 million (that is, 80 per cent × £10 million). Thus, goodwill is £4 million (that is, 12 − 8).

The group balance sheet will be as follows:

Balance sheet as at 30 September

	£m	£m
Fixed assets (at cost less depreciation)		
Goodwill arising on consolidation		
(12 − (80% × 10))		4
Land (40 + 5)		45
Plant (30 + 2)		32
Vehicles (20 + 2)		22
		103
Current assets		
Stocks (20 + 3)	23	
Debtors (30 + 2)	32	
Cash (8 + 2)	10	
	65	
Less **Creditors: amounts falling due within one year**		
Creditors (20 + 6)	26	
Net current assets		39
Total assets less current liabilities		142
Less **Creditors: amounts falling due after more than one year**		
Debentures (30 + 0)		30
		112
Capital and reserves		
Called-up share capital:		
ordinary shares of £1 each, fully paid		70
Share premium account		10
Profit and loss account		30
Minority interests		2
		112

Activity 8.10

The balance sheets of Large plc and Small plc, on the date that Large plc bought the shares in Small plc, were as follows:

Balance sheets as at 30 June

	Large plc £m	Large plc £m	Small plc £m	Small plc £m
Fixed assets (at cost less depreciation)				
Land		55		–
Plant		43		21
Vehicles		25		17
Investment in 15 million shares of Small plc		21		–
		144		38
Current assets				
Stocks	42		18	
Debtors	18		13	
Cash	35		13	
	95		44	
Less **Creditors: amounts falling due within one year**				
Creditors	25		20	
Net current assets		70		24
Total assets less current liabilities		214		62
Less **Creditors: amounts falling due after more than one year**				
Debentures		50		30
		164		32
Capital and reserves				
Called-up share capital:				
ordinary shares of £1 each, fully paid		100		20
Share premium account		–		5
Profit and loss account		64		7
		164		32

Have a try at preparing the group balance sheet.

The minority interest will be £8 million (that is, 25 per cent of £32 million).

To discover goodwill/capital reserve, we need to compare what was paid (£21 million) with what was obtained (75 per cent of £32 million = £24 million). Thus, we have a capital reserve of £3 million.

The group balance sheet will be as follows:

Balance sheet as at 30 June

	£m	£m
Fixed assets (at cost less depreciation)		
Land (55 + 0)		55
Plant (43 + 21)		64
Vehicles (25 + 17)		42
		161
Current assets		
Stocks (42 + 18)	60	
Debtors (18 + 13)	31	
Cash (35 + 13)	48	
	139	
Less **Creditors: amounts falling due within one year**		
Creditors (25 + 20)	45	
Net current assets		94
Total assets less current liabilities		255
Less **Creditors: amounts falling due after more than one year**		
Debentures (50 + 30)		80
		175
Capital and reserves		
Called-up share capital:		
ordinary shares of £1 each, fully paid		100
Capital reserve arising on consolidation [(75% × 32) − 21]		3
Profit and loss account		64
Minority interests (25% × 32)		8
		175

Trading has taken place since the shares were purchased

Except very rarely, most group balance sheets will be prepared some time after the parent company purchased the shares in the subsidiary. This does not in any way raise major difficulties, but we need to backtrack to the position at the time of the purchase to establish the goodwill/capital reserve.

We shall look at another example, this time a new one will be introduced, just to provide a little variety.

Example 8.7

The balance sheets of Mega plc and Micro plc, as at 31 December, are set out below. Mega plc bought its shares in Micro plc some time ago at which time the latter's share capital was exactly as shown below and the profit and loss account balance stood at £30 million.

Balance sheets as at 31 December

	Mega plc £m	Mega plc £m	Micro plc £m	Micro plc £m
Fixed assets (at cost less depreciation)				
Land		53		18
Plant		34		11
Vehicles		24		9
Investment in 6 million shares of				
Micro plc		33		–
		144		38
Current assets				
Stocks	27		10	
Debtors	29		11	
Cash	11		1	
	67		22	
Less **Creditors: amounts falling due within one year**				
Creditors	23		5	
Net current assets		44		17
Total assets less current liabilities		188		55
Less **Creditors: amounts falling due after more than one year**				
Debentures		50		10
		138		45
Capital and reserves				
Called-up share capital:				
ordinary shares of £1 each, fully paid		100		10
Profit and loss account		38		35
		138		45

We can see that the investment in the balance sheet of Mega plc (£33 million) comes nowhere near cancelling with the £45 million owners' claim of Micro plc. We need to separate out the elements.

Let us start with minority interests. Here we are not concerned at all with the position at the date of the takeover. If the owners' claim of Micro plc totals £45 million at the balance sheet date and the minorities own 4 million of the 10 million shares, their contribution to the financing of the group's assets must be £18 million (that is, 40 per cent × £45 million).

Next let us ask ourselves what Mega plc got when it paid £33 million for the shares. At that time, the capital and reserves part of Micro plc's balance sheet looked like this:

	£m
Called-up share capital:	
ordinary shares of £1 each, fully paid	10
Profit and loss account	30
	40

This means that the net assets of Micro plc must have also been worth (in terms of balance sheet values) £40 million; otherwise the balance sheet would not have balanced. Since Mega plc bought 6 million of 10 million shares, it paid £33 million for net assets worth £24 million (that is, 60 per cent of £40 million). Thus, there is goodwill arising on consolidation of £9 million (that is 33 – 24).

We shall assume that no steps have been taken since the takeover to alter this goodwill figure. We shall consider why such steps may have been taken a little later in this chapter.

In dealing with minority interests and goodwill we have, in effect, picked up the following parts of the owners' claim of Micro plc at 31 December:

■ The minorities' share of both the share capital and reserves (as minority interests).
■ Mega plc's share of the share capital and its share of the reserves as they stood at the date of the takeover (in the calculation of the goodwill figure).

The only remaining part of the owners' claim of Micro plc at 31 December is Mega plc's share of the reserves that have built up since the takeover, that is, its share of £35 million – £30 million = £5 million. This share is £3 million (that is, 60 per cent of £5 million). This is Mega plc's share of the profits that have been earned by its subsidiary since the takeover, to the extent that profits have not already been paid out as dividends. As such, it is logical for this £3 million to be added to the profit and loss account balance of the parent company in arriving at the group reserves.

This treatment of the share capital and reserves of Micro plc can be represented in a tabular form as shown in Figure 8.3.

Figure 8.3

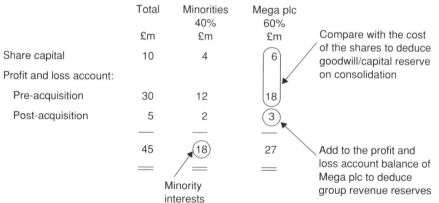

The treatment of the share capital and reserves of Micro plc in producing the group balance sheet

	Total £m	Minorities 40% £m	Mega plc 60% £m	
Share capital	10	4	6	Compare with the cost of the shares to deduce goodwill/capital reserve on consolidation
Profit and loss account:				
Pre-acquisition	30	12	18	
Post-acquisition	5	2	3	Add to the profit and loss account balance of Mega plc to deduce group revenue reserves
	45	18	27	

Minority interests

The minority interest total is simply the appropriate percentage of the subsidiary's total share capital and reserves, without reference to when the reserves arose. The parent's share of the subsidiary's total of share capital and reserves, at the date of the takeover, is compared with the price paid by the parent to deduce the goodwill/capital reserve arising on consolidation. The parent's share of the subsidiary's post-acquisition reserves is added to the parent's reserves to find the total reserves.

The group balance sheet will be as follows:

Balance sheet as at 31 December

Fixed assets (at cost less depreciation)	£m	£m
Goodwill arising on consolidation (33 − (6 + 18))		9
Land (53 + 18)		71
Plant (34 + 11)		45
Vehicles (24 + 9)		33
		158
Current assets		
Stocks (27 + 10)	37	
Debtors (29 + 11)	40	
Cash (11 + 1)	12	
	89	
Less **Creditors: amounts falling due within one year**		
Creditors (23 + 5)	28	
Net current assets		61
Total assets less current liabilities		219
Less **Creditors: amounts falling due after more than one year**		
Debentures (50 + 10)		60
		159
Capital and reserves		
Called-up share capital:		
ordinary shares of £1 each, fully paid		100
Profit and loss account (38 + 3)		41
Minority interests (40% × 45)		18
		159

Activity 8.11

The balance sheets of Grand plc and Petit Ltd, as at 30 June, are set out below. Grand plc bought its shares in Petit Ltd some time ago at which time the latter's share capital was the same as it is currently and the profit and loss account balance stood at £14 million.

Balance sheets as at 30 June

	Grand plc		Petit Ltd	
Fixed assets (at cost less depreciation)	£m	£m	£m	£m
Land		12		10
Plant		14		8
Vehicles		3		6
Investment in 7.5 million				
shares of Petit Ltd		21		–
		50		24
Current assets				
Stocks	10		5	
Debtors	9		4	
Cash	2		2	
	21		11	
Less **Creditors: amounts falling due within one year**				
Creditors	7		3	
Net current assets		14		8
Total assets less current liabilities		64		32

	Grand plc		Petit Ltd	
Less **Creditors: amounts falling due after more than one year**	£m	£m	£m	£m
Debentures		20		–
		44		32
Capital and reserves				
Called-up share capital:				
ordinary shares of £1 each, fully paid		30		10
Profit and loss account		14		22
		44		32

Prepare the balance sheet for the group as at 30 June.

Your answer should be something like this:

Minority interests
25% × £32 million = £8 million

Goodwill arising on consolidation
£21 million − [75% × (£10 million + £14 million)] = £3 million

Grand plc's share of Petit Ltd's post-acquisition reserves
75% × (£22 million − £14 million) = £6 million

Assuming that no steps have been taken since the takeover to alter the goodwill figure, the group balance sheet will be as follows:

Balance sheet as at 30 June

	£m	£m
Fixed assets (at cost less depreciation)		
Goodwill arising on consolidation		3
Land (12 + 10)		22
Plant (14 + 8)		22
Vehicles (3 + 6)		9
		56
Current assets		
Stocks (10 + 5)	15	
Debtors (9 + 4)	13	
Cash (2 + 2)	4	
	32	
Less **Creditors: amounts falling due within one year**		
Creditors (7 + 3)	10	
Net current assets		22
Total assets less current liabilities		78
Less **Creditors: amounts falling due after more than one year**		
Debentures (20 + 0)		20
		58
Capital and reserves		
Called-up share capital:		
ordinary shares of £1 each, fully paid		30
Profit and loss account (14 + 6)		20
Minority interests		8
		58

Goodwill arising on consolidation and balance sheet values

Goodwill on consolidation represents the difference between the cost of acquiring the shares in a subsidiary and the **fair value** of the net assets acquired. In the examples that we have considered so far, we have assumed that the balance sheet values are the same as the fair values of the assets of the subsidiary company. Thus, it has been possible to deduce goodwill by making a comparison of the cost of acquiring the subsidiary with the balance sheet values of the subsidiary. Unfortunately, things are not usually that simple!

Balance sheet values often differ from the fair values of assets. Generally speaking, balance sheet values are lower because accounting conventions, such as prudence and historic cost, conspire to produce a conservative bias. This means that, to calculate goodwill on consolidation, we cannot rely on balance sheet values. We must find out what the fair values of the assets acquired really are.

One further point that should be mentioned is that both the law and the relevant accounting standard require that, when preparing group accounts, the fair values of the subsidiary's assets, at the date on which the parent acquired the subsidiary, are substituted for the balance sheet values of those assets.

Example 8.8 below seeks to illustrate these points.

Example 8.8

The balance sheets of Parent plc and of Subsidiary Ltd (which we last met in Example 8.6) on the date that the former bought the shares in the latter, were as follows:

Balance sheets as at 30 September

	Parent plc £m	Parent plc £m	Subsidiary Ltd £m	Subsidiary Ltd £m
Fixed assets (at cost less depreciation)				
Land		40		5
Plant		30		2
Vehicles		20		2
Investment in 5 million shares of Subsidiary Ltd		15		–
		105		9
Current assets				
Stocks	20		3	
Debtors	30		2	
Cash	5		2	
	55		7	
Less Creditors: amounts falling due within one year				
Creditors	20		6	
Net current assets		35		1
Total assets less current liabilities		140		10
Less Creditors: amounts falling due after more than one year				
Debentures		30		–
		110		10

Capital and reserves	Parent plc £m	£m	Subsidiary Ltd £m	£m
Called-up share capital:				
ordinary shares of £1 each, fully paid		70		5
Share premium account		10		–
Profit and loss account		30		5
		110		10

When Parent plc was valuing the shares of Subsidiary Ltd, it was judged that most of the balance sheet values were in line with the fair values, but that the following values should be applied to the three categories of fixed assets:

	£m
Land	7
Plant	3
Vehicles	3

In addition it was recognised that the subsidiary has a good reputation, which was valued at £1 million. When these fair values are incorporated into the group balance sheet, it will be as follows:

Balance sheet as at 30 September

Fixed assets (at cost less depreciation)	£m	£m
Goodwill		1
Land (40 + 7)		47
Plant (30 + 3)		33
Vehicles (20 + 3)		23
		104
Current assets		
Stocks (20 + 3)	23	
Debtors (30 + 2)	32	
Cash (5 + 2)	7	
	62	
Less **Creditors: amounts falling due within one year**		
Creditors (20 + 6)	26	
Net current assets		36
Total assets less current liabilities		140
Less **Creditors: amounts falling due after more than one year**		
Debentures (30 + 0)		30
		110
Capital and reserves		
Called-up share capital:		
ordinary shares of £1 each, fully paid		70
Share premium account		10
Profit and loss account		30
		110

This example takes the simple case of no minority interests (that is, a 100 per cent subsidiary) and no post-acquisition trading (the balance sheets are at the date of acquisition), but these 'complications' would not alter the principles.

It should be noted that there is no need for the balance sheet of the subsidiary to be adjusted for fair values, just the group balance sheet. In fact, adjusting the subsidiary's balance sheet would contravene the historic cost convention since, as far as the subsidiary is concerned, no change occurs with the takeover except a change in the names on the list of shareholders. No transaction has occurred regarding its assets.

It should also be noted that goodwill is not normally left on the balance sheet. It is written off over its useful life, which is normally taken to be a maximum of twenty years. However, the relevant accounting standard (FRS 10, Goodwill and Intangible Assets) recognises that, in some cases, goodwill may have a longer life, or even an indefinite life.

Intercompany assets and claims

Though members of a group are separate legal entities, the element of control exercised by the parent, and generally close relations between them, tends to lead to intercompany trading and other intercompany transactions. This, in turn, means that a particular asset in one company's balance sheet could relate to an equally sized liability in the balance sheet of another member of the same group.

The principle underlying the group balance sheet is that it should represent the situation as if all the assets and claims of individual group members were directly the assets and claims of the parent company. Since the parent company cannot owe itself money, where there are intercompany balances these must be eliminated when preparing the group balance sheet.

Example 8.9

Delta plc and its subsidiary Gamma plc are the only members of a group. Delta plc sells goods on credit to Gamma plc. At the balance sheet date the following balances existed in the books of the companies:

	Debtors £m	Creditors £m
Delta plc	34	26
Gamma plc	23	18

Included in the debtors of Delta plc, and the creditors of Gamma plc, is £5 million in respect of some recent intercompany trading.

In deducing the figures to be included in the group balance sheet, we have to eliminate the intercompany balance, as follows:

$$\text{Debtors} = 34 - 5 + 23 = £52 \text{ million}$$

$$\text{Creditors} = 26 + 18 - 5 = £39 \text{ million}$$

Note that these consolidated debtors and creditors figures represent what is, respectively, owed by and owed to individuals and organisations outside of the group. This is what they are intended to represent, according to the principles of group accounting.

Exhibit 8.2 is the group balance sheet of Marks and Spencer plc (M&S), the food and clothes retailer as at 31 March 2001. Note the entry for minority interests. This £15.6 million represents that part of the assets of the group that has been financed by those who are not M&S shareholders. M&S shareholders have contributed the remaining £4,645.4 million, so the minorities are not very significant for M&S. This is because most of the subsidiaries are 100 per cent owned by M&S.

Exhibit 8.2	Marks and Spencer plc Group balance sheet at 31 March 2001	
		£m
Fixed assets		
Goodwill		–
Tangible assets:		
Land and buildings		2,735.2
Fit out, fixtures, fittings and equipment		1,291.9
Assets in the course of construction		91.8
		4,118.9
Investments		58.3
		4,177.2
Current assets		
Stocks		472.5
Debtors:		
Receivable within one year		917.2
Receivable after more than one year		1,712.1
Investments		260.0
Cash at bank and in hand		154.4
		3,516.2
Current liabilities		
Creditors: amounts falling due within one year		(1,981.6)
Net current assets		1,534.6
Total assets less current liabilities		5,711.8
Creditors: amounts falling due after more than one year		(735.1)
Provisions for liabilities and charges		(315.7)
Net assets		4,661.0
Capital and reserves		
Called up share capital		716.9
Share premium account		375.6
Revaluation reserve		455.6
Capital redemption reserve		2.6
Profit and loss account		3,094.7
Shareholders' funds (all equity)		4,645.4
Minority interests (all equity)		15.6
Total capital employed		4,661.0

Preparing the group profit and loss account

→ The **group profit and loss account** follows very similar principles to those which apply to the balance sheet. These are:

- Like items are added together. For example, the turnover of each subsidiary is added to that of the parent company to discover group turnover.
- All the amounts appearing under each heading in the profit and loss accounts of subsidiaries are included in the total, even where it is not a wholly owned subsidiary. For example, the turnover of a subsidiary, say 60 per cent owned by the parent, is included in full.
- The interests of minorities are separately identified towards the bottom of the profit and loss account.

Example 8.10

Holder plc owns 75 per cent of the ordinary shares of Sub Ltd. At the date of the acquisition, Sub Ltd's profit and loss account balance stood at £7 million. The outline profit and loss accounts of the two companies for the year ended on 31 December are as follows:

Profit and loss accounts for the year ended 31 December

	Holder plc		Sub Ltd	
	£m	£m	£m	£m
Turnover		83		40
Cost of sales		41		15
Gross profit		42		25
Administration expenses	18		10	
Distribution expenses	6	24	3	13
		18		12
Income from shares in group companies		3		–
Profit before tax		21		12
Taxation		8		4
Profit after tax		13		8
Profit and loss account balance brought forward from the previous year		25		19
		38		27
Dividend on ordinary shares		6		4
Profit and loss account balance carried forward to the following year		32		23

Preparing the group profit and loss account is a very simple matter of adding like items together, except for three issues:

- Dealing with the dividend paid by Sub Ltd to its parent. From Sub Ltd's point of view this is a normal dividend payment to a shareholder. Since Holder plc owns 75 per cent of the shares of Sub Ltd, it will be paid 75 per cent (£3 million) of the dividend paid (£4 million). From Holder plc's point of view, this dividend is part of its income and should be reflected in the profit and loss account as such. From a group point of view, however, it is simply a transfer of money from one member of the group to another and should not, therefore, appear in the group profit and loss account. We deal with this by ignoring both Sub Ltd's dividends and the income from dividends of Holder plc. The £1 million, which is the dividend entitlement of the minorities, is dealt with as part of the minority interests.

■ Not all of the profit after tax of the subsidiary 'belongs' to the group. Twenty-five per cent (£2 million) of it belongs to the minorities. We recognise this in the group profit and loss account by deducting the 25 per cent of the after-tax profit of the subsidiary from the combined after-tax profit. This also takes account of the minorities' entitlement to £1 million dividend.

■ Only the group's share of the post-acquisition reserves (that is, those that have arisen since Sub Ltd became a subsidiary of Holder plc) of Sub Ltd should be included in the group profit and loss account. This is exactly the same point as we encountered when considering the group balance sheet. The post-acquisition profit and loss account balance brought forward is £12 million (that is, £19 million – £7 million). Of this, only £9 million (75 per cent) 'belongs' to the group and should be added to Holder plc's reserves.

The group profit and loss account will be as follows:

Profit and loss account for the year ended 31 December

	£m	£m
Turnover (83 + 40)		123
Cost of sales (41 + 15)		56
Gross profit		67
Administration expenses (18 + 10)	28	
Distribution expenses (6 + 3)	9	37
Profit before tax		30
Taxation (8 + 4)		12
Profit after tax		18
Attributable to minorities		2
Profit after tax attributable to Holder plc shareholders		16
Profit and loss account balance brought forward from the previous year (25 + 9)		34
		50
Dividend on ordinary shares		6
Profit and loss account balance carried forward to the following year		44

This statement says that the assets under the control of the group generated net profit after tax of £18 million. Of this, £2 million is the share of the 'outside' shareholders of Sub Ltd. This follows the normal approach of group accounts of treating all assets, claims, revenues and expenses of group companies as if they were those of the group. Where the subsidiaries are not 100 per cent owned by the parent, this fact is acknowledged by making an adjustment to reflect the minority interests.

Activity 8.12

Ajax plc owns 60 per cent of the ordinary shares of Exeter plc. At the date of the acquisition, Exeter plc's profit and loss account balance stood at £25 million. The outline profit and loss accounts of the two companies for the year ended on 31 December are as follows:

Profit and loss accounts for the year ended 31 December

| | Ajax plc | | Exeter plc | |
	£m	£m	£m	£m
Turnover		120		80
Cost of sales		60		40
Gross profit		60		40
Administration expenses	20		5	
Distribution expenses	10	30	15	20
		30		20
Income from shares in group companies		6		–
Profit before tax		36		20
Taxation		12		10
Profit after tax		24		10
Profit and loss account balance brought forward from the previous year		60		45
		84		55
Dividend on ordinary shares		10		10
Profit and loss account balance carried forward to the following year		74		45

Have a try at preparing a consolidated (group) profit and loss account.

Your answer should look something like this:

Group profit and loss account for the year ended 31 December

	£m	£m
Turnover (120 + 80)		200
Cost of sales (60 + 40)		100
Gross profit		100
Administration expenses (20 + 5)	25	
Distribution expenses (10 + 15)	25	50
Profit before tax		50
Taxation (12 + 10)		22
Profit after tax		28
Attributable to minorities (40% × 10)		4
Profit after tax attributable to Ajax plc shareholders		24
Profit and loss account balance brought forward from the previous year [60 + ((45 − 25) × 60%)]		72
		96
Dividend on ordinary shares		10
Profit and loss account balance carried forward to the following year		86

Exhibit 8.3 is the group profit and loss account of Rexam plc, the consumer packaging and beverage can maker for the year ended 31 December 2000. Note the entry for minority interests. This £3 million represents that part of the after-tax profit of the Rexam group that is attributable to those who are not Rexam shareholders. Rexam shareholders have attributed to them the remaining £10 million. (As an aside, the other interesting feature of this profit and loss account is the size of the ordinary dividend in relation to the profit attributable to ordinary shareholders for the year.)

Exhibit 8.3	**Consolidated profit and loss account for the year ended 31 December**		
		2000 Total £m	1999 Total £m
Turnover			
Continuing operations		2,085	2,007
Acquisitions		639	–
		2,724	2,007
Discontinued operations		60	382
		2,784	2,389
Turnover of associates		(54)	(18)
		2,730	2,371
Operating expenses			
Continuing operations		(1,870)	(1,824)
Acquisitions		(593)	–
		(2,463)	(1,824)
Discontinued operations		(59)	(356)
		(2,522)	(2,180)
Operating profit			
Continuing operations		201	166
Acquisitions		6	–
		207	166
Discontinued operations		1	25
		208	191
Profit on fixed assets – continuing operations		5	5
Disposals of businesses		(64)	31
Profit on ordinary activities before interest		149	227
Interest (Note 6)		(89)	(40)
Profit on ordinary activities before taxation		60	187
Taxation on ordinary activities		(47)	(53)
Profit on ordinary activities after taxation		13	134
Equity minority interests		(3)	(2)
Profit for the financial year		10	132
Dividends on non equity shares		(5)	(6)
Profit attributable to ordinary shareholders		5	126
Ordinary dividends on equity shares		(59)	(58)
Retained (loss)/profit for the financial year		(54)	68

Group cash flow statements

Groups must normally prepare a cash flow statement that follows the same logic as the balance sheet and profit and loss account. That is, to show the movements in all of the cash that is in the control of the group, for the period under review.

→ The preparation of a **group cash flow statement** follows the same rules as apply to the preparation of the statement for individual companies. In view of this we need not spend time looking separately at cash flow statements in a group context.

? Self-assessment question 8.1

The balance sheets, as at 31 December last year, and profit and loss accounts, for the year ended last 31 December, of Great plc and Small plc are set out below. Great plc bought its shares in Small plc on 1 January last year at which time the latter's share capital was the same as it is currently and the profit and loss account balance stood at £35 million.

At the time of the acquisition, the fair value of all the assets of Small plc was thought to be the same as their balance sheet values, except for land whose fair value was thought to be £5 million more than the balance sheet value. It has been decided that any goodwill arising on consolidation, after taking account of the fair value of Small plc's land, should be depreciated in the group profit and loss account at the rate of 20 per cent each year for last year and the next four years.

Balance sheets as at 31 December last year

	Great plc £m	Great plc £m	Small plc £m	Small plc £m
Fixed assets (at cost less depreciation)				
Land		80		14
Plant		33		20
Vehicles		20		11
Investment in 16 million				
shares of Small plc		53		–
		186		45
Current assets				
Stocks	20		9	
Debtors	21		6	
Cash	17		5	
	58		20	
Less Creditors: amounts falling due within one year				
Creditors	17		5	
Net current assets		41		15
Total assets less current liabilities		227		60

	Great plc		Small plc	
	£m	£m	£m	£m
Less **Creditors: amounts falling due after more than one year**				
Debentures		50		–
		177		60
Capital and reserves				
Called-up share capital:				
ordinary shares of £1 each, fully paid		100		20
Profit and loss account		77		40
		187		60

Profit and loss accounts for the year ended 31 December last year

	Great plc		Small plc	
	£m	£m	£m	£m
Turnover		91		53
Cost of sales		46		24
Gross profit		45		29
Administration expenses	10		7	
Distribution expenses	7	17	4	11
		28		18
Income from shares in group companies		4		–
Profit before tax		32		18
Taxation		9		8
Profit after tax		23		10
Profit and loss account balance brought forward from the previous year		65		35
		88		45
Dividend on ordinary shares		11		5
Profit and loss account balance carried forward to the following year		77		40

Required:
Prepare the balance sheet and profit and loss account for the group.

Accounting for less than a controlling interest – associate companies

You may wonder what happens when a group makes a substantial investment in a company but this does not provide the group with a controlling interest. In other words, the company whose shares have been acquired does not become a subsidiary. Well, one approach would be to simply include the investment of shares in the company at cost in the group's consolidated balance sheet. Assuming the shares are held on a long-term basis, they would be treated as a fixed asset. Any dividends received from the investment would be treated as income in the relevant consolidated profit and loss account.

The problem with this approach, however, is that companies normally pay out in dividends much less than the profits earned for the period. The profits that are not distributed, but are ploughed back in order to generate more profits for the future, still belong to the shareholders. From the perspective of the group, the treatment described would not, therefore, reflect fully the investment made. Where the investment made by the investing group does not involve the purchase of a substantial shareholding in the company, this problem is over-looked and so the treatment of the investment described above is applied. However, where the investment involves the purchase of a significant number of voting shares in the company, a different kind of accounting treatment may be adopted.

Associate companies

To deal with the problem identified above, a particular type of company – an **associate company** has been defined. An associate company is one in which an investing company or group has a substantial but not a controlling interest in it. To be more precise, it is a company in which another company or group has a long-term interest and can exercise significant influence over the operating and financial policies of that company. This influence is usually achieved through representation on the Board of Directors of the company and is supported by a substantial interest in the voting shares of the company. A holding of at least 20 per cent of the voting shares of a company would suggest (but not guarantee) that the investing company or group is in a position of significant influence. The relevant accounting standard (FRS 9, Associates and Joint Ventures) will pro-vide you with more detailed guidelines concerning what constitutes an associate company.

The accounting treatment of an associate company falls somewhere between consolidation and the treatment of small share investments, as described at the beginning of this section. Let us assume, that a group invests in a company, which then becomes an associate of the group. The accounting treatment will be as follows:

- In the consolidated profit and loss account, the group's share of the operating profit of the associate company will be shown and will be added to the operating profit of the Group. As operating profit represents the profit before interest and tax, the group's share of any interest payable and tax relating to the associate company will also be shown and will be deducted in order to derive the net profit after tax for the group and its associate company.
- In the consolidated balance sheet, the investment made in the associate com-pany will be shown and the group's share of any post-acquisition reserves will be added to the investment. This will have the effect of showing more fully the investment made in the associate company.
- Dividends received by the group from the associate company will not be included in the consolidated profit and loss account. This is because the group's share of the associated company's profit will already be fully reflected in the accounts.

To illustrate these points, let us take a simple example.

Example 8.11

Group A owns 25 per cent of the ordinary shares of company B. The price paid for the shares was £26m and there was no goodwill arising from the purchase. Group A bought its shares in company B, when the latter's reserves stood at £24m. The reserves of company B have increased to £40m by the current year ended 31 March.

The profit and loss account for group A and company B for the current year are as follows:

Profit and loss accounts for the current year ended 31 March

	Group A Consolidated P&L account	Company B P&L account
	£000	£000
Sales	800,000	100,000
Cost of sales	500,000	60,000
Gross profit	300,000	40,000
Operating expenses	120,000	12,000
Operating profit	180,000	28,000
Dividend – company B	10,000	
	190,000	
Interest payable	30,000	8,000
Profit from ordinary activities		
before tax	160,000	20,000
Corporation tax payable	40,000	4,000
Profit after tax	120,000	16,000
Minority interest	30,000	–
	90,000	16,000
Dividends payable	30,000	12,000
Retained profit	60,000	4,000

To comply with the relevant standard (FRS 9, Associates and Joint Ventures), the dividend received from company B will be eliminated from the consolidated profit and loss account of group A. However, group A's share of the operating profit of company B as well as its share of interest payable and taxation relating to company B will be incorporated within the consolidated profit and loss account of the group. The revised profit and loss account for the group will, therefore, be as follows:

	£000	Group A Consolidated P&L account £000	
Sales		800,000	
Cost of sales		500,000	
Gross profit		300,000	
Operating expenses		120,000	
Group operating profit		180,000	
Share of operating profit of			
associate – company B		7,000	(25% × £28,000)
Total operating profit		187,000	

	£000	Group A Consolidated P&L account £000	
Interest payable			
Group	30,000		
Associate – company B	2,000	32,000	(25% × £8,000)
Profit on ordinary activities			
before tax		155,000	
Corporation tax payable			
Group	40,000		
Associate – company B	1,000	41,000	(25% × £4,000)
Profit after tax		114,000	
Minority interest		30,000	
		84,000	
Dividends payable[a]		30,000	
Retained profit		54,000	

[a] The only dividends reflected are those of Group A.

The consolidated balance sheet of Group A, treating company B as an associate company, would include an amount for the investment in company B that is calculated as follows:

Extract from Group A's balance sheet as at 31 March (current year)

	£000	
Cost of investment in associated company	26,000	
Share of post-acquisition reserves	4,000	(that is, 25% × (40 − 24))
	£30,000	

Activity 8.13

What is the crucial difference between the approach taken when consolidating subsidiary company results and incorporating the results of associated companies, as far as the balance sheet and profit and loss account are concerned?

In preparing group accounts, all of the items in the statements are added together, as if the parent owned them all, even when the subsidiary is less than 100 per cent owned. For example, the sales figure in the consolidated profit and loss account is the sum of all the sales made by group companies, the stock figure in the balance sheet is the sum of all the stock held by all members of the group.

When dealing with associated companies, we only deal with the shareholding company's share of the profit of the associate and its effect on the value of the shareholding.

Exhibit 8.4 is the group profit and loss account of Cadbury Schweppes plc, the confectionery and drinks manufacturer, for the year ended 31 December 2000. The group's share of the operating profit of its associates is clearly shown on the face of the consolidated profit and loss account. However, to avoid excessive detail, the group's share of interest payable and tax of the associated companies has been relegated to notes to the accounts. Most of the company's associated companies are overseas companies that are involved in some aspect of confectionary and beverages, but they also include a 26.7% stake in Camelot Group plc, the business which operates the UK national lottery.

Exhibit 8.4

Cadbury Schweppes plc
Group Profit and Loss Account for the year ended 31 December 2000

	2000 £m	1999 £m
Turnover		
Continuing operations	4,575	4,234
Discontinued operations	–	67
	4,575	4,301
Operating costs		
Trading expenses	(3,813)	(3,603)
Major restructuring costs	(49)	(64)
Exceptional items	–	–
	(3,862)	(3,667)
Trading Profit		
Continuing operations	713	618
Discontinued operations	–	16
Group Operating Profit	713	634
Share of operating profit in associates	65	35
Total Operating Profit including associates	778	669
Profit on sale of subsidiaries and investments	27	350
Profit on Ordinary Activities before Interest	805	1,019
Net interest	(49)	(61)
Profit on Ordinary Activities before Taxation	756	958
Taxation		
–On operating profit, associates and interest	(224)	(181)
–On profit on sale of subsidiaries and investments	–	(34)
	(224)	(215)
Profit on Ordinary Activities after Taxation	532	743
Equity minority interests	(12)	(79)
Non-equity minority interests	(24)	(22)
Profit for the Financial Year	496	642
Dividends paid and proposed to ordinary shareholders	(209)	(202)
Profit Retained for the Financial Year	287	440

The argument against consolidation

There seems to be a compelling logic for consolidating the results of subsidiaries controlled by a parent company, to reflect the fact that the shareholders of the parent company effectively control all of the assets of all of the companies in the group. There is also, however, a fairly strong argument against doing so.

Anyone reading the consolidated accounts of a group of companies could be misled into believing that trading with any member of the group would, in effect, be the same as trading with the group as a whole. The person might imagine that all of the group's assets could be called upon to meet any amounts owed by any member of the group. This would be untrue, however. Only the assets owned by the particular group member would be accessible to any creditor of that group member. The reason for this is, of course, the legal separateness of the limited company and its shareholder(s), which in turn leads to limited liability of individual group members. There would be absolutely no legal obligation on a parent company, nor a fellow subsidiary, to meet the debts of a struggling subsidiary. In fact this is a reason why some businesses operate through a series of subsidiaries, a point that was made early in this chapter.

Despite this criticism of consolidation it is a very popular legal requirement throughout the world.

Summary

Most larger businesses operate not through one company but through a group structure. The reasons for this include establishing and/or maintaining a sense of identity and 'ring fencing' individual parts of the business to gain separate limited liability for each part. As well as individual members of the group being required to produce annual accounts, the parent company is also required, by law, to produce accounts for the group as a whole. The basic principle of group accounting is that the various statements should reflect transactions as if the assets of subsidiaries were owned directly by the parent company. This means that, in essence, the group statements consist of the sum of the various like items which appear in the accounts of the individual companies. Thus the turnover for the group, which will be shown in the profit and loss account of the group, is the sum of the turnover figures of all individual group members. Certain minor complications arise, for example where the parent does not completely own all the shares of a particular subsidiary, but these are fairly easy to cope with.

Where a company has a significant holding in another, but less than that which is necessary to exercise control, the latter is said to be an associated company of the former. Special rules apply to the manner in which the results of the associated company are incorporated into the accounts of the shareholding company.

→ Key terms

Parent company   p. 241
Subsidiary company   p. 241
Group of companies   p. 241
Group accounts   p. 241
Takeover   p. 242
Holding company   p. 242
Target company   p. 245
Group balance sheet   p. 252
Consolidated (financial statement)
   p. 252

Minority interests   p. 257
Goodwill arising on consolidation
   p. 259
Capital reserve arising on consolidation
   p. 259
Fair values   p. 271
Group profit and loss account   p. 275
Group cash flow statement   p. 279
Associate company   p. 281

Further reading

If you would like to explore the topics covered in this chapter in more depth, we recommend the following books:

Financial Reporting, *Alexander, D.* and *Britton, A.*, 6th edn, Thomson Learning 2001, chapter 24.
Financial Accounting and Reporting, *Elliott, B.* and *Elliott, J.*, 5th edn, Financial Times/Prentice Hall 2001, chapters 19–22.
Financial Accounting, *Melville, A.*, 2nd edn, Financial Times/Prentice Hall 1999, chapter 18.

? REVIEW QUESTIONS

8.1   When does a group relationship arise and what are its consequences for accounting?

8.2   What does a group balance sheet show?

8.3   Quite often, when an existing company wishes to start a new venture, perhaps to produce a new product or render a new service, it will form a subsidiary company as a vehicle for the new venture. Why is this, why not have the new venture conducted by the original company?

8.4   What is an associated company and what are the consequences for accounting of one company being the associated company of a group of companies?

? EXERCISES

Exercises 8.1–8.4 are more advanced that 8.5–8.8. Those with coloured numbers have answers at the back of the book.

8.1   Giant plc bought a majority shareholding in Jack Ltd, on the 31 March. On that date the balance sheet of the two companies were as follows:

Balance sheets as at 31 March

	Giant plc		Jack Ltd	
	£m	£m	£m	£m
Fixed assets (at cost less depreciation)				
Land		27		12
Plant		55		8
Vehicles		18		7
Investment in 10 million shares				
of Jack Ltd		30		–
		130		27
Current assets				
Stocks	33		13	
Debtors	42		17	
Cash	22		5	
	97		35	
Less **Creditors: amounts falling**				
due within one year				
Creditors	41		19	
Net current assets		56		16
Total assets *less* current liabilities		186		43
Less **Creditors: amounts falling**				
due after more than one year				
Debentures		50		13
		136		30

	Giant plc		Jack Ltd	
	£m	£m	£m	£m
Capital and reserves				
Called-up share capital:				
ordinary shares of £1 each, fully paid		50		10
Share premium account		40		5
Revaluation reserve		–		8
Profit and loss account		46		7
		136		30

Assume that the balance sheet values of Jack Ltd's assets represent 'fair' values. Prepare the group balance sheet immediately following the takeover.

8.2   The balance sheets of Jumbo plc and of Nipper plc, on the date that Jumbo plc bought the shares in Nipper plc, were as follows:

Balance sheets as at 31 March

	Jumbo plc		Nipper plc	
	£m	£m	£m	£m
Fixed assets (at cost less depreciation)				
Land		84		18
Plant		34		33
Vehicles		45		12
Investment in 12 million shares				
of Nipper plc		24		–
		187		63
Current assets				
Stocks	55		32	
Debtors	26		44	
Cash	14		10	
	95		86	
Less **Creditors: amounts falling**				
due within one year				
Creditors	41		39	
Net current assets		54		47
Total assets *less* current liabilities		241		110
Less **Creditors: amounts falling**				
due after more than one year				
Debentures		100		70
		141		40
Capital and reserves				
Called-up share capital:				
ordinary shares of £1 each, fully paid		100		20
Share premium account		–		12
Profit and loss account		41		8
		141		40

Assume that the balance sheet values of Nipper plc's assets represent fair values. Prepare the group balance sheet immediately following the share acquisition.

8.3 An abridged set of consolidated financial statements for Toggles plc is given below.

Toggles plc
Consolidated profit and loss account for the year ended 30 June

	£m
Turnover	172.0
Operating profit	21.2
Less Taxation	6.4
Profit after taxation	14.8
Less Minority interest	2.4
Profit for year	12.4
Less Dividends	8.5
Retained profit for year	3.9

Consolidated balance sheet as at 30 June

	£m	£m
Intangible assets		
Goodwill on consolidation		7.2
Tangible assets		
Fixed assets		85.6
Current assets		
Stock	21.8	
Debtors	16.4	
Cash	1.7	
	39.9	
Creditors: amounts falling due within one year		
Trade creditors	15.3	
Net current assets		24.6
		117.4
Capital and reserves		
Share capital		100.0
Retained profit		16.1
		116.1
Minority interest		1.3
		117.4

Required:
(a) Answer, briefly, the following questions:
   (i) What is meant by 'minority interest' in both the profit and loss account and the balance sheet?
   (ii) What is meant by 'goodwill on consolidation'?
   (iii) Why will the 'retained profit' figure on the consolidated balance sheet usually be different from the 'retained profit' as shown in the parent company's balance sheet?
(b) Explain the purposes and advantages in preparing consolidated accounts for the parent company's shareholders.

8.4 Arnold plc owns 75 per cent of the ordinary shares of Baker plc. At the date of the acquisition, Baker plc's profit and loss account balance stood at £17 million. The outline profit and loss accounts of the two companies for the year ended on 31 December are as follows:

Profit and loss accounts for the year ended 31 December

	Arnold plc £m	Arnold plc £m	Baker plc £m	Baker plc £m
Turnover		83		47
Cost of sales		36		19
Gross profit		47		28
Administration expenses	14		7	
Distribution expenses	21	35	10	17
		12		11
Income from shares in group companies		3		–
Profit before tax		15		11
Taxation		4		3
Profit after tax		11		8
Profit and loss account balance brought forward from the previous year		34		21
		45		29
Dividend on ordinary shares		12		4
Profit and loss account balance carried forward to the following year		33		25

Prepare the consolidated (group) profit and loss account for Arnold plc and its subsidiary for the year ended 31 December.

8.5 The summary balance sheets for Apple Limited and Pear Limited are set out below.

Balance sheets as at 30 September

	Apple Limited £000	Apple Limited £000	Pear Limited £000	Pear Limited £000
Fixed assets		950		320
Shares in Pear Limited		240		–
Current assets				
Stocks	320		160	
Debtors	180		95	
Cash at bank	41		15	
	541		270	
Less Creditors: amounts due within one year				
Trade creditors	108		87	
Taxation	54		55	
Dividend	62		–	
	224		142	
Net current assets		317		128
Long-term loan		(500)		(160)
		1,007		288
Capital and reserves:				
£1 fully paid ordinary shares		700		200
Reserves		307		88
		1,007		288

Apple Ltd purchased 150,000 shares in Pear Ltd at a price of £1.60 per share on 30 September (the above balance sheet date).

Prepare a consolidated balance sheet for Apple Ltd as at 30 September.

8.6 Abridged statements for Harvest Limited and Wheat Limited as at 30 June this year are set out below. On 1 July last year Harvest Limited acquired 800,000 ordinary shares in Wheat Limited for a payment of £3,500,000. At that date and at 30 June this year, the assets in the balance sheet of Wheat Limited were shown at fair market values.

Balance sheets as at 30 June this year

	Harvest Limited		Wheat Limited	
	£000	£000	£000	£000
Tangible fixed assets		10,850		4,375
Investment in Wheat Limited		3,500		–
Current assets	3,775		1,470	
Current liabilities	(2,926)		(1,395)	
		849		75
Creditors not falling due within one year				
Bank loans		(7,000)		(2,500)
		8,199		1,950
Share capital (£1 shares)		2,000		1,000
Share premium account		3,000		500
Revenue reserves at				
1 July last year	2,800		375	
Profit for current year	399		75	
		3,199		450
		8,199		1,950

Prepare the consolidated balance sheet for Harvest Ltd as at 30 June this year, using the data given above.

8.7 On 1 July 2000 Pod Limited purchased 225,000 £1 fully paid ordinary shares of Pea Limited for a consideration of £500,000. Simplified balance sheets for both companies for the year ended 30 June 2002 are set out below.

Balance sheets as at 30 June 2002

	Pod Limited		Pea Limited	
	£	£	£	£
Fixed assets		1,104,570		982,769
Investments				
Shares in subsidiary		500,000		–
Current assets				
Stocks	672,471		294,713	
Debtors	216,811		164,517	
Amounts due from subsidiary company	76,000		–	
Cash	2,412		1,361	
	967,694		460,591	
Creditors: amounts due within one year				
Creditors	184,719		137,927	
Amounts owing to holding company	–		76,000	
Overdraft	68,429		25,681	
	253,148		239,608	

	Pod Limited		Pea Limited	
	£	£	£	£
Net current assets		714,546		220,983
Creditors: amounts due after more than one year				
Bank loan		(800,000)		(750,000)
		1,519,116		453,752
Capital and reserves				
Share capital: £1 ordinary shares		750,000		300,000
Share premium		250,000		50,000
Reserves at 1.7.2001	449,612		86,220	
Profit for year	69,504		17,532	
Reserves at 30.6.2002		519,116		103,752
		1,519,116		453,752

Prepare a consolidated balance sheet for Pod Ltd and its subsidiary company as at 30 June 2002.

8.8 The balance sheets for Maxi Limited and Mini Limited are set out below.

Balance sheets as at 31 March this year

	Maxi Limited		Mini Limited	
	£000	£000	£000	£000
Fixed assets				
Tangible assets		23,000		17,800
1,500,000 shares in Mini Limited		5,000		–
Current assets				
Stocks	5,000		2,400	
Debtors	4,280		1,682	
Amounts owed by Maxi Limited	–		390	
Cash at bank	76		1,570	
	9,356		6,042	
Creditors: amounts owing within one year				
Trade creditors	3,256		2,400	
Other creditors	1,047		1,962	
Amounts owed to Mini Limited	390		–	
Dividend payment	400		–	
Overdraft	2,450		–	
	7,543		4,362	
Net current assets		1,813		1,680
Creditors: amounts due after more than one year				
Bank loans		(13,000)		(14,000)
		16,813		5,480

	Maxi Limited		Mini Limited	
	£000	£000	£000	£000
Capital and reserves				
10,000,000 £1 ordinary shares				
fully paid		10,000		
2,000,000 50p ordinary shares				
fully paid				1,000
Share premium account		3,000		2,000
Profit and loss account at				
beginning of year		3,100		2,080
Profit for the year		713		400
		16,813		5,480

On 1 April last year, Maxi Limited purchased 1,500,000 shares of Mini Limited for a consideration of £5m.

Prepare a consolidated balance sheet for Maxi Limited at 31 March this year.

CHAPTER 9

Expanding the annual financial report

Introduction

Over the years, there has been a trend towards greater disclosure of information in the annual financial reports of limited companies. Various reasons can be cited for this trend. The increasing complexity of business, the increasing sophistication of users and an increasing recognition of the responsibilities of businesses towards a variety of stakeholder groups are some of the more important of these reasons.

In this chapter we consider some additional reports that may be provided by companies. We shall see that some of these reports, such as environmental reports, go beyond the conventional boundaries of accounting and imply a rethinking of the way in which we define and measure business success.

OBJECTIVES   When you have completed this chapter, you should be able to:

- Explain the nature and purpose of the value added statement and prepare a simple value added statement from available information.
- Discuss the effect of inflation on the conventional financial statements and explain how the problem of inflation may be dealt with.
- Discuss the need for environmental and social reports and explain the key issues that confront a business seeking to publish such reports.
- Explain the concept of sustainable development and the nature of triple bottom line reporting.

The value added statement

➡ The **value added statement (VAS)** came to prominence in the mid-1970s following publication of an influential discussion document entitled *The Corporate Report* (see reference (1) at the end of the chapter). This report argued that the VAS should be seen as an important financial statement that:

> elaborates on the profit and loss account and in time may come to be regarded as a preferable way of describing performance . . .

Following publication of *The Corporate Report*, two government reports lent further support for the inclusion of the VAS within the annual reports of limited companies.

The VAS is similar to the profit and loss account in certain respects and, indeed, can be seen as a modified form of the profit and loss account. Both financial statements are concerned with measuring the operating performance of a business over a period of time and both are based on the matching convention. However, the VAS differs from the profit and loss account in so far as it is concerned with measuring the *valued added* by a business rather than the *profit earned*.

A business can be viewed as buying in goods and services to which it then 'adds value'. The method of calculating value added is set out in Figure 9.1.

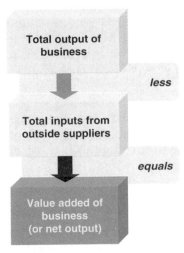

| Figure 9.1 | Calculating value added by a business |

The figure indicates that value added is, like profit, a residual figure. It represents the amount remaining after the cost of total inputs has been deducted from the value of total outputs received by the business.

The total output of the business will normally be the sales revenues for the period. The total inputs will be the bought-in materials and services such as stock purchases, rent, rates, electricity, telephone and so on. The resulting figure of net output, or value added, represents the income which has been generated from the collective effort of employees, suppliers of capital and government.

The VAS is seen as providing a broader focus than the profit and loss account. The problem with the conventional profit and loss account, so it is argued, is that it takes an owner perspective. It is concerned only with measuring the income attributable to the shareholders of the business. However, there are other groups who contribute to, and have a stake in, the wealth generated by a business. These other stakeholders include the employees, government and lenders. The VAS provides a measure of income generated by all the stakeholders and shows how this income, or value added, is then distributed between them.

Example 9.1 shows a value added statement.

Example 9.1

Value added statement for the year ended 30 June

	£m	£m
Turnover		130.6
Less Bought-in materials and services		88.4
Value added		42.2

Applied in the following way:

	£m	£m
To employees		
Wages, pensions and fringe benefits		28.1
To suppliers of capital		
Interest payable on loans	2.6	
Dividends to shareholders	3.8	6.4
To pay government		
Corporation tax payable		3.2
To provide for maintenance and expansion of assets		
Depreciation of fixed assets	3.0	
Retained profits	1.5	4.5
		42.2

From Example 9.1 we can see that the value added statement consists of two elements. The first is concerned with deriving a measure of value added for the period (here £42.2 million), which is achieved by deducting the bought-in materials and services from sales revenue. The second element is concerned with showing how that value added is applied. That is, it shows how value added is divided between the various stakeholder groups and how much is retained within the business. The depreciation and profits retained within the business can be reinvested so as to maintain and expand the asset base.

An important point to note is that the VAS will not provide any information which is not already contained within the conventional profit and loss account. Rather, it rearranges this information so as to provide new insights concerning the performance of the business.

Activity 9.1

Ray Cathode (Lighting Supplies) plc has produced the following:

Profit and loss account for the year ended 31 December

	£m	£m
Sales		198
Less Cost of sales		90
Gross profit		108
Salaries and wages	35	
Rent and rates	18	
Insurance	3	
Light and heat	10	

	£m	£m
Interest payable	6	
Postage and stationery	1	
Advertising	4	
Depreciation	19	96
Net profit before taxation		12
Corporation tax payable		4
Net profit after taxation		8
Dividends payable		3
Retained profit for the year		5

From this information, see if you can produce a value added statement for the year. (Use the format in the illustration above to guide you.)

Your answer should be as follows:

Value added statement for the year ended 31 December

	£m	£m
Turnover		198
Less Bought-in materials and services		
(90 + 18 + 3 + 10 + 1 + 4)		126
Value added		72
Applied in the following way:		
To employees		
Salaries and wages		35
To suppliers of capital		
Interest payable on loans	6	
Dividends to shareholders	3	9
To pay government		
Corporation tax payable		4
To provide for maintenance and expansion of assets		
Depreciation of fixed assets	19	
Retained profits	5	24
		72

Activity 9.2

What useful information can you glean from the VAS in Activity 9.1?

The VAS in Activity 9.1 reveals that nearly half of the value added generated by the business is distributed to employees in the form of salaries and wages. This proportion is much higher than that distributed to suppliers of capital. A relatively high proportion of value added being distributed to employees is not unusual (which may explain the enthusiasm among some managers for publishing this statement). The business retains one third of the value added to provide for maintenance and expansion of assets. A high proportion of value added retained may suggest a concern for growth to be financed through internally generated sources. The proportion of value added required to pay corporation tax is relatively small.

Advantages of the value added statement

A major advantage claimed for the VAS is that it can contribute towards better relations between employees, managers and shareholders. It is said to encourage a team spirit among those with a stake in the business. It reflects the view that the business is a coalition of interests and that business success depends on co-operation between the various stakeholders. By identifying employees as an important stakeholder, it is hoped that they will feel more a part of the team and will respond by showing greater co-operation and commitment. In addition, the VAS should emphasise to managers that employees are an important part of the team and not simply an expense: which is how they are portrayed in the conventional profit and loss account.

A second major advantage claimed is that a number of useful ratios can be derived from this statement. These include:

- Value added to sales (per cent)
- Value added per £1 of wages
- Dividends to value added (per cent)
- Tax to value added (per cent)
- Depreciation and retentions to value added (per cent)
- Value added to capital employed (per cent)

Activity 9.3

Calculate each of the above ratios using the information contained in the solution to Activity 9.1 above. How could these ratios be useful? (For purposes of calculation, assume that the capital employed of the company is £80 million.)

Your answer should be as follows:

$$\text{Value added to sales} = \frac{72}{198} \times 100\%$$

$$= 36.4\%$$

The lower this ratio, the greater the reliance of the business on outside sources of materials and services. For example, a wine retailer that purchases its wine from a wholesaler is likely to have a relatively low value added to sales ratio whereas a wine retailer that owns its own vineyards and bottling facilities will have a much higher ratio. The lower the ratio the more vulnerable the business will be to difficulties encountered from external suppliers.

$$\text{Value added per £1 of wages} = \frac{72}{35}$$

$$= 2.1$$

This ratio is a measure of labour productivity. In this case, the employees are generating £2.1 of value added for every £1 of wages expended. The higher the ratio, the higher the level of productivity. This ratio may be useful when making comparisons between businesses. Normally, the ratio would be higher than 1.0. A ratio of less than 1.0 means that employees are earning more than the value of their output.

$$\text{Dividends to value added} = \frac{3}{72} \times 100\%$$

$$= 4.2\%$$

This ratio calculates that portion of value added which will be received in cash more or less immediately by shareholders. The trend of this ratio may provide an insight to the distribution policy of the business over time. It is important to remember, however, that shareholders also benefit, in the form of capital growth, from amounts reinvested in the business. Thus, the ratio is only a partial measure of the benefits received by shareholders.

$$\text{Tax to value added} = \frac{4}{72} \times 100\%$$

$$= 5.6\%$$

This ratio calculates that portion of the value added which is payable to government in the form of taxes. It may be useful in assessing whether or not the business has an unfair burden of taxation.

$$\text{Depreciation and retentions to value added} = \frac{24}{72} \times 100\%$$

$$= 33.3\%$$

This ratio may provide an insight to the ability or inclination of the business to raise finance for new investment from internal operations rather than from external sources. A high ratio may suggest a greater ability or inclination to raise finance internally than a low ratio.

$$\text{Value added to capital employed} = \frac{72}{80} \times 100\%$$

$$= 90\%$$

This ratio is a measure of the productivity of capital employed. A high ratio is, therefore, normally preferred to a low ratio. Once again, this may be a useful ratio for comparison between companies.

Problems of the value added statement

The proposal to include a VAS as part of the annual report was, at first, greeted with enthusiasm, particularly among large companies. A survey of 300 large companies revealed that, in 1980–81, almost 30 per cent of these companies included the VAS in their annual reports. However, this survey was taken at a point in time when the VAS was probably at the height of its popularity. Since then its fortunes have gone into sharp decline for the reasons described below.

Although the VAS simply rearranges information contained in the conventional profit and loss account, the effect of this rearrangement is to raise a number of difficult measurement and reporting problems. Many of these problems have not really been resolved and this has undermined greater acceptance of the statement. The more important of these problems are:

- The team concept
- Team membership
- The classification of items
- The importance of profit

The team concept

Some commentators are uncomfortable with the idea that employees, shareholders and managers can be viewed as part of a team which shares common objectives. An alternative view is to regard employees and suppliers of capital as antagonists with opposing interests which stem from the nature of capitalist society. If this view is accepted, the VAS may be regarded as no more than a public relations exercise designed to obscure the underlying conflict between suppliers of capital and employees.

Team membership

Even if the team concept is accepted, there is still an issue concerning who should be included in the team (and who should be excluded). You will recall that the team is defined as being employees, suppliers of capital and government. However, this may not reflect the key relationships within a business. For example, many businesses have a close and longstanding relationship with their major suppliers and this relationship may be an important contribution towards success. It may, therefore, seem inappropriate to exclude this particular group from team membership.

Activity 9.4	Why cannot suppliers be included as members of the team? What would be the implications for the VAS?

To derive a figure of value added, the cost of bought-in materials and services must be deducted from turnover. Thus, a statement of value added could not really be prepared if suppliers were brought into the team.

The inclusion of government as a team member may not necessarily reflect reality. Although government may well benefit from the performance of a business through the taxation system, it may not make any direct contribution towards business success (although an indirect contribution through infrastructure investment, such as roads, is made). However, businesses do sometimes benefit directly from subsidies and grants; in which case, government could more easily be regarded as a full team member.

The classification of items

The VAS is beset with classification issues and problems. For example, depreciation is shown in the example above as an application of value added and is placed under the heading 'To provide for the maintenance and expansion of assets'. However, there is an argument for placing this item under 'Bought-in materials and services' which means it will then be included in the calculation of the value added figure.

Activity 9.5	Can you think why depreciation might be reclassified as 'Bought-in materials and services'?

A fixed asset is purchased to provide a service to the business. Like bought-in materials and services, a fixed asset is consumed in the process of generating revenue. The only real difference is that the consumption of a fixed asset is likely to extend over more than one accounting period. Depreciation is a measure of the fixed asset consumed during the period and should, it is argued, be treated in the same way as the bought-in materials and services which are consumed in that period. It is worth pointing out that, if a fixed asset were on hire or lease rather than being purchased outright, the rental charges would probably be included as part of bought-in materials and services without any further consideration.

A further classification problem concerns the amounts which should be included under the heading 'To pay government'. In Example 9.1, corporation tax was included under this heading. Although there is little room for dispute concerning this particular item, there are other items which are more contentious. For example, should business rates be included as a form of taxation? On the one hand, business rates represent a form of local taxation, but, on the other hand, a business will be provided with certain services, such as refuse collection, in return for the rates charge. Tax and national insurance payments deducted from the pay of employees is another difficult item. Although gross wages to employees (that is, wages before tax and national insurance payments are deducted) are normally shown under the heading 'To employees', it is the government who receives the taxation and national insurance payments. Employees will receive their wages net of taxation.

One final illustration of the problems of classification within the VAS concerns rent payable. We saw earlier that this item will normally be included as part of the bought-in goods and services. However, there is an argument for including it under the heading 'To suppliers of capital'. This would mean that the item becomes an application of value added rather than an amount deducted in arriving at the value added figure.

Activity 9.6	What do you think is the argument for this alternative treatment of rent payable?

It can be argued that the landlord is providing capital to the business in the form of a building and that the rent represents a payment for the capital supplied. If the business purchases a building and this is funded by a loan, the interest payable would be treated as a payment to suppliers of capital. Both rent payable and interest on a building loan can be viewed as providing the same benefits to a business (the right to occupy and use the building) and so should be treated in the same way.

If these alternative methods of dealing with contentious items were used, a quite different figure for value added would be derived. The absence of an accounting standard concerning the VAS means that differences in treatment are likely to occur between companies and so comparisons of performance will become more difficult.

The importance of profit

The idea that the VAS could become a more important statement than the conventional profit and loss account, as suggested by some commentators, seems a rather fanciful idea. Profit will remain of central importance within a capitalist economy and so the conventional profit and loss account is likely to remain the centrepiece of financial reports. Shareholders are concerned with the returns from their investment in a business, and if the managers do not ensure the shareholders receive adequate returns then they are likely to be replaced by managers who will. There is a danger that if managers become overconcerned with the improvement of value added this will have an adverse effect on profit.

| Activity 9.7 | Ray Von (Manufacturers) plc is currently considering whether to make a particular component or purchase the item from an outside supplier. The component can be sold by the business for £40. Making the component would involve a labour cost of £12 per unit and a material cost of £18. The cost of buying the item from an outside supplier would be £26. Calculate the value added and profit arising under each option. |

Your answer should be as follows:

	Buy-in	Make
	£	£
Selling price	40	40
Less Bought-in materials	26	18
Value added	14	22
Less Labour costs	–	12
Profit	14	10

We can see that to make the item will provide the greater value added but the lower profit. Thus, a decision to maximise value added would be at the expense of profit.

Where a business has a high value added but a poor profit record, there is a danger that some users will be misled concerning the viability of the business.

It should be emphasised that the profit generated by a business is likely to be important to various stakeholders and not only the shareholders. Lenders will be interested in the profit generated to enable them to assess the riskiness of their investment, governments will be interested for taxation purposes and employees will be interested for the assessment of likely future pay increases and job security. Those who support the VAS have failed to demonstrate that this statement is useful for decision-making purposes in the way that the profit and loss account is useful.

Although the VAS does not now appear frequently in the annual reports of companies, a number of companies continue to use this statement where they provide separate reports of company performance to employees. The VAS is then often portrayed in diagrammatic form for ease of understanding. For example, the application of total value added of Ray Cathode (Lighting Supplies) plc shown earlier can be represented in the form of a pie chart, as in Figure 9.2.

Reporting value added to employees alone, however, raises an issue of credibility. Employees may ask why a financial report which is not regarded as being important to other users is being provided to them? They may feel the major motivation is to demonstrate the extent to which value added is taken up in salaries and wages. As mentioned earlier, a sizeable proportion of value added is often distributed to employees.

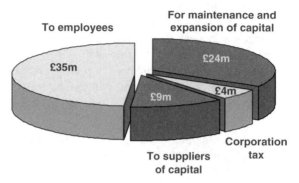

Figure 9.2

Distribution of total value added by Ray Cathode (Lighting Supplies) plc

Total value added £72m

To employees

For maintenance and
expansion of capital

£35m

£24m

£9m

£4m

To suppliers
of capital

Corporation
tax

The pie chart shows very clearly how the value added by the business has been distributed to the various stakeholders. We can see, for example, that almost half of the total value added is distributed to employees.

? **Self-assessment question 9.1**

The data set out below has been extracted from the accounting records of Samodiva Limited for the year ended 30 September

	£000
Sales	6,252
Bad debts	254
Non-recoverable value added tax	62
Cost of goods sold	1,630
Payments to other suppliers	858
Wages	628
Employers National Insurance	128
Corporation tax payable	244
Dividend to ordinary shareholders	500
Interest payable to debenture holders	320
Depreciation: plant and machines	632
office buildings and fittings	222
Cost of employees benefit-in-kind	82
Retained profit for the year	692

Required:
(a) Prepare a value added statement for Samodiva Limited for the year ended 30 September.
(b) Calculate any ratios that you consider appropriate for a better understanding of the information contained within the value added statement and comment on your results.

Inflation accounting and reporting

We saw in Chapter 2 that accounting measures items in monetary terms and that there is an assumption that this unit of measurement will remain stable over time. However, this assumption does not hold in reality, as each year the value of money changes. Usually, this is owing to inflation (that is, when the general purchasing power of money is reduced because of a rise in prices). However, it is also possible for deflation to occur (that is, for the general purchasing power of money to increase because of a fall in prices). The result of changes in the value of money is to undermine the measurement of performance and financial position as reflected in the conventional financial statements. In this section, we shall concentrate on the effect of inflation rather than deflation on the financial statements as it is the former rather than the latter that has created problems for UK businesses over the years. We shall see that inflation tends to result in an overstatement of profit and an understatement of financial position. In a later section we shall consider **inflation accounting** methods that attempt to deal with these problems.

The impact of inflation on profit measurement

During a period of inflation, profits tend to be overstated because of the time period which will often elapse between buying a particular resource and its subsequent use. Stock in trade is a good illustration of this, as Example 9.2 demonstrates.

Example 9.2

Kostova Car Sales Ltd acquired a new Mercedes motor car for £25,000 as part of its showroom stock. The car was held for several months before being sold to a customer for £30,000. The cost of replacing the vehicle from the manufacturers increased during the stockholding period to £26,250, which was in line with the general rate of inflation for that period. What is the profit made on the sale of the motor car?

The conventional approach to measuring profit involves matching the selling price of the vehicle to the original outlay cost. Thus, the profit will be calculated as follows:

	£
Sale of motor car	30,000
Less Cost of acquisition	25,000
Profit	5,000

Where the value of money is constant, the above approach can produce a valid result. However, when prices are rising, we encounter a problem, as the original cost will be an understatement of the resources consumed. We are told that during the stockholding period the cost of replacing the car increased in line with the rate of inflation (that is, the *average* purchasing power, as measured by the general rate of inflation, and the *specific* purchasing power of money, as measured by changes in the cost of the car, decreased by the same amount during the stockholding period). In view of this loss of purchasing power, the original cost of the stocks ceases to be a meaningful measure of the resources consumed during the period. It can be argued that it would be more realistic to calculate the profit for the period by taking the difference between the selling price and cost of the new car *expressed in current terms*. This means the profit will be as follows:

	£
Sale of motor car	30,000
Less Current purchase cost of car	26,250
Profit	3,750

We can see from Example 9.2 that the effect of substituting the original cost of stocks with costs expressed in current terms is to reduce the level of profit for the period.

The problem of time elapsing between the acquisition of a resource and its ultimate use is even more acute in the case of fixed assets. A fixed asset may be held for many years and the profit and loss accounts for each of the years during which the asset is held will be charged with depreciation relating to the asset. We saw in Chapter 3 that this depreciation charge is meant to represent that portion of the asset that is consumed during the period. However, the depreciation charge is based on the original cost of the asset and, during a period of inflation, this cost-based figure will become increasingly out of date. In practice, therefore, the profit and loss account will often match current sales with depreciation charges based on costs incurred many years earlier. This failure to match current sales with costs expressed in current terms will mean, once again, that profits are overstated.

The impact of inflation on financial position

Another problem of inflation is the risk that it may pose to the capital base of the business. Consider Example 9.3.

Example 9.3

Habbad Enterprises sells training videos to small businesses. The balance sheet of the business as at 31 March is as follows:

	£
Stock (20 videos @ £100)	2,000
Capital	2,000

Assume that, during the next period, the business managed to sell all of the videos for cash for £150 each. The reported profit for the period would be £1,000 (that is, $20 \times £(150 - 100)$) and the balance sheet at the end of the period would be as follows:

	£
Cash	3,000
Opening capital	2,000
Plus Profit for the period	1,000
	3,000

When prices are constant, it would be possible for Habbad Enterprises to pay a dividend equal to the whole of the reported profit for the period and still retain its capital base intact. That is, dividend distribution would not have an adverse effect on the purchasing power of the owners' investment in the business, or the ability of the business to maintain its scale of operations; there would still be the start-of-period £2,000.

Let us assume, however, that the general rate of inflation during the period was 10 per cent and the cost of the videos increased in line with this rate. To ensure that the owners' investment in the business is kept intact and the business is able to continue its current scale of operations, it would not now be possible to distribute all of the profits as conventionally measured.

Activity 9.8	What amount of profit do you think could be distributed to the owners of Habbad Enterprises without any adverse effect on the capital base?

As the general rate of inflation was 10 per cent during the period, and the cost of videos increased in line with this rate, the capital base must be increased by this amount to preserve the owners' investment and to ensure that the existing scale of operations can be maintained. The capital at the end of the period should, therefore, be:

$$£2,000 + (10\% \times £2,000) = £2,200$$

As the unadjusted capital at the end of the period is £3,000, the amount that can be distributed will be:

$$£3,000 - £2,200 = £800$$

Calculating profit by matching sales with the cost of purchases expressed in current terms will also provide this measure of the amount that can be safely distributed to owners. Hence:

	£
Sales (20 @ £150)	3,000
Less Cost of videos in current terms (20 @ £110)	2,200
Profit	800

During a period of inflation, the effect of reporting assets at their original cost on the balance sheet is also a problem as the cost or value of the asset expressed in current terms may be quite different. The higher the rate of inflation the greater this difference is likely to be. There is also the additional problem that the assets will normally be acquired at different dates. Thus, for example, the cost of plant purchased by a business on different dates, and appearing on the balance sheet, may be:

Plant at cost

	£
Acquired 31 March Year 1	18,000
Acquired 30 June Year 4	34,000
Acquired 20 September Year 8	42,000
	94,000

During a period of inflation, the purchasing power of the pound will be quite different at each acquisition date. The sum total of this group of assets (£94,000) will, therefore, be meaningless. In effect, the pounds spent at the various dates represent different currencies with different purchasing power.

Activity 9.9	Can you think what will be the effect of inflation on the calculation of profitability ratios such as net profit margin and ROCE?

As the net profit is overstated during a period of inflation, profitability ratios will tend to be higher. The problem will be more acute where profit is related to a measure of financial position such as the ROCE ratio. This is because the financial position of the business tends to be understated.

The problem of monetary items

Some items on the balance sheet have a fixed number of pounds assigned to them which cannot be changed as a result of inflation. These are known as
➡ **monetary items**.

Activity 9.10	Can you think of any items which would be categorised as monetary items?

Examples of monetary items on the asset side of the balance sheet would be debtors and cash. Examples on the liabilities side would be loans, overdrafts, tax owing and dividends outstanding.

The effect of holding monetary assets during a period of inflation will be to make a loss, whereas the effect of holding monetary liabilities will be to make a gain.

Activity 9.11	Explain the effects of holding £1,000 cash during a year when inflation was at the rate of 20 per cent.

The purchasing power of the cash held will be 20 per cent lower at the end of the year than at the beginning.

Beginning of period	End of period
Cash	Cash
£1,000	£1,000

Purchasing power compared with beginning of period
----------------------➤----------------------➤ £800 (that is, £1,000 less 20%)

This loss of purchasing power will have a real effect on the business to preserve the capital invested by the owners and on the ability of the business to maintain its scale of operations.

The reverse situation will apply where a monetary liability is held during a period of inflation. In real terms, the liability will be reduced and so the owners will make a gain at the expense of the lenders. These monetary gains and losses may be significant for a business but they are not revealed in the conventional financial statements.

Reporting the effect of inflation

The problems caused by inflation over the years have led to calls for additional financial statements that will help users understand the impact of inflation on the financial performance and position of the business. These additional financial statements take the form of a profit and loss account and balance sheet but differ from the conventional statements in that they incorporate the effect of price level changes.

There are two basic approaches to the problem of dealing with inflation. The first of these is concerned with ensuring that the *general purchasing power of owners* is maintained during a period of inflation. To do this, a general price index, such as the Retail Price Index, will be used to measure changes in the purchasing power of the pound. To maintain the owners' general purchasing power, the profit available for distribution must take account of price level changes. As a result, profit will be deduced by matching the sales for the period with the original cost of the goods expressed in terms of *current purchasing power*.

To illustrate how **current purchasing power (CPP) accounting** operates, let us look at Example 9.4.

Example 9.4	Konides and Co. purchased stock when the Retail Price Index was 100 and sold the stock ten months later when the index stood at 105. The goods were purchased for £2,000 and sold for £2,500.

To maintain the general purchasing power of the owners of the business, the profit for the period will be calculated as follows:

	£
Sales	2,500
Less Cost of sales (2,000 × 105/100)	2,100
Profit	400

The alternative approach to maintaining capital intact is concerned with ensuring that the *business is able to maintain its scale of operations*. To do this, the specific price changes which affect the business must be taken into account when preparing the financial statements. Here, the profit available for distribution will be deduced by matching the sales with the specific changes that arise in the cost of the goods acquired by the business.

In many cases, the price changes that affect a business may not correspond to the general price changes occurring within the economy (although for the sake of convenience, we assumed in earlier examples that the specific price of goods changed in line with the general rate of inflation). Referring to Example 9.5, let us assume that, although the general rate of inflation was 5 per cent during the period, the rise in the cost of the particular stocks traded was 10 per cent. Using the specific purchasing power approach to accounting for inflation, the profit for the period would be:

	£
Sales	2,500
Less Cost of sales (2,000 + (10% × £2,000))	2,200
Profit	300

Each approach is concerned with maintaining capital intact. However, the two approaches have different views concerning what form of capital should be kept intact. The general purchasing power approach is concerned with ensuring the *owners'* purchasing power over general goods and services within the economy is maintained, whereas the specific purchasing power approach is concerned with ensuring that the *business* is able to maintain its purchasing power over the specific goods and services that it needs in order to continue trading at the same level. Both views have their advantages and disadvantages and there has been a great deal of debate concerning which view should prevail. At present, the specific purchasing power approach probably has the greater support. However, the fairly low rates of inflation in recent years has meant that many companies no longer see this form of reporting as being as important as in earlier periods when inflation rates were much higher. In practice, few companies produce supplementary reports that account for the effects of inflation. Those that do normally use a particular form of specific purchasing power accounting referred to as **current cost accounting**. This method is based largely (but not exclusively) on the use of replacement cost (that is, the cost of replacing an item) figures rather than historic cost figures.

Exhibit 9.1

Very few UK companies make inflation adjustments as described above. However, the 2000 accounts of Railtrack Group plc, the business that owns and manages the UK's main railway network, included a set of current cost accounts as supplementary information. The profit for the year and the summary group balance sheet information on a current cost basis is shown. Despite the fairly low rates of inflation in the UK in recent years, the differences between the historic cost figures and current cost figures are quite marked. A comparison of some of the key figures in each set of accounts is set out below:

	Historic cost basis £m	Current cost basis £m
Profit for the year after tax	364	254
	£m	£m
Tangible fixed assets	12,341	28,514
Accumulated depreciation	5,637	19,078
	6,704	9,436

Source: Railtrack Group plc 2000 Annual Report.

Environmental reporting

In recent times there has been an increasing awareness of how fragile our natural environment is in the face of continuing economic development. There has been a growing concern that the policies pursued by businesses will inflict major environmental damage on our planet from which it may never recover. Environmental issues such as acid rain, destruction of the rainforests, the use of non-renewable resources, the treatment of hazardous waste, damage to the ozone layer and pollution of rivers have received much media coverage and this, in turn, has led to demands for businesses to be more accountable for their activities.

Conventional accounting fails to recognise the impact of the business on its environment. Accounting is based on transactions between parties who have property rights. The exchange of these rights (for example the purchase of an asset by a business for cash) will give rise to transactions that are quantifiable in monetary terms and which the accounting system can record. However, the impact of the business on aspects of the environment over which there are no property rights is not recorded by the accounting system and does not, therefore, appear in the financial statements. The principle that 'the polluter must pay' is, however, gaining greater recognition and this means that the financial statements will, at least, record the cost of negative environmental impacts.

Some businesses have responded to the increase in environmental awareness, and the criticisms levelled at the business community, by producing an **environmental report**. Generally speaking, large businesses have responded more readily to this new challenge than small and medium-sized ones which seem less convinced of the need for this kind of additional disclosure. Where environmental reports are being produced, it can be either as part of the annual financial reports or as separate reports to users. The motive for producing environmental reports will vary. For some businesses, it may be to reassure the public or regulatory authorities that the business is a good 'corporate citizen', whilst for others it may be to change the views of users and regulators about the activities of the business so to avoid any harmful reactions. Industrial sectors such as oil, chemicals and privatised utilities are well represented among those businesses producing such reports.

Styles of environmental reporting

Environmental reports are produced voluntarily and there is no consensus regarding 'best practice' in this area. As a result, the reports vary considerably in style, content and depth. It has been suggested, however, that they can be classified according to one of three levels (see reference (2) at the end of the chapter). These are:

- *Level 1* A statement simply setting out the environmental policies of the business and an explanation of its environmental management systems and responsibilities.
- *Level 2* A qualitative report that builds on the Level 1 statement and sets out the performance of the business on environmental matters in qualitative terms. For example, reports may indicate that the business is meeting, or exceeding, national, or international, standards on particular environmental matters.

- *Level 3*   A quantitative report providing a detailed breakdown of the performance of the business on environmental matters. Performance is set against
clear quantitative targets. The report may also quantify the financial impact of
managing the environment.

Most businesses that prepare environmental reports confine themselves to either
level 1 or level 2 reporting, although some companies (for example, British
Telecommunications plc) have introduced reporting using quantitative data.
Exhibit 9.2 outlines the environmental policy of Associated British Foods plc as
set out in its annual report of 1999.

Exhibit 9.2

Associated British Foods plc multinational food producer stated its environmental policy,
in its 1999 annual report, as follows:

One of the group's strategic objectives it to reduce, reuse and recycle waste where feasible. During
1999 an independent survey of our manufacturing sites was commissioned with the objective of
identifying waste and promoting waste minimisation. During the year the results of the survey will
be used to identity best practices and improve group performance.

Each division will review its environmental performance and produce an annual summary for the
Board. Reports from 2001 will contain data on relevant key performance indicators.

Source: Associated British Foods 1999 Annual Report.

Note the stated intention of the business to start reporting key indicators from 2001.
This reflects a trend towards increasing emphasis of reporting environmental targets.

Contents of environmental reports

A key issue facing businesses is what should be included in an environmental
report. One report (see reference (3) at the end of the chapter) suggests the
following:

- The environmental policy of the business.
- The identity of the director with overall responsibility for environmental issues.
- The environmental objectives of the business expressed in such a way that per-
formance can be measured against them. (In so far as possible, environmental
targets and performance should be expressed in quantifiable, technical or
financial terms.)
- Information on actions taken in pursuit of environmental objectives (includ-
ing details of expenditure incurred).
- The key impact of the business on the environment and, where practical, related
measures of environmental performance.
- The extent of compliance with any regulations industry guidelines.
- Significant environmental risks.
- Key features of external audit reports on the environmental activities of the
business.

However, there is no real consensus on this issue and other forms of reporting
have been proposed.

In addition to developing an appropriate report structure, the problem of
developing key indicators is an important issue.

| Activity 9.12 | **Can you think of criteria which might be applied in deciding whether or not a particular environmental indicator should be used?** |

The desirable characteristics of accounting information which we discussed in Chapter 1 might provide a useful starting point. These were:

- Relevance
- Reliability
- Comparability
- Understandability
- Materiality
- Cost/benefit

However, you may have thought of other criteria.

| Exhibit 9.3 | British Energy plc, a power generating business, produces environmental performance targets for each of its main sites. The targets for the Hartlepool site for 2000/2001 is shown below. The ticks and crosses indicate whether or not the targets were met during the year. |

Hartlepool
Environmental Performance
2000/2001 Targets

✓ **Maintain Certification to ISO 14001**
We continued our certification to ISO 14001, the international standard for Environmental Management Systems, following a successful re-certification audit by the EAQA.

✓ **Complete the audit programme for significant environmental aspects**
The 'top ten' significant environmental aspects form the environmental audit programme for the year. All 'top ten' significant environmental aspects were subjected to environmental compliance audits during the year.

✓ **Implement 80% of actions from the Environmental Management Team meetings**
Out of 73 actions placed, 63 have been successfully closed out, which corresponds to 86% implementation.

✗ **Complete the installation of the Reverse Osmosis Plant (to improve the quality of town water and reduce the need for bulk acids)**
This scheme was not pursued since it was decided to obtain supplies from a plant external to the site.

✓ **Improve leak detection capability of the radioactive gaseous discharge route**
We have completed an upgrade of the filter banks.

Other news

- There were no regulatory interventions or public complaints during the year.
- The maintenance programme for oil was reviewed and the continuing integrity of oil cooler nests confirmed. The project to move oil pipework above ground (for rapid detection and repair of any leakage) was completed.

Source: British Energy plc. Safety, Health and Environment Report (www.british-energy)

Problems of environmental reporting

Some commentators are unimpressed by the current quality of environmental reporting to date. It has been suggested that it lacks a clear framework which leads to partial and unsystematic reports. As environmental reporting is a voluntary exercise, there is little incentive for a business to disclose the adverse effects of its policies on the environment, although there may well be incentives to emphasise any positive effects. It has also been suggested that the general lack of quantitative measures and targets and the failure of many businesses to have their environmental management efforts audited by external bodies makes it difficult to assess how well businesses discharge their responsibilities towards the environment. This has led some to dismiss environmental reports as little more than a public relations exercise.

However, environmental reports are still at an early stage of development and there is evidence to suggest that the quality of these reports is improving each year. The pressure on businesses to produce environmental reports is likely to increase rather than decrease and it may well be that regulations will be imposed in the future. If this occurs, some of the problems mentioned above are likely to be reduced and faster progress will be made.

Exhibit 9.4

Environmental information will normally be disclosed in a separate environmental performance report or review. The kinds of items appearing in such a report have been discussed above. In addition, however, environmental information can be included within elements of the conventional annual report. Where items appear in the balance sheet and profit and loss account, they will normally reflect a provision for some future liability or a cost. This is because conventional accounting statements tend to reflect only the negative environmental impact of the business for reasons discussed above.

A suggested framework for reporting environmental information within elements of the annual report is set out below:

An environmental reporting framework for the annual report

Annual report element	Recommended environmental disclosure(s)
Chairman/CEOs report	■ corporate commitment to continuous environmental improvement ■ significant improvements since last report
Business segment review	■ segmented environmental performance data (if not provided in the environmental review) ■ improvements in key areas since previous report
Operating & financial review	■ key environmental issues facing the company ■ short/medium term and plans for addressing these ■ progress in addressing changes required by future legal requirements ■ actual and projected levels of environmental expenditure ■ legal matters pending
Report of the Directors	■ environmental policy statement (if not provided elsewhere)

Accounting policy disclosure	■ estimation of provisions and contingencies ■ capitalisation policies ■ impairment policies ■ de-commissioning and land remediation policies ■ depreciation policies
Profit & loss account	■ exceptional environmental charges (for example, for remediation, de-commissioning or impairment charges) ■ other environmental costs and benefits (if not disclosed in separate environmental review)
Balance sheet	■ environmental provisions ■ de-commissioning provisions ■ environmental costs capitalised ■ expected recoveries
Notes to the accounts	■ contingent environmental liabilities plus explanations
Other	■ Environmental data can also be put in the summary financial statements (for example, Body Shop, Scottish Hydro)

Source: Linking environmental and financial performance: a survey of best practice (ISAR/Adams 1998) Reported in Accounting and Business March 1998 p. 39.

Social reporting

A business has a number of groups, or stakeholders, that have an interest in, and will be affected by, its operations. The rights of shareholders and lenders concerning the business are well established in law. However, other stakeholders such as suppliers, customers, employees and the communities in which the business operates are increasingly recognised as having rights. Thus, modern businesses have a broad constituency to whom they are accountable and to whom they should report concerning the way in which they conduct their operations.

This wider responsibility has led a number of businesses to report the social aspects of their operations. Although such reports are still in their infancy, their importance is growing and they are being viewed increasingly as an integral part of the annual reporting cycle – at least for larger businesses.

Styles of social reports

➡ **Social reports**, like environmental reports, vary considerably in style, content and depth. Some businesses refer to particular social and environmental issues, almost as an aside, in their annual financial reports. Other companies will have a separate section, or sections, of the annual report devoted exclusively to these issues. In a few cases, such as the Body Shop and Royal Dutch Shell plc, there are quite separate and lengthy reports relating to social and environmental issues. The costs of producing and disseminating such reports have been reduced thanks to the Internet. It is now possible for a business to include these reports on its website and for them to be downloaded by those who are interested in doing so.

For the moment, a wide diversity of reporting practice persists. The social dimensions of business operations are not well defined and so it is inevitable that they are interpreted by different businesses in different ways. It seems that any form of interaction that a business has with society could be included within a social report. However, as our views on social performance crystallise, a growing consensus should emerge about what should be reported and how it should be reported.

It has been argued that a social report can be viewed as having three layers of information:

■ *Layer 1* This is descriptive information that provides details of employees (such as numbers employed and skills categories), involvement in community projects, and customer facilities.
■ *Layer 2* This provides details of the extent to which ethical and legal standards are being met. These standards may cover such areas as equal opportunities in employment, health and safety at work, fair trading relationships, and so on.
■ *Layer 3* This involves consultation with the various stakeholder groups concerning the way in which the business conducts its operations and then reporting what the stakeholders have to say about the business.

(See reference (4) at the end of the chapter.)

The reporting of feedback from stakeholders (layer 3) is a particularly novel idea. An example of the way in which a business may report the views of its stakeholders is shown in Exhibit 9.5 below.

Exhibit 9.5

The Body Shop, a retail chain selling cosmetics and toiletries, is at the forefront of social reporting and in 1997 produced a Value Report that reported its performance relating to social, environmental and animal protection issues. As part of this lengthy report, it reported the comments of various stakeholders regarding the way in which the business operated. To illustrate the reporting approach taken, a section relating to one of its stakeholder groups (owners of Body Shop franchises) is reproduced below. As we can see, the company is prepared to reveal itself 'warts and all'.

Comments on doing business with The Body Shop

'Judging by the in-house discussion and newspaper reports we did not treat our staff wisely during the restructuring – communication was bad.'

'We now have a detailed marketing strategy. There has been at last a recognition that we need to change to succeed.'

'Listen, respect, value our contribution and experience as a key core customer.'

'They should ask franchisees about what new products we want before they launch a new range.'

'Openness. Talk with us not to us.'

'A lot of emphasis is still London and company shops.'

'Treat us more like valued customers (for example, how other suppliers treat us) and less like a means to an end.'

'You should break down UK retail into departments and ask for the service levels to franchisees as customers, the service levels are inconsistent, depending on the departments, therefore it is hard to judge as a whole (for example, legal department, shop fitting and so on).'

'The Body Shop International does communicate reasonably well with the UK press but often before us! We find it frustrating to read things about the business from a newspaper before we hear it from The Body Shop International itself. They need to realise that we and our staff are on the front line when questions need answering from customers.'

'Social Audit process itself is brilliant. However we don't feel The Body Shop International are changing their policies quickly enough as a result of the survey.'

'At present we have absolutely no contact with anyone from the training dept – when we did (3 years ago) it provided an invaluable input to the business.'

'Senior managers with more feeling for what The Body Shop customers want from us. They are too remote from the high street.'

'Excellent service, but we need more courses and more spaces.'

'Advertise nationally (TV). Need to move with the times – retailing is more competitive than ever before!'

'The Body Shop still is not presenting itself well in the media – it is a great company and should do better.'

Source: www.the-body-shop.com Value Report 1997 p. 99.

Sustainable development

In recent years, there has been a growing recognition that environmental issues and social issues are inextricably linked. For example, when we debate issues relating to our natural environment, it will usually raise issues concerning the welfare of communities, the distributions of wealth, social justice and so on. This implies that a more complete approach to reporting would deal with *both* the environmental and social dimensions of business operations as well as reporting the effectiveness of the business in generating economic wealth.

A framework that can be used to bring together all three dimensions in a systematic way is based on the concept of **sustainable development**. This concept has been defined as: 'meeting the needs of the present without compromising the ability of future generations to meet their own needs' (see reference (5) at the end of the chapter).

Supporters of sustainable development believe that economic viability must go hand in hand with a concern for the environment and for social equity. In order for us to survive and prosper over the longer term, businesses must have proper regard for the effect on the natural and human resources that they use. This means that businesses should manage environmental and human resources with the same kind of commitment with which they manage their financial resources. This idea appears to be gaining ground and a number of companies are now committed to what has been termed 'sustainable value creation'.

Exhibit 9.6	BAA plc, an airport operator, is committed to the idea of sustainable development and tries to integrate environmental, social and economic factors into its strategic and operational decisions. The company has identified the following priority areas of performance:

Environment	Social	Economic
■ Noise	■ Diversity and equal opportunities	■ Direct and indirect employment
■ Air quality	■ Stakeholder engagement	■ National economic contribution
■ Surface transport	■ Staff involvement in community	■ Facilitating knowledge-driven economy & tourism
■ Climate change	■ Staff learning and development	■ Supply chain payments
■ Waste	■ Charitable donations	■ Meet the local supplier events
■ Biodiversity	■ Health and safety	
■ Water quality and consumption	■ Wide employment and skills opportunities	
■ Material and resource use	■ Major catalyst for regeneration	

Source: BAA plc website

Sustainable development and triple bottom line reporting

Some believe that the best way to assess the effectiveness with which a business implements environmental, social and economic policies is through **triple bottom line reporting**. This means that, in addition to reporting economic value added, a business should also report environmental value added and social value added. Environmental valued added would measure the renewable natural resources consumed (such as wood and fish stocks), as well as the non-renewable resources consumed (such as fossilised fuels). Social value added would attempt to measure the 'intellectual resources' (that is knowledge and skills) that the business has developed or lost and the extent to which it has developed or damaged the level of respect and trust within the communities in which it operates. The economic value added (such as profit) could then be viewed in the context of the environmental and social value added by the business. If all three forms could be quantified in monetary terms, it would be possible to deduce the *total net value added* by a business, which would be the sum of the three dimensions.

Triple bottom line reporting is an ambitious idea that raises huge problems and issues.

Activity 9.13	Can you think of some of the key issues that will have to be addressed in order to produce a triple bottom line for a business?

The issues that we thought of are:

■ How are environmental and social dimensions to be defined? In other words, what items should be included and what should be excluded?

■ How can environmental value added and social value added be measured in monetary terms?

■ How can there be an independent audit of these measures so as to lend credibility to the reporting process?

■ How can benchmarks be developed against which we can assess progress?

This is not an exhaustive list, you may have thought of others.

Despite the problems, there has already been some progress towards developing this type of reporting framework. A few progressive businesses have already begun to develop sustainable development frameworks. The BAA plc framework cited above is an example. A further example is the reports of Royal Dutch Shell plc the international oil company. This company has developed a huge array of social and environmental measures in order to help stakeholders assess their performance in these areas.

Key areas for triple bottom line reporting

Although the development of triple bottom line reporting is a mammoth task, a sensible starting point is to identify a small number of key areas for consideration. Having done this, we can then try to develop appropriate indicators and targets against which these indicators can be assessed. For environmental value added, it has been suggested that the following key areas should be considered:

■ *Materials usage*   The different types and amounts of materials consumed by the business.

■ *Energy usage*   The different types and amounts of energy consumed in carrying out business operations.

■ *Non-product output*   The types and amounts of waste created by the business, including details of recycling, disposal methods and so on.

■ *Pollutant releases*   The types and amounts of pollutants, such as harmful chemicals, that have been released into the environment.

In the area of social value added, the following key areas have been identified:

■ *Employment practices*   Health and safety at work, equal opportunities, job security and financial rewards.

■ *Ethical sourcing*   Fair trading principles, agreements with suppliers concerning child labour, fair wages, and working conditions.

■ *Community relations*   Contributions to the community in the form of donations to worthy projects, job creation, taxes contributed and employee involvement in community issues.

■ *Social impact of products*   The contribution of products to the well being of society, the way in which goods help to meet the needs of consumers.

(See reference (6) at the end of the chapter)

Exhibit 9.7

Severn Trent plc, a water utility, has structured its report covering economic, social and environmental issues according to the objectives and indicators recommended by the UK government.

The four main objectives and the 14 headline indicators used by the company are as follows:

Maintenance of high and stable levels of economic growth and employment	Social progress which recognises the needs of everyone	Effective protection of the environment	Prudent use of natural resources
Economic growth measured by company turnover measured by total annual investment	**Health** measured by population receiving water and waste services from Severn Trent	**Climate change** measured using the UK Government's greenhouse gases indicator	**Use of natural resources** measured by the amount of water leaking from our water mains
Employment measured by number of full time (equivalent) employees	**Education and training** measured by employee days training in a year	**Air pollution** measured by acidic gas emissions (NOx and SOx)	**Waste** measured by total waste disposed of from Severn Trent businesses
	Housing quality measured by all domestic properties receiving water, sewerage or refuse collection services from Severn Trent companies	**Transport** measured by total distance travelled for operational and business purposes	
		Water quality measured by proportion of rivers with 'good or fair' quality classification	
		Wildlife measured by number of trees planted by Severn Trent businesses	
		Land use measured by area of land restored	

Source: Severn Trent plc (Environmental Leadership. www.severn-trent.com)

Developing new reporting methodologies

In addition to matters relating to content, methods of developing and auditing environmental and social reports are also being developed. As an example, the methodology of The Body shop plc is shown in Exhibit 9.8 below.

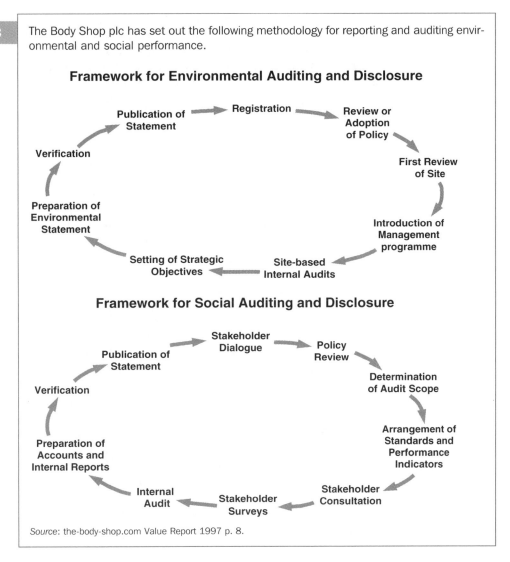

Exhibit 9.8

The Body Shop plc has set out the following methodology for reporting and auditing environmental and social performance.

Framework for Environmental Auditing and Disclosure

Publication of Statement → Registration → Review or Adoption of Policy → First Review of Site → Introduction of Management programme → Site-based Internal Audits → Setting of Strategic Objectives → Preparation of Environmental Statement → Verification → Publication of Statement

Framework for Social Auditing and Disclosure

Publication of Statement → Stakeholder Dialogue → Policy Review → Determination of Audit Scope → Arrangement of Standards and Performance Indicators → Stakeholder Consultation → Stakeholder Surveys → Internal Audit → Preparation of Accounts and Internal Reports → Verification → Publication of Statement

Source: the-body-shop.com Value Report 1997 p. 8.

Some of the reports published that deal with social and environmental issues, or with sustainable development, are subject to independent audit. As with conventional financial reports, the purpose of the audit is to lend credibility to the information provided. However, there are mixed views as to whether the audit of such reports is a good thing. This type of reporting is at a very early stage of development and there is a danger that experimentation with new measures and the inclusion of new forms of information will be hindered by the need to satisfy the auditors (who are often accountants or specialist consultants). There is also a danger that, as there are no clear rules about the content of such reports or the measures that should be used, the auditors' agenda will be set by the company and so the credibility of the audit process will be undermined.

It would be easy to dismiss the current attempts at sustainable development reporting as providing, with a few exceptions, inconsistent, incomplete and unverified information. However, the pressures on businesses in this area are mounting and so significant progress is likely in the future. Bodies such as the Global Reporting Initiative have been formed to help develop more comparable and credible reports relating to sustainable value creation, which will provide further impetus to progress.

Summary

In this chapter we examined a number of additional financial statements which can be included in the annual financial report. We began by considering the value added statement (VAS) which aims to foster a team spirit among the various stakeholders in the business. We saw, however, that there are problems in measuring and reporting value added and that nowadays relatively few companies incorporate this financial statement in their annual reports. However, they are still used in reports to employees.

We considered the impact of inflation on the conventional financial statements. We saw that during a period of rising prices, profits tend to be overstated and financial position to be understated. We examined the two major schools of thought on how the problem of inflation should be tackled. However, there is no real consensus on which approach should prevail.

Increasing concern for the environment has led to some businesses producing environmental reports. To date, the quality of these reports has been patchy and there is much work to be done in developing appropriate reporting structures and key indicators. There is also much work to be done in encouraging small and medium-sized businesses to produce environmental reports. Apart from overcoming the scepticism that such businesses may have towards such reports, there is often the added problem that they do not have the internal environmental management systems to produce them.

Finally, we considered the emerging topic of social reporting. We saw that this was still an ill-defined area and little progress has been made to date in determining the form and content of social reports. However, the growing interest in sustainable development and in triple bottom line reporting is likely to give impetus to the development of social reporting in the future.

 Key terms

Value added statement (VAS) p. 293	Current cost accounting (CCA) p. 308
Inflation accounting p. 303	Environmental report p. 309
Monetary items p. 306	Social reports p. 313
Current purchasing power (CPP) accounting p. 307	Triple bottom line reporting p. 316

Further reading

If you would like to explore the topics covered in this chapter in more depth, we recommend the following books:

Advanced Financial Accounting, *Lewis, R.* and *Pendrill, D.*, 6th edn, Prentice Hall/ Financial Times 2000, chapters 11, 15, 16.
Inflation Accounting: An Introduction to the Debate, *Whittington, G.*, Cambridge University Press, 1983.

The areas of environmental and social reporting are fast changing. You may find it useful to consult the following websites to discover the current state of progress:

www.sustainability.co.uk.
www.accountability.co.uk.
www.globalreporting.org.
www.totalvaluecreation.com

References

1. **The Corporate Report**, Accounting Standards Committee, ASC 1975.
2. 'Corporate environmental reporting in practice', by *Bullough, M.* and *Johnson, D.*, in **Business Strategy and the Environment**, Vol. 4, 1995, pp. 36–39.
3. **Business, Accountancy and the Environment: A policy and research agenda**, *Macve, R.* and *Carey, A.*, ICAEW, 1992.
4. 'Environment and Social Reporting', by *Gray, R.*, *Collison, D.* and *Debbington, J.*, in **Financial Reporting Today: Current Trends and Emerging Issues**, Accountancy Books, 1998.
5. **Our Common Future** (The Brundtland Report), World Commission on Environment and Development, 1987, p. 8.
6. **Sustainability Rulers: Measuring Corporate Environmental and Social Performance**, *Ranganathan, J.*, World Resources Institute, May, 1998.

? REVIEW QUESTIONS

9.1 It has been suggested that if an accountant is asked by the board of directors of a company, 'What is the value added for a period?', he or she could easily reply, 'What figure do you have in mind?' Explain why such a reply could be made.

9.2 Does environmental reporting and social reporting really fall within the scope of accounting? Are accountants really the best people to prepare and audit such reports?

9.3 Are there any arguments for using the historic cost method of accounting during a period of inflation?

9.4 Should reporting of sustainable value creation be a voluntary exercise or should there be a legal obligation to produce such reports?

? EXERCISES

Exercises 9.6–9.8 are more advanced than 9.1–9.5. Those with coloured numbers have answers at the back of the book.

9.1 'The value added statement simply rearranges information contained within the conventional profit and loss account. As a result it is of little value to users.' Discuss.

9.2 The following data have been taken from the accounts of Buttons Ltd, a retail company, for the year ended 30 September.

	£	£
Turnover		950,000
Cost of sales:		
Materials	220,000	
Wages and salaries	160,000	
Other expenses	95,000	
Interest	45,000	
Depreciation	80,000	
		600,000
		350,000
Taxation		110,000
		240,000
Dividends paid and proposed		120,000
Retained profit		120,000

Required:
(a) Prepare a value added statement for Buttons Ltd for the year ended 30 September.
(b) State and comment upon the reasons why a company may present a value added statement to its shareholders in addition to a profit and loss account.

9.3 Refer to your answer to exercise 9.2 above. Calculate ratios that you believe could be used to interpret the VAS for Buttons Ltd. Explain the purpose of each ratio.

9.4 Rose Limited operates a small chain of retail shops. Abbreviated and unaudited accounts are given below.

Profit and loss accounts for the years ended 31 March

	Last year £000	Last year £000	This year £000	This year £000
Sales		7,800		12,080
Cost of sales		4,370		6,282
Gross profit		3,430		5,798
Labour costs	2,106		2,658	
Depreciation	450		625	
Other operating costs	92		1,003	
		2,648		4,286
Net profit before interest		782		1,512
Interest payable		–		66
Net profit before tax		782		1,446
Tax payable		158		259
Net profit after tax		624		1,187
Dividend payable		250		300
Retained profit for year		374		887
Retained profit brought forward		498		872
Retained profit carried forward		872		1,759

Required:
Prepare a value added statement for the year ended 31 March this year.

9.5 Comment on each of the following statements:

(a) 'Inflation-adjusted accounts do not justify the additional cost of their preparation. The historic cost accounts are all that is required by users.'
(b) 'Publishing environmental reports may not be in the interests of a business.'

9.6 Most businesses that produce environment reports and/or social reports believe that
it is a good thing to have these reports independently audited. However, not everyone agrees with this.
   What do you think are the arguments for and against having these reports independently audited?

9.7 It is often argued that it is difficult to make comparisons between the environmental
reports of different companies even when they are in the same industry.
   Examine the most recent environmental report of Severn Trent plc and compare it
with another water utility company of your choice. What problems do you experience in making comparisons?

9.8 Milton Friedman, a famous economist, once wrote:

   there is one and only one social responsibility of business – to use its resources and
   engage in activities designed to increase profits.

Preparing social reports and pursuing social objectives can be costly and so it might
be argued that a company should not do this as it is not consistent with the need to
maximise profits over the long term.
   Do you agree with this view? Discuss.

Supplementary information

This section provides information that is supplementary to the main text of the book.

Appendix A takes the format of a normal textual chapter and describes the way in which financial transactions are recorded in books of accounts. Generally, this is by means of the 'double entry' system, described in basic terms in the Appendix.

Appendix B gives definitions of the key terms highlighted throughout the main text and summarised at the end of each chapter. The aim of the Appendix is to provide a single location to check on the meanings of the major accounting terms used in this book and in the world of finance.

Appendices C, D and E give answers to some of the questions set in the main text. Appendix C gives answers to the review questions, Appendix D gives answers to the self-assessment questions, and Appendix E to those of the exercises that are marked as having their answers provided in the book.

Recording financial transactions

Introduction

In Chapters 2 and 3, we saw how the accounting transactions of a business may be recorded by making a series of entries on the balance sheet and/or profit and loss account. Each of these entries had its corresponding 'double' such that, after both sides of the transaction had been recorded, the balance sheet continued to justify its name and to balance. Adjusting the balance sheet by hand for each transaction could be very messy and confusing. With a reasonably large number of transactions, it is pretty certain to result in mistakes.

For businesses whose accounting systems are on a computer, this problem is overcome because suitable software can deal with a series of 'plus' and 'minus' entries very reliably. Where the accounting system is not computerised, it would be helpful to have some more practical way of keeping accounting records. Such a system not only exists but, before the advent of the computer, was the routine way of keeping accounts. It is this system that is explained in this Appendix. You should be clear that the system we are going to consider follows exactly the same rules as those that you have already met. Its distinguishing feature is its ability to give those keeping accounting records by hand, a methodical approach to follow, where errors should be minimised.

OBJECTIVES When you have completed this Appendix you should be able to:

- Explain the basic principles of double-entry bookkeeping.
- Write up a series of business transactions and balance the accounts.
- Extract a trial balance and explain its purpose.
- Prepare a set of final accounts from the underlying double-entry accounts.

The basics of double-entry bookkeeping

➡ In **double-entry bookkeeping**, instead of having a balance sheet where plus and minus entries are made in various areas according to the aspects (for example, cash) that are concerned with a particular transaction, each aspect has its own 'mini
➡ balance sheet', known as an **account**, which, for cash, would appear as follows:

Cash	
£	£

As with the balance sheet, an increase in cash appears on the left-hand side of this account.

Suppose that the entries are for a new business with no cash, but it is started by the owner putting £5,000 in the new business's bank account as initial capital. This entry would appear in the cash account as follows:

Cash

	£		£
1 January Capital	5,000		

The corresponding entry would be made in the capital account as follows:

Capital

	£		£
		1 January Cash	5,000

In the same way as an increase in capital goes on the right-hand side of the balance sheet, we show an increase in capital on the right-hand side of the capital account. It is usual to show, in each account, where the other side of the entry will be found. Thus, someone looking at the capital account will know from the narrative that the £5,000 arose from a receipt of cash. This not only provides potentially useful information, but enables a 'trail' to be followed when checking for errors. Including the date of the transaction provides additional information to the reader of the accounts.

Let us now suppose that £600 of the cash is used to buy some stock. This would affect the cash account as follows:

Cash

	£		£
1 January Capital	5,000	2 January Stock	600

Now we have seen one of the crucial differences between the use of accounts (double-entry bookkeeping) and adjusting the balance sheet: when you reduce an asset or a claim, you do not put an entry in the same column with a minus sign against it but, instead, you put it on the opposite side of the account. This cash account in effect shows 'positive' cash of £5,000 and 'negative' cash of £600, a net amount of £4,400.

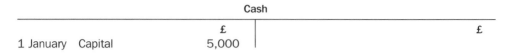

Activity A.1

As you know, we must somehow record the other side of the transaction involving the acquisition of the stock for £600. See if you can work out what to do in respect of the stock.

We must open an account for stock. Since stock is an asset, an increase in it will appear on the left-hand side of the account, as follows:

Stock

	£		£
2 January Cash	600		

What we have seen so far highlights the key rule of double-entry bookkeeping: each left-hand entry must have a right-hand entry of equal size. Using the jargon we can say **every debit must have a credit**. ('Debit' simply means the left-hand side of an account and 'credit' means the right-hand side.)

The rules of double entry also extend to 'trading' transactions – that is, making revenues (sales and so on) and incurring expenses. Thus, when on 3 January the business paid £300 to rent business premises (to include heat and light) for the month, we should normally open a 'rent account' and make the following entries in this account and in the cash account:

Rent

	£		£
3 January Cash	300		

Cash

	£		£
1 January Capital	5,000	2 January Stock	600
		3 January Rent	300

The treatment of the rent illustrates an important point: it is not just assets that appear on the debit side of accounts; expenses do as well. This is not altogether surprising since assets and expenses are closely linked. Assets actually transform into expenses as they are 'used up'. Rent, which, as here, is usually paid in advance, is an asset when it is first paid. It represents the value to the business of being entitled to occupy the premises for the forthcoming period (until the end of January in this case). As January progresses, this asset becomes an expense; it is 'used up'. This does not require that we make any adjustment to the rent account, but we need to remember that the debit entry in the rent account does not necessarily represent an asset nor an expense; it could be a mixture of the two. Strictly, by the end of the day on which it was paid (3 January), £29.03 would have represented an expense for the three days, the remaining £270.97 would have been an asset. As each day passes, £9.68 (that is, £300/31) more will transform from an asset into an expense. As we have already seen, it is not necessary for us to make any adjustment to the rent account as the days pass.

Assume, now, that on 5 January the business sold stock costing £200 for £300 on credit. As usual, when we are able to identify the cost of the goods sold at the time of sale, we need to deal with the sale and the cost of the stock sold as two separate issues, each having its own set of debits and credits.

Firstly, let us deal with the sale. We now need to open accounts for both 'sales' and 'trade debtors' – which do not, as yet, exist. The sale is an increase in a revenue; hence the credit entry, which creates an asset, and hence the debit entry in trade debtors:

Sales

	£		£
		5 January Trade debtors	300

Trade debtors

	£		£
5 January Sales	300		

Let us now deal with the stock sold. Since the stock sold has become the expense 'cost of sales', we need to reduce the figure on the stock account by making a credit entry and make the corresponding debit in a 'cost of sales' account, opened for the purpose:

Stock

	£			£
2 January Cash	600	5 January Cost of sales		200

Cost of sales

	£		£
5 January Stock	200		

Following the example of sales, we can make the general points that:

■ **Debits (left-hand entries) represent increases in assets and expenses and decreases in claims and revenues.**
■ **Credits (right-hand entries) represent increases in claims and revenues and decreases in assets and expenses.**

We shall now look at the other transactions for our hypothetical business for the remainder of January. These can be taken to be as follows:

January 8	Bought some stock on credit costing £800
January 11	Bought some office furniture for £400
January 15	Sold stock costing £600 for £900, on credit
January 18	Received £800 from trade debtors
January 21	Paid trade creditors £500
January 24	Paid wages for the month £400
January 27	Bought stock on credit for £800
January 31	Borrowed £2,000 from the Commercial Finance Company

Naturally, we shall have to open several additional accounts to enable us to record all of these transactions in any meaningful way. By the end of January, the set of accounts would appear as follows:

Cash

		£			£
1 January	Capital	5,000	2 January	Stock	600
18 January	Trade debtors	800	3 January	Rent	300
31 January	Comm. Fin Co	2,000	11 January	Office furniture	400
			21 January	Trade creditors	500
			24 January	Wages	400

Capital

	£			£
		1 January	Cash	5,000

Stock

		£			£
2 January	Cash	600	5 January	Cost of sales	200
8 January	Trade creditors	800	15 January	Cost of sales	600
27 January	Trade creditors	800			

Rent

		£		£
3 January	Cash	300		

Sales

	£			£
		5 January	Trade debtors	300
		15 January	Trade debtors	900

Trade debtors

		£			£
5 January	Sales	300	18 January	Cash	800
15 January	Sales	900			

Cost of sales

		£	£
5 January	Stock	200	
15 January	Stock	600	

Trade creditors

		£			£
21 January	Cash	500	8 January	Stock	800
			27 January	Stock	800

Office furniture

		£	£
11 January	Cash	400	

Wages

		£	£
24 January	Cash	400	

Loan creditor – Commercial Finance Company

£			£
	31 January	Cash	2,000

All of the transactions from 8 January onwards are quite similar in nature to those up to that date, which we discussed in detail, and so you should be able to follow them using the date references as a guide.

Balancing accounts and the trial balance

Businesses keeping their accounts in the way shown would find it helpful to summarise their individual accounts periodically – perhaps weekly or monthly – for two reasons:

- To be able to see at a glance how much is in each account (for example to see how much cash the business has left).
- To help to check the accuracy of the bookkeeping so far.

Let us look at the cash account again:

Cash

		£			£
1 January	Capital	5,000	2 January	Stock	600
18 January	Trade debtors	800	3 January	Rent	300
31 January	Comm. Fin. Co.	2,000	11 January	Office furniture	400
			21 January	Trade creditors	500
			24 January	Wages	400

Does this account tell us how much cash the business has at 31 January? The answer is partly yes and partly no!

We can fairly easily deduce the amount of cash simply by adding up the debit (receipts) column and deducting the sum of the credit (payments) column, but it would be easier if this were done for us.

To summarise or **balance** this account, we add up the larger column (the debit side) and put this total on both sides of the account. We then put in, on the credit side, the figure that will make that side add up to the same figure. We cannot put in this balancing figure only once or the double-entry rule will have been broken, and so we also put it in on the other side below the totals, as follows:

Cash

		£			£
1 January	Capital	5,000	2 January	Stock	600
18 January	Trade debtors	800	3 January	Rent	300
31 January	Comm. Fin Co	2,000	11 January	Trade creditors	400
			21 January	Trade creditors	500
			24 January	Wages	400
			31 January		
				Balance carried down	5,600
		7,800			7,800
1 February					
	Balance brought down	5,600			

Note that the balance carried down (usually abbreviated to 'c/d') at the end of one period becomes the balance brought down ('b/d') at the beginning of the next. Now we can see at a glance what the present situation is, without having to do any mental arithmetic.

Activity A.2   Have a try at balancing the stock account and then say what we know about the stock situation at the end of January.

Stock

		£			£
2 January	Cash	600	5 January	Cost of sales	200
8 January	Trade creditors	800	15 January	Cost of sales	600
27 January	Trade creditors	800	31 January	Balance c/d	1,400
		2,200			2,200
1 February	Balance b/d	1,400			

We can see at a glance that the business held stock that had cost £1,400 at the end of January. We can also see quite easily how this situation arose.

We can balance all of the other accounts in similar fashion. There is no point in formally balancing accounts that have only one entry at the moment (for example, the capital account) because we cannot summarise one figure; it is already in as summarised a form as it can be. After balancing, the other accounts will be as follows:

Capital

	£			£
		1 January	Cash	5,000

Rent

		£		£
3 January	Cash	300		

Sales

		£			£
31 January	Balance c/d	1,200	5 January	Trade debtors	300
			15 January	Trade debtors	900
		1,200			1,200
			1 February	Balance b/d	1,200

Trade debtors

		£			£
5 January	Sales	300	18 January	Cash	800
15 January	Sales	900	31 January	Balance c/d	400
		1,200			1,200
1 February	Balance b/d	400			

Cost of Sales

		£			£
5 January	Stock	200	31 January	Balance c/d	800
15 January	Stock	600			
		800			800
1 February	Balance b/d	800			

Trade creditors

		£			£
21 January	Cash	500	8 January	Stock	800
31 January	Balance c/d	1,100	27 January	Stock	800
		1,600			1,600
			1 February	Balance b/d	1,100

Office furniture

		£		£
11 January	Cash	400		

Wages

		£		£
24 January	Cash	400		

Loan creditor – Commercial Finance Company

	£			£
		31 January	Cash	2,000

Activity A.3

If we now separately total the debit balances and the credit ones, what should we expect to find?

We should expect to find that these two totals are equal. This must in theory be true since every debit entry was matched by an equally-sized credit entry.

Let us see if our expectation in Activity A.3 works in our example, by listing the debit and credit balances as follows:

	Debits £	Credits £
Cash	5,600	
Stock	1,400	
Capital		5,000
Rent	300	
Sales		1,200
Trade debtors	400	
Cost of sales	800	
Trade creditors		1,100
Office furniture	400	
Wages	400	
Loan creditor		2,000
	9,300	9,300

➡ This statement is known as a **trial balance**. The fact that it agrees gives us some indication that we have not made any bookkeeping errors.

This situation does not, however, give us total confidence that no error could have occurred. Consider the transaction that took place on 3 January (paid rent for the month of £300). In each of the following cases, all of which would be wrong, the trial balance would still have agreed:

- The transaction was completely omitted from the accounts; that is, no entries were made at all.
- The amount was misread as £3,000 but then (correctly) debited to the rent account and credited to cash.
- The correct amount was (incorrectly) debited to cash and credited to rent.

Nevertheless, a trial balance that agrees does give some confidence that accounts have been correctly written up.

Activity A.4	**Why do you think the words 'debtor' and 'creditor' are used to describe those who owe money or are owed money by a business?**

The answer simply is that debtors have a debit balance in the books of the business, whereas creditors have a credit balance.

Preparing final accounts

The next stage in the process is to prepare the profit and loss account and balance sheet. Preparing the profit and loss account is simply a matter of going through the individual accounts, identifying those balances that represent revenues and expenses of the period, and transferring them to a profit and loss account, which is part of the double-entry system.

We shall now do this for the example we have been using. To simplify matters, we shall assume that there is no depreciation on the office furniture, nor any interest due on the loan, nor any other prepaid or accrued expenses. You should be clear, however, that end-of-period adjustments of this type can very easily be dealt with in double-entry accounts, as we shall see later in this appendix.

The balances on the following accounts represent expenses or revenues for the month of January:

- Rent
- Sales
- Cost of sales
- Wages

The balances on these accounts will be transferred to a profit and loss account. The remaining balances represent assets and claims that continue to exist at the end of January.

The four accounts whose balances represent revenues or expenses, and the profit and loss account, are dealt with next. To transfer balances to the profit and loss account, we simply debit or credit the account concerned, such that any balance amount is eliminated, and make the corresponding credit or debit in the profit and loss account. Take rent, for example. This has a debit balance (because the balance represents an expense). We must credit the rent account with £300 and debit profit and loss account with the same amount. So a debit balance on the rent account becomes a debit entry in the profit and loss account which is then, along with the other expenses, compared with the sales. For the four accounts, then, we have the following:

Rent

		£			£
3 January	Cash	300	31 January	Profit and loss	300

Sales

		£			£
31 January	Balance c/d	1,200	5 January	Trade debtors	300
			15 January	Trade debtors	900
		1,200			1,200
31 January	Profit and loss	1,200	1 February	Balance b/d	1,200

Cost of Sales

		£			£
5 January	Stock	200	31 January	Balance c/d	800
15 January	Stock	600			
		800			800
1 February	Balance b/d	800	31 January	Profit and loss	800

Wages

		£			£
24 January	Cash	400	31 January	Profit and loss	400

Profit and loss account

		£			£
31 January	Cost of sales	800	31 January	Sales	1,200
31 January	Rent	300			
31 January	Wages	400			

We must now transfer the balance on the profit and loss account (a debit balance of £300).

Activity A.5

What does the balance on the profit and loss account represent, and where should it be transferred to?

The balance is either the profit or the loss (loss in this case) for the period. This loss must be borne by the owner, and it must therefore be transferred to the capital account.

The two accounts would now appear as follows:

Profit and loss account

		£			£
31 January	Cost of sales	800	31 January	Sales	1,200
31 January	Rent	300			
31 January	Wages	400	31 January	Capital (net loss)	300
		1,500			1,500

Capital

		£			£
31 January	Profit and loss (net loss)	300	1 January	Cash	5,000
31 January	Balance c/d	4,700			
		5,000			5,000
			1 February	Balance b/d	4,700

The last thing done was to balance the capital account.

Now all of the balances remaining on accounts represent either assets or claims as at 31 January. These balances can now be used to produce a balance sheet, as follows:

Balance sheet as at 31 January

	£	£
Fixed assets		
Office furniture		400
Current assets		
Stock	1,400	
Trade debtors	400	
Cash	5,600	
	7,400	
Current liabilities		
Trade creditors	1,100	
		6,300
		6,700
Less Loan creditor		2,000
		4,700
Capital		4,700

The profit and loss account could be written in a more stylish manner, for reporting to users, as follows:

Profit and loss account for the month ended 31 January

	£	£
Sales		1,200
Cost of sales		800
Gross profit		400
Less Rent	300	
Wages	400	
		700
Net loss for the month		(300)

Preparing final accounts – some further issues

As was stated early in the previous section some simplifying assumptions were made about the business, that we used to illustrate double-entry bookkeeping and its first month of trading. These were:

- the office furniture does not depreciate
- there was no interest due on the loan (not unreasonable because the loan was not taken out until the last day of the month), and
- there were no prepaid or accrued expenses. This is to say that the cash paid for expenses (rent and wages) equalled the expense for the month (for example the £400 paid for wages represented all the cash due to employees and no more).

We are now going to look at the accounts of a different business (Jane and Co), where these assumptions will not apply.

The trial balance of Jane and Co at 31 December last year, the end of its first year of trading, was as follows:

	Debits £	Credits £
Capital		27,400
Cash	2,700	
Cost of sales	38,200	
Electricity	4,900	
General expenses	12,700	
Loan creditor		10,000
Loan interest	300	
Machinery	12,500	
Rent	13,000	
Sales		85,500
Stock	3,400	
Trade creditors		3,500
Trade debtors	4,400	
Wages	34,300	
	126,400	126,400

The business started trading on 1 January last year. On that date it borrowed the £10,000, which is shown above as a loan creditor. The machinery (a fixed asset) was also bought on that date.

The trial balance is correct in that it accurately reflects the transactions that occurred during the year. No profit and loss account has been prepared so far. The following further information, none of which is taken into account in the trial balance, is also available:

1. At 31 December there was an electricity bill for the last three months of the year for £1,800 unpaid. This was paid early in January this year.
2. The loan carried an interest rate of 6% a year. This was due to be paid on 30 June and 31 December, but the payment due on 31 December was overlooked and not paid until 1 January this year.
3. The wages figure in the trial balance represents payments for all the work done by employees during the year, except that some extra hours worked in late December had not been paid by the end of the year. These hours were worth

£800 and this amount was paid to the relevant employees early in January this year.

4. The rent expense is £1,000 per month, payable at the beginning of each month. Late in December last year, the January payment for this year was made.

5. The machinery is estimated to have a useful life with the business of five years and then to have a disposal value of £4,500. It has been decided to use the 'straight-line' method of depreciation (that is equal annual depreciation charges).

Before we go on to prepare the final accounts for the business, let us first establish what general approach we need to take with the five further items of information listed above. Let us take the first one, dealing with electricity.

Activity A.6	What is the electricity expense for the year?

The figure in the trial balance (£4,900) is the expense for just the first nine months of the year. The full expense for the year is £6,700 (that is, £4,900 + £1,800).

If the profit and loss account is to provide a full picture of the year's trading, the electricity expense for the year must be £6,700.

Activity A.7	In view of the fact that the unpaid electricity bill must be included in the profit and loss account as an expense and the unpaid bill is settled shortly after the year end, should we increase the trial balance electricity figure and reduce the cash figure by the £1,800, as if the payment took place before the end of the year?

No. The cash at the end of the year was £2,700 and this fact must be reflected on the balance sheet.

The position at 31 December regarding electricity is that the expense for the year is £1,800 more than has been paid and the business has a creditor for that amount. The business has had the electricity, but not yet paid for it. This is an accrued expense.

The electricity account needs to be dealt with as follows:

Electricity

		£			£
31 Dec	Balance brought down	4,900	31 Dec	Profit and loss account	6,700
31 Dec	Balance carried down	1,800			
		6,700			6,700
			1 Jan	Balance brought down	1,800

The £4,900 balance brought down is the total of the payments made during the year. The credit balance brought down on 1 January represents the amount owed to the electricity supplier on that date. To complete the double entry, there needs to be a debit entry (balance carried down). The whole amount represents the expense for the year, reflected in the transfer to profit and loss account (£6,700). Thus the profit and loss account will have the correct expense figure and the £1,800 credit balance will be picked up in the balance sheet as a current liability (accrued expense).

Activity A.8	Have a try at showing both the loan interest and the wages accounts, in each case picking up the balance reflected in the trial balance and dealing with the accrued expenses.

Loan interest

		£			£
31 Dec	Balance brought down	300	31 Dec	Profit and loss account	600
31 Dec	Balance carried down	300			
		600			600
			1 Jan	Balance brought down	300

The loan is at the interest rate of 6% a year, so the expense for a year is £600 (that is, 6% × £10,000) or two payments of £300 each. This means that the amount owing at 31 December is £300. The account layout follows the same logic as the electricity account

Wages

		£			£
31 Dec	Balance brought down	34,300	31 Dec	Profit and loss account	35,100
31 Dec	Balance carried down	800			
		35,100			35,100
			1 Jan	Balance brought down	800

This is similar to the electricity and loan interest accounts. The accrued expense is carried down into the new accounting year, having the effect of increasing the profit and loss account figure from the trial balance one by the addition of the accrued expense.

The rent expense is similar to the first three of these 'adjustments' except that here we have a prepayment rather than an accrual. The rent is £1,000 for each month, £12,000 for the year. Since £13,000 was paid during the year, the owner of the premises owed the business £1,000 at 31 December. The rent account would look as follows:

Rent

		£			£
31 Dec	Balance brought down	13,000	31 Dec	Profit and loss account	12,000
			31 Dec	Balance carried down	1,000
		13,000			13,000
1 Jan	Balance brought down	1,000			

Since the balance represents a prepayment, it must be brought down as a debit, which in turn means that we need a credit entry of equal amount at 31 December. This means that the profit and loss account figure that makes the account balance is £12,000.

The last of the 'adjustments' relates to depreciation. This is rather different to the others, but is not difficult to deal with.

Since the machinery cost £12,500 and is expected to generate £4,500 when it is disposed of, the total depreciation expense over its five-year life will be £8,000 (that is, £12,500 – £4,500). Since the business intends that this depreciation should be shared equally over the five years, the annual depreciation expense for this machinery will be £1,600 (that is £8,000/5). We simply open a 'Provision for depreciation of machinery' account, and credit this with the £1,600 for the year; the corresponding double entry will be to the profit and loss account, as follows:

Provision for depreciation of machinery

	£			£
		31 Dec	Profit and loss account	1,600

There is no need to 'balance' this account as it only contains one figure. This credit balance will appear on the balance sheet as a deduction from the cost of the machinery, as we shall see shortly.

In the following year, a similar entry will be made, so the balance will increase. It will keep increasing until the machinery is disposed of.

We shall not bother to go through the other expenses and revenues (cost of sales, general expenses and sales) since it is simply a matter of transferring the balance to the profit and loss account, without carrying down a balance.

Of the remaining accounts, cash, loan creditor, machinery, stock trade creditors and debtors do not need further attention, simply to have the balance put onto the balance sheet. This leaves 'Capital' which must be credited with the profit, or debited with the loss, the other side of the double entry being in the profit and loss account.

Thus the final accounts will be as follows:

Jane and Co
Balance sheet as at 31 December last year

		£	£
Fixed assets			
Machinery	Cost		12,500
	Depreciation		1,600
			10,900
Current assets			
Stock		3,400	
Prepayments (rent)		1,000	
Trade debtors		4,400	
Cash		2,700	
		11,500	
Current liabilities			
Accruals (electricity, interest, wages)		2,900	
Trade creditors		3,500	
		6,400	
			5,100
			16,000
Less: Loan creditor			10,000
			6,000
Capital (27,400 – 21,400)			6,000

Profit and loss account for the year ended 31 December last year

		£	£
Sales			85,500
Cost of sales			38,200
Gross profit			47,300
Less:	Electricity	6,700	
	General expenses	12,700	
	Loan interest	600	
	Depreciation of machinery	1,600	
	Rent	12,000	
	Wages	35,100	
			68,700
Net loss for the month			21,400

The ledger and its division

The book in which the accounts are traditionally kept is known as the ledger and 'accounts' are sometimes referred to as 'ledger accounts', even where they are computerised.

In a handwritten accounting system, the ledger is often divided into various sections. This tends to be for two main reasons:

1. Having all of the accounts in one book means that it is only possible for one person at a time to use the accounts, either to make entries or to extract useful information.
2. Dividing the ledger along logical grounds can allow specialisation, so that various individual members of the accounts staff can look after their own part of the system. This can lead to more efficient record keeping. It can also lead to greater security, that is less risk of error and fraud by limiting an individual's access to only part of the entire set of accounts.

There are no clear, universal rules on the division of the ledger, but the following division is fairly common:

- *The cash book*
  This tends to be all of the accounts relating to cash either loose or in the bank.
- *The sales (or trade debtors) ledger*
  This contains the accounts of all of the business's individual trade debtors.
- *The purchases (or trade creditors) ledger*
  This consists of the accounts of all of the business's individual trade creditors.
- *The nominal ledger*
  These accounts tend to be those of expenses and revenues, for example, sales, wages, rent, and so on.
- *The general ledger*
  This contains the remainder of the business's accounts, mainly those to do with fixed assets and long-term finance.

Summary

In this appendix we have reviewed a system for keeping accounting records by hand, such that a relatively large volume of transactions can be handled effectively and accurately. In this system, known as double-entry bookkeeping, there is a separate account for each asset, claim, expense and liability that needs to be separately identified. Each account looks like a letter T and is sometimes referred to as a 'T-account'. On the left-hand (debit) side of the account we record increases in assets and expenses and decreases in revenues and claims. On the right-hand (credit) side we record increases in revenues and claims and decreases in assets and expenses. This means that there is an equal credit entry in one account for a debit entry in another.

We saw that not only can double-entry bookkeeping be used to record the day-to-day transactions of the organisation, but it can also follow through to generate the profit and loss account. The balance sheet is then simply a list of the net figure (the 'balance') on each of the accounts after appropriate transfers have been made to the profit and loss account.

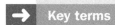 **Key terms**

Double-entry bookkeeping   p. 327   **Credit**   p. 329
Account   p. 327   **Balance**   p. 332
Debit   p. 329   **Trial balance**   p. 334

The full set of accounts of a business is often referred to as the ledger. The ledger is often divided into sections. This can lead to more efficient and secure accounting record keeping.

Further reading

If you would like to explore the topics covered in this appendix in more depth, we recommend the following books:

Foundations of Business Accounting, *Dodge, R.*, 2nd edn, Thompson Business Press, 1997, chapter 3.

An Introduction to Financial Accounting, *Thomas, A.*, 2nd edn, McGraw-Hill, 1996, chapters 4 and 5.

Practical Accounting, *Benedict, A.* and *Elliott, B.*, Financial Times Prentice Hall, 2001, chapters 2–5.

Financial Accounting, *Bebbington, J., Gray, R.* and *Laughlin, R.*, 3rd edn, Thomson Learning, 2001, chapters 2–7.

? EXERCISES

All of these exercises have answers at the back of the book.

A.1 | In respect of each of the following transactions, state in which two accounts must an entry be made and whether the entry is a debit or a credit. (For example, if the transaction were purchase of stock for cash, the answer would be debit the stock account and credit the cash account.)

(a) Purchased stock on credit.
(b) Owner made cash drawings.
(c) Paid interest on a business loan.
(d) Purchased stock for cash.
(e) Received cash from a credit customer.
(f) Paid wages to employees.
(g) The owner received some cash from a credit customer, which was taken as drawings rather than being paid into the business's bank account.
(h) Paid a credit supplier.
(i) Paid electricity bill.
(j) Made cash sales.

A.2 | (a) Record the following transactions in a set of double-entry accounts:

1 February	Lee (the owner) put £6,000 into a newly-opened business bank account to start a new business
3 February	Purchased stock for £2,600 for cash
5 February	Purchased some equipment (fixed asset) for cash for £800
6 February	Purchased stock costing £3,000 on credit
9 February	Paid rent for the month of £250
10 February	Paid fuel and electricity for the month of £240
11 February	Paid general expenses of £200
15 February	Sold stock for £4,000 in cash; the stock had cost £2,400
19 February	Sold stock for £3,800 on credit; the stock had cost £2,300
21 February	Lee withdrew £1,000 in cash for personal use
25 February	Paid £2,000 to trade creditors
28 February	Received £2,500 from trade debtors

(b) Balance the relevant accounts and prepare a trial balance (making sure that it agrees).
(c) Prepare a profit and loss account for the month and a balance sheet at the month end. Assume that there are no prepaid or accrued expenses at the end of the month and ignore any possible depreciation.

A.3 | The following is the balance sheet of David's business at 1 January of last year.

Fixed assets		£	Capital	£ 25,050
Buildings		25,000		
Fittings: cost	10,000		Loan	12,000
depreciation	2,000	8,000		
			Current liabilities	
			Trade creditors	1,690
Current assets			Accrued electricity	270
Stock of stationery		140		
Stock in trade		1,350		
Prepaid in rent		500		
Trade debtors		1,840		
Cash		2,180		
		39,010		39,010

The following is a summary of the transactions that took place during the year:

1. Stock was purchased on credit for £17,220.
2. Stock was purchased for £3,760 cash.
3. Credit sales amounted to £33,100 (cost £15,220).
4. Cash sales amounted to £10,360 (cost £4,900).
5. Wages of £3,770 were paid.
6. Rent of £3,000 was paid. The annual rental amounts to £3,000.
7. Electricity of £1,070 was paid.
8. General expenses of £580 were paid.
9. Additional fittings were purchased on 1 January for £2,000, The cash for this was raised from an additional loan of this amount. The interest rate is 10% a year, the same as for the existing loan.
10. £1,000 of the loan was repaid on 30 June.
11. Cash received from debtors amounted to £32,810.
12. Cash paid to creditors amounted to £18,150.
13. The owner withdrew £10,400 cash and £560 stock.

At the end of the year it was found that:

(a) The electricity bill for the last quarter of the year for £290 had not been paid.
(b) It was also found that trade debts amounting to £260 were unlikely to be received.
(c) The value of stationery remaining was estimated at £150. Stationery is included in general expenses.
(d) The loan carried interest of 10% per annum.
(e) Depreciation to be taken at 20% on the cost of the fittings owned at the year end. Buildings are not depreciated.

Required:
(1) Open ledger accounts and bring down all of the balances in the opening balance sheet.
(2) Make entries to record the transactions (1) to (13) (above), opening any additional accounts as necessary.
(3) Open a profit and loss account (part of the double entry, remember). Make the necessary entries for the items (a) to (e) (above) and the appropriate transfers to the profit and loss account.
(4) List the remaining balances in the same form as the opening balance sheet (above).

Glossary of key terms

Account A section of a double-entry bookkeeping system that deals with one particular asset, claim, expense or revenue. p. 327

Accounting The process of identifying, measuring and communicating information to permit informed judgements and decisions by users of the information. p. 1

Accounting conventions Accounting rules that have evolved over time in order to deal with practical problems rather than to reflect some theoretical ideal. p. 13

Accounting information system The system used within a business to identify, record, analyse and report accounting information. p. 9

Accounting (financial reporting) standards Rules established by the UK accounting profession, which should be followed by preparers of the annual accounts of companies. p. 133

Accrued expenses Expenses that are outstanding at the end of the accounting period. p. 61

Acid-test ratio A liquidity ratio that relates the current assets (less stocks) to the current liabilities. p. 203

Allotted share capital See Issued share capital.

Asset A resource held by a business that has certain characteristics. p. 24

Associate company A company over which considerable influence, but not full control, may be exercised by another company. p. 281

Auditors Professionals whose main duty is to make a report as to whether, in their opinion, the accounting statements of a company do that which they are supposed to do, namely, to show a true and fair view and comply with statutory, and accounting standard requirements. p. 138

Authorised share capital The maximum amount of share capital that directors are authorised by the shareholders to issue. p. 107

Average settlement period for debtors/creditors The average time taken for debtors to pay the amounts owing or for a business to pay its creditors. p. 198

Average stock turnover period An efficiency ratio that measures the average period for which stocks are held by a business. p. 197

Bad debt Amount owed to the business that is considered to be irrecoverable. p. 81

Balance The net of the debit and credit totals in an account in a double-entry bookkeeping system. p. 332

Balance sheet A statement of financial position that shows the assets of a business and the claim on those assets. p. 19

Bonus issue   Reserves that are converted into shares and given 'free' to shareholders. p. 106

Bonus shares   See Bonus issue.

Business entity convention   The convention that holds that, for accounting purposes, the business and its owner(s) are treated as quite separate and distinct. p. 40

Called-up share capital   That part of a company's share capital for which the shareholders have been asked to pay the agreed amount. Part of the claim of the owners against the business. p. 107

Capital   The owner's claim on the assets of the business. p. 26

Capital expenditure   The outlay of funds on fixed assets. p. 164

Capital reserve   A reserve that arises from a 'capital' profit or gain rather than from normal trading activities. p. 103

Capital reserve arising on consolidation   Any amount paid below the underlying net asset value of a subsidiary by a parent company. p. 259

Cash flow   The movement of cash. p. 159

Cash flow statement   A statement that shows the sources and uses of cash for a period. p. 19

Claim   An obligation on the part of the business to provide cash or some other benefit to an outside party. p. 24

Combined Code   A code of practice for companies listed on the London Stock Exchange that deals with corporate governance matters. p. 98

Common costs   Costs that relate to more than one business segment. p. 148

Common-size financial statements   Normal financial statements (such as the P and L account, balance sheet and cash flow statement) that are expressed in terms of some base figure. p. 220

Comparability   The requirement that items, which are basically the same, should be treated in the same manner for measurement and reporting purposes. Lack of comparability will limit the usefulness of accounting information. p. 6

Consistency convention   The accounting convention that holds that when a particular method of accounting is selected to deal with a transaction, this method should be applied consistently over time. p. 80

Consolidated financial statement   A group financial statement (balance sheet and so on) where the results of subsidiary companies are 'consolidated' into the results of the parent company. p. 252

Consolidating   Reducing the number of shares in issue and simultaneously increasing the nominal value per share to maintain the same total nominal value of the shares issued. p. 104

Corporate governance   Systems for directing and controlling a company. p. 97

Corporation tax   Taxation that a limited company is liable to pay on its profits. p. 96

Cost of sales   The cost of the goods sold during a period. Cost of sales can be derived by adding the opening stock held to the stock purchases for the period and then deducting the closing stocks held. p. 57

Creative accounting   Adopting accounting policies to achieve a particular view of performance and position that preparers would like the users to see rather than what is a true and fair view. p. 218

Credit   An entry made in the right-hand side of an account in double-entry bookkeeping. p. 329

Current asset An asset that is not held on a continuing basis. Current assets include cash itself and other assets that are expected to be converted to cash at some point in the future. p. 31

Current cost accounting A method of accounting for inflation, based on maintaining the existing scale of business operations. It seeks to maintain the purchasing power of the business over specific goods and services utilised. p. 308

Current liabilities Amounts due for repayment to outside parties within twelve months of the balance sheet date. p. 33

Current purchasing power (CPP) accounting A method of accounting for inflation based on maintaining the owners' purchasing power over general goods and services within the economy. p. 307

Current ratio A liquidity ratio that relates the current assets of the business to the current liabilities. p. 202

Debenture A long-term loan, usually made to a company, that is evidenced by a trust deed. p. 108

Debit An entry made in the left-hand side of an account in double-entry bookkeeping. p. 327

Depreciation A measure of that portion of the cost (less residual value) of a fixed asset that has been consumed during an accounting period. p. 64

Direct method An approach to deducing the cash flows from trading operations, in a cash flow statement, by analysing the business's cash records. p. 168

Directors Individuals who are elected to act as the most senior level of management of a company. p. 97

Directors' Report A report containing information of a financial and non-financial nature that the directors must produce as part of the annual financial report to shareholders. p. 131

Dividend Transfer of assets made by a company to its shareholders. p. 102

Dividend cover ratio An investment ratio that relates the earnings available for dividends to the dividend announced to indicate how many times the former covers the latter. p. 211

Dividend payout ratio An investment ratio that relates the dividends announced for the period to the earnings available for dividends which were generated in that period. p. 211

Dividend per share An investment ratio that relates the dividends announced for a period to the number of shares in issue. p. 210

Dividend yield ratio An investment ratio that relates the cash return from a share to its current market value. p. 212

Double-entry bookkeeping A system for recording financial transactions where each transaction is recorded twice, once as a debit and once as a credit. p. 327

Dual aspect convention The accounting convention that holds that each transaction has two aspects and that each aspect must be recorded in the financial statements. p. 40

Earnings per share An investment ratio that relates the earnings generated by the business during a period, and available to shareholders, to the number of shares in issue. p. 212

Environmental report A report that accounts for the impact of the business on the environment. p. 309

Equity Ordinary shares and reserves of a company. p. 102

Equity dividends paid A section of the cash flow statement that deals with the cash flows arising from ordinary share dividends paid. p. 164

Expense A measure of the outflow of assets (or increase in liabilities) that is incurred as a result of generating revenues. p. 54

Fair values (in group accounts) Market values of subsidiary company assets that are to be included in the group balance sheet. p. 271

Final accounts The profit and loss account, balance sheet and cash flow statement taken together. p. 23

Financial accounting The measuring and reporting of accounting information for external users (those users other than the managers of the business). p. 10

Financial gearing The existence of fixed payment bearing securities (for example, loans) in the capital structure of a business. p. 206

Financing A section of the cash flow statement that deals with the cash flows arising from raising and repaying long-term finance. p. 164

First in, first out (FIFO) A method of stock valuation that assumes that the earlier stocks are to be sold first. p. 76

Fixed asset An asset held with the intention of being used to generate wealth rather than being held for resale. Fixed assets can be seen as the tools of the business and are held on a continuing basis. p. 31

Fully paid shares Shares on which the shareholders have paid the full issue price. p. 107

Gearing See financial gearing.

Gearing ratio A ratio that relates the contribution of long-term lenders to the total long-term capital of the business. p. 207

Going concern convention The accounting convention that holds that the business will continue operations for the foreseeable future. In orther words, there is no intention or need to liquidate the business. p. 39

Goodwill arising on consolidation Anything paid in excess of the underlying net asset value of the subsidiary's shares. p. 259

Gross profit The amount remaining (if positive) after trading expenses (for example, cost of sales) have been deducted from trading revenues (for example, sales). p. 56

Gross profit margin A profitability ratio relating the gross profit for the period to the sales for the period. p. 195

Group accounts Sets of financial accounting statements that combine the performance and position of a group of companies which are under common control. p. 241

Group balance sheet A balance sheet for a group of companies, prepared from the perspective of the parent company's shareholders. p. 252

Group cash flow statement A cash flow statement for a group of companies, prepared from the perspective of the parent company's shareholders. p. 279

Group of companies A situation that arises where one company is able to exercise control over another or others. p. 241

Group profit and loss account A profit and loss account for a group of companies, prepared from the perspective of the parent company's shareholders. p. 275

Historic cost What an asset cost when it was originally acquired. p. 39

Historic cost convention The accounting convention that holds that assets should be recorded at their historic (acquisition) cost. p. 39

Holding company   See Parent company. p. 242

Indirect method   An approach to deducing the cash flows from trading operations, in a cash flow statement, by analysing the business's final accounts. p. 168

Inflation accounting   A means of accounting for a fall in the purchasing power of money. p. 303

Intangible assets   Assets that do not have a physical substance (for example, patents, goodwill and debtors). p. 26

Interest cover ratio   A gearing ratio that divides the net profit before interest and taxation by the interest payable for a period. p. 209

Issued share capital   That part of the authorised share capital that has been issued to shareholders. Also known as allotted share capital. p. 107

Last in, first out (LIFO)   A method of stock valuation that assumes that the latest stocks are the first to be sold. p. 76

Liabilities   Claims of individuals and organisations, apart from the owner, that have arisen from past transactions or events such as supplying goods or lending money to the business. p. 26

Limited company   An artificial legal person that has an identity separate from that of those who own and manage it. p. 15

Limited liability   The restriction of the legal obligation of shareholders to meet all of the company's debts. p. 95

Long-term liabilities   Those amounts due to other parties that are not liable for repayment within the next twelve months after the balance sheet date. p. 33

Management accounting   The measuring and reporting of accounting information for the managers of a business. p. 10

Management of liquid resources   A section of the cash flow statement that deals with the cash flows arising from movements in short-term liquid resources. p. 164

Matching convention   The accounting convention that holds that, in measuring income, expenses should be matched to revenues, which they helped generate, in the same accounting period as those revenues were realised. p. 60

Materiality   The requirement that material information should be disclosed to users of financial reports. p. 7

Materiality convention   The accounting convention that states that, where the amounts involved are immaterial, only what is expedient should be considered. p. 63

Minority interests   That part of the net assets of a subsidiary company that is financed by shareholders other than the parent company. Also known as 'outsiders interests'. p. 257

Monetary items   Items appearing on the balance sheet that have a fixed number of £s attached to them and which cannot be changed as a result of inflation. p. 306

Money measurement convention   The accounting convention that holds that accounting should deal only with those items that are capable of being expressed in monetary terms. p. 38

Net cash flow from operating activities   A section of the cash flow statement that deals with the cash flows from trading operations. p. 162

Net profit   The amount remaining (if positive) after the total expenses for a period have been deducted from total revenues. p. 56

Net profit margin A profitability ratio relating the net profit for the period to the sales for the period. p. 195

Nominal value The face value of a share in a company. p. 101

Objectivity convention The convention that holds that, in so far as is possible, the financial statements prepared should be based on objective verifiable evidence rather than matters of opinion. p. 43

Operating and financial review A narrative report that helps users to understand the operating and financial results of a business for a period. p. 149

Operating cash flow per ordinary share An investment ratio that relates the operating cash flows available to ordinary shareholders to the number of ordinary shares. p. 213

Operating cash flows to maturing obligations ratio A liquidity ratio that compares the operating cash flows to the current liabilities of the business. p. 205

Ordinary shares Shares of a company owned by those who are due the benefits of the company's activities after all other stakeholders have been satisfied. p. 102

Overtrading The situation arising when a business is operating at a level of activity that cannot be supported by the amount of finance which has been committed. p. 218

Paid-up share capital That part of the share capital of a company that has been called and paid. p. 107

Parent company A company that is able to exercise control over another (subsidiary) company, usually, but not necessarily, because it owns a majority of the shares of the subsidiary. Sometimes known as a 'holding' company. p. 241

Partnership A form of business unit where there are at least two individuals, but usually no more than twenty, carrying on a business with the intention of making a profit. p. 15

Preference shares Shares of a company owned by those who are entitled to the first part of any dividend which the company may pay. p. 102

Prepaid expenses Expenses that have been paid in advance at the end of the accounting period. p. 63

Price/earnings ratio An investment ratio that relates the market value of a share to the earnings per share. p. 214

Private company A limited company for which the directors can restrict the ownership of its shares. p. 95

Profit The increase in wealth attributable to the owners of a business that arises through business operations. p. 53

Profit and loss account A financial statement that measures and reports the profit (or loss) the business has generated during a period. It is derived by deducting from total revenues for a period, the total expenses associated with those revenues. p. 19

Provision for doubtful debts An amount set aside out of profits to provide for anticipated losses arising from debts that may prove irrecoverable. p. 81

Prudence convention The accounting convention that holds that financial statements should err on the side of caution. p. 41

Public company A limited company for which the directors cannot restrict the ownership of its shares. p. 95

Realisation convention The accounting convention that holds that revenue should be recognised only when it has been realised. p. 60

Reducing balance method   A method of calculating depreciation that applies a fixed percentage rate of depreciation to the written-down value of an asset in each period. p. 66

Relevance   The ability of accounting information to influence decisions. Relevance is regarded as a key characteristic of useful accounting information. p. 6

Reliability   The requirement that accounting should be free from material error or bias. Reliability is regarded as a key characteristic of useful accounting information. p. 6

Replacement cost   The cost of replacing an asset with a similar one. p. 308

Reserves   Part of the owners' claim on a limited company that has arisen from profits and gains, to the extent that these have not been distributed to the shareholders. p. 103

Residual value   The amount for which a fixed asset is sold when the business has no further use for it. p. 66

Return on capital employed (ROCE)   A profitability ratio expressing the relationship between the net profit (before interest and taxation) and the long-term capital invested in the business. p. 194

Return on ordinary shareholders' funds (ROSF)   A profitability ratio that compares the amount of profit for the period available to the ordinary shareholders with their stake in the business. p. 193

Returns from investment and servicing of finance   A section of the cash flow statement that deals with the cash flows arising from interest and dividends received and from interest paid. p. 164

Revenue   A measure of the inflow of assets (for example, cash or amounts owed to a business by debtors), or a reduction in liabilities, that arises as a result of trading operations. p. 53

Revenue reserve   Part of the owners' claim on a company that arises from realised profits and gains, including after-tax trading profits and gains from disposals of fixed assets. These profits and gains have been re-invested in the company rather than distributed to the owners. p. 102

Rights issue   An issue of shares for cash to existing shareholders on the basis of the number of shares already held. p. 106

Sales per employee   An efficiency ratio that relates the sales generated during a period to the average number of employees of the business. p. 200

Sales to capital employed ratio   An efficiency ratio that relates the sales generated during a period to the capital employed. p. 199

Segmental financial report   Reports that break down the operating results of a business according to its business or geographical segments. p. 146

Share   A portion of the ownership, or equity, of a company. p. 5

Share premium account   A capital reserve reflecting any amount above the nominal value of shares that is paid for those shares. p. 104

Social reports   Reports that are produced to reveal the way in which a business interacts with society. p. 313

Sole proprietorship   An individual in business on his or her own account. p. 14

Stable monetary unit convention   The accounting convention that holds that money, which is the unit of measurement in accounting, will not change in value over time. p. 41

Statement of recognised gains and losses   A statement that shows the change in the owners' claim on a limited company from the date of one published balance sheet to the next. p. 135

Straight-line method   A method of accounting for depreciation that allocates the amount to be depreciated evenly over the useful life of the asset. p. 66

Subsidiary company   A company over which another (parent) company is able to exercise control, usually, but not necessarily, because a majority of its shares are owned by the parent company. p. 241

Summary financial statements   A summarised version of the complete annual financial statements, which shareholders may receive as an alternative to the complete statements. p. 132

Takeover   Where one company buys a majority of the shares of another company and so controls it. p. 242

Tangible assets   Those assets that have a physical substance (for example, plant and machinery, motor vehicles). p. 26

Target company   A company that is the subject of a takeover bid. p. 245

Taxation   A section of the cash flow statement that deals with the cash flows arising from taxes paid and refunded. p. 164

Trading and P and L account   A type of profit and loss account prepared by merchandising businesses (for example, retailers and wholesalers) that measures and reports the gross profit (loss) from trading and then deducts overhead expenses to derive the net profit (loss) for the period. p. 56

Transfer price   The price at which goods or services are sold, or transferred, between divisions of the same business. p. 148

Trial balance   A totalled list of the balances on each of the accounts in a double-entry bookkeeping system. p. 334

Triple bottom line reporting   The combined reporting of economic value added, environmental value added and social value added by a business. p. 316

Understandability   The requirement that accounting information should be capable of being understood by those for whom the information is primarily compiled. Lack of understandability will limit the usefulness of accounting information. p. 7

Value added statement   A performance statement, based on a rearrangement of the information contained in the profit and loss account, that reveals the income (value added) attributable to employees, government and suppliers of capital. p. 293

Weighted average cost (AVCO)   A method of valuing stocks which assumes that stocks entering the business lose their separate identity and any issues of stock reflect the weighted average cost of the stocks held. p. 76

Written down value   The difference between the cost (or revalued amount) of a fixed asset and the accumulated depreciation relating to the assets. The written down value is also referred to as the net book value. p. 66

Solutions to review questions

1.1 The following users will have an interest in a university.

■ *Government* Information about the financial resources of a university may be helpful in deciding on the level of funding the university should receive. Information concerning the way in which the funds are applied will be useful in assessing whether taxpayer's money has been used in an effective and efficient manner.

■ *Students* Students may be interested in the financial state of the university to see whether it can increase, or at least maintain, the level of facilities that is currently on offer. Where the university seeks to impose additional costs on students (for example, higher charges from rented accommodation), students may wish to see financial evidence that such charges are justified.

■ *Management* Managers will need financial information to plan and control the activities of the university. They will require information about all aspects of the university's activities as they are accountable for the way in which university funds are employed.

■ *Lenders/employees/suppliers of goods and services/community* These groups will have much the same information needs relating to a university as they would have for a private-sector business.

1.2 In order to be justified in producing a particular piece of accounting information, strictly the person authorising its production should be satisfied that the economic cost of providing it is less than the economic benefit which will be derived from its production. This is to say that there should be a net economic benefit of producing it. Otherwise it should not be produced.

There are obvious problems in determining what is the value of the benefit. There are also likely to be difficulties in determining the amount of the cost. Thus, the judgement is not easy to make.

Economics is not the only issue, particularly in the context of financial accounting. Social and other factors may well be involved. It can be argued that society has a right to certain information about a large business, even though the information may not have an economic value to society.

1.3 Since we can never be sure what is going to happen in the future, the best that we can do is to make judgements made on the basis of past experience. Thus, information concerning flows of cash and of wealth in the recent past is likely to be a useful source on which to base judgements about possible future outcomes. In addition, information concerning the past can be helpful in checking on the accuracy of earlier predictions and judgements. By undertaking this kind of checking, we may decide to revise our view of the future.

1.4 The idea that we should provide simplified financial reports for less sophisticated users has gained increasing acceptance in recent years. Many large companies now offer simplified annual reports to private shareholders and to employees. However, there are dangers associated with this type of report. Companies are complex organ-isations and any attempt to simplify their activities or encapsulate their performance in a relatively few pages runs the risk that the message will be distorted. Perhaps we should not expect accountants to achieve what may be an impossible task. Instead, we should expect unsophisticated users to seek professional help or to study accounting!

2.1 The confusion arises because the owner seems unaware of the business entity con-vention in accounting. This convention requires a separation of the business from the owner(s) of the business for accounting purposes. The business is regarded as a separ-ate entity and the balance sheet is prepared from the perspective of the business rather than that of the owner. As a result, funds invested in the business by the owner will be regarded as a claim which the owner has on the business. In a balance sheet prepared using the horizontal format, this claim will be shown alongside other claims on the business from outsiders.

2.2 A balance sheet does not show what a business is worth for two major reasons:

- The money measurement convention ensures that only those items which can be measured reliably are shown on the balance sheet. Thus, things of value such as the reputation for product quality, skills of employees, etc. will not normally appear in the balance sheet.
- The historic cost convention results in assets being recorded at their outlay cost rather than their current value. In the case of certain assets, the difference between historic cost and current value may be significant.

2.3 The balance sheet is a statement of financial position. In the US, the balance sheet is, therefore, referred to as the 'position statement'. You may think this name conveys more meaning to users than the name that is used in the UK.

2.4 Some object to the idea of humans being treated as assets for inclusion on the balance sheet. It can be seen as demeaning for humans to be listed alongside stocks, plant and machinery and other assets. However, others argue that humans are often the most valuable resource of a business and placing a value on this resource will help bring to the attention of managers the importance of nurturing and developing this 'asset'. There is a saying in management that 'the things that count are the things that get counted'. As the value of the 'human assets' is not stated in the financial statements, there is a danger that managers will treat these 'assets' less favourably than other assets which are on the balance sheet.

Humans are likely to meet the first criterion of an asset listed in the chapter; that is, a probable future benefit exists. There would be little point in employing people if this were not the case. The second criterion concerning exclusive right of control is more problematic. Clearly a business cannot control humans in the same way as most other assets. However, a business can have the exclusive right to the employment services that a person provides. This distinction between control over the services pro-vided, rather than control over the person, makes it possible to argue that the second criterion can be met.

Humans sign a contract of employment with the business and so the third criterion is normally met. The difficulty, however, is with the fourth criterion; that is, whether the value of humans (or their services) can be measured with any degree of reliability. To date, none of the measurement methods proposed enjoys widespread acceptance.

3.1 At the time of preparing the profit and loss account, it is not always possible to determine accurately the expenses incurred during the period. It will only be at some later point in time that the true position becomes clear. However, it is still necessary to try and include all relevant expenses in the profit and loss account and so estimates of the future will have to be made. Examples of estimates that may have to be made include:

- Expenses accrued at the end of the period such as the amount of telephone expenses incurred since the last quarter's bill.
- The amount of depreciation based on estimates of the life of the fixed asset and future residual value.
- The amount of bad and doubtful debts incurred.

3.2 Depreciation attempts to allocate the cost (less any residual value) of the asset over its useful life. Depreciation does not attempt to measure the fall in value of the asset during the period. Thus, the written down value of the asset appearing on the balance sheet normally represents the unexpired cost of the asset rather than its current market value.

3.3 The convention of consistency is designed to provide a degree of uniformity concerning the application of accounting policies. We have seen that in certain areas there may be more than one method of accounting for an item, for example stock valuation. The convention of consistency states that, having decided on a particular accounting policy, a business should continue to apply the policy in successive periods. Whilst this policy helps to ensure that users can make valid comparisons concerning business performance *over time* it does not ensure that valid comparisons can be made *between businesses*. This is because different businesses may consistently apply different accounting policies.

3.4 Costs incurred by a business may have two elements – an asset element and an expense element. The major difference between the two elements is the period over which the benefits accrue. An expense is that element of the cost incurred that is used up during the accounting period. An asset is that element of cost that is carried forward on the balance sheet and which will normally be used up in future periods. Thus, interest payable is normally treated as an expense in the financial statements as the benefits are normally used up during the accounting period. However, where the interest is incurred to fund the production of an asset that will benefit future periods, it may be capitalised and treated as part of the cost of the asset and written off over the period of the asset's life. This would, of course, be a less prudent approach than writing off the interest charges on financing the cost of production immediately.

4.1 It does not differ. In both cases they are required to meet their debts to the full extent that there are assets available. To this extent they both have a liability that is limited to the extent of their assets. This is a particularly important fact for the shareholders of a limited company because they know that creditors of the company cannot demand that the shareholders contribute additional funds to help meet debts. Thus the liability of the shareholders is limited to the amount that they have paid for their shares, or have agreed to pay in the case of partially unpaid shares. This contrasts with the position of the owner or part owner of an unincorporated (non-company) business. Here all of the individual's assets could be required to meet the unsatisfied liabilities of the business.

4.2 A private limited company may place restrictions on the transfer of its shares; that is, the directors can veto an attempt by a shareholder to sell his or her shares to another person to whom the directors object. Thus, in effect, the majority can avoid having as a shareholder someone to whom they object. A public company cannot do this.

A public limited company must have a share capital of at least £50,000. There is no minimum for a private limited company.

The main advantage of being a public limited company is that they may offer their shares and debentures to the general public; private companies cannot make such an offer.

4.3 A reserve is that part of the owners' claim of a company that is not share capital. Reserves represent gains or surpluses that enhance the claim of the shareholders above the nominal value of their shares. For example the share premium account is a reserve that represents the excess over the nominal value of shares that is paid for them on a share issue. Retained profit or profit and loss account balance is a reserve that arises from ploughed-back profits earned by the company.

4.4 Called-up share capital is that part of the issued shares of a company that has been called for payment. Sometimes companies issue shares that are not to be paid fully on issue, but the unpaid balance called up subsequently.

5.1 Accounting is still an evolving subject. It is not static and so the principles that are laid down at any particular point in time may become obsolete as a result of changes in our understanding of the nature of accounting information and its impact on users and changes in the economic environment within which accounting is employed. We must accept, therefore, that accounting principles will continue to evolve and existing principles must be regularly reviewed.

5.2 Apart from increases in accounting regulation, financial reports have increased because of:

■ Increasing demands by influential users groups, such as shareholders and financial analysts, for financial information relating to the company.
■ The increasing sophistication of influential user groups, such as financial analysts, to deal with financial information.
■ The increasing complexity of business operations requiring greater explanation.
■ Increasing recognition of the need for greater accountability towards certain user groups (such as employees and community groups) requiring the need for additional reports, such as environmental reports and social reports (see Chapter 9).

5.3 There are various problems associated with the measurement of business segments. These include:

■ The definition of a segment
■ The treatment of inter-segmental transactions, such as sales
■ The treatment of common costs

There is no single correct method of dealing with these problems and variations will arise in practice. This, in turn, will hinder comparisons between businesses.

5.4 Preparing an ORF may present a problem for accountants. In order for information that they produce to be credible to all interested parties, the accountants should be as neutral as possible in measuring and reporting the financial performance and position of the business. The OFR requires some interpretation of results and there is a danger that the directors will wish to portray the business activities in as favourable a light as possible. This will affect what items are reported and how they are reported. The OFR is not normally independently audited and so the risks of bias in reporting are therefore increased. The board of directors should therefore accept full responsibility for preparing the OFR and this should be made clear to users.

6.1 People and organisations will not normally accept other than cash in settlement of their claims against the business. If a business wants to employ people it must pay them in cash. If it wants to buy a new fixed asset to exploit a business opportunity, the seller of the fixed asset will normally insist on being paid in cash, normally after a short period of credit. When businesses fail, it is their inability to find the cash to pay claimants which actually drives them under. These factors lead to cash being the pre-eminent business asset and, therefore, the one which analysts and others watch carefully in trying to assess the ability of the business to survive and/or to take advantage of commercial opportunities as they arise.

6.2 With the 'direct method', the cash records of the business are analysed for the period concerned. The analysis reveals the amounts of cash, in total, which have been paid and received in respect of each category of the cash flow statement. This is not difficult in principle, nor in practice if it is done by computer as a matter of routine.

The 'indirect method' takes the approach that, while the net profit (loss) is not equal to the net inflow (outflow) of cash from operations, they are fairly closely linked to the extent that appropriate adjustment of the profit (loss) figure will produce the correct cash flow one. The adjustment is concerned with depreciation charge for, and movements in relevant working capital items over, the period.

6.3 (a) *Cash flow from operations* This would normally be positive, even for a business with small profits or even losses. The fact that depreciation is not a cash flow tends to lead to positive cash flows in this area in all but unusual cases.
    (b) *Cash flow from returns from investments and servicing of finance* This tends to be negative since most businesses have more finance to service than they have investments generating returns. Only rarely would this area generate a positive cash flow.
    (c) *Cash flow from taxation* Though a business sustaining losses following a period of taxed profits could be obtaining tax refunds, normally this area would give negative cash flows.
    (d) *Cash flow from capital expenditure* Normally this would be negative in cash flow terms since assets become worn out and need to be replaced in the normal course of business. This means that, typically, old fixed assets are generating less cash on their disposal than is having to be paid out to replace them.
    (e) *Cash flow from equity dividends* This will always be an outflow or zero, where no dividend is paid.
    (f) *Cash flow from management of liquid resources* This will have no particular pre-dominating direction of cash flow. Cash will tend to flow in and out of short-term investments as cash surpluses emerge and dissipate.

(g) *Cash flow from financing* There is a tendency for businesses either to expand or to fail. In either case, this is likely to mean that over the years more finance will be raised than will be redeemed or retired.

6.4 There are several reasons for this. These include the following:

- Changes in stock, debtors and creditors. For example an increase in debtors during an accounting period would mean that the cash received from credit sales would be less than the credit sales for the same period.
- Cash may have been spent on new fixed assets or received from disposals of old fixed assets; these cash payments and receipts would not directly affect profit.
- Cash may have been spent to redeem or repay a financial claim or received as a result of the creation or the increase of a claim. These cash payments and receipts would not directly affect profit.

The tax charged in the profit and loss account would not be the same tax that is paid during the same accounting period.

7.1 The fact that a business operates on a low profit margin indicates that a small percentage of profit is being produced for each £1 of sales generated. However, this does not mean necessarily that the return on capital employed will be low as a result. If the business is able to generate a large amount of sales during a period the total profit may be very high even though the net profit per £1 of sales is low. If the net profit generated is high, this can lead, in turn, to a high return on capital employed as it is the total net profit which is used as the numerator in this ratio.

7.2 The balance sheet is drawn up at a single point in time – the end of the financial period. As a result, the figures shown on the balance sheet represent the position at that single point in time and may not be representative of the position during the period. Wherever possible, average figures (perhaps based on monthly figures) should be used. However, an external user may only have access to the opening and closing balance sheets for the year and so a simple average based on these figures may be all that is possible to calculate. Where a business is seasonal in nature or is subject to cyclical changes, this simple averaging may not be sufficient.

7.3 Although ratios help eliminate certain problems relating to size, it is important to bear size differences in mind when interpreting the results of ratios relating to different businesses. For example, large businesses may be more profitable because of the benefits which size can bring, such as economies of scale, market domination, access to cheap sources of finance, and so on. Thus differences in market share, the relative size of profits and capital employed, and so on. should be used to help interpret the differences revealed by ratios between businesses.

7.4 The P/E ratio may vary between companies within the same industry for the following reasons:

- *Accounting conventions* Differences in the methods used to compute profit (for example, stock valuation, depreciation, etc.) can lead to different profit figures and, therefore, different P/E ratios.
- *Different prospects* One company may be regarded as having a much brighter future due to factors such as the quality of management, the quality of products, location, etc. This will affect the market price investors are prepared to pay for the share and, hence, the P/E ratio.

■ *Different asset structure* The underlying asset base of one company may be much higher and this may affect the market price of the shares.

8.1 A group situation arises when one company is in a position to exercise control over another company. This almost always means that the parent owns a majority of the voting shares of the subsidiary.

Where a group relationship exists, all companies in the group must prepare annual accounts in the normal way, but, in addition, the parent company must prepare and publish a set of group accounts.

8.2 The group balance sheet shows the assets and external claims of all members of the group (including the parent company) as if they were those of the parent company. Where there are minority shareholders in any of the subsidiary companies, the fact that not all of the equity finance of the group is supplied by the parent company shareholders is recognised. This recognition takes the form of an item 'minority interests' in the financing area of the group balance sheet.

8.3 There are probably two reasons for this:

■ *Limited liability* Each company has its own limited liability. Thus, one company's financial collapse will not affect the others directly. The group is a number of independent units as far as liability is concerned.
■ *Individual identity* Running a large business as a group of separate semi-autonomous departments is generally seen as good management. One means of emphasising the autonomy is to run each department or division as a separate company. This arrangement may also be seen as a good marketing ploy since customers may prefer to deal with, what they see as, a smaller unit.

8.4 One company will be treated as an associate of another where another company or group has a long-term interest and can exercise significant influence over the operating and financial policies of that company. This is usually achieved through representation on the Board of Directors of the company and is supported by a substantial interest in the voting shares in the company.

The accounting consequences are that the group must include its share of the post-acquisition reserves of the associate in its own balance sheet. It must also show its share of the operating profit, interest charges and tax charges relating to the associate in its profit and loss account.

9.1 The measurement of value added can be regarded as highly subjective. In the absence of any clear accounting rules, different approaches to measurement can be employed. In the chapter, a number of these differences were described. These included:

■ The inclusion of depreciation as a bought-in service
■ The treatment of business rates as a form of taxation
■ The treatment of rent payable as a distribution to suppliers of capital
■ Tax deducted from employees treated as a payment to government and so on.

Different practices can lead to quite different measures of value added.

9.2 Environmental and social reporting certainly go beyond the conventional boundaries of accounting. The reports contain non-financial data, some of which may be of a highly technical, scientific nature. There is a case, therefore, for others to undertake the preparation and auditing of such reports.

However, environmental and social reports have financial elements to them and it may be that environmental and social items will be increasingly expressed in financial terms in the future. Thus, it can be argued that accountants have a useful role to play. The qualities often associated with accountants such as their professional judgement, independence and forensic skills may also be important in lending credibility to the reports. This may be more important ultimately than a deep understanding of technical points.

9.3 Despite the fact that inflation has reached very high levels over the past two decades, the historic cost method has proved to be very resilient. A number of things contributed towards its continued survival. These include:

- Lack of an agreed alternative. We saw in the chapter that there is no real consensus concerning what should replace historic cost accounting.
- Objective verifiable information is provided. The historic cost accounting method is not as open to subjective judgement and manipulation as methods requiring estimates of current costs and values.

9.4 Some believe that the danger caused to the planet as a result of business activity (such as pollution, consumption of non-renewable resources and so on) is something that requires action from government. The government should, therefore, lay down the rules concerning sustainable development and should make businesses account for their behaviour. One way in which this can be done is through the publication of annual sustainable development reports. However, the government has yet to impose such rules and so reporting on sustainable development is a voluntary exercise.

Some believe, however, that sustainable development reports should remain a voluntary exercise. Such reporting is costly, so it is argued, and does not have to be borne by many international competitors. By imposing additional regulatory burdens on businesses, there is a danger that they will become less competitive. (However, any additional costs incurred will be determined by the nature and extent of the legal rules imposed.)

Solutions to self-assessment questions

2.1 Kunalan Manufacturing Company

The balance sheet provides an insight into the mix of assets held. Thus, it can be seen that, in value terms, approximately 60 per cent of assets held are in the form of fixed assets and that freehold premises comprise more than half of these fixed assets. Current assets held are largely in the form of stock (approximately 46 per cent of current assets) and trade debtors (approximately 42 per cent of current assets).

The balance sheet also provides an insight into the liquidity of the business. The current assets are £104,000 and can be viewed as representing cash or near-cash assets held, compared with £42,000 in current liabilities. In this case, it appears that the business is fairly liquid as the current assets exceed the current liabilities by a large amount. Liquidity is very important in order to maintain the capacity of the business to pay its debts.

The balance sheet gives an indication of the financial structure of the business. It can be seen in this case that the owner is providing £63,000 and long-term lenders are providing £160,000. This means that outsiders contribute 72 per cent (£160,000/£223,000) of the total long-term finance required and the business is, therefore, heavily reliant on outside sources of finance. The business is under pressure to make profits that are at least sufficient to pay interest and to make capital repayments when they fall due.

3.2 TT Limited

Balance sheet as at 31 December 2000

Assets	£	Claims	£
Delivery van		Capital	
(12,000 − 2,500)	9,500	(50,000 + 26,900)	76,900
Stock in trade (143,000 +			
12,000 − 74,000 − 16,000)	65,000	Trade creditors	
		(143,000 − 121,000)	22,000
Trade debtors (152,000 −			
132,000 − 400)	19,600	Accrued expenses	
		(630 + 620)	1,250
Cash at bank (50,000 − 25,000 −			
500 − 1,200 − 12,000 − 33,500 −			
1,650 − 12,000 + 35,000 − 9,400 +			
132,000 − 121,000)	750		
Prepaid expenses			
(5,000 + 300)	5,300		
	100,150		100,150

Profit and loss account for the year ended 31 December 2000

	£	£
Sales (152,000 + 35,000)		187,000
Less Cost of stock sold		
(74,000 + 16,000)		90,000
Gross profit		97,000
Less		
Rent	20,000	
Rates (500 + 900)	1,400	
Wages (33,500 + 630)	34,130	
Electricity (1,650 + 620)	2,270	
Bad debts	400	
Van depreciation ($\frac{12,000 - 2,000}{4}$)	2,500	
Van expenses	9,400	
		70,100
Net profit for the year		£26,900

The balance sheet could now be rewritten in a more stylish form as follows:

Balance sheet as at 31 December 2000

	£	£	£
Fixed assets			
Motor van			9,500
Current assets			
Stock in trade	65,000		
Trade debtors	19,600		
Prepaid expenses	5,300		
Cash	750		
		90,650	
Less **Current liabilities**			
Trade creditors	22,000		
Accrued expenses	1,250		
		23,250	
			67,400
			76,900
Capital			
Original			50,000
Retained profit			26,900
			76,900

4.1 Dev Ltd

(a) The summarised balance sheet of Dev Ltd, immediately following the rights and bonus issue, is as follows:

Balance sheet as at 31 December 2001

	£
Net assets [235 + 40 (cash from the rights issue)]	275,000
Capital and reserves	
Share capital: 100,000 shares @ £1 [(100 + 20) + 60]	180,000
Share premium account (30 + 20 − 50)	–
Revaluation reserve (37 − 10)	27,000
Profit and loss account balance	68,000
	275,000

Note that the bonus issue of £60,000 is taken from capital reserves (reserves unavailable for dividends) as follows:

	£
Share premium account	50,000
Revaluation reserve	10,000
	60,000

More could have been taken from the revaluation reserve and less from the share premium account without making any difference to dividend payment possibilities.

(b) There may be pressure from a potential creditor for the company to limit its ability to pay dividends. This would place creditors in a more secure position because the maximum buffer or safety margin between the value of the assets and the amount owed by the company is maintained. It is not unusual for potential creditors to insist on some measure to lock up shareholders' funds in this way as a condition of granting the loan.

(c) The summarised balance sheet of Dev Ltd, immediately following the rights and bonus issue, assuming a minimum dividend potential objective, is as follows:

Balance sheet as at 31 December 2001

	£
Net assets [235 + 40 (cash from the rights issue)]	275,000
Capital and reserves	
Share capital: 100,000 shares @ £1 ((100 + 20) + 60)	180,000
Share premium account (30 + 20)	50,000
Revaluation reserve	37,000
Profit and loss account balance (68 − 60)	8,000
	275,000

(d) Before the bonus issue, the maximum dividend was £68,000. Now it is £8,000. Thus the bonus issue has had the effect of locking up an additional £60,000 of the assets of the company in terms of the company's ability to pay dividends.

(e) Before the issues Lee had 100 shares worth £2.35 (£235,000/100,000) each or £235 in total. Lee would be offered 20 shares in the rights issue at £2 each or £40 in total. After the rights issue, Lee would have 120 shares worth £2.2917 (£275,000/120,000) each or £275 in total.

The bonus issue would give Lee 60 additional shares. After the bonus issue, Lee would have 180 shares worth £1.5278 (£275,000/180,000) each or £275 in total.

None of this affects Lee's wealth. Before the issues, Lee had £235 worth of shares and £40 more in cash. After the issues, Lee has the same total wealth but all £275 is in the value of the shares.

(f) The things that we know about the company are as follows:

(i)   It is a private (as opposed to a public) limited company, for it has 'Ltd' (limited) as part of its name, rather than plc (public limited company).

(ii) It has made an issue of shares at a premium, almost certainly after it had traded successfully for a period. (There is a share premium account. It would be very unlikely that the original shares, issued when the company was first formed, would have been issued at a premium.)

(iii) Certain of the assets in the balance sheet have been upwardly revalued by at least £37,000. (There is a revaluation reserve of £37,000. This may just be what is left after a previous bonus issue had taken part of the balance.)

(iv) The company has traded at an aggregate profit (though there could have been losses in some years), net of tax and any dividends paid. (There is a positive balance on the profit and loss account.)

5.1 J. Sainsbury plc

The following ratios may be calculated for each of the main business segments:

	2000 %	1999 %
Net profit to sales		
Food retailing – UK	4.1	5.6
Food retailing – USA	3.3	2.8
DIY retailing – UK	4.5	5.6
Banking – UK	2.2	(3.8)
Property development – UK	9.7	28.1
Sales growth		
Food retailing – UK	5.8	
Food retailing – USA	20.6	
DIY retailing – UK	2.5	
Banking – UK	16.2	
Property development – UK	515.6	
Net profit to capital employed (net assets)		
Food retailing – UK	10.7	16.1
Food retailing – USA	9.9	10.9
DIY retailing – UK	10.5	15.4
Banking – UK	2.6	(5.9)
Property development – UK	13.0	6.9

In all segments of the business, sales increased in 2000 compared with the previous year. We do not know from the information provided in the question to what extent this growth came from expanding operations – for example opening new stores. Inflation would be expected to cause a 2–3 per cent increase in turnover. Sainsbury's annual report gives details of each segment's progress.

In all three retailing segments, the net profit to capital employed fell in 2000 relative to 1999. Only in banking and property development did the business improve its performance, but these segments accounted for relatively little of the total turnover and profit of the business.

6.1 Touchstone plc

Cash flow statement for the year ended 31 December 2001

	£m	£m
Net cash inflows from operating activities		66
(see calculation below)		
Returns from investment and servicing of finance		
Interest received	2	
Interest paid	(4)	
Net cash outflow from returns on investment and servicing of finance		(2)

	£m	£m
Taxation		
Corporation tax paid	(12)	
Net cash outflow for taxation		(12)
Capital expenditure		
Land and buildings	(22)	
Plant and machinery (see note below)	(19)	
Net cash outflow for capital expenditure		(41)
		11
Equity dividends paid		
Dividends paid (see note below)	(16)	
Net cash outflow for equity dividends		(16)
		(5)
Management of liquid resources		–
Financing		
Issue of debenture stock	20	
Net cash inflow from financing		20
Net increase in cash		15

To see how this relates to the cash of the business at the beginning and end of the year, it is useful to show a reconciliation as follows:

Reconciliation of cash movements during the year ended 31 December 2001

	£m
Balance at 1 January 2001	4
Net cash inflow	15
Balance at 31 December 2001	19

Calculation of net cash inflow from operating activities

	£m	£m
Net operating profit (from the profit and loss account)		62
Add Depreciation		
Land and buildings	6	
Plant and machinery	10	
		16
		78
Less Increase in debtors (26 – 16)	10	
Decrease in creditors (26 – 23)	3	13
		65
Add Decrease in stocks (25 – 24)		1
		66

Notes
Dividends

	£m
Amount owed at the start of the year	12
Dividend for the year	18
	30
Amount owed at the end of the year	(14)
Dividend paid during the year	16

Taxation	£m
Amount owed at the start of the year	4
Taxation for the year	16
	20
Amount owed at the end of the year	(8)
Tax paid during the year	12

Fixed asset acquisitions	Land and buildings £m	Plant and machinery £m
Position at 31 December 2000	94	53
Less 2001 depreciation	6	10
	88	43
Position at 31 December 2001	110	62
Acquisitions	22	19

7.1 Financial ratios

In order to answer this question you may have used the following ratios:

	A plc	B plc
Current ratio	$\dfrac{853.0}{422.4} = 2.0$	$\dfrac{816.5}{293.1} = 2.8$
Acid-test ratio	$\dfrac{(853.0 - 592.0)}{422.4} = 0.6$	$\dfrac{(816.5 - 403.0)}{293.1} = 1.4$
Gearing ratio	$\dfrac{190}{(687.6 + 190)} \times 100 = 21.6\%$	$\dfrac{250}{(874.6 + 250)} \times 100 = 22.2\%$
Interest cover ratio	$\dfrac{(131.9 + 19.4)}{19.4} = 7.8 \text{ times}$	$\dfrac{(139.4 + 27.5)}{27.5} = 6.1 \text{ times}$
Dividend payout ratio	$\dfrac{135.0}{99.9} \times 100 = 135\%$	$\dfrac{95.0}{104.6} \times 100 = 91\%$
Price/earnings ratio	$\dfrac{£6.50}{31.2p} = 20.8 \text{ times}$	$\dfrac{£8.20}{41.8p} = 19.6 \text{ times}$

A plc has a much lower current ratio and acid test-ratio than does B plc. The reasons for this may be partly due to the fact that A plc has a lower average settlement period for debtors. The acid-test ratio of A plc is substantially below 1.0: this may suggest a liquidity problem.

8.1 Great plc

Group balance sheet as at 31 December last year

	£m	£m
Fixed assets (at cost less depreciation)		
Goodwill arising on consolidation[a]		4
Land (80 + 14 + 5)		99
Plant		53
Vehicles		31
		187

	£m	£m
Current assets		
Stocks	29	
Debtors	27	
Cash	22	
	78	
Less **Creditors: amounts falling due within one year**		
Creditors	22	
Net current assets		56
Total assets less current liabilities		243
Less **Creditors: amounts falling due after more than one year**		
Debentures		50
		193
Capital and reserves		
Called-up share capital: ordinary shares of £1 each, fully paid		100
Profit and loss account $(77 + ((40 - 35) \times 80\%) - 1)$		80[b]
Minority interests $(60 + 5) \times 20\%$		13
		193

[a] Goodwill arising on consolidation: $53 - (80\% \times (20 + 35 + 5)) = 5$, less depreciation (20 per cent) = £4 million. The depreciation will be assumed to be part of the cost of sales.
[b] Apart from the fact that this is the closing profit and loss account balance (see below), it can be shown to be correct as:

	£m
Great plc's balance	77
Great plc's share of Small plc's post-acquisition profits $(40 - 35) \times 80\%$	4
	81
Less the year's depreciation of the goodwill arising on consolidaiton	1
	80

Group profit and loss account for last year

	£m	£m
Turnover		144
Cost of sales (46 + 24 + 1 (goodwill))		71
Gross profit		73
Administration expenses	17	
Distribution expenses	11	28
Profit before tax		45
Taxation		17
Profit after tax		28
Attributable to minorities $(20\% \times 10)$		2
Profit after tax attributable to Great plc shareholders		26
Profit and loss account balance brought forward from the previous year (there was no post-acquisition balance brought forward for Small plc)		65
		91
Dividend on ordinary shares		11
Profit and loss account balance carried forward to the following year		80

9.1
Samodiva Limited
Value added statement for the year ended 30 September

	£000	£000	%
Sales (less bad debts)		5,998	
Less bought-in goods and services		2,488	
Value added		3,510	
Distributed to			
Employees –			
Wages	628		
Benefits	82	710	20.2
Government – taxation (62 + 128 + 244)		434	12.4
Providers of capital			
Shareholders	500		14.3
Debenture holders	320	820	9.1
Retained within company			
Depreciation	854		24.3
Retained earnings	692	1,546	19.7
		3,510	100.0

The ratios reveal that a large percentage of total value added (44.0%) is retained within the business. Providers of capital take 23.4% of value added and employees take only 20.2%. This last figure seems quite low. It is not unusual for 70 per cent or more of value added by a business to be paid to employees.

Solutions to selected exercises

Chapter 2

2.1

Cash flow statement for day 4

	£
Opening balance (from day 3)	49
Cash from sale of wrapping paper	47
	96
Cash paid to purchase wrapping paper	(53)
Closing balance	43

Profit and loss account for day 4

	£
Sales	47
Cost of goods sold	(33)
Profit	14

Balance sheet at the end of day 4

	£
Cash	43
Stock of goods for resale (28 + 53 − 33)	48
Total business wealth	91

2.2

	£
Cash introduced by Paul on day 1	40
Profit of day 1	15
Profit of day 2	13
Profit of day 3	9
Profit of day 4	14
	91

Thus the wealth of the business, all of which belongs to Paul as sole owner, consists of the cash he put in to start the business plus the profit earned each day.

Profit and loss account for day 1

	£
Sales (70 × £0.80)	56
Cost of sales (70 × £0.50)	(35)
Profit	21

Cash flow statement for day 1

	£
Opening balance	40
Add Cash from sales	56
	96
Less Cash for purchases (80 × £0.50)	40
Closing balance	56

Balance sheet as at end of day 1

	£
Cash balance	56
Stock of unsold goods (10 × £0.50)	5
Helen's business wealth	61

Profit and loss account for day 2

	£
Sales (65 × £0.80)	52.0
Cost of sales (65 × £0.50)	(32.5)
Profit	19.5

Cash flow statement for day 2

	£
Opening balance	56.0
Add Cash from sales	52.0
	108.0
Less Cash for purchases (60 × £0.50)	30.0
Closing balance	78.0

Balance sheet as at end of day 2

	£
Cash balance	78.0
Stock of unsold goods (5 × £0.50)	2.5
Helen's business wealth	80.5

Profit and loss account for day 3

	£
Sales (20 × £0.80) + (45 × £0.40)	34.0
Cost of sales (65 × £0.50)	(32.5)
Profit	1.5

Cash flow statement for day 3

	£
Opening balance	78.0
Add Cash from sales	34.0
	112.0
Less Cash for purchases (60 × £0.50)	30.0
Closing balance	82.0

Balance sheet as at end of day 3

	£
Cash balance	82.0
Stock of unsold goods	–
Helen's business wealth	82.0

2.4

Joe Conday
Balance sheet as at 1 March

	£		£
Bank	20,000	Capital	20,000

Balance sheet as at 2 March

	£		£
Bank (20,000 − 6,000)	14,000	Capital	20,000
Fixtures and fittings	6,000	Creditors	8,000
Stock	8,000		
	28,000		28,000

Balance sheet as at 3 March

	£		£
Bank (14,000 + 5,000)	19,000	Capital	20,000
Fixtures and fittings	6,000	Creditors	8,000
Stock	8,000	Loan	5,000
	33,000		33,000

Balance sheet as at 4 March

	£		£
Bank (19,000 − 7,200)	11,800	Capital	19,800
Fixtures and fittings	6,000	Creditors	8,000
Stock	8,000	Loan	5,000
Motor car	7,000		
	32,800		32,800

Balance sheet as at 5 March

	£		£
Bank (11,800 − 2,500)	9,300	Capital	19,300
Fixtures and fittings	6,000	Creditors	8,000
Stock	8,000	Loan	5,000
Motor car	9,000		
	32,300		32,300

Balance sheet as at 6 March

	£		£
Bank (9,300 + 2,000 − 1,000)	10,300	Capital	21,300
Fixtures and fittings	6,000	Creditors	8,000
Stock	8,000	Loan	4,000
Motor car	9,000		
	33,300		33,300

2.5 (a) Crafty Engineering Ltd

Balance sheet as at 30 June last year

	£000	£000	£000
Fixed assets			
Freehold premises			320
Machinery and tools			207
Motor vehicles			38
			565
Current assets			
Stock in trade		153	
Debtors		185	
		338	
Less **Current liabilities**			
Creditors	86		
Bank overdraft	116	202	
			136
			701
Less **Long-term liabilities**			
Loan from Industrial Finance Co.			260
			441
Capital (missing figure)			441

(b) The balance sheet reveals a high level of investment in fixed assets. In percentage terms, we can say that more than 60 per cent of the total investment in assets has been in fixed assets. The nature of the business may require a heavy investment in fixed assets. The investment in current assets exceeds the current liabilities by a large amount (approximately 1.7 times). As a result, there is no obvious sign of a liquidity problem. However, the balance sheet reveals that the company has no cash balance and is therefore dependent on the continuing support of the bank (in the form of a bank overdraft) in order to meet obligations when they fall due. When considering the long-term financing of the business, we can see that about 37 per cent [260/(260 + 441)] of the total long-term finance for the business has been supplied by loan capital and about 63 per cent [441/(260 + 441)] by the owners. This level of borrowing seems quite high but not excessive. However, we would need to know more about the ability of the company to service the loan capital (that is, make interest payments and loan repayments) before a full assessment could be made.

Chapter 3

3.1 (a) Capital does increase as a result of the owners introducing more cash into the business, but it will also increase as a result of introducing other assets (for example, a motor car) and by the business generating revenues by trading. Similarly, capital decreases not only as a result of withdrawals of cash by owners but also by withdrawals of other assets (for example, stock for the owners' personal use) and through trading expenses being incurred. For the typical business in a typical accounting period, capital will alter much more as a result of trading activities than for any other reason.

(b) An accrued expense is not one that relates to next year. It is one that needs to be matched with the revenues of the accounting period under review, but that has yet to be met in terms of cash payment. As such, it will appear on the balance sheet as a current liability.

(c) The purpose of depreciation is not to provide for asset replacement. Rather, it is an attempt to allocate the cost of the asset (less any residual value) over its useful life. Depreciation is an attempt to provide a measure of the amount of the fixed asset that has been consumed during the period. This amount will then be charged as an expense for the period in order to derive the profit figure. Depreciation is a book entry (the outlay of cash occurs when the asset is purchased) and does not normally entail setting aside a separate amount of cash for asset replacement. Even if this were done, there would be no guarantee that sufficient funds would be available at the end of the asset's life for its replacement. Factors such as inflation and technological change may mean that the replacement cost is higher than the original cost of the asset.

(d) In the short term, it is possible for the current value of a fixed asset to exceed its original cost. However, nearly all fixed assets will wear out over time as a result of being used to generate wealth for the business. This will be the case for freehold buildings. As a result, some measure of depreciation should be calculated to take account of the fact that the asset is being consumed. Some businesses revalue their freehold buildings where the current value is significantly different from the original cost. Where this occurs, the depreciation charged should be based on the revalued amount. This will normally result in higher depreciation charges than if the asset remained at its historic cost.

3.3 The upward movement in profit and downward movement in cash may be for various reasons, which include the following:

- The purchase of assets for cash during the period (for example, motor cars and stock), which were not all consumed during the period and are therefore not having as great an effect on expenses as they are on cash.
- The payment of an outstanding liability (for example, a loan), which will have an effect on cash but not on expenses in the profit and loss account.
- The withdrawal of cash by the owners from the capital invested, which will not have an effect on the expenses in the profit and loss account.
- The generation of revenues on credit where the cash has yet to be received. This will increase the sales for the period but will not have a beneficial effect on the cash balance until a later period.

3.4 (a) **FIFO**

	Purchases			Cost of sales		
	Tonnes	Cost/tonne £	Total £	Tonnes	Cost/tonne £	Total £
1 Sept	20	18	360			
2 Sept	48	20	960			
4 Sept	15	24	360			
6 Sept	10	25	250			
7 Sept				20	18	360
				40	20	800
	93		1,930	60		1,160
Opening stock + purchases			1,930			
Cost of sales			(1,160)			
Closing stock			770	[(8 × £20) + (15 × £24) + (10 × £25)]		

(b) LIFO

	Purchases			Cost of sales		
	Tonnes	Cost/tonne £	Total £	Tonnes	Cost/tonne £	Total £
1 Sept	20	18	360			
2 Sept	48	20	960			
4 Sept	15	24	360			
6 Sept	10	25	250			
7 Sept				10	25	250
				15	24	360
				35	20	700
	93		1,930	60		1,310

Opening stock + purchases	1,930
Cost of sales	(1,310)
Closing stock	620 [(20 × £18) + (13 × £20)]

(c) AVCO

	Purchases			Cost of sales		
	Tonnes	Cost/tonne £	Total £	Tonnes	Cost/tonne £	Total £
1 Sept	20	18	360			
2 Sept	48	20	960			
4 Sept	15	24	360			
6 Sept	10	25	250			
	93	20.8	1,930			
7 Sept				60	20.8	1,248

Opening stock + purchases	1,930
Cost of sales	(1,248)
Closing stock	682

3.5
(a) Rent payable – expense for period   £9,000
(b) Rates and insurance – expense for period   £6,000
(c) General expenses – paid in period   £7,000
(d) Loan interest payable – prepaid   £500
(e) Salaries – paid in period   £6,000
(f) Rent receivable – received during period   £3,000

3.8 An examination of the trading and profit and loss accounts for the two years reveals a number of interesting points, which include:

■ An increase in sales value and gross profit of 9.9 per cent in 2001.
■ The gross profit expressed as a percentage of sales remaining at 70 per cent.
■ An increase in salaries of 7.2 per cent.
■ An increase in selling and distribution costs of 31.2 per cent.
■ An increase in bad debts of 392.5 per cent.
■ A decline in net profit of 39.3 per cent.
■ A decline in the net profit as a percentage of sales from 13.3 per cent to 7.4 per cent.

Thus, the business has enjoyed an increase in sales and gross profits, but this has failed to translate to an increase in net profit because of the significant rise in overheads. The increase in selling costs during 2001 suggests that the increase in sales was achieved by greater marketing effort, and the huge increase in bad debts suggests that the increase in sales may be attributable to selling to less creditworthy customers or to a weak debt-collection policy. There appears to have been a change of policy in 2001 towards sales, and this has not been successful overall as the net profit has shown a dramatic decline.

Chapter 4

4.1 Limited companies can no more set a limit on the amount of debts they will meet than can human beings. They must meet their debts up to the limit of their assets, just as we as individuals must. In the context of owners' claim, 'reserves' mean part of the owners' claim against the assets of the company. These assets may or may not include cash. The legal ability of the company to pay dividends is not related to the amount of cash that it has.

Preference shares do not carry a guaranteed dividend. They simply guarantee that the preference shareholders have a right to the first slice of any dividend that is paid. Shares of many companies can, in effect, be bought by one investor from another through the Stock Exchange. Such a transaction has no direct effect on the company, however. These are not new shares being offered by the company, but existing shares that are being sold 'second-hand'.

4.2 (a) The first part of the quote is incorrect. Bonus shares should not, of themselves, increase the value of the shareholders' wealth. This is because reserves, belonging to the shareholders, are used to create bonus shares. Thus, each shareholder's stake in the company has not increased.

Share splits should not increase the wealth of the shareholder, and so that part of the quote is correct.

(b) This statement is incorrect. Shares can be issued at any price, provided that it is not below the nominal value of the shares. Once the company has been trading profitably for a period, the shares will not be worth the same as they were (the nominal value) when the company was first formed. In such circumstances, issuing shares at above their nominal value would not only be legal, but essential to preserve the wealth of the existing shareholders relative to any new ones.

(c) This statement is incorrect. From a legal perspective, the company is limited to a maximum dividend of the current extent of its revenue reserves. This amounts to any after-tax profits or gains realised that have not been eroded through, for example, payments of previous dividends. Legally, cash is not an issue; it would be perfectly legal for a company to borrow the funds to pay a dividend – although whether such an action would be commercially prudent is another question.

(d) This statement is partly incorrect. Companies do indeed have to pay tax on their profits. Depending on their circumstances, shareholders might also have to pay tax on their dividend.

| 4.4 | Iqbal Ltd |

Year	Maximum dividend £	
1998	0	No profit exists out of which to pay a dividend
1999	0	There remains a cumulative loss of £7,000. Since the revaluation represents a gain that has not been realised, it cannot be used to justify a dividend
2000	13,000	The cumulative net realised gains are derived as (– £15,000 + £8,000 + £15,000 + £5,000)
2001	14,000	The net realised profits and gains for the year
2002	22,000	The net realised profits and gains for the year

| 4.6 | Pear Limited |

Balance sheet as at 30 September 2001

	£000	£000
Fixed assets		
Cost (1,570 + 30)	1,600	
Depreciation (690 + 12)	702	
		898
Current assets		
Stock	207	
Debtors (182 + 18 – 4)	196	
Cash at bank	21	
	424	
Less **Creditors: amounts due within one year**		
Trade creditors	88	
Other creditors (20 + 30 + 15 + 2)	67	
Taxation	17	
Dividend proposed	25	
Bank overdraft	105	
	302	
Net current assets		122
Less **Creditors: amounts due after more than one year**		
10% debenture – repayable 2008		(300)
		720
Capital and reserves		
Shares capital		300
Share premium account		300
Retained profit at beginning of year	104	
Retained profit for year	16	120
		720

Profit and loss account for the year ended 30 September 2001

	£000	£000
Turnover (1,456 + 18)		1,474
Cost of sales		(768)
Gross profit		706
Less Salaries	220	
Depreciation (249 + 12)	261	
Other operating costs [131 + (2% × 200) + 2]	137	
		(618)
Operating profit		88
Interest payable (15 + 15)		(30)
Profit before taxation		58
Taxation (58 × 30%)		(17)
Profit after taxation		41
Dividend proposed		(25)
Retained profit for the year		16

4.7 Chips Limited

Balance sheet as at 30 June 2001

	£000	£000	£000
Fixed assets	Cost	Depreciation	
Buildings	800	112	688
Plant and equipment	650	367	283
Motor vehicles (102 − 8); (53 − 5 + 19)	94	67	27
	1,544	546	998
Current assets			
Stock		950	
Debtors (420 − 16)		404	
Cash at bank (16 + 2)		18	
		1,372	
Less **Creditors due within one year**			
Trade creditors (361 + 23)		(384)	
Other creditors (117 + 35)		(152)	
Taxation		(26)	
Dividends proposed		(28)	
		(590)	
Net current assets			782
Less **Creditors due after more than one year**			
Secured 10% loan			(700)
			1,080
Capital and reserves			
Ordinary shares of £1, fully paid			500
6% Preference shares of £1			300
Reserves at 1 July 2000		248	
Retained profit for year		32	280
			1,080

Profit and loss account for the year ended 30 June 2001

	£000	£000
Turnover (1,850 − 16)		1,834
Cost of sales (1,040 + 23)		1,063
Gross profit		771
Less Depreciation [220 − 2 − 5 + 8 + (94 × 20%)]	(240)	
Other operating costs	(375)	
		(615)
Operating profit		156
Interest payable (35 + 35)		(70)
Profit before taxation		86
Taxation (86 × 30%)		(26)
Profit after taxation		60
Dividends proposed: Preference (300 × 6%)	(18)	
Ordinary (500 × 2p)	(10)	(28)
		32

Chapter 5

5.1 Many believe that the annual reports of companies are becoming too long and contain too much information. To illustrate this point, a few examples of the length of the 2000 accounts of large companies are as follows:

Rolls-Royce plc	76 pages
The Boots Company plc	76 pages
Cadbury Schweppes plc	148 pages
National Express Group plc	76 pages

There is a danger that users will suffer from 'information overload' if they are confronted with an excessive amount of information and that they will be unable to cope with it. This may, in turn, lead them to:

- Fail to distinguish between important and less important information.
- Fail to approach the analysis of information in a logical and systematic manner.
- Feel a sense of confusion and avoid the task of analysing the information.

The problem of lengthy annual reports is likely to be a particular problem for the less sophisticated user. This problem, however, has been recognised and many companies publish abridged accounts for private investors, which include only the key points. However, for sophisticated users the problem may be that the annual reports are still not long enough. They often wish to glean as much information as possible from the company in order to make investment decisions.

5.3

I. Ching (Booksellers) plc
Profit and loss account for the year to 31 December

	£m	£m
Turnover		943
Cost of sales		460
Gross profit		483
Distribution costs	110	
Administration expenses	314	424
		59
Other operating income		86
		145

	£m	£m
Income from other fixed asset investments	42	
Other interest receivable and similar income	25	67
		212
Interest payable and similar charges		40
		172
Tax on profit or loss on ordinary activities (25%)		43
Profit on ordinary activities after taxation		129
Retained profit brought forward from last year		285
		414
Transfer to general reserve	100	
Proposed dividend on ordinary shares (30% × £129)	39	139
Retained profit carried forward		275

5.4

G. Stavros and Co plc
Balance sheet as at end of financial period

	£m	£m	£m
Fixed assets:			
Intangible assets:			
Patents and trademarks		170	
Tangible assets:			
Land and buildings	165		
Plant and machinery	143		
Motor vehicles	22	330	500
Current assets:			
Stocks:			
Raw materials and consumables	120		
Work-in-progress	18		
Finished goods and goods for resale	96	234	
Debtors:			
Trade debtors	86		
Prepayments and accrued income	15	101	
Cash at bank and in hand		12	
		347	
Creditors: amounts falling due within one year			
Trade creditors	75		
Other creditors including taxation and social security	23		
Accruals and deferred income	47	145	
Net current assets			202
Total assets less current liabilities			702
Creditors: amounts falling due after more than one year			
Debenture loans		230	
Provisions for liabilities and charges			
Pensions		54	284
			418
Capital and reserves			
Called-up share capital (balancing figure)			50
Share premium account			30
Revaluation reserve			100
General reserves			163
Profit and loss account			75
			418

5.5 Some of the arguments that are relevant to this question are already contained within the chapter and so will not be restated here. However, some further points that might be made concerning accounting regulation and accounting measurement are:

For
- It seems reasonable that companies, particularly given their limited liability, should be required to account to their members and to the general public and that the law should prescribe how this should be done – including how particular items should be measured. It also seems sensible that accounting standards should amplify these rules, to try to establish some uniformity of practice. Investors could be misled if the same item appeared in the accounts of two separate companies but had been measured in different ways.
- Companies would find it difficult to attract finance, credit and possibly employees without publishing credible information about themselves. An important measure of performance is profit, and investors often need to make judgements concerning relative performance within an industry sector. Without clear benchmarks by which to judge performance, investors may not invest in a company.

Against
- Some would argue that it is up to the companies to decide whether or not they can survive and prosper without publishing information about themselves. If they can, then so much the better for them since they will have saved large amounts of money by not doing so. If it is necessary for a company to provide financial information in order to be able to attract investment finance and other necessary factors, then the company can make the necessary judgement of how much information is necessary and what form of measurements are required.
- Not all company management view matters in the same way. Allowing companies to select their own approaches to financial reporting enables them to reflect their personalities. Thus, a conservative management will adopt conservative accounting policies such as writing off research and development expenditure quickly, whereas more adventurous management may adopt less conservative accounting policies such as writing off research and development expenditure over several years. The impact of these different views will have an effect on profit and will give the reader an insight to the approach adopted by the management team.

5.8 **Electricity distribution business**

(a) The following ratios may be calculated for each of the three main business segments:

	2002 %	2001 %
Net profit to sales		
Distribution	41.1	41.1
Supply	1.3	1.1
Retail	3.8	4.3
Sales growth		
Distribution	7.7	
Supply	0.4	
Retail	34.4	
Net profit to capital employed (net assets)		
Distribution	30.1	30.7
Supply	*	64.9
Retail	5.0	6.8

* As the net assets are negative (liabilities exceed assets), a ratio is not computed.

The above ratios reveal a high net profit to sales ratio for the distribution area which has remained constant over the two-year period. The distribution area also enjoys a high return on capital employed. Although there was a slight dip in this return in 2002, the increase in sales for the period ensured that net profits increased substantially over the period.

The net profit to sales ratio for the supply area is very low and there has been little sales growth over the period. This area contributes the largest part of the company's turnover but a relatively small part of its total profits for each period. However, the level of investment required is much lower than the other areas (indeed, it was negative in 2002). The return on capital employed in 2001 was very high compared with other areas of activity.

The net profit to sales ratio in the retail area was quite low and declined in 2002 to 3.8 per cent. However, the company managed to increase sales dramatically during the period and this led to a significant increase in profits. The growth in retail sales was accompanied by a significant increase in the level of investment in this area. As a result, there was a decline on the ROCE in 2002.

(b) The intersegment adjustments could be presented so as to show the impact on each operating segment. In the annual reports, it is not possible to identify which segments are most affected by the intersegmental transactions.

Chapter 6

6.1 (a) An increase in the level of stock in trade would, ultimately, have an adverse effect on cash.

(b) A rights issue of ordinary shares will give rise to a positive cash flow, which will be included in the 'financing' section of the cash flow statement.

(c) A bonus issue of ordinary shares has no cash flow effect.

(d) Writing off some of the value of the stock has no cash flow effect.

(e) A disposal for cash of a large number of shares by a major shareholder has no cash-flow effect as far as the business is concerned.

(f) Depreciation does not involve cash at all. Using the indirect method of deducing cash flow from operations involves the depreciation expense in the calculation, but this is simply because we are trying to find out from the profit (after depreciation) figure what the profit before depreciation must have been.

6.3

Torrent plc
Cash flow statement for the year ended 31 December 2001

	£m	£m
Net cash inflows from operating activities		247
(see calculation below)		
Returns from investment and servicing of finance		
Interest received	14	
Interest paid	(26)	
Net cash outflow from returns on investment		
and servicing of finance		(12)
Taxation		
Corporation tax paid (see note below)	(41)	
Net cash outflow for taxation		(41)
Capital expenditure		
Payments to acquire tangible fixed assets	(67)	
Net cash outflow for capital expenditure		(67)
		127

	£m	£m
Equity dividends paid		
Dividends paid (see note below)	(50)	
Net cash flow for equity dividends paid		(50)
		77
Management of liquid resources		–
Financing		
Repayments of debenture stock	(100)	
Net cash outflow from financing		(100)
Net increase(decrease) in cash		(23)

Reconciliation of cash movements during the year ended 31 December 2001

	£m
Balance at 1 January 2001	(6)
Net cash outflow	(23)
Balance at 31 December 2001	(29)

Notes

(i) *Dividend* Since all of the dividend for 2001 was unpaid at the end of 2001, it seems that the business pays just one final dividend each year, some time after the year end. Thus it is the *2000* dividend that will have led to a cash outflow in 2001.

(ii) *Taxation:*

	£m
Amount owed at 1 January 2001	23
Tax charge for the year	36
	59
Amount owed at 31 December 2001	18
Cash paid during the year	41

(iii) *Debentures* It has been assumed that the debentures were redeemed for their balance sheet value. This is not always the case, however.

(iv) *Shares* The share issue was effected by converting the share premium account balance and £60 million of the revaluation reserve balance to ordinary share capital. This involved no flow of cash.

Calculation of net cash inflow from operating activities

	£m	£m
Net operating profit (from the profit and loss account)		182
Add Depreciation:		
Plant etc. (325 + 67 − 314)*		78
		260
Less Increase in debtors (132 − 123)	9	
Decrease in creditors (39 − 30)	9	
Decrease in accruals (15 − 11)	4	22
		238
Add Decrease in stocks (41 − 35)	6	
Decrease in prepayments (16 − 13)	3	9
		247

* Since there were no disposals, the depreciation charges must be the difference between the fixed asset values at the start and end of the year, adjusted by the cost of any additions.

The following comments can be made about the Torrent plc's cash flow as shown by the cash flow statement for the year ended 31 December 2001:

- There was a positive cash flow from operating activities.
- There was a net cash outflow in respect of financing.
- The outflow of cash to acquire additional tangible fixed assets was very comfortably covered by cash generated by operating activities, even after allowing for the net cash outflows for financing and tax. This is usually interpreted as a 'strong' cash-flow situation.
- There was a fairly major repayment of debenture loan.
- Overall, there was a fairly significant reduction in cash over the year, leading to a negative cash balance at the year end.

6.4 Cheng plc

Cash flow statement for the year ended 31 December 2001

	£m	£m
Net cash inflows from operating activities (see calculation below)		48
Returns from investment and servicing of finance		
Interest paid	(4)	
Net cash outflow from returns on investment and servicing of finance		(4)
Taxation		
Corporation tax paid	(11)	
Net cash flow for taxation		(11)
Capital expenditure		
Land and buildings	(30)	
Plant and machinery (see note below)	(6)	
Net cash outflow for capital expenditure		(36)
		(3)
Equity dividends paid		
Dividends paid (see note below)	(18)	
Net cash flow for equity dividends paid		(18)
		(21)
Management of liquid resources		–
Financing		–
Net decrease in cash		(21)

Reconciliation of cash movements during the year ended 31 December 2001

	£m
Balance at 1 January 2001	19
Net cash outflow	(21)
Balance at 31 December 2001	(2)

Calculation of net cash inflow from operating activities

	£m	£m
Net operating profit (from the profit and loss account)		29
Add Depreciation:		
Land and buildings	10	
Plant and machinery	12	
		22
		51
Less Increase in stocks (25 – 24)	1	
Decrease in creditors (23 – 20)	3	4
		47
Add Decrease in debtors (26 – 25)		1
		48

Notes

Dividends

	£m
Amount due at 1 January 2001	14
Dividend for the year	18
	32
Amount due at 31 December 2001	(14)
Cash paid during the year	18

Fixed asset acquisitions

	Land and buildings £m	Plant and machinery £m
Position at 1 January 2001	110	62
Less 2001 depreciation	10	12
	100	50
Position at 31 December 2001	130	56
Acquisitions	30	6

Taxation

	£m
Amount due at 1 January 2001	8
Charge for the year	6
	14
Amount due at 31 December 2001	(3)
Cash paid during the year	11

6.5 Nailsea Ltd

Cash flow statement for the year ended 30 June 2002

	£000	£000
Net cash inflows from operating activities (Note 1)		397
Returns from investment and servicing of finance		
Interest paid	(27)	
Net cash outflow from returns on investment and servicing of finance		(27)
Taxation		
Corporation tax paid (Note 2)	(125)	
Net cash outflow for taxation		(125)

	£000	£000
Capital expenditure		
Land and buildings	(400)	
Plant and machinery	(250)	
Net cash outflow from capital expenditure		(650)
		(405)
Equity dividends paid (Note 3)		
Dividends paid	(80)	
Net cash outflow for equity dividends paid		(80)
		(485)
Management of liquid resources		–
Financing		
Additional share capital (200 + 100)	300	
Debentures	300	
Net cash inflow from financing		600
Net increase in cash		115

Reconciliation of cash movements during the year ended 30 June 2002

	£000
Balance at 1 July 2001	(32)
Net cash inflow	115
Balance at 30 June 2002	83

Notes

Note 1: Calculation of net cash inflow from operating activities

	£000	£000
Net operating profit (from the profit and loss account)		342
Add Depreciation		
Plant and machinery		320
		662
Less Increase in stocks (450 – 275)	175	
Increase in debtors (250 – 100)	150	325
		337
Add Increase in creditors (190 – 130)		60
		397

Note 2: Taxation

	£000
Amount due at 1 July 2001	55
Charge for the year	140
	195
Amount due at 30 June 2000	70
Cash paid during the year	125

Note 3: Dividends
It is clear that the dividend declared in one year is paid in the next, and so the 2001 dividend will be paid in 2002.

6.6	Blackstone plc

Cash flow statement for the year ended 31 March 2002

	£m	£m
Net cash inflows from operating activities (Note 1)		2,541
Returns from investment and servicing of finance		
Interest paid	(456)	
Net cash outflow from returns on investment and servicing of finance		(456)
Taxation (Note 2)		
Corporation tax paid	(300)	
Net cash outflow for taxation		(300)
Capital expenditure		
Proceeds of sales	54	
Goodwill	(700)	
Plant and machinery	(2,970)	
Fixtures and fittings	(1,608)	
Net cash outflow for capital expenditure		(5,224)
		(3,439)
Equity dividends paid (Note 3)		
Dividends paid	(300)	
Net cash outflow for equity dividends paid		(300)
		(3,739)
Management of liquid resources		–
Financing		
Additional bank loan	2,000	
Net cash inflow from financing		2,000
Net decrease in cash		(1,739)

Reconciliation of cash movements during the year ended 31 March 2002

	£m
Balance at 1 April 2001	(77)
Net cash outflow	(1,739)
Balance at 31 March 2002	(1,816)

Notes

Note 1: Calculation of net cash inflow from operating activities

	£m	£m
Net operating profit (from the profit and loss account)		2,309
Add Depreciation:		
Land and buildings	225	
Plant and machinery	745	
Fixtures and fittings	281	
Loss on disposals (54 – 581 + 489)	38	1,289
		3,598
Less Increase in stocks (2,410 – 1,209)	1,201	
Increase in debtors (1,573 – 941)	632	1,833
		1,765
Add Increase in creditors (1,507 – 731)		776
		2,541

Note 2: Taxation

	£m
Amount due at 1 April 2001	105
Charge for the year	390
	495
Amount due at 31 March 2002	(195)
Cash paid during the year	300

Note 3: Dividends

It seems that dividends declared by the company in one year are paid in the next, and so the 2002 payment will be the 2001 dividend.

Chapter 7

7.1 I. Jiang (Western) Ltd

The effect of each of the changes on ROCE is not always easy to predict.

(a) An increase in the gross profit margin *may* lead to a decrease in ROCE in particular circumstances. If the increase in the margin resulted from an increase in price, which in turn led to a decrease in sales, a fall in ROCE can occur. A fall in sales can reduce the net profit (the numerator in ROCE) if the overheads of the business did not decrease correspondingly.

(b) A reduction in sales can reduce ROCE for the reasons mentioned above.

(c) An increase in overhead expenses will reduce the net profit and this in turn will result in a reduction in ROCE.

(d) An increase in stocks held will increase the amount of capital employed by the business (the denominator in ROCE) where long-term funds are employed to finance the stocks. This will, in turn, reduce ROCE.

(e) Repayment of the loan at the year end will reduce the capital employed and this will increase the ROCE, provided that the loan repayment does not affect the scale of operations.

(f) An increase in the time taken for debtors to pay will result in an increase in capital employed if long-term funds are employed to finance the debtors. This increase in long-term funds will, in turn, reduce ROCE.

7.2 (a) This part of the question has been dealt with in the text of the chapter. Review as necessary.

(b) The ratios for business A and business B reveal that the debtors turnover ratio for business A is 63 days whereas for business B the ratio is only 21 days. Business B is therefore much quicker in collecting amounts outstanding from customers. Nevertheless, there is not much difference between the two businesses in the time taken to pay trade creditors: business A takes 50 days to pay its creditors whereas Business B takes 45 days. It is interesting to compare the difference in the debtor and creditor collection periods for each business. As business A allows an average of 63 days' credit to its customers, yet pays creditors within 50 days, it will require greater investment in working capital than business B, which allows an average of only 21 days to its debtors but takes 45 days to pay its creditors.

Business A has a much higher gross profit percentage than business B. However, the net profit percentage for the two businesses is identical. This suggests that business A has much higher overheads than business B. The stock turnover period for business A is more than twice that of business B. This may be due to the fact that business A maintains a wider range of goods in stock in order to meet customer requirements. The evidence therefore suggests that business A is the business that prides itself on personal service. The higher average settlement period is consistent with a more relaxed attitude to credit collection (thereby maintaining customer goodwill) and the high overheads are consistent with the incurring of additional costs in order to satisfy customer requirements. The high stock levels of business A are consistent with maintaining a wide range of stock in order to satisfy a range of customer needs.

Business B has the characteristics of a more price-competitive business. Its gross profit percentage is much lower than business A's, indicating a much lower gross profit per £1 of sales. However, overheads are kept low in order to ensure the net profit percentage is the same as business A's. The low stock turnover period and average collection period for debtors are consistent with a business that wishes to minimise investment in current assets, thereby reducing costs.

7.4 Helena Beauty Products Ltd

	2000	2001
Profitability ratios		
Net profit margin	$\frac{80}{3,600} \times 100\% = 2.2\%$	$\frac{90}{3,840} \times 100\% = 2.3\%$
Gross profit margin	$\frac{1,440}{3,600} \times 100\% = 40\%$	$\frac{1,590}{3,840} \times 100\% = 41.4\%$
ROCE	$\frac{80}{2,668} \times 100\% = 3.0\%$	$\frac{90}{2,874} \times 100\% = 3.1\%$
Efficiency ratios		
Stock turnover period	$\frac{(320+400)/2}{2,160} \times 365 = 61$ days	$\frac{(400+500)/2}{2,250} \times 365 = 73$ days
Average collection period	$\frac{750}{3,600} \times 365 = 76$ days	$\frac{960}{3,840} \times 365 = 91$ days
Sales/capital employed	$\frac{3,600}{2,668} = 1.3$	$\frac{3,840}{2,874} = 1.3$

The above ratios reveal a low net-profit margin in each year. The gross profit margin, however, is quite high in each year, suggesting that the company has high overheads. There was a slight improvement of 1.4 percentage points in the gross profit margin during 2001, but this appears to have been largely swallowed up by increased overheads. As a result, the net profit margin improved by only 0.1 percentage points in 2001. The low net profit margin is matched by a rather low sales to capital employed ratio in both years. The combined effect of this is a low ROCE in both years. The ROCE for each year is lower than might be expected from investment in risk-free government securities and should be regarded as unsatisfactory.

The stock turnover period and average collection period for debtors have both increased significantly over the period. The average collection period seems to be high and should be a cause for concern. Although both profit (in absolute terms) and sales improved during 2001, the directors should be concerned at the low level of profitability and efficiency of the business. In particular, an investigation should be carried out concerning the high level of overheads and the higher investment in stocks and debtors.

7.7 Harridges Ltd

(a)

	2001	2002
ROCE	$\dfrac{310}{1,600} = 19.4\%$	$\dfrac{350}{1,700} = 20.6\%$
ROSF	$\dfrac{155}{1,100} = 14.1\%$	$\dfrac{175}{1,200} = 14.6\%$
Gross profit margin	$\dfrac{1,040}{2,600} = 40\%$	$\dfrac{1,150}{3,500} = 32.9\%$
Net profit margin	$\dfrac{310}{2,600} = 11.9\%$	$\dfrac{350}{3,500} = 10\%$
Current ratio	$\dfrac{738}{400} = 1.8$	$\dfrac{660}{485} = 1.4$
Acid-test ratio	$\dfrac{485}{400} = 1.2$	$\dfrac{260}{485} = 0.5$
Days debtors	$\dfrac{105}{2,600} \times 365 = 15$ days	$\dfrac{145}{3,500} \times 365 = 15$ days
Days creditors	$\dfrac{235}{1,560} \times 365 = 55$ days	$\dfrac{300}{2,350^*} \times 365 = 47$ days
Stock turnover period	$\dfrac{250}{1,560} \times 365 = 58$ days	$\dfrac{400}{2,350} \times 365 = 62$ days
Gearing ratio	$\dfrac{500}{1,600} = 31.3\%$	$\dfrac{500}{1,700} = 29.4\%$
EPS	$\dfrac{155}{490} = 31.6\text{p}$	$\dfrac{175}{490} = 35.7\text{p}$

* Used because the credit purchases figure is not available.

(b) There has been a considerable decline in the gross profit margin during 2002. This fact, combined with the increase in sales by more than one-third, suggests that a price-cutting policy has been adopted in order to stimulate sales. The resulting increase in sales, however, has led to only a small improvement in ROCE and returns to equity. Similarly, there has only been a small improvement in EPS.

Despite a large cut in the gross profit margin, the net profit margin has fallen by less than 2 per cent. This suggests that overheads have been tightly controlled during 2002. Certainly, overheads have not risen in proportion to sales.

The current ratio has fallen and the acid-test ratio has fallen by more than half. Even though liquidity ratios are lower in retailing than in manufacturing, the liquidity of the company should now be a cause for concern. However, this may be a passing problem. The company is investing heavily in fixed assets and is relying on internal funds to finance this growth. When this investment ends, the liquidity position may improve quickly.

The debtors period has remained unchanged over the two years, and there has been no significant change in the stock turnover period in 2002. The gearing ratio is quite low and provides no cause for concern given the profitability of the company.

Overall, the company appears to be financially sound. Although there has been rapid growth during 2002, there is no real cause for alarm provided that the liquidity of the company can be improved in the near future. In the absence of information concerning share price, it is not possible to say whether or not an investment should be made.

7.8 Genesis Ltd

(a) and (b) These parts have been answered in the text of the chapter and you are referred to it for a discussion on overtrading and its consequences.

(c)

$$\text{Current ratio} = \frac{232}{550} = 0.42$$

$$\text{Acid-test ratio} = \frac{104}{550} = 0.19$$

$$\text{Stock turnover period} = \frac{128}{1,248} \times 365 = 37 \text{ days}$$

$$\text{Average settlement period for debtors} = \frac{104}{1,640} \times 365 = 23 \text{ days}$$

$$\text{Average settlement period for creditors} = \frac{184}{1,260} \times 365 = 53 \text{ days}$$

(d) Overtrading must be dealt with either by increasing the level of funding in order to match the level of activity, or by reducing the level of activity to match the funds available. The latter option may result in a reduction in profits in the short-term but may be necessary to ensure long-term survival.

Chapter 8

8.1

Group balance sheet of Giant and its subsidiary as at 31 March

	£m	£m
Fixed assets (at cost less depreciation)		
Land		39
Plant		63
Vehicles		25
		127
Current assets		
Stocks	46	
Debtors	59	
Cash	27	
	132	
Less **Creditors: amounts falling due within one year**		
Creditors	60	
Net current assets		72
Total assets less current liabilities		199
Less **Creditors: amounts falling due after more than one year**		
Debentures		63
		136

	£m	£m
Capital and reserves		
Called-up share capital:		
ordinary shares of £1 each, fully paid		50
Share premium account		40
Profit and loss account		46
		136

Note that the group balance sheet is prepared by adding all like items together. The investment in 10 million shares of Jack Ltd (£30m), in the balance sheet of Giant plc, is then compared with the capital and reserves (in total) in Jack Ltd's balance sheet. Since Giant paid exactly the balance sheet values of Jack's assets *and* bought all of Jack's shares, these two figures are equal and can be cancelled.

8.2 The balance sheet of Jumbo plc and its subsidiary will be as follows:

Balance sheet as at 31 March

	£m	£m
Fixed assets (at cost less depreciation)		
Land		102
Plant		67
Vehicles		57
		226
Current assets		
Stocks	87	
Debtors	70	
Cash	24	
	181	
Less **Creditors: amounts falling due within one year**		
Creditors	80	
Net current assets		101
Total assets less current liabilities		327
Less **Creditors: amounts falling due after more than one year**		
Debentures		170
		157
Capital and reserves		
Called-up share capital:		
ordinary shares of £1 each, fully paid		100
Profit and loss account		41
		141
Minority interests		16
		157

Note that the normal approach is taken with various assets and external claims. The 'minority interests' figure represents the minorities' share (8 million of 20 million ordinary shares) in the capital and reserves of Nipper plc.

8.3 Toggles plc

(a) (i) 'Minority interests' represents the portion, either of net assets (balance sheet) or after tax profit (profit and loss account), which is attributable to minority shareholders. Minority shareholders are those shareholders in the subsidiaries other than the parent company. Since, by definition, the parent company is the major shareholder in each of its subsidiaries, any other shareholders in any other subsidiary must be a minority, in terms of number of shares owned.

(ii) 'Goodwill arising on consolidation' is the difference, at the time that the parent acquires the subsidiary, between what is paid for the subsidiary company shares and what they are 'worth'. 'Worth' normally is based on the fair values of the underlying assets which appear in the balance sheet of the subsidiary. This is not necessarily, nor usually, the balance sheet values. Goodwill, therefore, represents the excess of what was paid over the fair values of the assets which appear in the balance sheet of the subsidiary. As such it is an intangible asset which represents the amount that the parent was prepared to pay for the reputation, staff loyalty, and so on of the subsidiary, that is what we normally refer to as goodwill.

Normally goodwill on consolidation is depreciated over a period, starting from the date of acquisition of the subsidiary company shares by the parent company.

(iii) The retained profit of the parent company will be its own cumulative profits net of tax and dividends paid. This will include dividends received from its subsidiaries, which represent part of the company's income.

When the results of the subsidiaries are consolidated with those of the parent, the parent's share of the post-acquisition retained profits of its subsidiaries is added to its own retained profit figure. In this way the parent is, in effect, credited with its share of all the subsidiaries' after tax profit, not just with the dividends which the subsidiaries have paid.

(b) The objective of preparing consolidated accounts is to reflect the underlying economic reality that the assets of the subsidiary companies are as much under the control of the shareholders of the parent, acting through their board of directors, as are the assets owned directly by the parent. This will be true despite the fact that the subsidiary is strictly a separate company from the parent. It is also despite the fact that the parent may not own all of the shares of the subsidiaries.

Consolidated accounts provide an example where accounting tends to put 'content' before 'form' in the UK. That is to say that it tries to reflect economic reality rather than the strict legal position. This is to try to provide more useful information.

Chapter 9

9.1 The VAS is, in effect, a rearrangement of the information already contained within the profit and loss account. However, it does not automatically follow that the VAS will be of little value to users. Its purpose is different from that of the profit and loss account, which is geared towards providing a measure of income for the shareholders of the business. However, there are other groups with a stake in the business and which benefit from its activities. The VAS attempts to measure the value added by the collective effort of the various groups and the benefits that each group has received from the business. It is, therefore, a much broader measure of income than the profit and loss account. The benefits of the VAS have been dealt with in the chapter. However, it is worth mentioning again the use of the VAS in promoting a team spirit among the various stakeholders.

Some, however, believe the VAS is a child of its time. It was first proposed at a time when industrial relations in the UK were at a low ebb and employee/management disputes were widespread. Promoting team spirit and showing the proportion of value added that employees receive from the business was therefore seen as a good idea. However, the combined effects of recession, high levels of unemployment, industrial relations legislation and increased global competitiveness over the past few decades have resulted in far fewer disputes and managers are less concerned with this aspect of their duties. This may help to explain, in part, the fall in popularity of the VAS.

9.2 | Buttons Ltd

(a) The value added statement for the year ended 30 September is:

	£000	£000
Sales turnover		950
Less Bought in materials and services (220 + 95)		315
Value added		635
Applied as follows:		
To employees		160
To pay government		110
To suppliers of capital:		
Interest	45	
Dividends	120	165
For maintenance and expansion of assets:		
Depreciation	80	
Retained profit	120	200
		635

(b) The VAS is seen as promoting a measure of income which is generated through the collective effort of the key 'stakeholders' of the business. The VAS tries to encourage a team spirit among managers, shareholders, employees and so on, and to reduce conflict. The VAS also permits the calculation of various ratios (as seen in the chapter) which may help in assessing financial performance.

As the amount of value added received by employees is often high in relation to that received by other groups, the VAS is useful in reinforcing the fact that employees are significant beneficiaries of the business. However, some are suspicious of the motives of management in presenting financial information in this way.

9.3 |

$$\text{Value added to sales} = \frac{635}{950} \times 100\%$$

$$= 66.8\%$$

The lower this ratio, the greater the reliance of the business on outside sources of materials and services and the more vulnerable the business will be to difficulties encountered by external suppliers.

$$\text{Value added per £1 of wages} = \frac{635}{160}$$

$$= 4.0$$

This ratio is a measure of labour productivity. In this case, the employees are generating £4.0 of value added for every £1 of wages expended. The higher the ratio, the higher the level of productivity. This ratio may be useful when making comparisons between businesses.

$$\text{Dividends to value added} = \frac{120}{635} \times 100\%$$

$$= 18.9\%$$

This ratio calculates that portion of value added that will be received in cash more or less immediately by shareholders. The trend of this ratio may provide an insight to the distribution policy of the business over time. It is important to remember, however, that shareholders also benefit, in the form of capital growth, from amounts reinvested in the business. Thus, the ratio is only a partial measure of the benefits received by shareholders.

$$\text{Depreciation and retentions to value added} = \frac{200}{635} \times 100\%$$

$$= 31.5\%$$

This ratio may provide an insight to the ability or willingness of the business to raise finance for new investment from internal operations rather than external sources. A high ratio may suggest a greater ability or willingness to raise finance internally than a low ratio.

9.5 (a) Although the historic cost accounts have certain redeeming features, such as objectivity, it is difficult to argue that they are all that users require. During a period of inflation, historic cost accounting tends to result in an overstatement of profit and an understatement of financial position for the business. In the absence of additional information, users of the historic cost accounts will be required to make their own adjustments in order to take into account the effects of inflation on the financial statements.

The value of inflation-adjusted accounts will depend on the levels of inflation within the economy. The higher the rates of inflation, the greater the distortion of the historic cost accounts and, therefore, the greater the need for some sort of inflation-adjusted statement. However, the problems which exist during periods of inflation still persist during periods of low inflation and their cumulative effect can be significant over a number of years.

We should always bear in mind the fact that the preparation of inflation-adjusted information has a cost to the business, and the benefits of preparation should exceed the costs. This means, amongst other things, that the form of inflation-adjusted accounts should be given careful consideration. We saw in Chapter 9, however, that there is more than one approach to dealing with the problem of inflation adjustment. The debate as to which is the best method to use has not been resolved. Until this is done, the case for inflation-adjusted accounts is certainly weakened.

(b) Publishing environmental reports can have its drawbacks. There is a danger that publication could open up opportunities for litigation against the business if any shortcomings are exposed. There is also the danger that the expectations of stakeholders will be raised as a result of publishing such information and the business will be required to adopt increasingly stringent environmental standards which will prove very costly. For many businesses, the publication of environmental reports would, first of all, require the development of an internal environmental management system, which could be both time consuming and costly.

However, there are likely to be costs associated with not providing such information. Businesses are under increasing pressure from a variety of sources including customers, other businesses within the same industry and green campaigners to produce such reports. Failure to respond to such pressures may not be in the longer-term interests of the business. Unless these groups can be reassured by environmental policies adopted by the business, there is the risk of strict legislation being imposed (leading to higher costs) and lost sales.

Appendix A

A.1 A.1

Account to be debited	Account to be credited
(a) Stock	Trade creditors
(b) Capital (or a separate drawings account)	Cash
(c) Loan interest	Cash
(d) Stock	Cash
(e) Cash	Trade debtors
(f) Wages	Cash
(g) Capital (or a separate drawings account)	Trade debtors
(h) Trade creditors	Cash
(i) Electricity (or heat and light)	Cash
(j) Cash	Sales

Note that the precise name given to an account is not crucial so long as those who are using the information are clear as to what each account deals with.

A.2 (a) and (b)

Cash

		£			£
1 Feb	Capital	6,000	3 Feb	Stock	2,600
15 Feb	Sales	4,000	5 Feb	Equipment	800
28 Feb	Trade debtors	2,500	9 Feb	Rent	250
			10 Feb	Fuel and electricity	240
			11 Feb	General expenses	200
			21 Feb	Capital	1,000
			25 Feb	Trade creditors	2,000
			28 Feb	Balance c/d	5,410
		12,500			12,500
1 Mar	Balance b/d	5,410			

Capital

		£			£
21 Feb	Cash	1,000	1 Feb	Cash	6,000
28 Feb	Balance c/d	5,000			
		6,000			6,000
			1 Mar	Balance b/d	5,000
28 Feb	Balance c/d	7,410	28 Feb	Profit and loss	2,410
		7,410			7,410
			1 Mar	Balance b/d	7,410

Stock

		£			£
3 Feb	Cash	2,600	15 Feb	Cost of sales	2,400
6 Feb	Trade creditors	3,000	19 Feb	Cost of sales	2,300
			28 Feb	Balance c/d	900
		5,600			5,600
1 Mar	Balance b/d	900			

Equipment

		£			£
5 Feb	Cash	800			

Trade creditors

		£			£
25 Feb	Cash	2,000	6 Feb	Stock	3,000
28 Feb	Balance c/d	1,000			
		3,000			3,000
			1 Mar	Balance b/d	1,000

Rent

		£			£
9 Feb	Cash	250	28 Feb	Profit and loss	250

Fuel and electricity

		£			£
10 Feb	Cash	240	28 Feb	Profit and loss	240

General expenses

		£			£
11 Feb	Cash	200	28 Feb	Profit and loss	200

Sales

		£			£
28 February	Balance c/d	7,800	15 Feb	Cash	4,000
			19 Feb	Trade debtors	3,800
		7,800			7,800
28 Feb	Profit and loss	7,800	28 Feb	Balance b/d	7,800

Cost of sales

		£			£
15 Feb	Stock	2,400	28 Feb	Balance c/d	4,700
19 Feb	Stock	2,300			
		4,700			4,700
28 Feb	Balance b/d	4,700	28 Feb	Profit and loss	4,700

Trade debtors

		£			£
19 Feb	Sales	3,800	28 Feb	Cash	2,500
			28 Feb	Balance c/d	1,300
		3,800			3,800
1 Mar	Balance b/d	1,300			

(b) Trial balance as at 28 February

	Debits £	Credits £
Cash	5,410	
Capital		5,000
Stock	900	
Equipment	800	
Trade creditors		1,000
Rent	250	
Fuel and electricity	240	
General expenses	200	
Sales		7,800
Cost of sales	4,700	
Trade debtors	1,300	
	13,800	13,800

(c)

Profit and loss account

		£			£
28 Feb	Cost of sales	4,700	28 February	Sales	7,800
28 Feb	Rent	250			
28 Feb	Fuel and electricity	240			
28 Feb	General expenses	200			
28 Feb	Capital (net profit)	2,410			
		7,800			7,800

Balance sheet as at 28 February

	£	£
Fixed assets:		
Equipment		800
Current assets:		
Stock	900	
Trade debtors	1,300	
Cash	5,410	
	7,610	
Current liabilities		
Trade creditors	1,000	
		6,610
		7,410
Capital		7,410

Profit and loss account for the month ended 28 February

	£	£
Sales		7,800
Cost of sales		4,700
Gross profit		3,100
Less Rent	250	
Fuel and electricity	240	
General expenses	200	
		690
Net profit for the month		2,410

A.3

Buildings

		£			£
1 Jan	Balance brought down	25,000			

Fittings – cost

		£			£
1 Jan	Balance brought down	10,000	31 Dec	Balance carried down	12,000
	Cash	2,000			
		12,000			12,000
1 Jan	Balance brought down	12,000			

Fittings – depreciation

		£			£
31 Dec	Balance carried down	4,400	1 Jan	Balance brought down	2,000
			31 Dec	Profit and loss	
				(£12,000 × 20%)	2,400
					4,400
		4,400			
			1 Jan	Balance brought down	4,400

General expenses

		£			£
1 Jan	Balance brought down	140	31 Dec	Profit and loss	570
	Cash	580		Balance carried down	150
		720			720
1 Jan	Balance brought down	150			

Stock in trade

		£			£
1 Jan	Balance brought down	1,350	31 Dec	Cost of sales	15,220
31 Dec	Trade creditors	17,220		Cost of sales	4,900
	Cash	3,760		Capital	560
				Balance carried down	1,650
		22,330			22,330
1 Jan	Balance brought down	1,650			

Cost of sales

		£			£
31 Dec	Stock in trade	15,220	31 Dec	Profit and loss	20,120
	Stock in trade	4,900			
		20,120			20,120

Rent

		£			£
1 Jan	Balance brought down	500	31 Dec	Profit and loss	3,000
31 Dec	Cash	3,000		Balance carried down	500
		3,500			3,500
1 Jan	Balance brought down	500			

Trade debtors

		£			£
1 Jan	Balance brought down	1,840	31 Dec	Cash	32,810
31 Dec	Sales	33,100		Profit and loss (bad debt)	260
				Balance carried down	1,870
		34,940			34,940
1 Jan	Balance brought down	1,870			

Cash

		£			£
1 Jan	Balance brought down	2,180	31 Dec	Stock in trade	3,760
31 Dec	Sales	10,360		Wages	3,770
	Loan	2,000		Rent	3,000
	Trade debtors	32,810		Electricity	1,070
				General expenses	580
				Fittings	2,000
				Loan	1,000
				Trade creditors	18,150
				Capital	10,400
				Balance carried down	3,620
		47,350			47,350
1 Jan	Balance brought down	3,620			

Capital

		£			£
31 Dec	Stock in trade	560	1 Jan	Balance brought down	25,050
	Cash	10,400		Profit and loss (profit)	10,900
	Balance carried down	24,990			
		35,950			35,950
			1 Jan	Balance brought down	24,990

Loan

		£			£
30 June	Cash	1,000	1 Jan	Balance brought down	12,000
31 Dec	Balance carried down	13,000		Cash	2,000
		14,000			14,000
			1 Jan	Balance brought down	13,000

Trade creditors

		£			£
30 June	Cash	18,150	1 Jan	Balance brought down	1,690
31 Dec	Balance carried down	760	31 Dec	Stock in trade	17,220
		18,910			18,910
			1 Jan	Balance brought down	760

Electricity

		£			£
31 Dec	Cash	1,070	1 Jan	Balance brought down	270
31 Dec	Balance carried down	290	31 Dec	Profit and loss	1,090
		1,360			1,360
			1 Jan	Balance brought down	290

Sales

		£			£
31 Dec	Profit and loss	43,460	31 Dec	Trade debtors	33,100
				Cash	10,360
		43,460			43,460

Wages

		£			£
31 Dec	Cash	3,770	31 Dec	Profit and loss	3,770

Loan interest

		£			£
31 Dec	Balance carried down	1,350	31 Dec	Profit and loss	1,350
				$[(6/12 \times 14,000) +$	
				$(6/12 \times 13,000)] \times 10\%$	
			1 Jan	Balance brought down	1,350

Profit and loss

		£			£
31 Dec	Cost of sales	20,120	31 Dec	Sales	43,460
	Depreciation	2,400			
	General expenses	570			
	Rent	3,000			
	Bad debts (Trade debtors)	260			
	Electricity	1,090			
	Wages	3,770			
	Loan interest	1,350			
	Profit (Capital)	10,900			
		43,460			43,460

Balance sheet as at 31 December last year

Fixed assets	£	£		£
Buildings		25,000	Capital	24,990
Fittings: cost	12,000			
depreciation	4,400	7,600	Loan	13,000
			Current liabilities	
Current assets			Trade creditors	760
Stock of stationery		150	Accrued electricity	290
Stock in trade		1,650	Accrued loan interest	1,350
Prepaid rent		500		
Trade debtors		1,870		
Cash		3,620		
		40,390		40,390

Index

Page numbers in **bold** refer to definitions in glossary.